THE MARKET REVOLUTION IN AMERICA

THE MARKET REVOLUTION IN AMERICA

Social, Political, and Religious Expressions, 1800–1880

Edited by
MELVYN STOKES
and
STEPHEN CONWAY

UNIVERSITY PRESS OF VIRGINIA
Charlottesville and London

The University Press of Virginia
Copyright © 1996 by the Rector and Visitors
of the University of Virginia

First published 1996

Library of Congress Cataloging–in–Publication Data

The market revolution in America : social, political, and religious
expressions, 1800–1880 / edited by Melvin Stokes and Stephen Conway.
    p.   cm.
Includes index.
ISBN 0-8139-1649-6 (cloth : alk. paper). — ISBN 0-8139-1650-X
(pbk. : alk. paper)
1.Capitalism—United States—History. 2.Capitalism—Political aspects—
United States—History. 3.Capitalism—Religious aspects—History.
4.Capitalism—Social aspects—United States—History. 5.Democracy—United
States—History. I.Stokes, Melvin. II.Conway, Stephen, 1957– .
HC110.C3M37 1996
330.973'05—dc20   95-42346
                                               CIP

Printed in the United States of America

Contents

Acknowledgments

T HE EDITORS HAVE ACQUIRED a large number of debts in the preparation of this volume. It is a pleasure to acknowledge them here. We are particularly grateful to Eric Foner for his help and support for the project from the beginning. We were greatly assisted by John Ashworth, Richard Carwardine, Christopher Clark, Daniel Walker Howe, Michael F. Holt, Peter J. Parish, Donald J. Ratcliffe, and Harry L. Watson at all stages. The conference at which early versions of many of these essays were discussed was planned with the aid of Christopher Abel, Tony Badger, Martin Daunton, Michael Heale, and Gary L. McDowell.

Charles Sellers, Richard E. Ellis, Peter J. Parish, and Sean Wilentz made major contributions to the conference itself. Without financial support from the Commonwealth Fund and Graduate School of University College London, the conference could not have taken place. Financial assistance is also gratefully acknowledged from the British Academy, the David Bruce Center for American Studies at Keele University, the History Faculty of Cambridge University, London University's Institute of United States Studies, the *Journal of American Studies,* and the Royal Historical Society. The Cultural Affairs Office of the United States Embassy provided funds to help bring twelve American graduate students to London for the conference. William Armbruster, deputy cultural attaché, was particularly helpful in this regard. Chairs of sessions at the conference included Louis Billington, Bruce Collins, Martin Crawford, Michael Heale, Peter J. Parish, Derek Roberts, David Turley, and Peter Way. Jane Hubben and Andrew Strouthous provided assistance at the conference itself, and Nazneen Razwi contributed greatly to the arrangements.

As the book took shape once the conference was over, new or revised essays had to be submitted on a very tight schedule. We are grateful to all who labored hard to meet deadlines. Charles Sellers, Richard E. Ellis, and Amy Dru Stanley, who provided new contributions, were particularly helpful. Harry L. Watson, with great generosity, expanded his essay to encompass areas he had not been asked to cover at first. Sean Wilentz, despite family illness, managed to attend the conference and later to produce a revised version of his essay. Daniel Walker Howe, Donald J. Ratcliffe, and Christopher Clark rendered valuable assistance in the final preparation of the manuscript. Richard Holway of the University Press of Virginia was encouraging and highly supportive throughout. Nazneen Razwi typed one chapter with characteristic accuracy and dedication. The manuscript was copyedited with care and thoroughness by Suzanne Schafer and Marilyn Martin of Elizabeth Shaw Editorial and Publishing Services. Leigh Priest prepared the index with great efficiency and under considerable pressure of time. Finally, when push came to shove, and allegedly "user-friendly" software programs proved anything but, Rachel Aucott, Nafisa Taylor, and Simon Renton helped sort it all out.

Introduction

MELVYN STOKES

I N THE LAST FEW YEARS, growing attention has been paid by historians to the idea of a "market revolution" in early nineteenth-century America. A largely subsistence economy of small farms and tiny workshops, satisfying mostly local needs through barter and exchange, gave place to an economy in which farmers and manufacturers produced food and goods for the cash rewards of an often distant marketplace. Such a change had major implications for household arrangements, social institutions, political ideology and practice, and cultural patterns. Charles Sellers was using the concept of a market revolution at least as early as the 1960s.[1] In 1975, Sellers's Berkeley colleague Michael P. Rogin structured a chapter of his study of Jacksonian Indian policy around the market revolution.[2] Sean Wilentz used the term in a 1982 essay and developed a broader application of the idea eight years later.[3] Harry L. Watson adopted the market revolution as a major organizing theme of his important 1990 reappraisal of Jacksonian politics. Since 1990, scholars including Daniel Feller, Paul Goodman, William E. Gienapp, Paul E. Johnson, and Donald J. Ratcliffe have incorporated it into their work.[4] In 1991, Sellers published what is clearly destined to remain the major synthesis of early nineteenth-century history from the perspective of the market revolution.[5]

Though *market revolution* may be a relatively new term to most American historians, the ideas underpinning it are by no means original. The general characteristics of the transition from a local agricultural and handicrafts-based economic system to an industrial-type economy oriented toward markets were first mapped out by political economists around the turn of the century. These writers were concerned to apply Darwinian ideas on evolution to economics by identifying the varying "stages" of economic development. They were aware that economic changes involved modifications in human thought and behavior.[6] They also realized that politics was affected: the last years of the nineteenth century saw the emergence of the idea that early American politics could be explained as a contest between social groups at varying stages of economic development. Over a century ago, it seemed evident to one historian that American farmers of the early republic were divided on subsistence-commercial lines. Orin G. Libby, who had studied with Frederick Jackson Turner, made the differences between the two groups an

1

integral part of his analysis of the struggle over ratifying the Constitution.[7] The subsistence-commercial dichotomy also appeared in Charles A. Beard's account of the making of the Constitution. It played a major role in the later work of Jackson Turner Main.[8]

More relevant, perhaps, to the modern market revolution thesis is that key elements of the thesis were prefigured in George R. Taylor's *Transportation Revolution* (1951). The United States, Taylor wrote, was still primarily an agricultural country in 1815. Though he said little about agriculture itself (a subject reserved for a later volume in the same series), it is clear that he regarded most farming as being of a subsistence character. Commercial farming took place only near rivers and the coast; *Niles' Weekly Register* asserted, with conceivable exaggeration, in 1818 that two-thirds of South Carolina's market crops were grown within five miles of a river. Such manufacturing as there was took place predominantly in the countryside, where it was carried on by households and mills producing goods for domestic or neighborhood use.[9] The cost of inland transportation appeared to block any hope of change toward a less local, more market-oriented type of economy. In 1816, a U.S. Senate report pointed out that a ton of goods could be brought from Europe to America for roughly nine dollars, while the same amount would pay for shipment over only thirty miles by land. Better communications, in the form of turnpike roads, canals, river steamboats, plank roads, and railroads, brought the cost of overland transportation down sharply during the following decades. Taylor listed other factors—a swiftly expanding population, a wealth of manufacturing resources, a stable government favorable to enterprise, and the lack of social or political restraints on entrepreneurial activities—that contributed to the development of the American economy. Ultimately, however, it was improved transportation he saw as the main reason for the rise of an increasingly industrial and commercial society.[10]

The attempt in recent years to use the market revolution as a synthesis to bring together so many features of the history of the early nineteenth century prompts the obvious question: why now? Scholarly interest in the market may have reflected, or been a critical response to, the market rhetoric of right-wing governments of the 1980s in both the United Kingdom and the United States. It may also be connected to the collapse of communism in eastern Europe and the extension of the capitalist marketplace to the countries concerned. For the most part, however, the current focus seems to reflect changes and new priorities within the field of American history itself. Four movements in particular may be singled out: the challenge to ideas of liberal capitalism from writers on rural *mentalité*; the often analogous findings by new labor historians on the outlook and values of late eighteenth- and early nineteenth-century workers; the challenge to the ethnocultural approach to politics presented by scholars exploring the relationship between economic issues and politics; and recent work on the linkage between the rise of a market society and social and cultural change.

Consensus historians of the postwar years regarded America as capitalist from the start. European capitalism, according to Max Weber, had its origins in Calvinist puritanism. Puritan values, including the dedication to hard work and the aversion to extravagance and luxury, encouraged the accumulation of capital. Early Puritan settlers brought these values with them to the New World. When Carl Degler declared, in a famous phrase, that American capitalism "came in the first ships," he was articulating this point of view.[11] To this account of religiously inspired capitalism, consensus history added in the 1950s the perception of an exceptionalist American ideology. In the absence of a feudal system, argued Louis Hartz, "Lockian liberalism" had come to be the outlook shared by most Americans. Although never clearly defined, this was understood to mean equal rights, equality of opportunity in the capitalist marketplace, security of property, and a laissez-faire philosophy of government.[12]

Consensus historians saw farmers as part of this capitalist tradition. In Richard Hofstadter's view, the early American farmer had been committed to moneymaking objectives, but his commercial goals had often been circumscribed by limited opportunities. Self-sufficiency, far from being his yeoman-esque choice, "was usually forced upon him by a lack of transportation or markets, or by the necessity to save cash to expand his operations."[13] This perception of farmers as frustrated capitalists survived as the prevailing historical paradigm until the late 1970s, when it was challenged by a number of historians trying, consciously or unconsciously, to meet the demand of Lucien Febvre and the *Annales* school for a "total history."[14]

The study of precommercial farming *mentalité* was launched in articles by Michael Merrill, James Henretta, and Christopher Clark. Merrill criticized the notion that farmers of the late eighteenth and early nineteenth centuries were primarily individualists seeking profits from markets. They labored to produce surpluses because few rural households were completely self-sufficient. The surplus was produced not for cash sale but as a means of exchange within the local community. Though the goods produced were frequently given a cash value, this was a use value for bookkeeping purposes rather than a means of measuring profit in the capitalist sense. Precapitalist farmers, Henretta maintained, were more interested in protecting the integrity of their households and passing on land and possessions to future generations of their family than in the search for profit. Like Merrill, Henretta saw farmers as belonging to a social and cultural world that emphasized community rather than the individual and in which farming households cooperated together, exchanging goods and work. Only when land became less available did farmers become more attuned to, and dependent on, production for the market. Christopher Clark, looking at the Connecticut River Valley, found a similar pattern of household production at the end of the eighteenth century. This gave way, in later decades, to the pursuit of profit through market relations. In a 1979 article, Clark advanced a social explanation for the rise of rural capitalism, refining and extending it in his later book.[15]

The consequences of changes in manufacturing have been explored by a number of scholars. In the first half of the nineteenth century, household manufacture tended to give place to production for the market. Better transportation facilities helped the changeover, as did growing demand from an expanding population, but the principal initiative came from merchant capitalists. These men employed various strategies to increase production and profits. In cities like New York and Cincinnati, they divided up traditional craft skills and paid outworkers, usually the most exploited groups in society, to do piecework at low rates. Where a specific industry already dominated a town, as shoemaking did in Lynn, Massachusetts, they put out work to women in farming families. Another alternative was to concentrate production in large units employing mechanization—the beginnings of the factory system. These processes helped bring about the downfall of the old craft system. Cast on the market as a commodity—unskilled labor—many artisans looked back on a world that in many respects paralleled the precapitalist rural *mentalité,* with its emphasis on household production, cooperation, and reciprocal, nonmonetary exchanges between households. They sought to check the advance of the market by engaging in new forms of organization and protest.[16] In their fight against capitalist exploitation and inequality on behalf of a traditional "moral economy," they developed a working-class variant of the republican creed—"labor republicanism," in Daniel T. Rodgers's phrase—that emphasized individual independence, equal rights, and the need to restrain private power.[17]

While social historians have expanded our knowledge of rural and urban worlds, political historians have followed a trajectory of their own. In *The Age of Jackson* (1945), Arthur M. Schlesinger, Jr., depicted the core of Jacksonian politics as a class struggle between artisans and businessmen.[18] This interpretation was attacked by consensus scholars, who saw Schlesinger's artisan-workers as small capitalists and Jackson's closest supporters in the Bank War as champions of a rising, entrepreneurial middle class.[19] The main challenge to the idea that the politics of the Jacksonian period were class based, however, came with Lee Benson's *Concept of Jacksonian Democracy* (1961). Using voting records and statistics, Benson argued that ethnic and religious factors were more crucial than class in determining how Americans voted.[20] Following Benson, a whole school of ethnocultural history arose.[21] It did not, however, go uncriticized. Ethnocultural historians were challenged on a variety of counts: their methodology, the difficulty of applying their thesis to regions that were not particularly diverse ethnically and religiously (such as the South), their failure to account for the formation of the Jacksonian party system or its collapse in the years before the Civil War, and their portrayal of a strange kind of stasis in which ethnic and religious conflicts survived largely unaffected by economic and social transformations.[22] Perhaps most crucially, it was alleged, they had no satisfactory explanation of the correlation (if it existed) between voting behavior and government policymaking.[23]

It is now nearly a century since Guy S. Callender criticized the idea that early nineteenth-century American governments followed laissez-faire policies, and many other historians have followed in his footsteps. It has been clear for some time that, in the eight decades between Revolution and Civil War, government at all levels interfered constantly and with major consequences in American economic life.[24] Not only were these interventions frequently the result of conflict within government, they often stimulated conflict outside it. Ethnocultural historians, while disregarding the question of how economic policies were made, saw voters reacting to them primarily in terms of cultural symbolism rather than material concerns.[25]

This view of politics has been challenged in the last two decades from several different directions. Some of the pioneers of ethnocultural history, including Michael F. Holt and Ronald P. Formisano, broadened their analytical approach to include study of economic issues and controversies. At the same time, other scholars, including J. Mills Thornton III and Harry L. Watson, produced state or local studies that clarified the connection between political alignments and economic points of view.[26] In an analysis of political culture, Daniel Walker Howe found that a dozen prominent Whigs were united by, among other things, a belief in moral and economic progress and the need for expanded market relations.[27] Differing attitudes toward the advance of capitalism were seen as crucial in two important studies of political rhetoric: John Ashworth argued that the conflict of Whigs and Jacksonians was in reality a clash between capitalism and democracy, while Lawrence F. Kohl believed that an individual's partisan allegiance was determined on the basis of his psychological response to market changes.[28] Many of these themes were brought together in Harry L. Watson's elegant synthesis, *Liberty and Power* (1990).

While political historians explored the links between economic issues and politics, many scholars were working on the connection between an expanding market and wider patterns of social and cultural change. Some investigated the effects on women and family life. Nancy F. Cott argued that the transition to bourgeois family life and the growth of a separate "women's sphere" imposed two kinds of "bondage" on women: that of subjection (to male authority and a new concept of marriage) and that of strength (as women sought influence outside the home and formed supportive relationships with each other). Mary P. Ryan traced the growth of a new ethos of family life centered around maternal affection. Middle-class women found their role in the family redefined: they were expected to become loving child rearers, teachers of morality, and protectors, through the domestic environment they created, of the well-being of market-ravaged men.[29] Both Cott and Ryan saw women as playing a major part in the dissemination of middle-class values through their role in reform activities and in the churches. Other scholars reinforced the view that reform movements and revivalistic religion were deeply influenced by the new social and cultural needs of an expanding market.[30] Legal historians demonstrated how law was revised to meet the requirements of a property-owning, entrepreneurial society.[31] Because of the great expansion of goods and services it encouraged, moreover, the market can be seen to have influenced many details of everyday life.[32]

It might be argued that these studies of the last decades of the eighteenth and the first decades of the nineteenth century exaggerate the novelty of the market in society. James M. Redfield has written about the emergence of a market economy in Greece between 800 and 600 B.C. Richard H. Britnell locates the commercialization of English society in the years between 1000 and 1500.[33] Jean-Christophe Agnew, analyzing what he perceives as the ongoing tension between the market (representing work) and the theater (symbolizing play) in "Anglo-American thought" in the years 1550 to 1750, assumes the market arrived at the same time as the first British settlers. Recently, the traditional consensus view of capitalism's spread has been restated in a sophisticated manner by Jack P. Greene. In *The Pursuits of Happiness* (1988), Greene argues that seventeenth- and eighteenth-century England exported its "profoundly acquisitive and accumulating spirit" to its North American colonies, which were commercial in orientation from the beginning.[34]

Charles Sellers, in his important synthesis of work on early nineteenth-century history, confronts this problem at the outset. *The Market Revolution: Jacksonian America, 1815–1846* (1991) is constructed around the great divide between land and market. Since the arrival of the first European settlers, he maintains, each pulled in opposite directions. The market meant seaboard towns, the maintenance of trading links with Europe, and the pursuit of profit. Land stood for the development of the interior, subsistence agriculture, and a nonprofitmaking way of life. Sellers agrees that the first colonial settlements, growing up in coastal areas or in the lower parts of river valleys, were closely tied to European markets. In the eighteenth century, however, a population explosion tilted the balance in favor of land. Settlers flooded into the interior, and soon a majority of Americans, cut off from the market by poor communications, lived a primarily subsistence life in conditions very different from those that prevailed in commercialized areas (Sellers, *Market Revolution*, 4–5).[35]

Most Americans, producing the essentials of life for themselves and exchanging goods and labor with neighbors, created a highly localized, community-oriented way of life (12–13). In a subsistence culture, farming families solved their labor problem by having many children. The system of family labor was policed, and protection and security provided, by patriarchal authority (8–9). Yet labor itself on the farm was not as arduous as in market occupations. It was often sociable, heavily dependent on weather and season, and—because the aim of subsistence farmers was not accumulating wealth but passing on land to children in order to maintain their way of life— far less pressured (10–14). Subsistence life, according to Sellers, had both strengths and flaws. While amply "meeting human needs for security, sociability, and trust," it also exacted a price "in patriarchy, conformity, and circumscribed horizons" that made it vulnerable to market penetration (17).

What ultimately doomed the subsistence culture, in Sellers's view, was a combination of rising land prices and expanding population. Subsistence families, in order to provide for their numerous offspring, needed continuous supplies of cheap land (9, 17). When this was no longer available in long-settled areas of the Northeast, an agrarian crisis began. Fathers, desperate to meet increasing tax burdens and pass on the expected patrimony to their children, attempted to raise supplementary income through market activities. Womenfolk stepped up their production of yarn and cloth, and "putting-out" systems of manufacture stretched far into the countryside (17–19, 156–57). In the struggle to maintain a traditional way of life, the farming families of southeastern New England were pioneering the changeover to capitalist methods of production (19).

For Americans in the southern and western interior, Sellers argues, it was the boom following the end of the War of 1812 that led to the beginnings of capitalist transformation (19). The role of government was crucial here (5, 32, 40). The ascendancy of Jefferson had, since 1801, effectively denied entrepreneurial elites the assistance of the federal government (39). Yet, in many states, influential members of the local Republican party were just as much in favor of government aid to enterprise as were their Federalist opponents (40). The increasing significance of this so-called National Republican viewpoint was clearly on show when the Fourteenth Congress assembled in December 1815 (70). By passing a range of probusiness measures (71–79), the new Congress set out to reverse existing federal policy and commit the United States "irrevocably" to a process of capitalist development (69). At virtually the same moment, complementing the earlier work of lawyers ("the shock troops of capitalism") and state judges, the Supreme Court embarked upon a series of decisions that were profoundly favorable to business enterprise (47–59, 84–90, 100–102). Sellers is aware, however, that although public policy and legal rules played an important part in the success of the market revolution, as did capitalist entrepreneurs, they cannot account for it completely. Following recent work on patterns of consumption, he traces the rise of social pressure for store-bought goods and clothing within farming families (154–56). Moreover, in the tradition of E. P. Thompson, he analyzes cultural as well as economic factors. "Arminianism," he argues, by linking human effort to the idea of salvation, had created a theology of "capitalist accommodation" that helped many reconcile themselves to market ways by providing religious sanction for "competitive individualism" and the pursuit "of wealth and status" (29–31).

Although powerful forces had thus emerged to back market expansion, they soon encountered resistance in the subsistence world. The first signs of the strength of that resistance came when the country's "small-farming majority" decisively repudiated a "market-oriented leadership" in the congressional elections of 1816 (103–6). In subsequent years, a drive for greater democratic controls was accompanied by a rising "antinomian" (or "New Light") rebellion in religion that defended traditional subsistence values of egalitarianism and communal love in the face of the competitive ethics of the marketplace (30–31, 108). The hard times after the panic of 1819 (which introduced the United States to the capitalist cycle of boom and bust) reinforced these trends and led to the emergence of a class-based politics in many states (138, 157–61, 164–65). The central issues of this new politics in the North and West concerned farmers' and workers' opposition to paper money and banks (122–24, 161–64, 168–71). The South was an exception to this trend as hardpressed planters, newly aroused to the vulnerability of slavery, hastened to ally themselves with backcountry farmers on the basis of opposition to tariffs and to developmentalism in general (273–81).

With Andrew Jackson's election to the presidency in 1828, the antimarket forces gained an "indomitable" leader (321). Though himself a member of the slave-owning gentry, Jackson shared the subsistence culture's "anti-Indian animus," patriarchal standpoint, and hard-money sentiments (90, 177, 180). As president, according to Sellers, he adopted a twofold strategy. Through an emphasis on his own opposition to banks, internal improvements, and Indian rights, Jackson attempted to drive a wedge between southern planters who championed "nullifier heresy" and yeomen farmers opposed to market ways, thereby undermining the threat posed by "planter power" to "democratic Union" (308–13, 316, 328–29). He also set out to bring the market revolution to a halt by attacking paper money and credit. His Bank veto of 1832 won him widespread producer-class support against an agent of control over that class. Yet, although Biddle's Bank was eventually destroyed, the market revolution continued (321–22, 325–26, 331–37, 342–48). Sellers explains this failure as a result of several factors: constitutional provisions that prevented Jackson's interference with state banks (321–22); the inadequacy of hard money as a corrective, especially when accompanied by the "inflationary firestorm" of the mid-1830s (342–45); and, above all, Jackson's need to act through the party system and Congress. The president found, in the climactic struggle between democracy and capitalism, that many politicians within his own party could not be trusted. By using democratic rhetoric, these men hid their entrepreneurial sympathies (322–23, 342–48). The Whigs soon learned to do the same. In 1840, successfully blurring the distinction between capitalism and democracy, they defeated a reelection bid by Jackson's chosen hard-money successor (350–51, 355–56, 361–62).

Sellers sees the move to a market economy as accompanied by increasing stress on individuals and human relationships. It meant exchanging the "unpressured security" of the subsistence world for the uncertainties of the capitalist system. Businessmen sought wealth and feared failure. Under pressure from competitors, they worked hard for success. They also extracted as much labor as possible from an alienated workforce. Yet, in personal terms, they often worried at the abandonment of "traditional ethics" for "tough-minded capitalist egotism" (152–53, 215–16). Religion helped resolve many of these doubts and difficulties. Arminian faith, particularly as cast in "Moderate Light" form, not only met the "psychic needs" of businessmen with its emphasis on effort and good works; as adapted by Charles G. Finney and others, it helped meet their economic needs as well. Combining traditional moral rigor with the promise of universal forgiveness and salvation, Finney reached out to the New Light–antinomian majority, undermining opposition to the advance of the market while at the same time conditioning workers to the need for disciplined effort (203, 210–18, 225–26, 228–30, 238).

The triumph of the market revolution was both aided and legitimized, Sellers argues, by the development of a hegemonic bourgeois culture.[36] A professionalized, two-party political system and a revamped Moderate Light–arminian religion played their part in building that hegemony (363, 216). So, too, did women robbed of a traditional role in household production. Restricted by market development to domestic roles of "childbearing, daily family subsistence, and child nurture and socialization," many sought escape in religion and in support for moral reform movements (226–28, 243–45, 374–75). An emerging market, Sellers maintains, required the inculcation of farmers and workers with bourgeois habits of disciplined effort and self-restraint (211, 214, 229–30, 237, 245–51, 258–59). Many of the reform movements of the antebellum era were not so much an expression of liberal conscience as a means of building this middle-class hegemony (251–54, 259–68). By the 1840s, aided by better schooling and increased literacy, a growing tide of printed literature, and a literary romanticism produced by a new class of intellectuals to sentimentalize the harsher features of a market world, this bourgeois culture was far along the road to supremacy (264, 365–72, 375–80). Distracting its working-class opponents through jingoism, nativism, and racism, it moved to attain total hegemony by confronting its own "great contradiction," slavery (386–91, 395–96, 427).

Among the initial reactions to Sellers's book were a review by Sean Wilentz in the *New Republic* and a symposium, incorporating contributions from Mary H. Blewett, Amy Bridges, Richard E. Ellis, Joel H. Silbey, Harry L. Watson, and Major L. Wilson, along with a response from Sellers himself, published in the *Journal of the Early Republic*.[37] Though many of these scholars paid specific tribute to the range and power of the book, they also challenged a number of its features. Sellers's terminology ("Presbygational," and the "Moderate Light/New Light" or "arminian/antinomian" divide) was believed by some to be idiosyncratic, at times misleading.[38] A number felt that Marxist conviction had led him to exaggerate the contrast between the virtues of the precapitalist world and the vices of its capitalist successor.[39] Sellers, it was suggested, had accepted too uncritically the idea of separate male and female "spheres," and seemed at times ambivalent in his views of the role of women in the market revolution. Although conceding the racism of many market critics, he had largely ignored the role of African-American slaves as actors in the drama of capitalist transformation.[40] Other matters neglected, it was alleged, included republican ideology and political conflicts more easily explicable in ethnoreligious than market terms. In his response, Sellers called for a "critical historical perspective" on the costs and benefits of capitalism, an acceptance of the significance of "class dynamics" in explaining historical change, and a recognition that the depth and strength of resistance to the market undermines the prevailing myth of "consensual democratic capitalism."[41]

The response to Sellers's work and the growing salience of the market revolution as a paradigm for explaining nineteenth-century history prompted the idea of a book to examine the varied expressions of the market revolution from the perspectives of a number of scholars working in differing fields of nineteenth-century history.[42] It was intended that the essays to be brought together would embody a variety of approaches and represent a number of fields. Some would deal with the market revolution thesis itself; others would use it only as a starting point. Some would analyze the usefulness of the concept generally for a particular area of history, while several would engage specifically with the arguments in Sellers's book. In order that the essays themselves might be exposed to scholarly analysis and criticism, first drafts were circulated for discussion at the Commonwealth Fund Conference in London on February 11–12, 1994.[43] The essays were subsequently revised—and additional essays added—to meet many of the points raised at the conference.

One crucial difficulty was chronology. While Sellers's discussion of social and cultural changes ranges back to the eighteenth century, his narrative of political development opens with the final act of the War of 1812 and closes with the Wilmot Proviso. The transformation of a mainly subsistence society into a largely market-oriented one took considerably longer than this.[44] Robert Gross wrote about the tensions produced by commercial pressures in revolutionary Concord. Winifred Rothenberg has documented the emergence of a market economy in Massachusetts between 1785 and 1800. Joyce Appleby saw liberal capitalism as appealing strongly to farmers in the Middle Atlantic states in the 1790s, and the Jeffersonian victory of 1800 as the triumph of a new capitalist social order.[45]

At the other end of the timescale, as Joel H. Silbey points out, the market's conquest remained patchy in many areas long after 1850.[46] Economist John R. Commons recalled in his autobiography that his father, who had been at home in the subsistence economy of exchange and barter, proved incapable of making the transition to the world of money and credit. In this, it is likely that he was not alone, even in the years after the Civil War. William Allen White, in his autobiography, painted a dramatic portrait of what happened to one small town in Kansas when the market arrived in the late 1870s. Among present-day scholars, Steven Hahn has argued that the growth of the Farmers' Alliance in upcountry Georgia in the 1880s was largely a response to the growing commercialization of agriculture.[47]

It was clear that to end a study of the market revolution around 1850 would eliminate any consideration of the rise to power of the Republican party, which brought the Federal government to adopt promarket policies over banking and railroads. It would be to ignore the fact that without the success of the Union armies, no national market could have existed[48]—or that it was only with Reconstruction that former African-American slaves gained full access to the market and that market ways spread deep into the southern backcountry.[49] Taking into account these considerations, it was decided to extend the range of the book (though not of each individual essay) to include the period from approximately 1800 to 1880.

The essays themselves are concentrated in a number of broad areas. Christopher Clark, Harry L. Watson, and Amy Dru Stanley examine the social and economic consequences of the market revolution. Clark, while finding the market revolution a useful explanatory concept in the history of the North, warns against seeing it as an inevitable process. It was a product of changes that were mostly contested, might not have happened at all or in the way they did, and in many areas produced results significantly at variance with what many historians have believed. Watson examines the impact of the market revolution on the South's distinctive dual economy of seaboard plantations and largely subsistence uplands. Each experienced the market revolution in different ways. The plantation economy was subjected to growing commercial pressures. This had paradoxical implications for African-American slaves: it increased the danger of their sale but also made it possible for many of them to engage in market activities on their own behalf. In the uplands, by contrast, most white farmers resisted pressures for commercial development. This reluctance would seem only too correct in the years after the Civil War, as growing market relations created patterns of poverty and dependency throughout the rural South. Stanley explores the connections between gender relations and the development of a market society. Those relationships, she argues, were far more complex than the "separate spheres" model, initially advanced by Cott and Ryan and later used by Sellers, acknowledges. Many women carried on work at market-related tasks, in as well as outside the home. Yet, as a legitimating ideology, separate spheres helped mark the boundary not only between men and women but also—in the hands of the abolitionists—between slave labor and free.

In a market society, ideals of republican independence gave way, for most citizens, to the reality of dependent labor. The latter was excused and validated through the ideology of "free labor." Eric Foner's essay examines changes to the free labor concept in the light of recent developments in the study of labor, gender, the law, and political language. These changes, he maintains, have emphasized that the term *free labor* had divergent meanings. In common with many ideologies, moreover, it was defined by exclusion, often along lines of race and gender. The Reconstruction era saw free labor principles enacted into federal law and their boundaries extended to include African Americans, but women continued to be excluded. John Ashworth argues that a major problem with the view of free labor originally advanced by Foner was that it failed to differentiate clearly between supporters of the Republican party and the adherents of other contemporary parties in the North (particularly the Democrats) or of previous political groupings. Ashworth contends that the commitment to free labor had, for the Republicans, evolved into a commitment to wage labor. It was this commitment that distinguished them from northern Democrats in the 1850s and from Jeffersonians and Jacksonians in earlier times.

In the first of four essays on politics, Richard E. Ellis analyzes the implications of the market revolution for the political process from Jefferson's first election as president to Jackson's retirement. Ellis begins with a discussion of the so-called American System, which he regards as a result of the victory of commercially oriented Jeffersonians. By 1819–20, a national economy had been created, but this had unexpected consequences: increasing political apathy, more inequality, the strengthening of slavery, and the arrival of the capitalist boom and bust cycle. The depression after 1819, according to Ellis, gave birth to Jacksonian democracy. Once in power, however, the Jacksonians failed to develop a positive program for dealing with the market revolution. This was inevitable; by the 1830s, the national economy was no longer subject to control by the federal government. Donald J. Ratcliffe advances a new thesis on when the market revolution had its principal impact on politics. Between 1819 and 1833, he argues, American politics reflected, above all, the sharpening of the sectional tensions, ethnocultural affiliations, and partisan loyalties inherited from the pre-1815 era as well as popular demands for a more responsive government. This picture altered considerably between 1834 and 1844. During this period, Ratcliffe asserts, voters were being asked to approve or contest positions taken by state and national leaders on policies relating to economic growth and its social effects, and these questions had a direct connection with the personal experience of voters themselves. Because the market revolution happened in different places at different times, their attitudes were deeply polarized. Thus the middle and later 1830s, in Ratcliffe's view, formed the critical period when the market revolution had its greatest impact on national political alignments, crystallizing and invigorating the second party system.

The market revolution theory has recovered part of the historical reputation of the Jacksonians. They are now seen, once again, by many historians as fighting against inequalities of wealth and for greater democracy. Yet they still remain vulnerable to criticism because of their racist views of African Americans and Native Americans. Sean Wilentz suggests a reappraisal of this interpretation, at least so far as slavery is concerned. In the 1830s, he points out, a few Democratic party dissidents supported abolitionism. These party members became hostile to slavery because it seemed to be shoring up capitalism (the "money power") or because it threatened the idea of equal political rights among white men. But, by the 1840s, some Democrats were attacking slavery itself rather than merely its implications for whites. They argued, in characteristically Jacksonian manner, that producers had the right to compensation for their labor. Increasingly, they applied this principle to blacks as well as whites. Strict construction of the Constitution—another major tenet of Jacksonianism—also led many to oppose allowing slavery to expand into the territories. This was seen as an important first step on the road to abolition. Despite the deficiencies of some of the antislavery Democrats, Wilentz argues, they offered an alternative approach to the slavery issue and the racism that justified slavery itself.

Michael F. Holt's chapter examines the manner in which issues raised by the market revolution were of crucial significance in politics after the panic of 1837, but had been moved to the periphery of partisan conflict in the years after the panic of 1873. This was a result of a range of factors, including the growing maturity of the third party system, an ethnocultural strategy deliberately pursued by the Republicans who were in power in the 1870s, and increasing geographical and factional divisions within each party. The growth of the market economy by 1880, Holt asserts, had prepared the ground for a new form of political conflict determined more by interest group loyalties than generalized interparty struggle over particular economic issues.

In the final part of the book, two essays engage directly with Charles Sellers's view of the relationship between the market revolution and religion. Daniel Walker Howe criticizes Sellers's New Light–Moderate Light, antinomian-arminian terminology on historical grounds. Sellers's dismissal of ideas of human dignity and free will as mere capitalist ideology seems to Howe both reductionist and perverse. He also disparages Sellers's conception of the market revolution as a Kulturkampf. Sellers, he maintains, reifies the market, making it an actor in the story of economic and social transformation rather than a resource created and exploited by human beings for their own purposes. A more balanced, less negative assessment of the effects of the market revolution, Howe maintains, would help us understand how it succeeded. He links its progress to middle-class aspirations for a better life, as reflected not only in material things but also in perceptions of manners and taste—the growth of what is called "polite culture." In his essay, Richard Carwardine looks at Sellers's arminian-antinomian divide in terms of Methodism. Though Sellers writes of Methodists as part of his antinomian coalition, the theology of Methodism, Carwardine points out, was fundamentally Arminian. Not all Methodists were Jacksonians, and Carwardine's essay considers the variety of their political involvements. Though religion helped ordinary men and women deal with the results of the market revolution, and may at times have aided its advance, Carwardine believes it is false to see the religious loyalties and enthusiasms of the era purely in such functional terms.

Charles Sellers, in his essay, concludes that attitudes concerning the benefits and defects of capitalism have biased historians' views of the results of the market revolution. He traces the growth of the consensus paradigm relating capitalism to democracy and provides reasons for rejecting that paradigm. His own interpretation, he insists, best explains—in accordance with Lee Benson's "ascertainable facts"—the link between democracy and capitalism. The triumph of the latter, Sellers believes, shows that the majority—at least on important questions—does not rule. Yet, in a sentiment that would surely be echoed by all the contributors to this volume, he also appeals for the development of yet more paradigms to enlarge our understanding of nineteenth-century history.

NOTES

1. See Charles Sellers and Henry May, *A Synopsis of American History* (Chicago, 1963), chaps. 9–11. The idea, if not the term itself, influenced the publications of Sellers's graduate students in later decades. See James Roger Sharp, *Jacksonians versus the Banks: Politics in the States after the Panic of 1837* (New York, 1970); Kim T. Phillips, "The Pennsylvania Origins of the Jackson Movement," *Political Science Quarterly* 91 (1976): 489–508; Donald J. Ratcliffe, "Politics in Jacksonian Ohio: Reflections on the Ethnocultural Interpretation," *Ohio History* 88 (1979): 5–36.

2. Michael P. Rogin, "The Market Revolution and the Reconstruction of Paternal Authority," in his *Fathers and Children: Andrew Jackson and the Subjugation of the American Indian* (New York, 1975).

3. Sean Wilentz, "On Class and Politics in Jacksonian America," in Stanley I. Kutler

and Stanley N. Katz, eds., *The Promise of American History* (Baltimore, 1982); Sean Wilentz, "Society, Politics, and the Market Revolution, 1815–1848," in Eric Foner, ed., *The New American History* (Philadelphia, 1990), pp. 51–71.

4. Harry L. Watson, *Liberty and Power: The Politics of Jacksonian America* (New York, 1990); Daniel Feller, "Politics and Society: Toward a Jacksonian Synthesis," *Journal of the Early Republic* 10 (1990): 135–61; Paul Goodman, "The Emergence of Homestead Exemption in the United States: Accommodation and Resistance to the Market Revolution, 1840–1880," *Journal of American History* 80 (1993): 470–98; William E. Gienapp, "The Antebellum Era," and Paul E. Johnson, "The Market Revolution," in Mary K. Cayton, Elliott J. Gorn, and Peter W. Williams, eds., *Encyclopedia of American Social History*, 3 vols. (New York, 1993), 1:105–30, 545–60; Donald J. Ratcliffe, "The Market Revolution and Party Alignments in Ohio, 1828–1840," in Andrew R. L. Cayton and Jeffrey P. Brown, eds., *The Pursuit of Public Power: Political Culture in Ohio, 1787–1861* (Kent, Ohio, 1994).

5. Charles Sellers, *The Market Revolution: Jacksonian America, 1815–1846* (New York, 1991).

6. See Richard T. Ely, *Studies in the Evolution of Industrial Society* (New York, 1903), pp. 6–7, 12–13, 25–26, 43–73. Cf. Franklin H. Giddings, "The Economic Ages," *Political Science Quarterly* 16 (1901): 193–221, and Carl Bücher, *Industrial Evolution*, trans. S. Morley Wickett (New York, 1901).

7. Orin G. Libby, *The Geographical Distribution of the Vote of the Thirteen States on the Federal Constitution, 1787–88* (Madison, Wis., 1894).

8. Charles A. Beard, *An Economic Interpretation of the Constitution* (New York, 1913), pp. 27, 29, 254–55, 281, 284, 288; Jackson Turner Main, *The Antifederalists: Critics of the Constitution, 1781–1788* (Chapel Hill, N.C., 1961), pp. 1–2, 5–6, 26–28, 29–30, 33–37, 40–41, 52–54, 70, 86–87, 100, 109, 112, 223, 233, 240, 271–74; Jackson Turner Main, *The Social Structure of Revolutionary America* (Princeton, N.J., 1965), pp. 18–34, 40–41, 50–54, 56–59, 61–63, 196.

9. George R. Taylor, *The Transportation Revolution, 1815–1860* (New York, 1951), pp. 3, 56, 210.

10. Ibid., pp. 17–103, 132–38, 207.

11. Max Weber, *The Protestant Ethic and the Spirit of Capitalism*, trans. Talcott Parsons (New York, 1930); Carl Degler, *Out of Our Past* (New York, 1959), p. 1.

12. Louis Hartz, *The Liberal Tradition in America: An Interpretation of American Thought since the Revolution* (New York, 1955).

13. Richard Hofstadter, *The Age of Reform: From Bryan to F.D.R.* (New York, 1955), p. 23.

14. For a dissenting view, see Michael A. Lebowitz, "The Jacksonians: Paradox Lost?" in Barton J. Bernstein, ed., *Towards a New Past: Dissenting Essays in American History* (New York, 1968), pp. 71–74. A number of political historians, including Charles Sellers, also questioned the view of the farmer as capitalist.

15. Michael Merrill, "Cash Is Good to Eat: Self-Sufficiency and Exchange in the Rural Economy of the United States," *Radical History Review* 4 (1977): 42–71; James Henretta, "Families and Farms: *Mentalité* in Pre-Industrial America," *William and Mary Quarterly* 35 (1978): 3–32; Christopher Clark, "Household Economy, Market Exchange, and the Rise of Capitalism in the Connecticut River Valley, 1800–1860," *Journal of Social History* 13

(1979): 169–90; Christopher Clark, *The Roots of Rural Capitalism: Western Massachusetts, 1780–1860* (Ithaca, N.Y., 1990).

16. See Alan Dawley, *Class and Community: The Industrial Revolution in Lynn* (Cambridge, Mass., 1976); Thomas Dublin, *Women at Work: The Transformation of Work and Community in Lowell, Massachusetts, 1820–1860* (New York, 1979); Sean Wilentz, *Chants Democratic: New York City and the Rise of the American Working Class, 1788–1850* (New York, 1984); Steven J. Ross, *Workers on the Edge: Work, Leisure, and Politics in Industrializing Cincinnati, 1788–1890* (New York, 1985); Christine Stansell, *City of Women: Sex and Class in New York, 1789–1860* (New York, 1986).

17. See Daniel T. Rodgers, "Republicanism: The Career of a Concept," *Journal of American History* 79 (1992): 24–31.

18. Arthur M. Schlesinger, Jr., *The Age of Jackson* (Boston, 1945).

19. See Richard Hofstadter, "Andrew Jackson and the Rise of Liberal Capitalism," in his *The American Political Tradition and the Men Who Made It* (New York, 1948); Bray Hammond, *Banks and Politics in America from the Revolution to the Civil War* (Princeton, N.J., 1957); Walter Hugins, *Jacksonian Democracy and the Working Class: A Study of the New York Workingman's Movement, 1829–1837* (Stanford, Calif., 1960).

20. Lee Benson, *The Concept of Jacksonian Democracy: New York as a Test Case* (Princeton, N.J., 1961).

21. See, for example, Michael F. Holt, *Forging a Majority: The Formation of the Republican Party in Pittsburgh, 1848–1860* (New Haven, Conn., 1969); Paul Kleppner, *The Cross of Culture: A Social Analysis of Midwestern Politics, 1850–1900* (New York, 1970); Richard Jensen, *The Winning of the Midwest: Social and Political Conflict, 1888–1896* (Chicago, 1971); Ronald P. Formisano, *The Birth of Mass Political Parties: Michigan, 1827–1861* (Princeton, N.J., 1971); William G. Shade, *Banks or No Banks: The Money Issue in Western Politics, 1832–1865* (Detroit, 1972); Joel H. Silbey, *Political Ideology and Voting Behavior in the Age of Jackson* (Englewood Cliffs, N.J., 1973); Paul Kleppner, *The Third Electoral System, 1853–1892: Parties, Voters, and Political Cultures* (Chapel Hill, N.C., 1979); Joel H. Silbey, *The Partisan Imperative: The Dynamics of American Politics before the Civil War* (New York, 1985).

22. On these issues, see the perceptive comments by Daniel Feller in "Politics and Society," 141–44.

23. Richard L. McCormick, "Ethnocultural Interpretations of Nineteenth-Century American Voting Behavior," in his *The Party Period and Public Policy: American Politics from the Age of Jackson to the Progressive Era* (New York, 1986), pp. 55–63. It seemed for a while that one means of linking electoral behavior to policymaking was the "realignment thesis" initially advanced by Walter Dean Burnham. American politics since the 1790s, Burnham argued, had included five successive party systems, each with its particular policies and voting patterns. Realignments (Burnham and others argued) took place by means of "critical elections," with subsequent party-led governments altering policy to meet voters' expressed wishes and priorities. Some political historians disliked Burnham's chronological divisions—Joel Silbey proposed an alternative periodization—and realignment theory itself is now perceived as subject to a range of conceptual and practical difficulties. See Walter Dean Burnham, "Party Systems and the Political Process," in William N. Chambers and Walter Dean Burnham, eds., *The American Party Systems:*

Stages of Political Development (New York, 1967), pp. 277–307; Walter Dean Burnham, *Critical Elections and the Mainsprings of American Politics* (New York, 1970); Jerome M. Clubb, William H. Flanigan, and Nancy H. Zingale, *Partisan Realignment: Voters, Parties, and Government in American History* (Beverly Hills, Calif., 1980); Joel H. Silbey, *The American Political Nation, 1838–1893* (Stanford, Calif., 1991); Byron E. Shafer, *The End of Realignment? Interpreting American Electoral Eras* (Madison, Wis., 1991).

24. Guy Stevens Callender, "The Early Transportation and Banking Enterprises of the States in Relation to the Growth of Corporations," *Quarterly Journal of Economics* 17 (1902): 111–62; Louis Hartz, *Economic Policy and Democratic Thought: Pennsylvania, 1776–1860* (Cambridge, Mass., 1948); Oscar and Mary F. Handlin, *Commonwealth: A Study of the Role of Government in the American Economy* (New York, 1947); Milton S. Heath, *Constructive Liberalism: Role of the State in Economic Development in Georgia to 1860* (Cambridge, Mass., 1954); Carter Goodrich, *Government Promotion of American Canals and Railroads, 1800–1890* (New York, 1960); Carter Goodrich, ed., *Canals and American Economic Development* (New York, 1961); Nathan Miller, *Enterprise of a Free People: Economic Development in New York State, 1792–1838* (Ithaca, N.Y., 1962); Frank Bourgin, *The Great Challenge: The Myth of Laissez-Faire in the Early Republic* (New York, 1989). The history of this last work is curious. Written as a doctoral thesis under Charles E. Merriam at the University of Chicago in the 1940s, it was set aside for reasons that are now irrecoverable (but may have included a political bias against New Deal planning) and finally published over half a century later (pp. xi–xiv).

25. McCormick, "Ethnocultural Interpretations," p. 60.

26. Michael F. Holt, *The Political Crisis of the 1850s* (New York, 1978); Ronald P. Formisano, *The Transformation of Political Culture: Massachusetts Parties, 1790s–1840s* (New York, 1983); J. Mills Thornton III, *Politics and Power in a Slave Society: Alabama, 1800–1860* (Baton Rouge, La., 1978); Harry L. Watson, *Jacksonian Politics and Community Conflict: The Emergence of the Second Party System in Cumberland County, North Carolina* (Baton Rouge, La., 1981).

27. Daniel Walker Howe, *The Political Culture of the American Whigs* (Chicago, 1979).

28. John Ashworth, *"Agrarians" and "Aristocrats": Party Political Ideology in the United States, 1837–1846* (London, 1983); Lawrence F. Kohl, *The Politics of Individualism: Parties and the American Character in the Jacksonian Era* (New York, 1989).

29. Nancy F. Cott, *The Bonds of Womanhood: "Woman's Sphere" in New England, 1780–1835* (New Haven, Conn., 1977); Mary P. Ryan, *Cradle of the Middle Class: The Family in Oneida County, New York, 1790–1865* (New York, 1983).

30. See Anthony F. C. Wallace, *Rockdale: The Growth of an American Village in the Early Industrial Revolution* (New York, 1972); Ronald G. Walters, *American Reformers, 1815–1860* (New York, 1975); Paul Boyer, *Urban Masses and Moral Order in America, 1820–1920* (Cambridge, Mass., 1978); Paul E. Johnson, *A Shopkeeper's Millennium: Society and Revivals in Rochester, New York, 1815–1837* (New York, 1978).

31. On this point, see Morton J. Horwitz, *The Transformation of American Law, 1780–1860* (Cambridge, Mass., 1977); William E. Nelson, *The Americanization of the Common Law: The Impact of Legal Change on Massachusetts Society, 1760–1830* (Cambridge, Mass., 1975).

32. Jack Larkin, *The Reshaping of Everyday Life, 1790–1840* (New York, 1988).

33. James M. Redfield, "The Development of the Market in Archaic Greece," in B. L. Anderson and A. J. H. Latham, eds., *The Market in History,* proceedings of a symposium held at St. George's House, Windsor Castle, Sept. 9–13, 1984 (London, 1986), pp. 29–58; Richard H. Britnell, *The Commercialisation of English Society, 1000–1500* (Cambridge, Eng., 1993). Donald J. Ratcliffe kindly drew my attention to the second of these works.

34. Jean-Christophe Agnew, *Worlds Apart: The Market and the Theater in Anglo-American Thought, 1550–1750* (Cambridge, Eng., 1986); Jack P. Greene, *Pursuits of Happiness: The Social Development of Early Modern British Colonies and the Formation of American Culture* (Chapel Hill, N.C., 1988), pp. 8, 10, 12, 31, 34–35, 48–52, 99, 107–8, 124–25, 138–39, 141–42 (quotation on p. 50). Greene's model applies to the colonies on the Chesapeake, to the middle colonies (a point corroborated by James T. Lemon in his study of southeastern Pennsylvania), and the colonies of the Lower South. But, as he himself conceded, it does not apply to New England, where soil and climate militated against the rise of single-crop, commercial-type agriculture of the kind common further south, and where community attachments limited spatial mobility. While Greene draws attention to an increasing market orientation in New England during the eighteenth century, he acknowledges that the vast majority of New Englanders continued to live on farms and that they remained—when compared to colonists further south—less commercial. Ibid., pp. 25–26, 61–67; James T. Lemon, *The Best Poor Man's Country: A Geographical Study of Early Southeastern Pennsylvania* (Baltimore, 1972), esp. pp. 2–3, 220, 223, 226–27.

35. There is consequently no contradiction between the work of scholars who have emphasized the commercial orientation of the colonies and the idea of market revolution in the nineteenth century. Greene, for example, has noted that, in New England as elsewhere, the dramatic population growth of the eighteenth century combined with the increasing cost and scarcity of land in long-settled areas to persuade many settlers to leave in search of cheaper and more available land. As they moved inland, they cut or greatly reduced their links to the market, thus preparing the ground for the market revolution of the nineteenth century. Greene, *Pursuits of Happiness,* pp. 56–58, 125–27, 177–81. Agnew, though apparently believing in the continuity of market pressures in the "Anglo-American world," soon concedes that nearly all his "Anglo-American" texts are by British authors, that American markets lagged by up to a century behind their British equivalents, and that it was only in the years after the Revolution that most Americans developed an awareness of how market processes worked. Agnew, *Worlds Apart,* pp. xiii, 192–93.

36. On the vogue for Gramscian ideas in recent American scholarship, see T. J. Jackson Lears, "The Concept of Cultural Hegemony: Problems and Possibilities," *American Historical Review* 90 (1985): 567–93.

37. Sean Wilentz, "The Original Outsider," *New Republic,* June 22, 1992, pp. 34–38; symposium, *Journal of the Early Republic* 12 (1992): 445–76 (hereafter cited as "symposium").

38. Symposium, 449, 452, 469. Amy Bridges points out that the schematic divide between "arminian market" and "antinomian land" left Sellers "inattentive to the mixed stakes many citizens had in the advance of commerce, and the mixed feelings they had about it" (ibid., 472). The attempt to generalize in this way also disguises crucial anoma-

lies, especially on the "land" side of the war: small producers, particularly from the North, who enthusiastically embraced commercial opportunity; the strange presence of free-thinking urban workers in an antinomian coalition, and the curious support given by southern planters to antimarket forces. Wilentz, "The Original Outsider," 35; symposium, 464, 472.

39. Symposium, 448–49, 469; Wilentz, "The Original Outsider," 35.

40. Symposium, 452, 469.

41. Ibid., 455–56, 462–63, 474–75.

42. Donald J. Ratcliffe played an important part in persuading me of the significance of the market revolution. I am also grateful to John Ashworth, Richard Carwardine, Christopher Clark, Daniel Walker Howe, Eric Foner, Peter J. Parish, and Sean Wilentz for advice and assistance at the beginning of the project.

43. Steven Hahn and Jonathan Prude noted, while editing an excellent collection of essays on rural history, that this type of early comment and criticism is much rarer with essay collections than with completed monographs. Steven Hahn and Jonathan Prude, *The Countryside in the Age of Capitalist Transformation: Essays in the Social History of Rural America* (Chapel Hill, N.C., 1985), acknowledgments.

44. Recent historians of agricultural society have perceived the term *subsistence* as misleading. It is explicitly rejected, for example, by Christopher Clark in his *Roots of Rural Capitalism*. Yet the word is still employed by many scholars, including Charles Sellers, and—if suitably qualified—retains a certain value as a kind of descriptive shorthand.

45. Robert Gross, *The Minutemen and Their World* (New York, 1976); Winifred Barr Rothenberg, *From Market-Places to a Market Economy: The Transformation of Rural Massachusetts, 1750–1850* (Chicago, 1992); Joyce Appleby, *Capitalism and a New Social Order: The Republican Vision of the 1790s* (New York, 1984). Similar considerations are raised by Allan Kulikoff, *The Agrarian Origins of American Capitalism* (Charlottesville, Va., 1992), and James Henretta, "The War for Economic Independence and American Economic Development," in his *The Origins of American Capitalism: Collected Essays* (Boston, 1991).

46. Symposium, 458. It is notable, for example, that Taylor's "transportation revolution" lasted until 1860, Goodman's study of homestead exemption laws covered the period up to 1880, and Goodrich's analysis of government aid to internal communications ended in 1890.

47. John R. Commons, *Myself* (New York, 1934), p. 11; William Allen White, *The Autobiography of William Allen White* (New York, 1946), pp. 43, 66; Steven Hahn, *The Roots of Southern Populism: Yeoman Farmers and the Transformation of the Georgia Upcountry, 1850–1890* (New York, 1983).

48. Paul E. Johnson argues that the transportation revolution did not create a national market "at least until the 1850s." Even this is probably premature. George R. Taylor emphasized that the United States still lacked an integrated railroad system in 1860. There were many small independent lines and a variety of gauges, and only in one place— Bowling Green, Kentucky—did the northern and southern railroad systems physically meet. Johnson, "Market Revolution," 548; Taylor, *Transportation Revolution*, p. 86.

49. Eric Foner, *Reconstruction: America's Unfinished Revolution, 1863–1877* (New York, 1988).

PART I

The Market Revolution

1

The Consequences of the Market Revolution
in the American North

CHRISTOPHER CLARK

OVER THE PAST QUARTER-CENTURY many historians have bemoaned the fragmentation of their specialist fields and called for the return of the kind of overall synthesis that once seemed to provide clear interpretive frameworks for professional scholars and the public. Now, in the 1990s, American historians of the nineteenth century—one of the most rapidly growing and fragmented fields in the whole profession—have been offered just such an interpretive tool. The work of Charles Sellers and other scholars has presented the period between the American Revolution and the Civil War, and particularly the Jacksonian period, as dominated by a market revolution that transformed American economic life, linking farmers, planters, and merchants to national and international patterns of production and trade, laying the robust foundations of industrial power and creating commercial and financial institutions essential to a dynamic capitalist society. This transformation influenced much of American society, politics, and culture, producing fundamental shifts in the way American people conducted their lives and constructed their relationships with one another and shaping many of the rifts, conflicts, and inequalities that divided them.[1]

The concept of market revolution in nineteenth-century America has many strengths. Above all, it unites interpretations of politics, ideology, and culture with the findings of social and economic historians. It also links historians' traditional focus on elites with the newer emphasis on "history from below" and the perspective of the powerless and oppressed. It sweeps these findings and viewpoints together into a coherent synthesis that both reflects the powerful currents of change in early America and embraces the myriad varieties of circumstance and experience that framed the lives of an expanding, fragmenting, dynamic population.

Though I have reservations about it, I have no doubt that the concept of market revolution is a valuable general explanation of the period. Touching, as it does, the concerns of historians with widely divergent ideological perspectives, it is likely to remain so, precisely because it helps highlight, rather than obscure, the deep conflicts in American society.[2] As Charles Sellers shows, although early in the nineteenth century market developments did much to bind the new United States together and erase some of its regional distinctions, they also exacerbated the contradictions and tensions that would drive North and South into conflict and war, divide the Union, and almost destroy it. The market revolution did not prevent North and South from following their different social and economic trajectories. Only the northern victory in the Civil War, by ensuring the destruction of slavery and thwarting southern secession, guaranteed the political conditions for a single United States market. By the end of Reconstruction, the South had accepted neocolonial domination by a dynamic northern economy in return for the freedom to continue to oppress and exploit its former slave population.[3]

Yet my primary purpose in examining the *consequences* of the market revolution in the North is to suggest that, so far, these have often been assumed, rather than carefully examined. The debate has focused much more on its origins and development. The concept of market revolution arose mainly from scholarship that compared nineteenth-century society with the patterns of the colonial and revolutionary periods. It is novel because, until a decade or two ago, most historians accepted that, whatever *political* upheavals had resulted from the Revolution, American *society* had been largely unaffected, and continued to evolve within frameworks that had essentially been established by colonial settlement. America was usually assumed to have been "capitalist from the start," a set of colonial enterprises whose conduct and purpose was structured by the growing Atlantic market.[4] Since markets had always shaped American experience, the notion of a market revolution in the nineteenth century was unthinkable.

A generation of scholarship in several fields, particularly in the rural history of the American North, has altered these assumptions. Markets existed, of course, but their significance was often smaller than had been assumed. Rural societies, and the towns that handled commercial transactions, were essentially precapitalist. Production and exchange were usually household based, and used family or other forms of dependent labor. Only after the American Revolution did these circumstances start to alter radically: both production for market and wage labor became more significant and more dynamic aspects of social and economic life.[5] The market revolution consisted in the fabric of these changes, and in the marked contrasts that nineteenth-century society began to present with its colonial and revolutionary antecedents.

Historians' focus on the origins and processes of the market revolution has tended, so far, to distract them from a thorough evaluation of where all this change was leading. As I hope to show by looking at the period roughly from the 1820s to the 1870s, portrayals of the consequences have been selective and have tended to point in particular directions that contain only a partial account of the northern society that emerged in the mid-to late nineteenth century. Just as the concept of market revolution itself arose when scholars put together the varied findings from studies of the eighteenth century, so analysis of its effects will need to take account of a more rounded evaluation of the society it helped to shape.

At one level, we can see the market revolution embracing the kinds of economic changes that historians long associated with the early nineteenth century and that are now commonly associated with the emergence of American industrial capitalism. Broadly, we can identify four related sets of changes, all connected with the replacement of locally oriented, regionally self-sufficient rural economies by a national market network. First, the creation of a national market led to the coordination over long distances of the production, distribution, and consumption of goods of all kinds, so that families and individuals throughout the North were drawn into the various facets of this market. Second, market developments promoted significant concentrations of many forms of economic activity. Urban centers that serviced and directed trade grew in size and significance, and commercial power tended to become concentrated in fewer of these centers. During the middle of the century, for instance, Chicago emerged as the single most important urban center in the Midwest, taking over some of the functions of earlier centers such as Cincinnati and St. Louis; at the same time New York achieved a dominant position, both as a regional commercial hub and as a financial center that helped coordinate and profit from activities in Chicago and elsewhere. Capital, generated in trade, manufactures, and the land speculation that accompanied white settlement of the West, was increasingly channeled through urban banks and other lenders, and was invested in canals, railroads, factories, and mines on an unprecedented scale. Corporations, initially formed to handle investments too large for individuals or partnerships, began to emerge as significant economic actors. Third, all this activity entailed increasing mobility: of capital and the financial instruments essential for trade and investment; of goods, transported far and fast on canalboats, ships, and trains; of labor, drawn from rural and urban settings both in America and Europe, freed from traditional obligations to families and masters and carried across sea and land to build cities and transportation or to operate factories and farms. Powerful ideological currents validated a system based on the superiority of free and wage labor to the slavery of the South. Fourth, all these developments were accompanied by innovations in the structure and policies of government and legal systems that facilitated rapid change and smoothed the way for capital, labor, and goods to circulate in quantities and at a velocity that earlier generations could not have imagined. Government land policies, encouragement for transportation, and military action played a vital role, in particular, in the rapid settlement of the West. These processes of coordination, concentration, mobility, and state assistance were facets of the market revolution that most clearly promoted the material side of American economic development. In them we find many familiar facets of industrial change: mechanization, labor-saving devices, increases in productivity, economic booms and slumps, the relationships between economic activity and internal and international migration, the North's long shift from rural, agricultural republic to urban, industrial core economy. In the 1860s they permitted the mobilization of the labor and resources needed to win the Civil War. In these many manifestations of the market revolution, new ways of organizing economic life overwhelmed and replaced old patterns. Contemporaries and historians alike have dwelled on the power and profundity of these changes.[6]

The recent scholarship that Sellers and others drew upon has also illuminated many other facets of these changes. The market revolution was not merely a set of economic events; it tied material change to equally important patterns of cultural and political transformation. Markets were not just to do with production and distribution: historians are increasingly aware of the important cultural implications of changes in consumption that both drove and were facilitated by new patterns of manufacture and transport, and of the wider effects of this "consumer revolution" on politics, social relations, and individuals' construction of their own identities.[7] Participation in markets, both as producers and consumers, often obliged people to alter their assumptions and behavior. Today, it does not seem strange to us that farmers should send their best produce to market, but in the more locally oriented, household-based economies of the early nineteenth century, this was not the obvious course of action. Agricultural journals criticized farm families for eating their best food, rather than selling it; Fanny Kemble, on her visit to the United States in the 1830s, was told by a farmer that his family's poultry produced good eggs, but "the *very* fresh ones, we eat ourselves." Over time, such attitudes changed, as more and more farmers were drawn into market production. To people able to observe their contemporaries under such conditions, the change in behavior it brought about was often striking. When Wilhelmina Stille moved from rural Westphalia to an Ohio River settlement in the 1830s, she wrote of her brother, who had migrated four years earlier: "Wil-

helm is so much smarter here than he was in Germany I wouldn't have believed it." She attributed this to conditions we would associate with a market
society: "I think it's because he has so little work that is easy and he goes
around and talks with all the clever people about all kinds of business and so
on."[8] Participation in a market economy, whether as farmer, dealer, or wage
worker, often implied new values and attitudes. As Sellers amply reflects in
his book, historians have traced such changes in virtually every aspect of personal life: in religious belief and observance, in marriage, family structures,
child rearing, education, and attitudes toward sexuality. Plausibly, the development of "market" behavior was connected with all of them.

Moreover, these changes entailed material, cultural, and political upheavals, divisions, and conflicts. Practitioners of the new ecological history have
drawn attention to the alterations to the landscape that accompanied the
introduction of market-dedicated farming and logging and the growth of
industries dependent on water or mineral resources—changes that often
brought lasting damage to ecological systems—and to the profound transformation of the West as white settlement, the expropriation of Native
Americans, and the exploitation of animals, land, and minerals permanently
changed the face of half a continent in little more than a generation.[9] Patterns
of material life and cultural position became more varied. Family farming,
for example, remained at the heart of northern agriculture even as farmers
became market oriented, but their position as owners of property and producers of their own goods set farmers increasingly apart from the growing
numbers of agricultural and industrial wage workers, whose relationship to
the means of production were quite different. Class divisions within industrial districts and cities became more apparent, as distinctions grew between
"masters" and "hands" and as residential segregation by class became common. Political changes accompanied—even if they did not perfectly reflect—
these conflicts. In general terms, as Sean Wilentz has written, the market
revolution engendered new forms of mass party politics. More specifically, as
Sellers argues in his book, politics in the Jacksonian period became a conduit
for the deep antagonisms that arose between market-oriented and market-
resistant groups in American society; the emergence of mass democracy was
also accompanied by changes in legal and political practice that helped fend
off resistance to economic change and, in Sellers's words, "made democracy
safe for capitalism."[10] From the 1830s on, the North's rapid expansion and
change, with its political and ideological accompaniments, also deepened its
differences with the slave South, sharpening what Sellers calls "the great contradiction" in American society that would be resolved only by civil war.

So the evidence, both of material and economic conditions and of cultural and political circumstances, all points to deep changes in which the market revolution can be attributed a primary or contributory role. However, complex and multifaceted as these contributions were, and divided as historians' opinions are as to their precise significance, most interpretations on which the market revolution thesis rests share a series of assumptions in common about the directions American society took in the nineteenth century—assumptions essentially rooted in a set of binary comparisons between conditions before and after the market revolution had its effects.

To a considerable extent, discussions of market revolution agree in portraying the creation of a new American society and culture from a fixed menu of characteristics. Community gave way before individualism and competitiveness. The rise of long-distance trade, the growth of urban areas, and the decline of older patterns of neighborhood and reciprocity all produced greater impersonality, a greater need to deal with strangers, greater anonymity, and a more abstract system of transactions. Class divisions, mobility, and anonymity all made life more atomistic. Among other things, the market revolution helped instill a greater value on private life, on withdrawal from the world, on a focus on family above community, and on a guardedness about personal matters. These new patterns were mediated and legitimized, moreover, by the arguments of political economy—that "free" economic relationships conformed to the patterns of nature and should be exempt from interference by government or moral concerns—and by the ideology of free labor, which at once seemed to explain characteristics of the emergent society in the North and to sharpen its conflict with the ambitions of the slave South. The market revolution, in other words, embodied the emergence of American liberalism and its political, ideological, and institutional forms.

Such consequences, and their contrasts with an older, different culture, have long been familiar to historians. What is striking is that so many new studies have been shaped to fit them rather than to call them into question. My argument is not that these things did not happen, or that they are not an accurate reflection of tangible, powerful changes in nineteenth-century culture, but rather that they are in many ways a selective, mutually reinforcing collection of observations that direct attention away from a much richer tapestry of circumstances. In suggesting the need for a different approach, I shall first discuss some of the conceptual bases of the market revolution thesis and then set out some of the social and cultural features that are often missed in assessments of its consequences.

Arguments about the market revolution have tended to confirm older assumptions about the direction of social and cultural change because the very concept embodies a notion of irrevocable and irresistible pressure that rapidly influenced almost every aspect of American life and behavior. Sellers, more than many scholars, makes it abundantly clear that this pressure was resisted, and that the resistance structured American politics in the 1820s and 1830s; but even he, in the end, implies that the struggle would be lost. A crucial methodological question arises out of Sellers's employment of the market revolution concept: was it a set of events, or was it a process that *caused* those events and serves to explain them? Early in his book, Sellers employs the term in the first sense, but by the end he has adopted the second. The market and the market revolution change imperceptibly from descriptive categories of activities to reified explanatory forces. Somewhere in the process the cultural outcomes of the changes they brought about come to be assumed, and hence to seem inevitable. When markets and market values come to be seen as penetrating American society, we start to lose a sense of the intricate processes entailed in bringing this about. The market then becomes an abstract, catch-all explanation, resistant to detailed examination.

There are several objections to this interpretation. One is that it pays too little attention to the social-structural and cultural conditions that brought particular people, localities, and regions into new relationships with distant buyers and sellers of goods in the first place and that continued to shape their interaction as markets grew and became more integrated. On the eastern seaboard, for instance, Pennsylvania Germans and their English neighbors, as well as New England farmers, followed distinct paths toward a market-oriented society because their different social structures, family organization, labor patterns, and cultural practices all shaped the terms on which they would engage with it. Immigrant settlers in the West, too, developed their links with wider markets in the context of religious and cultural ties that they sustained in their new homes.[11] Further, the concept of the market is too abstract and general to capture adequately the complex systems of organization and practice that people created to handle the production, transportation, and processing of goods of all kinds. Though, undoubtedly, these practices shared much in common and it becomes possible to refer to the commodification of vast arrays of products and services, we need to understand the specific historical paths taken by separate markets in particular types of product. As William Cronon has recently shown, even in the late nineteenth century, as Chicago exercised its powerful influence as a concentrator of market forces throughout the West, the systems created to handle grain, lumber, and meat products each had a distinct history and a distinct set of social and institutional relationships. Neither in its origins nor in its consequences was the market revolution a single process. It entailed a complex reordering of social relations of many kinds.[12]

Two further issues arise from the complexity of the social structures and practices from which markets were created. *Market* is too often conflated with *capitalism;* historians have already begun to use the terms *market revolution* and *transition to capitalism* as if they were interchangeable.[13] But, while adaptation to dependence on markets entailed changes in the practices of production and consumption, it did not necessarily bring about changes in social relations: family farming, as we have seen, remained dominant in northern agriculture. The transition to capitalism was, on the other hand, essentially a shift in social relations, particularly the growth of wage labor, and in the commercial and institutional relationships that handled finance, production, and distribution on a larger and larger scale. The two processes were closely linked, but they were not identical. Indeed, as I have argued elsewhere, their connection was often paradoxical: because much agriculture in the North and West continued to be dominated by freehold farming on a scale manageable by family labor, direct capitalist exploitation of farmed land was rarely profitable. Merchants and manufacturers instead invested in handling, moving, and processing the products of the land, or in hiring surplus rural labor to work in workshops and factories to manufacture goods for profit. The market revolution on the land and the creation of capitalist industry were of course complementary: the creation of a national market was the organization on a monumental scale of the exchange of foodstuffs and manufactures between different people. But the processes were distinct.[14]

Second, though the importance and integration of the market economy grew steadily over time, it was not a simple linear process. As Sellers and others readily point out, the very conditions of markets made them unstable and subject to repeated booms and busts. At a local and family level, as well as in the minds of merchants and others with some power in the system, the constant reversals of market fortunes created doubts and resistance to its formal logic. Ideological changes did not, therefore, occur simply to keep pace with economic developments. They accompanied, instead, the much more complex interaction of perceptions about the market with actual social relations. Joyce Appleby, for instance, has argued that in the 1790s the prospects of competitive individualism and access to wage work presented a vision of opportunity to ordinary, poor Americans bounded by the constraints of a relatively hierarchical, household-centered, patriarchal society.[15] But this vision did not always remain fixed for such people. While many undoubtedly continued to share it, others found that the new social relationships and conditions of capitalist society set new bounds on them that—especially in the 1820s and 1830s and again after the Civil War—they entered labor or political movements to contest.[16]

Similarly, the effects of the evangelical revivals of the 1830s, combined with the unnerving experience of depression and bankruptcy at the end of that decade, led figures such as Lewis Tappan to urge new forms of moral restraint on the freewheeling market. Temperance reform, credit reporting, and other facets of individual self-control may have become part of the cultural apparatus of the market revolution during the course of its development, but they were neither part of its script at the outset nor inevitably bound to become so.[17] However, their intrusion helped redirect both aspects of economic life and the wider political debates about it. In so doing they made the process of market development more interrupted and less unidirectional than we are often inclined to conceive of it. For example, as Ann Fabian has argued, a moral critique of gambling grew up during the nineteenth century strongly in opposition to the assumptions and behavior of dealers in commodity markets and imposing standards and restraints that were clearly at odds with the earning of profits from particular markets.[18]

These points matter because they relate to the wider cultural and political consequences of people's engagement with market conditions and values. The precise character of market developments, the complex reordering of social relationships, the often paradoxical relations between capitalism and markets, and the moral and ideological contests that altered the direction of change all lead us to question our assumptions about the character of the society that emerged from all this. Undoubtedly the North became, to a great extent, more amoral, atomized, individualistic, and private than the colonial North had been, but it had other characteristics as well, and to portray it mainly in these terms is to be unjustifiably selective. If we look at four areas— moral economy, gender, collective behavior, and public life—we can see aspects of social and cultural practice that do not easily fit conventional interpretations. If we look at a fifth area, the practice and operation of the law, we can start to identify some of the terrain on which conflicts over economic and social power were waged in a market society.

While there is plenty of evidence that writers on political economy in the second half of the nineteenth century frequently argued for a separation of economic calculation from moral considerations, and so sought to insulate individual economic behavior from wider public scrutiny, there is room to doubt that this separation was so widely made at a popular level. Anecdotes

and jokes about trade and its tricks circulated in northern newspapers, al-
manacs, and journals, drawing on and recycling material into oral traditions
of storytelling and "yarning" that took place over farm gates and at taverns,
stores, and other places of trade. This genre had a double-edged character.
On the one hand, many stories depicted individuals being duped by the tricks
of trade, or getting their own back on merchants, peddlers, or dealers who
had sought to pull a fast one on them; much of the humor in these jokes and
tales bespoke an absence of sympathy with their victims and exemplified the
dangers, anxieties, and fearfulness of making transactions on which liveli-
hoods would depend. On the other hand, there was also an undercurrent of
indignation and moral repulsion at these circumstances, suggesting sympathy
among tellers and listeners for the dilemmas that trade imposed.[19]

The storytelling tradition supports other evidence, from a variety of
sources, for the continuation of values of "moral economy" among American
workers and farmers throughout the nineteenth century. Among farmers in
Massachusetts, New York, and elsewhere, the ethics of local exchange could
continue to govern transactions between neighbors well after dealings with
merchants and distant traders had begun to follow the rules of the market.
Support for the Granger movement in the 1870s, and for the Farmers' Alliance and Populist upsurge of the 1880s and 1890s, was based not just on "instrumentalist" complaints about low prices for marketable crops and the
amount of the cut taken by merchants, railroads, and commodity dealers,
but on deeper conceptions of community that implied moral standards of
fair dealing widely seen as violated by the commercial system.[20] Comparable
values continued to inform labor movements. Mary Blewett, for instance, has
shown that values of moral economy lay behind the protests of New England
workers in the 1850s and 1870s, while concepts of community and solidarity
helped to sustain the American labor movement during its most difficult
struggles in the 1880s and 1890s, even as the more instrumentalist strategies of Samuel Gompers's "bread-and-butter unionism" came to hold sway
among large groups of skilled workers.[21] Acceptance of the notion that the
market was morally neutral was, therefore, uneven and contested.

Class, race, gender, and occupation all influenced individuals' and groups'
perceptions of economic values. Historians generated many of their assumptions about the effects of the market revolution before they had begun to
incorporate an understanding of the influence of gender on the social and
cultural patterns they were studying. Evidence suggests that effects were variable and contested, and undermines confidence in overarching generalizations. Interpretations in this field have so far fallen roughly into two categories. Sellers, on one hand, follows earlier accounts of the history of women in

suggesting that men's and women's experiences were divided into "separate spheres." The full implications of the market revolution, he suggests, were faced mainly by men. It was they who adopted individualist, competitive behavior that separated economic concerns from morality. Men addressed commerce and production, while matters of nurture, morality, and conscience became the preserve of women. But, on the other hand, much recent work on gender relations has called into question the accuracy of the concept of separate spheres: it was based on contemporary prescriptive notions that, at most, presented an idealized vision of the lives of certain parts of the middle class. In practice, the connections between gender and market were much more complex than this vision suggested. Under most circumstances, in rural and urban areas, women remained directly involved in production of various kinds. Indeed, only the male-centered free labor ideology led to the increasing undervaluation of women's contributions either in the marketplace (where their labor was systematically underpaid) or in nonmarket, household tasks (which received no monetary compensation).[22]

We have, moreover, increasing evidence of the importance of women's participation in the marketplace as consumers and of the morally charged debates that these activities promoted among contemporary commentators on middle-class, farming, and working-class communities.[23] The notion of separate spheres is an ideological construct of commentators who were trying to impose order on a complex set of relationships; it is not an adequate guide to the varied terrain on which issues concerning gender were fought over. Historians continue to uncover the ironies of this struggle. A recent study of Holyoke, Massachusetts, for example, reveals that labor unions became strong there among sections of the Irish-American working class, but only as male institutions; in the middle decades of the nineteenth century, however, women formed a larger proportion of the city's Irish-American factory workforce than did men.[24] Concepts of work, community, and morality were therefore riven in many directions that interacted awkwardly with the logic of market participation.

Not only gender but also the organization of work and other activities should lead us to question the common assumption that the overwhelming outcome of the market revolution was to promote individualism and social atomization. Undoubtedly these things were important, but they do not alone adequately embrace the variety of experience of nineteenth-century Americans. We have, for one thing, too much evidence of the importance of churches and other voluntary organizations to accept without question the view that a market society merely corroded aspects of community. Moreover, the demands of production in an increasingly concentrated capitalist economy created new, unprecedented loci of collective activity—above all, in factories. Studies of urban life do not unequivocally support the contention that it was atomized and impersonal; many groups and individuals found in the neighborhoods and institutions they created new concepts of community and group identity. It is no coincidence, either, that many of the new forms of leisure and popular culture that emerged after midcentury were collective ones, based on the participation of large numbers of people as players, spectators, or consumers. While this collective experience was evidently promoted by entrepreneurs seeking to commercialize leisure, such market pressures were as often the result of popular collective action as the cause of it.[25]

Such evidence, in turn, suggests the need to reconceptualize our common assumptions about the role and importance of private life in a market-oriented society. Some notion of a shift from community and public culture toward private and individual experience has underlain many studies of the eighteenth- and nineteenth-century North, and it continues to hold sway as historians find new areas to explore. It is the strongest organizing theme, for instance, in Richard L. Bushman's recent book *The Refinement of America,* which traces the transmutation of eighteenth-century concerns with the public aspects of personal deportment and material culture into a growing nineteenth-century preoccupation with internalized self-discipline and the organization of private domestic space.[26] Yet, as Bushman's own evidence shows, these material and behavioral changes had profound public as well as private aspects. One of the highlights of the book is his account of the influence of private middle-class styles on the furnishing and architecture of churches: carpets, heating, and a growing preference for the Gothic helped, within a generation in the middle of the nineteenth century, to transform once chaste and simple meeting houses and churches into public versions of bourgeois parlors. But this does not support an argument for increasing private concerns; it reflects, rather, the terms on which certain people in a commercial society could use their power to shape aspects of public life. Bushman himself observes that this process of enrichment of nineteenth-century churches— which had to be paid for, of course, by congregations or wealthy benefactors—introduced new boundaries into the experience of religion, with profound effects on the later development of American Christianity. These boundaries, however, were not those between public and private; they were largely those of class. Acted out in the public sphere, the increasing distinction between sumptuous middle-class churches and denominations that held to older notions of public asceticism marked the growth of patterns of exclusivity in American society that supported other deep divisions between rich and poor.

"Individualism" was therefore gendered, and the "private" sphere marked by class division. In ways we do not yet fully understand, these emerging distinctions in society rearranged the terrain on which public life was conducted; but they did not destroy public life itself. Politics, religion, leisure, parades, the organization of urban amenities and space—all continued to be conducted in the public view; indeed, repeated and often successful efforts were made to resist their appropriation by private interests, or to reverse it if it had occurred.[27] The very concept of political culture, applied increasingly since the 1970s to studies of nineteenth-century politics, implies a notion that there existed shared perceptions of activities and behavior that remained predominantly in the public sphere. These perceptions changed with social and economic transformations, and also helped shape them, but they did not decline in importance.[28]

One major exception here was the law. There is evidence of an increasing tendency for those with economic power to make use of legal principles and court judgments that could shield their interests from public scrutiny or interference. With the rise of a historically based "critical legal studies" over the past generation, scholars have become increasingly aware of the fundamental role of the law in setting the ground rules and regulating the terms by which a market economy and industrial capitalism could establish themselves and expand. Charles Sellers referred to early nineteenth-century lawyers as the "shock troops" of American capitalism, "the main purveyors of capitalist ideology."[29] Certainly, in a host of legal disputes and decisions, state courts (particularly in the Northeast) worked out the means by which property, labor, and financial instruments would be brought together to accomplish unprecedented volumes of production and trade. This was not, of course, a process limited in time or scope. It would never end. Lawyers turned out to be not only the shock troops of a new development but a permanent and growing part of the scene. Throughout the United States, the principal work of county and state courts was to adjudicate disputes arising from the conduct of transactions, debt, and the disposition of property.[30] Important initiators of the market system, lawyers subsequently became its engineers, maintenance staff, and garbage collectors.

In the 1970s, the legal historian Morton Horwitz interpreted the courts and judge-made law as acting "instrumentally" to favor policies of economic development and capital accumulation, and hence the interests of the most advanced proponents of new developments in transportation, trade, and manufacturing.[31] Critics of this view have argued that legal principles evolved autonomously from social and economic interests; that lawyers and judges, as an increasingly large, specialist and professionalized group, drew on their common training, traditions, and practices to evolve distinctive "legal discourses" independent of class-based conceptions of economic interest or policy. In a recent study of labor law, Christopher L. Tomlins has sought to strike a balance between these opposing viewpoints.[32] His argument leads to some useful reflections on the relationships between law, culture, and the implications of the market revolution.

One of Tomlins's concerns is a problem that has confronted historians for a long time: how do we reconcile the pervasiveness of a free labor ideology in the mid-nineteenth-century North with the growing realization that the realities of wage labor were far from free or equal? Employment for wages entailed great inequalities of power and reward that the early labor movement increasingly sought to redress. Tomlins shows that the operation of the law in a variety of areas concerned with employment upheld the notion that the wage relation was an equitable contract freely entered into by employer and worker, while simultaneously it accorded to employers considerable private authority over the workers they hired.

Until the 1840s, charges could be brought against trade unions for criminal conspiracy to interfere with the free bargaining of individual workers with their bosses. Although a landmark Massachusetts decision in the case of *Commonwealth* v. *Hunt* (1842) effectively removed this threat to the existence of unions as such, the law of criminal conspiracy still closely restricted the kind of action workers could legally take collectively to assert or defend their rights. Similarly, a series of cases in the 1830s and 1840s severely limited employers' liability to pay damages for injuries suffered by workers in industrial accidents. Above all, however, Tomlins shows that courts during the early nineteenth century progressively extended the scope of old common-law "master and servant" rules to secure to employers widespread rights to regulate the conduct of their employees while they were at the workplace. Employers' power was essentially private, and only loosely constrained; workers, having made contracts of employment, had little scope to seek governmental regulation or political oversight of the day-to-day conditions they were obliged to accept.[33]

These developments in employment law evolved, Tomlins argues, not simply out of an instrumentalist conception of the law that drove judges to protect the interests of capital, but from the deeper origins of legal discourse in common law and Lockean principles of the defense of property. The position of employers as owners of capital and other property put them at an advantage in legal tussles with wage workers, who were bereft of such interests for the courts to acknowledge. Moreover, American law and the legal profession had, in the period after the Revolution, taken on a primary role in sheltering the interests of property from the claims of democracy that the Revolution itself had generated. Courts themselves, particularly in the Northeast, were not democratic institutions, and legal judgments tended to place decisions about property rights beyond the risk of legislative interference.

Issues central to the development of markets and industrial capitalism were therefore placed largely outside the realm of politics. When Tocqueville visited the United States in the early 1830s, he noted not only the abundance of lawyers and their importance in the conduct of public affairs, but also that "lawyers as a body form the most powerful, if not the only, counterpoise to the democratic element," being "secretly opposed to the instincts of democracy."[34] Linked to Tocqueville's further reflections on American democracy, however, this conclusion comes to more than just an astute observation. In democracies, Tocqueville argued, elites would withdraw themselves from public life to cultivate their interests in private. Lawyers and the law provided the crucial medium by which the chief beneficiaries of the market revolution could insulate themselves from popular power and, at the same time, exercise profitable, legally sanctioned power over the very people they perceived as a threat. "Privacy" was not so much a politically neutral social consequence of a market economy, as a carefully evolved, necessary condition of its continuation in a democratic context.

The consequences of the market revolution were therefore even more complex and charged with conflict than has sometimes been assumed. New public as well as private spheres, new collectivities and communities as well as individualism, grew out of the profound economic and social transformation of the early nineteenth century. The point is, though, of course, that this was by no means a completed transformation: the market revolution and the evolution of industrial capitalism have, with other developments (including strong inclinations to collective and public economic provision), continued to shape American society ever since, sometimes continuing, sometimes reversing the cultural trends that they helped initiate in the nineteenth century. Yet widespread beliefs in individualism, privacy, free labor, inventiveness, competition, and entrepreneurship have continued to underpin American capitalism and to influence both popular and scholarly interpretations of its emergence. The conventional historical interpretation of the effects of the market revolution that this essay has sought to qualify is, to a great extent, rooted in the broader set of popular beliefs about capitalism that, using the proper sense of the term, we can call a mythology.

Why did this particular mythology emerge? Why did it focus on the individualist, contractual, private aspects of the market revolution, rather than the collective, moral, public characteristics that, as Sellers and others have shown, so often formed the basis for resistance to the market's more grasping and destructive implications? The stress on certain consequences and not others has not merely been selective. It has supported a set of ideological assumptions that endorsed the changes favored by certain types of market actors. Like any ideology, it has also effectively hidden from view other aspects of the culture these changes helped bring into being. One view would be that the mythology was a product of the ideological hegemony of the beneficiaries and supporters of American capitalism, who by care and manipulation turned a particular set of contested notions about society into what seemed natural "common sense." But hegemony does not have to work that way. Rather than being a conscious process, it is more likely to have emerged as an unconscious result of a number of circumstances. Chief among these were the double-edged character of market dealings, and the appealing half-truth that wage labor was "free" of burdensome obligations. Under the particular conditions of the American North, it became possible to emphasize exclusively one side of a set of more complex social and cultural conditions.

Individualism, inventiveness, mobility, freedom, and entrepreneurialism were not the conditions under which most nineteenth-century people lived. They describe most closely, even if not completely, the circumstances of adult white males, especially those with property. Women, the poor, and dependent people were usually excluded from their benefits. They represent the circumstances of those most readily able to take action in a market economy: artisans able to set up their own shops; farmers who could sustain themselves on their land, or alternatively could move to settle new areas in the West; workers with the skill or good fortune to be able to bargain effectively for wages and move to a new job if conditions were not right in the existing one.

However, as labor historian Charles Stephenson has pointed out, in an industrial economy where employment was often seasonal and intermittent and in which unemployment was endemic, mobility and entrepreneurship were qualities necessary even among workers with little or no property, not in order to make fortunes but as strategies for survival. Enough people did move, enough did invent some new technique or machine, enough did gain from buying cheap and selling dear that the selected aspects of popular mythology were at least partially in accordance with many people's experience.[35]

Above all, though the democratic system was bypassed by important court decisions that affected the terms on which so many people lived and worked, the achievement of some popular aspirations—including squatters' preemption rights, homestead exemptions, abolition of imprisonment for debt, mechanics' lien laws, and the homestead law itself—meant that politics, too, continued to be widely perceived as a worthwhile and legitimate channel for people's interest and support.

But the mythology did not present the whole picture. I hope, in reviewing these issues, to have opened the way for discussion of the wider ramifications of the market revolution for people's experience in the nineteenth century. Matters that were, on the face of it, material ones, segregated into the increasingly private spheres of property and business calculation and held by political economists to be beyond the bounds of moral discussion or political interference, were in practice constantly contested in the wider public culture of politics, religion, and ideologies. Interpreting the market revolution's public and collective consequences is essential for understanding some of the most crucial aspects of American cultural change: the impact of religious revivals, reform movements, and abolitionism; the vibrant role of politics in so many people's lives; the moral roots of labor and populist protest; and the concepts of public duty and national identity that drove so many tens of thousands of farming people and wage workers to flock to military and voluntary service on the North's behalf during the Civil War.

NOTES

1. Charles Sellers, *The Market Revolution: Jacksonian America, 1815–1846* (New York, 1991). See also Harry L. Watson, *Liberty and Power: The Politics of Jacksonian America* (New York, 1990); Sean Wilentz, "Society, Politics, and the Market Revolution, 1815–1848," in Eric Foner, ed., *The New American History* (Philadelphia, 1990); and Paul E. Johnson, "Market Revolution," in Mary K. Cayton, Elliott J. Gorn, and Peter W. Williams, eds., *Encyclopedia of American Social History*, 3 vols. (New York, 1993), 1:545–60.

2. A sign of this is that much early critical appraisal of Sellers's book has addressed facets of his argument rather than attacking his overall theme. See, for example, "A Symposium on Charles Sellers, *The Market Revolution: Jacksonian America, 1815–1846*," *Journal of the Early Republic* 12 (1992): 445–76, with contributions from Richard E. Ellis, Mary H. Blewett, Joel H. Silbey, Major L. Wilson, Harry L. Watson, and Amy Bridges, and a response by Charles Sellers.

3. James M. McPherson, *Abraham Lincoln and the Second American Revolution* (New York, 1991), chap. 1.

4. This argument, widely accepted in the 1950s and 1960s, was summarized by Carl Degler in *Out of Our Past* (New York, 1970).

5. New findings in rural history are briefly summarized in Sellers, *Market Revolution,* chap. 1. The reinterpretation began with two articles published in the late 1970s: Michael Merrill, "Cash Is Good to Eat: Self-Sufficiency and Exchange in the Rural Economy of the United States," *Radical History Review* 4 (1977): 42–71, and James A. Henretta, "Families and Farms: *Mentalité* in Pre-Industrial America," *William and Mary Quarterly* 35 (1978): 3–32. The debate they touched off is summarized in Allan Kulikoff, "The Transition to Capitalism in Rural America," *William and Mary Quarterly* 46 (1989): 120–44.

6. Many of the economic and technological aspects of these changes were described by George Rogers Taylor, *The Transportation Revolution, 1815–1860* (New York, 1951). Stuart Bruchey, *Enterprise: The Dynamic Economy of a Free People* (Cambridge, Mass., 1990), provides a more recent thematic discussion by an economic historian. On national markets and their effect on regional manufacturing patterns, see David R. Meyer, "Emergence of the American Manufacturing Belt: An Interpretation," *Journal of Historical Geography* 9, no. 2 (1983): 145–74. On Chicago's growth and its relationships to other cities, see William Cronon, *Nature's Metropolis: Chicago and the Great West* (New York, 1991), esp. chaps. 2 and 6.

7. On the growing new literature on American consumption in the eighteenth and nineteenth centuries, see Timothy H. Breen, "'Baubles of Britain': The American and Consumer Revolutions of the Eighteenth Century," *Past and Present* 119 (1988): 73–104; Elizabeth A. Perkins, "The Consumer Frontier: Household Consumption in Early Kentucky," *Journal of American History* 78, no. 2 (1991): 486–510; and David Jaffee, "Peddlers of Progress and the Transformation of the Rural North, 1760–1860," *Journal of American History* 78, no. 2 (1991): 511–35.

8. Wilhelmina Stille to her parents, Powhatan Point, Ohio, [Oct. 1837?], in Walter D. Kamphoefner, Wolfgang Helbich, and Ulrike Sommer, eds., *News from the Land of Freedom: German Immigrants Write Home,* trans. Susan C. Vogel (Ithaca, N.Y., 1991), p. 71.

9. On commercial farming's impact on the New England landscape, see Carolyn Merchant, *Ecological Revolutions: Nature, Gender, and Science in New England* (Chapel Hill, N.C., 1989); on its transformation of midwestern grain-, lumber-, and meat-raising regions, see Cronon, *Nature's Metropolis,* chaps. 3–5. An excellent case study of manufacturing's impact on landscape is Theodore Steinberg, *Nature Incorporated: Industrialization and the Waters of New England* (Cambridge, Eng., 1991). For general statements concerning the rapacity of Americans' appropriation of the West, see Patricia Nelson Limerick, *The Legacy of Conquest: The Unbroken Past of the American West* (New York, 1987). On the complex human geography of exploitation see William Cronon, "Kennecot Journey: The Paths out of Town," in William Cronon, George Miles, and Jay Gitlin, eds., *Under an Open Sky: Rethinking America's Western Past* (New York, 1992), pp. 28–51; and Clyde A. Milner, Carol A. O'Connor, and Martha A. Sandweiss, eds., *The Oxford History of the American West* (New York, 1994).

10. Wilentz, "Society, Politics, and the Market Revolution," p. 18; Sellers, *Market Revolution,* p. 348.

11. Barry Levy, *Quakers and the American Family: British Settlement in the Delaware Valley* (New York, 1988), pp. 14, 125, 152; Lucy Simler and Paul G. E. Clemens, "The 'Best Poor Man's Country' in 1783: The Population Structure of Rural Society in Late-Eighteenth-Century Southeastern Pennsylvania," *Proceedings of the American Philosophical Society* 133, no. 2 (1989): 234–61; Christopher Clark, *The Roots of Rural Capitalism: Western Massachusetts, 1780–1860* (Ithaca, N.Y., 1990), esp. chap. 3; on German immigrants see Kamphoefner, Helbich, and Sommer, *News from the Land of Freedom*, and on Scandinavians, Jon Gjerde, *From Peasants to Farmers: The Migration from Balestrand, Norway, to the Upper Middle West* (Cambridge, Eng., 1985), chap. 8.

12. Cronon, *Nature's Metropolis*, chaps. 3–5.

13. Johnson, "Market Revolution," p. 545.

14. Christopher Clark, "Agrarian Societies and Economic Development in Nineteenth-Century North America," in Walther L. Bernecker and Hans Werner Tobler, eds., *Development and Underdevelopment in America: Contrasts of Economic Growth in North and Latin America in Historical Perspective* (Berlin, 1993), esp. pp. 195–206.

15. Joyce O. Appleby, *Capitalism and a New Social Order: The Republican Vision of the 1790s* (New York, 1983).

16. Bruce Laurie, *Working People of Philadelphia, 1800–1850* (Philadelphia, 1980), pp. 85–104; Sean Wilentz, *Chants Democratic: New York City and the Rise of the American Working Class, 1788–1850* (New York, 1984), pp. 219–54; David Montgomery, *Beyond Equality: Labor and the Radical Republicans, 1862–1872* (New York, 1967), esp. chap. 6.

17. On aspects of self-control and responses to the market, see for example Bertram Wyatt-Brown, *Lewis Tappan and the Evangelical War against Slavery* (Cleveland, 1969); Clark, *Roots of Rural Capitalism*, chap. 6; Stephen Nissenbaum, *Sex, Diet, and Debility in Jacksonian America: Sylvester Graham and Health Reform* (Westport, Conn., 1980).

18. Ann Fabian, *Card Sharps, Dream Books, and Bucket Shops: Gambling in Nineteenth-Century America* (Ithaca, N.Y., 1990), pp. 2–5, 10. Fabian points out, moreover, that nineteenth-century constraints on gambling were reversed in the second half of the twentieth century.

19. The preceding paragraphs are based on my own research for an as yet unpublished paper, "Trading Tales: Economy and Culture in Rural New England, 1750–1830" (1990).

20. Clark, *Roots of Rural Capitalism*, pp. 273–74; Nancy Grey Osterud, *Bonds of Community: The Lives of Farm Women in Nineteenth-Century New York* (Ithaca, N.Y., 1991), pp. 61, 204–10, 277–78; Robert C. McMath, *Populist Vanguard: The Origins of the Southern Farmers' Alliance* (Chapel Hill, N.C., 1975); Bryan Palmer, *Man over Money* (Chapel Hill, N.C., 1980).

21. Mary H. Blewett, "Society and Economic Change," in "Symposium on Charles Sellers, *Market Revolution*," 452–53.

22. On gender and work, see Jeanne Boydston, *Home and Work: Housework, Wages, and the Ideology of Labor in the Early Republic* (New York, 1990); and Thomas Dublin, *Transforming Women's Work: New England Lives in the Industrial Revolution* (Ithaca, N.Y., 1994). On rural areas, see Nancy Grey Osterud, "Gender and the Transition to Capitalism in Rural America," *Agricultural History* 67, no. 2 (1993): 14–29; and Osterud, *Bonds of Community*, esp. pp. 1–13. On urban working women, see Thomas L. Dublin, *Women at Work: The Transformation of Work and Community in Lowell, Massachusetts, 1826–1860*

(New York, 1979); Christine Stansell, *City of Women: Sex and Class in New York, 1780–1860* (New York, 1986); and Mary H. Blewett, *Men, Women, and Work: Class, Gender, and Protest in the New England Shoe Industry, 1790–1910* (Urbana, Ill., 1988).

23. Daniel Horowitz, *The Morality of Spending: Attitudes toward the Consumer Society in America* (Baltimore, 1985).

24. William F. Hartford, *Working People of Holyoke: Work and Ethnicity in a Massachusetts Mill Town, 1850–1960* (New Brunswick, N.J., 1990).

25. On urban neighborhoods, see Kenneth A. Scherzer, *The Unbounded Community: Neighborhood Life and Social Structure in New York City, 1830–1875* (Durham, N.C., 1992); on leisure, see Roy Rosenzweig, *Eight Hours for What We Will: Workers and Leisure in an Industrial City, 1870–1920* (Cambridge, Eng., 1983) and Warren Goldstein, *Playing for Keeps: A History of Early Baseball* (Ithaca, N.Y., 1989).

26. Richard L. Bushman, *The Refinement of America: Persons, Houses, Cities* (New York, 1992).

27. Mary Ryan, "The American Parade," in Lynn Hunt, ed., *The New Cultural History* (Berkeley, Calif., 1989), chap. 5; Roy Rosenzweig and Elizabeth Blackmar, *The Park and the People: A History of Central Park* (Ithaca, N.Y., 1992); on the reversal of policies leaving public works in private hands, see Robin L. Einhorn, *Property Rules: Political Economy in Chicago, 1833–1872* (Chicago, 1991).

28. Daniel Walker Howe, *The Political Culture of the American Whigs* (Chicago, 1979); Ronald P. Formisano, *The Transformation of Political Culture: Massachusetts Parties, 1790s–1840s* (New York, 1983). See also Jean Fagan Yellin and John C. Van Horne, eds., *The Abolitionist Sisterhood: Women's Political Culture in Antebellum America* (Ithaca, N.Y., 1994).

29. Sellers, *Market Revolution*, p. 47.

30. This was so even in newly settled regions; see, for example, Gordon Morris Bakken, *Practicing Law in Frontier California* (Lincoln, Nebr., 1991).

31. Morton Horwitz, *The Transformation of American Law, 1780–1860* (Cambridge, Mass., 1977).

32. Christopher L. Tomlins, *Law, Labor, and Ideology in the Early American Republic* (Cambridge, Eng., 1993).

33. Tomlins, *Law, Labor, and Ideology*, esp. chaps. 6–8, 10.

34. Alexis de Tocqueville, *Democracy in America*, quoted in Sellers, *Market Revolution*, p. 47.

35. Charles Stephenson, "'There's Plenty Waitin' at the Gates': Mobility, Opportunity, and the American Worker," in Charles Stephenson and Robert Asher, eds., *Life and Labor: Dimensions of American Working-Class History* (Albany, N.Y., 1986), pp. 72–91; on inventions by "ordinary people with relatively common knowledge," see Kenneth L. Sokoloff and B. Zorina Khan, "The Democratization of Invention during Early Industrialization: Evidence from the United States, 1790–1846," *Journal of Economic History* 50, no. 2 (1990): 363–78 (quotation from p. 364).

2

Slavery and Development in a Dual Economy:
The South and the Market Revolution

HARRY L. WATSON

T HE MARKET REVOLUTION of the nineteenth century had no more enthusiastic supporter than Edward Lee Winslow, president of a plank
road that was under construction between western North Carolina
and the Cape Fear River, a potential highway to the Atlantic Ocean. Speaking
to his stockholders in 1850, Winslow rhapsodized over the future prospects
of transportation development. By his calculations, a backcountry farmer
with twenty-five barrels of flour and a two-horse wagon could use the road
to reduce his traveling time to market by as much as three days in each direction, while the volume of traffic on the road would bring annual profits of 10
to 12 percent to the investors. The consequences could be vast, he predicted,
in a tone that was both hortatory and optimistic: "Man was placed on the
earth to subdue and conquer it . . . , and there are no barriers which Nature
has erected, which may not be overcome with energy and exertion. Improve
and cheapen the means of transportation,—relieve the productive labor of
the country of the evils arising from bad roads,—give a quick and healthful
circulation through all the arteries of trade,—and you raise the value of all
descriptions of property, to say nothing of the blessings of the improvement
in the social and religious condition of the population consequent thereon."[1]

Winslow described the material advantages of plank roads in such alluring
detail that one wonders why the farmers and stockholders needed so much
persuasion, and what accounted for the mysterious "veil," as Winslow put it,
"which has so long covered their eyes and blinded them to their interests."
The corporate executive gave a partial hint somewhat later in his report. "Our
people in North Carolina," he admitted, "must become accustomed to paying Tolls."[2]

Edward Lee Winslow was in many ways typical of the commercial boosters
of internal improvements in the antebellum South. He came from a long-
established mercantile family in the fall-line market town of Fayetteville. He
promised extravagant profits to customers and investors and widespread advantages to regional development if only an impatient audience would carry

his project a little bit further. In addition to material gains, he longed for cultural improvements and promised unspecified benefits to "the social and religious condition of the population." Above all, he railed against the ignorance and apathy that somehow hobbled his efforts at every turn.[3]

What can account for Winslow's defensiveness and frustration? Why, as late as 1850, were some southern Americans apparently still indifferent to the benefits of internal improvements? Why was it so hard to get farmers to submit to the cash requirements of a toll road system, despite the seemingly obvious benefits of cheaper and faster transportation? Why, half a century after North Carolina's embrace of the Great Revival, did a commercial booster long for the religious improvements that he expected to follow from a deeper commitment to the market economy? Above all, historians could ask, did the difficulties Winslow faced have something to do with the values and assumptions that grew up around the institution of slavery and the South's plantation economy?

The emerging concept of a market revolution in the nineteenth-century United States can help us to answer these questions. As articulated in Charles Sellers's exciting synthesis, the concept ties together contemporary movements in the economy, the society, the religion, the politics, and the larger culture of antebellum America.[4] The economic and cultural circumstances of the South make clear, however, that the regional impact of commercialization was highly uneven.

Parts of the South had been fully integrated into the Atlantic market economy ever since the development of the tobacco plantation and its export trade in the early seventeenth century. Remoter sections were still isolated in the middle of the nineteenth century, and even then were not always eager to expand their market connections. As the antebellum period advanced, however, a corps of local reformers struggled to hasten this transition, to bring the isolated parts of the South within the sphere of dominant market relations, to transform what they regarded as the backward culture of inland regions, and to cement thereby the loyalties of nonslaveholding whites to the threatened institution of African slavery. Their success in this effort was limited at best, and the South began its war for independence with serious and persisting divisions between its slaveholding and nonslaveholding sectors.

The history of the market revolution in the South is thus the story of a "dual economy." Students of twentieth-century economic development first applied this term to colonial societies that were divided between commercial, western-dominated sectors and highly traditional forms of production that were relatively isolated from the pressures of contemporary capitalism. Morton Rothstein has extended the term to describe the difference between the plantation and semisubsistence sectors of the Old South. The concept must not be applied too rigidly: even the most heavily commercialized plantations were usually self-sufficient in food, and some cash exchanges with the outside world took place in the most isolated yeoman communities. As a heuristic device, however, the notion of a dual economy is indeed very useful as we seek to understand the bewilderment of Mr. Edward Lee Winslow and the whole range of Dixie's diverse responses to the market revolution.[5]

Sellers's account of the market revolution begins with the favorable ratio of free population to land in eighteenth-century America. This basic circumstance gave most white Americans an unusual opportunity to live well without depending on landlords, creditors, or restrictive commercial relationships. Matters began to change at the end of the eighteenth century, however, and kept changing at an ever-increasing pace through the middle of the nineteenth century and beyond. Despite the safety valve of a frontier, rising population pressed heavily against natural resources and forced free Americans into a greater division of labor, a new class structure, a search for comparative advantages in town and country, a commodification of labor and its products, and a sometimes grudging submission to the dictates of prices and markets in arranging the basic patterns of their lives. Seeking to protect the autonomy of the household (more precisely, of its patriarchal head), rural families took up domestic manufacturing, urban artisans suffered the humiliations and privations of the sweatshop, infant industries began their streamside clatter, and the power of the bank, the bank note, and the countinghouse spread across the country. Among the middle and upper classes, moreover, the opportunities for upward mobility, residential segregation by class, and the divorce of home and work all encouraged a new emphasis on female domesticity, masculine self-discipline and self-denial, and evangelical reform.[6]

The advantages of this process were obvious to many: cash incomes rose and consumer goods became more accessible to a widening circle of customers. Historians are also aware of the possibilities for increased liberty and personal growth for middle-class women, who benefited from their gradual abandonment of household production and their enhanced moral standing under the cult of domesticity. The disadvantages were more subtle. Deepened involvement in the market economy subjected millions to the power of the business cycle for the first time, and previously independent producers, whether urban artisans or rural yeomen, felt the demeaning sting of dependence on their social and economic superiors.

The reaction, Sellers tells us, was the powerful populist clamor for American democracy. Starting in the realm of religion, American plain folk claimed immediate personal access to divine knowledge and a moral and spiritual superiority to clerical and worldly elites. In the secular realm, kindred spirits to Sellers's "antinomians" demanded limits on the powers of the bourgeois classes who promoted and fattened on the growing power of the marketplace. Drawing on republican traditions, they insisted on political equality and curbs on economic transformation, and adopted Andrew Jackson as their champion. Opposing them, the friends of commercial progress sought support in the Whig party and the reforming, uplifting, and disciplining power of the moderately evangelical churches. Ultimately, however, ordinary citizens' commitment to private property blunted their radical impulses, and America became a bourgeois republic with an unresolved tension between capitalism and democracy.[7]

When stated in this manner, the concept of a market revolution seems especially tailored for the world of the urbanizing and industrializing Northeast. On the surface, the experience of the South seems vastly different. For one thing, the South's population did not grow nearly as much between 1790 and 1860 as the North's did, although the territory for southern migration was ample. Specifically, the states south of Pennsylvania had held almost 2 million of the nation's 3.9 million inhabitants at the time of the first federal census in 1790, but the slave states contained only 12.2 out of 31.4 million on the eve of the Civil War. According to Sellers's model, a lower ratio of people to land removed one obvious stimulus for market-driven change in the antebellum South.[8] Despite the best efforts of men like Edward Lee Winslow, moreover, the South also lagged in the growth of cities, the development of manufactures, the construction of canals and railroads, and the general increase of wealth. Though cliometricians now insist that southern incomes were as much as 80 percent of the national average by 1860, evidence of the South's near-colonial dependency and underdevelopment seemed as powerful to most contemporaries as it has to generations of nonquantitative historians.[9]

Properly understood, however, the market revolution has very important implications for southern history. The most obvious consequence was the massive geographical expansion of the slave states as the Cotton Kingdom took shape. The growth of the factory system in old and New England sent southerners westward in search of fresh land to grow cotton, especially in the aftermath of the War of 1812. The resulting mass migration extended the "South" from the shores of the Atlantic Ocean to the borders of Mexico and touched off fantasies of a continental empire based on slavery. The consequences of expansion were vast, not only for the ambitious planters who gained the most from it, but more especially for the slaves who were torn away from friends and family and "sold down the river," in the slave trade's ultimate commodification of human life and labor.

Southern experience of the market revolution did not stop with western migration. The rise of white man's democracy, the growth of evangelical religion, and the political conflict of the second party system were prominent features of antebellum history in both major sections of the country. The market revolution had a different impact in the South, however, owing to important preexisting features of its economy, geography, and society. The cumulative impact of these differences was to create a prolonged struggle to "modernize" the slave South, a struggle that was only partially successful. In the final analysis, the institution of slavery had a powerful, paradoxical influence in pushing the South toward ever-greater commercialization, yet also in slowing its progress toward that end, leaving a unique regional coloration to the market revolution and its consequences.

The paradoxical effects of the market revolution in the South stemmed directly from its dual economy. The most fertile and accessible parts of the Atlantic seaboard had long been active in world trade. Favored with flat terrain, fertile soil, and navigable rivers, these regions traditionally produced semitropical staples for export abroad, using waterborne transportation and slave labor in plantation settings. The favorite crops at the time of American independence were tobacco, rice, and indigo. Over time, cotton and sugar joined the list and indigo disappeared, but the dependence of southern planters on export agriculture and the vagaries of international prices and credit terms remained constant.[10]

Inland regions of the South faced differing circumstances. In the states that bordered the Atlantic, a rising scarp of land cut across the coastal plain at a distance between fifty and two hundred miles from the coast, placing rapids in the river systems and cutting off easy access to the coast. Beyond this fall line, a plateau known as the Piedmont stretched to the Appalachian mountains. Climate and topography imposed obstacles to plantation agriculture in the Piedmont; while the region supported a sprinkling of large slaveholding estates, most inhabitants were modest farmers with small landholdings and few or no slaves. Using their own labor, these farmers and their families produced corn and pork for their own consumption and largely clothed themselves with homespun textiles. They carried some foodstuffs to fall-line market towns to exchange for the few articles they could not make themselves, but their communities remained far more self-sufficient than the plantation districts of the low country or tidewater. Similar conditions prevailed in the swampy or infertile portions of the coastal plain, where dense pine forests prevailed against the expansion of the plantation region.[11]

As the South expanded in the early nineteenth century, the same division between slaveholding and nonslaveholding regions was reproduced in the transappalachian West. The valleys of navigable rivers fostered cotton plantations tilled by slaves, while the adjoining upland regions supported more isolated communities of yeoman farmers with fewer slaves and limited market connections. In this dual economy, therefore, one sector was closely connected to the world market while the other was relatively isolated from it. Any major economic change in the region was likely to affect these two sectors very differently.[12]

Over the last generation, considerable historiographical strife has swirled over the question of whether the plantation sector of this economy should be called capitalist. Building on the earlier insights of Ulrich B. Phillips, Eugene D. Genovese has called the planters "pre-capitalist" and "quasi-seigneurial," while critics such as Charles Sellers, Kenneth M. Stampp, Robert W. Fogel, and Stanley Engerman dismiss such claims.[13] In the end, the issue boils down to a question of definition and perspective. Historians who focus on the relationship of planters to the outside world—on their interactions with factors, bankers, and suppliers—will always see them as capitalists in a capitalist world. The slave plantation came into existence as part of the expanding capitalism of the sixteenth century, these scholars point out, and it remained a part of the capitalist world until it perished.[14] Historians who study the master-slave relationship, however, are more likely to see the planter as something other than an ordinary capitalist who exploits nominally free proletarians by a system of meager wages. In this view, slaves were not free and planters paid no wages, so slavery could never be capitalism. Unlike true capitalists, moreover, masters could not threaten their workers with dismissal. To get their slaves to work efficiently, masters had no choice but to offer a system of rewards as well as punishments, a practice that evolved into a system of reciprocal obligations Genovese has called *paternalism*. Some scholars have rejected this concept vehemently, understanding Genovese to mean that planters were characteristically kind and benevolent to their human chattels, but I would not share such a reading.

Deriving as it does from rival definitions of capitalism, this debate could easily go on forever. It is worth observing, however, that in a recent summary of cliometric findings on slavery, a perceptive admirer of that school notes the superior efficiency of slave agriculture and the impeccably capitalist credentials of the slave owners, only to ask why the South invested so heavily in slavery, "when rates of return in many antebellum southern industries were three to eight times higher than the rate of return on slaves?"[15] From a purely cliometric perspective there is no clear answer, but Phillips's dictum, quoted approvingly by Genovese, that the plantation was "less a business than a life" seems to have renewed relevance in this context.[16] While planters seem to have been acutely sensitive to the profit motive generally and to good business practices within the setting of the plantation world itself, they would not abandon plantations for a higher return in industry. In other words, even the cliometric evidence reveals that cultural and psychological satisfactions made the investment in slaves (and the death-struggle to retain them) a matter of cultural and emotional commitment, and more than a simple business calculation.

Phillips's remark reminds us why the argument over slavery-as-capitalism broke out in the first place. By the late 1950s, revisionist historians had persuaded themselves that the North and the South were compatible societies with little of substance to fight over, and study of the causes of the Civil War had worn itself out in what Eric Foner called "a fruitless metaphysical debate over the problem of inevitability."[17] Genovese's early work challenged this impasse with a powerful depiction of two fundamentally different societies. "From the moment that slavery passed from being one of several labor systems into being the basis of the southern social order," he insisted, "material and ideological conflict with the north came into being and had to grow worse."[18] On the whole, subsequent scholarship has vindicated this fundamental insight, even as other historians have largely eschewed Genovese's terminology. Though they differ on many details, for example, J. Mills Thornton III and William J. Cooper, Jr., have both reminded us how the existence of slavery gave a special tinge to southern politics, even when abolitionism itself was not an issue.[19]

To insist on "capitalism" and "precapitalism" as the source of crucial social differences between North and South would shackle historians to a rigid and useless teleology, but it would be equally foolish to ignore these differences. The best solution is simply to say that the market sector of the South's dual economy was a slave society that depended on the technology and institutions of the capitalist world, even as its dominant individuals sometimes feared and resisted the subversive power of those same institutions.[20]

The South's twisted relationship to the world of the marketplace was most directly felt by the slaves themselves. Legally defined as chattel property, enslaved persons were not only participants in commerce but also the objects of it. Too often, the most significant aspect of the market revolution for slaves was the increased possibility of being sold in it. The expansion of cotton production that followed Whitney's gin brought a vastly expanded domestic slave trade, and year after year the auction block parted thousands of husbands and wives, parents and children, friends and other relatives, imposing slavery's most enduring grief. At the same time, scholars are becoming increasingly aware of slaves' own role as marketplace participants who used their access to gardens and free time to produce goods for sale, to buy and sell independently, and to accumulate property. Joining the market economy—however marginally—gave slaves the opportunity to improve their standards of living and to enjoy a few benefits of personal autonomy. Like worship, or music, or storytelling, the internal economy of the slave community is emerging from the shadows as one of many means that African Americans used to press for freedom and assert their own humanity.[21]

In truth, there were many slave trades. Raiding and kidnapping to supply the demands of European or Arab traders had been a brutal and disruptive influence in the society of West Africa and did not fully disappear with the legal abolition of the international slave trade in 1807. Another round of buying and selling took place in America, as captains disposed of their human cargoes from Bahía to the Chesapeake and beyond. From the earliest years, masters traded slaves in local markets, as death or financial reverses or changing business strategies dictated a resort to the auction block. There was also a lively rental market, in which the hired slave might change masters as often as once a year. All of these markets exposed their victims to brutality and humiliation and the devastating possibility of separation from friends and family.

The best-known slave trade of all, and the one most affected by the complex transformation we are calling the market revolution, was the enterprise that carried surplus slaves from old tobacco regions around the Chesapeake and other areas of the Upper South down to the cotton and cane fields of the Deep South. Frederic Bamcroft published the first systematic account of this business in 1931. More recently, Michael Tadman has produced an invaluable monograph and Edmund L. Drago has edited a remarkable collection of trading correspondence.[22] Tadman's careful quantitative analysis has mapped the contours of the South's human traffic over time and space. He confirms that the growing demand for cotton first sparked a sizable domestic trade in North American slaves during the 1790s, as Upper South masters sent surplus chattels to the expanding plantations of the Deep South and later to the Old Southwest. The approaching end of the African slave trade in 1807 only increased the activity of the domestic market. Whereas previous scholars had attributed most of the interregional movement of slaves to migrating planters who carried whole communities of slaves with them to new territories, Tadman finds that professional slave traders accounted for a large portion of the migration from the start. In the decade of the 1820s, he estimates that professional "Negro speculators" carried about 112,090 individuals from slave-exporting to slave-importing regions, amounting to 70 percent of the inter-regional slave migration of that decade. The subsequent volume of the traffic fluctuated with the business cycle but roughly doubled in size before the outbreak of the Civil War curtailed (but did not halt) the business.[23] The trade might capture slaves of any age or sex, including young children sold separately from their mothers, but the principal victims were teenagers and young adults. Contrary to earlier impressions, most of these young people were offered for sale as a deliberate business decision; they were not caught up in the trade by the accident of their owner's death or indebtedness. For slave children living in the upper South in 1820, Tadman cautiously concludes, the cumulative chance of being "sold South" might have been something like 30 percent by 1860.[24]

Recent scholars agree that tales of slave "stud farms" are largely the product of lurid popular fantasies. The supportive culture of the slave community that historians have now carefully documented could hardly have sustained itself without a corps of stable and cohesive families to bear and rear each rising generation of African Americans. Generally speaking, masters encouraged the formation of slave families, only to sell off some of the growing children as they reached adolescence.

Tadman uses his evidence on this systematic and widespread trade in slaves to challenge the importance of paternalism in master-slave relations. When masters were buying and selling their bond servants as a regular source of profit, routinely destroying black families for the sake of gain, how could they sustain any notion of slavery as a mutually beneficial system of reciprocal obligations within "our family black and white?"

There can be no doubt that a profound racism shaped masters' every thought of slave relations, convincing most that blacks' attachments to their loved ones were trivial and transitory, unworthy of serious consideration where business was concerned. Instead of characterizing the mentality of the average slave owner, the paternalist defense of slavery seems to have originated among intellectuals allied to the largest planters, those whose estates could absorb their own increase without strain, who could thus avoid the regular, systematic sale of young slaves, and whose positions of political and social leadership imposed on them a heavy obligation to defend the morality of the system.[25] Even the brutality of the regular trade in human flesh, however, could not change the pressure on masters to make concessions to those they held in bondage, simply to make the process of exploitation work smoothly. The complex tangle of paternalist reciprocity arose from that necessity, not through any genuine benevolence on the part of masters. No-where is this clearer than in the emergent story of the slaves' own market activities.

Theoretically, slaves were property themselves and therefore could not hold or exchange property on their own. As a practical matter, moreover, lawmakers reasoned that a slave's right to property would only abet the wide-spread problem of theft by slaves, allowing a culprit to claim that the stolen property was his own. A 1705 Virginia statute forbade slaves from owning "horses, cattle, and hogs," and similar prohibitions appeared in most other slaveholding jurisdictions.[26]

Despite all laws and theories to the contrary, however, masters seem to have recognized the advantages of allowing slaves the privileges of ownership and the concomitant opportunity to buy and sell in open or semi-open mar-kets. Except in cases of emergency, slaves normally enjoyed a holiday on Sun-days, in the week after Christmas, and again at "laying by" time in midsum-mer. During these periods, slaves were free to work on their own, and many did so. Some slaves worked for wages during their "free" time, either for their own masters or for neighboring farmers. Other slaves made handicrafts and sold them. A few, like Frederick Douglass, hired their time from the master and retained the balance of their wages for self-support. Most commonly, masters allowed slaves sufficient land for a family garden plot, which they tended on evenings and holidays. Sometimes these plots were quite extensive and allowed slaves to raise their own small crops of cotton.

Masters made these concessions as part of a conscious management strategy. Garden plots put the burden of varying and enriching the slave diet on the slaves themselves, they reasoned, and kept them busy when they might otherwise be troublesome. Planters also hoped that slaves who learned to care for their own property would more readily care for the master's. To provide an extra incentive for exertion, masters often agreed to pay cash for the chick-ens, eggs, and vegetables their slaves produced, or even to allow slaves to market their produce off the plantation and to spend the proceeds as they chose.[27]

Even where the gang labor system kept most slaves fully occupied from sunrise to sunset, the opportunity to work independently led to a wide-ranging internal economy in the slave quarters. Numerous plantation records show regular payments to field hands for small to moderate sums, and store accounts show regular slave purchases of food, clothing, and personal items. To the masters' endless dismay, fencing of stolen goods with marginal white folk and illicit trading for alcohol were also widely reported features of this internal economy.[28]

Where the task system gave slaves greater command of their time, the internal economy was even more extensive, though it apparently never equaled the level of market activity that dominated the Caribbean islands. In the Sea Islands of Georgia and South Carolina, a few enslaved entrepreneurs accumulated sizable property holdings of cattle, hogs, and even horses. After emancipation, for example, a white witness from Liberty County, Georgia, assured the Southern Claims Commission that former driver Paris Jones had owned a horse and wagon, eight cows, sixteen sheep, and twenty-six hogs before the war, making him a "substantial man . . . [who] was more like a free man than any slave." [29]

What are we to make of these slaves who haggled and profited in the marketplace, even as they lived in constant danger of being sold themselves? Was it true, as runaway Charles Ball claimed, that the slave who worked for himself was "a kind of freeman on Sunday?" [30] Or were slaves' activities in the marketplace so minor that they could offer no serious challenge to the coercion that otherwise ruled their lives?

Masters certainly recognized the liberating power of the market. Even as planters longed to expand their own access to markets, they recognized that marketing contacts could loosen slave discipline, and they sometimes fought internal improvements for that reason. In the early days of steam, for example, at least one group of sarcastic Virginians fulminated against an approaching railroad on the grounds that "there may & will be established on it Men to superintend, who no doubt will supply us with . . . blessings such as trading with us your Humble Petitioners (and our Negroes in particular)." [31] For their part, slaves clearly seized on the chance to work independently and to join the market economy, both as a means of enhancing their material well-being and as a opportunity to experience the feeling of freedom. Just as scholars have come to recognize folklore, religion, and family life as free spaces that slaves used to assert their own humanity within the system of bondage, historians must recognize the internal economy of the plantation as an arena for the exercise of African-American independence.

Over time, however, the safe and circumscribed character of this independence became clear even to the masters. While the problems of theft and illicit trading never disappeared, planters realized that slave businesses, much like slave families and slave religion, ultimately bolstered the established order even as they challenged it. As one overseer explained, "No Negro, with a well stocked poultry house, a small crop advancing, a canoe partly finished, or a few tubs unsold, all of which he calculates soon to enjoy, will ever run away." [32] Market opportunities apparently increased for slaves as the antebellum period advanced, especially in the Sea Island region, but powerful restrictions were also well established there. Though Philip D. Morgan reported numerous slaves who purchased cows and horses in the low country, tightened state laws eventually prevented slaves from buying the most valuable thing they could have wanted: their freedom. When the Reverend Charles Colcock Jones decided to part company with Cassius and his family, the conscientious minister scrupulously paid his slave the eighty-five dollars that was credited to his plantation account, but sold him all the same.[33]

Though slaves gained experience with buying and selling before the war, Morgan finds that they were much slower to adopt the aggressive marketing mentality of genuine entrepreneurs. In the early days of Reconstruction, northern observers in the Sea Islands commented that the former slaves shunned wage labor and preferred to "raise a little corn and sweet potatoes, and with their facilities for catching fish and oysters, and shooting wild game, they have as much to eat as they want, and now are quite satisfied with that." In other words, slaves had used the market to enlarge the small sphere of their freedoms, but declined all cash incentives that would put them back under the control of others. Their primary objective, it seems, was independence rather than income.[34]

In that respect, the slaves and the southern yeomanry were much alike. Indeed, if any sector of the antebellum southern economy deserved the label "precapitalist," it was the upland region of small farms and limited market involvement. Blessed with warm weather, plenty of land, easy subsistence, and few incentives for extra toil, the inhabitants of these regions soon developed a reputation for laziness and complacency. As early as 1728, the words of William Byrd II spoke specifically of North Carolinians but captured an enduring stereotype of southern poor whites:

> Surely there is no place in the World where the Inhabitants live with less Labour than in N Carolina. It approaches nearer to the Description of Lubberland than any other, by the great felicity of the Climate, the easiness of raising Provisions, and the Slothfulness of the People.
>
>   Indian Corn is of so great increase, that a little Pains will Subsist a very large Family with Bread, and then they may have meat without any pains at all, by the Help of the Low Grounds, and the great Variety of Mast that grows on the High-land. The men, for their parts, just like the Indians, impose all the Work upon the Poor Women. . . .
>
>   Thus they loiter away their Lives, like Solomon's Sluggard, with their Arms across, and at the Winding up of the Year Scarcely have Bread to Eat.[35]

A similar reputation persisted well into the 1850s. Speaking of the inhabitants of North Carolina's "piney woods," Frederick Law Olmsted described the majority as "entirely uneducated, poverty-stricken vagabonds," gripped by pre-Christian superstitions and locked into an economy and a lifestyle that had apparently changed little in more than a century:

> They will cultivate a little corn, and possibly a few roods of potatoes, cow-peas, and coleworts [collards]. They will own a few swine, that find their living in the forest; and pretty certainly, also, a rifle and dogs; and the men, ostensibly, occupy most of their time in hunting. . . . A gentleman of Fayetteville told me that he had, several times, appraised, under oath, the whole household property of families of this class at less than $20. . . . The farmers and [turpentine] distillers say, that they do not like to employ them, because they cannot be relied upon to finish what they undertake, or to work according to directions; and because, being white men, they cannot "drive" them.[36]

Olmsted spoke specifically about landless squatters, but "the Proprietors," he added, "are people but a grade superior to these vagabonds." Despite his distaste, moreover, Olmsted understood the cause of the poverty and ignorance of the people he encountered. "Owing . . . to the difficulty and expense of reaching market with bulky produce from the interior and western districts, population and wealth are more divided than in the other Atlantic States," he explained. "Industry is almost entirely rural, and there is but little communication or concert of action among the small and scattered proprietors of capital. For the same reason, the advantages of education are more difficult to be enjoyed."[37]

Taken together, Byrd and Olmsted described a way of life that spread far beyond North Carolina. Small farmers, either landowners or squatters, flourished on easy terms by cultivating corn and raising hogs and cattle on the open range. Transportation difficulties protected them from market-driven pressures to live differently. Above all, these southerners treasured the privileges of race and liberty. Because they were white, they could not be driven like slaves. In other words, they would not submit to the time and work discipline typical of the early factory system or to the strict organization of labor to which Fogel and Engerman attribute the superior efficiency of the slave plantation.[38] They were thus only minimally affected by the onset of the market revolution.[39]

As Christopher Clark has shown, the equally isolated regions of the rural North began to break out of their confinement as a growing population pressed increasingly against limited natural resources.[40] Neither sector of the South's dual economy followed this path of development very closely. Slavery itself tended to discourage the development of skilled crafts, minor workshops, or intensifying market relationships between the two segments of free white society. The largest staple producers ordered manufactured products from their agents in New York or London, largely bypassing local markets.

Planters also felt an understandable pressure to keep their expensive and po-
tentially unruly workers busy and productive at all times. Food crops could
be tended during slack periods of the growing season, when the staple crops
needed minimal attention. Most plantations were therefore self-sufficient in
food for workers and animals, with enough to spare for minor trading or
charity in the neighborhood. Similar pressures encouraged the largest slaveholders to maintain their own force of slave artisans to make and repair the
plantation's tools, equipment, and buildings and to manufacture textiles and
clothing for the workforce as well. These practices naturally limited the
growth of trade between the plantations and free farmers and artisans, inhib-
iting the kinds of changes that gave rise to New England's remarkable economic development in the same period.[41]

Gavin Wright has found that the possibility of increased commercial agriculture could seem threatening to the South's "plain folk," even when transportation for their products was available. Farmers who reduced their production of foodstuffs (especially corn) to produce a larger amount of a cash
crop like cotton were gambling on a steady or rising price for the staple. If
the price of cotton tumbled, they could be left with a worthless crop and little
to eat. Heavily capitalized planters could absorb this risk, but marginal producers might starve their families or lose their farms if a market venture went
badly. Wright believes that the yeomanry therefore practiced "safety-first"
agriculture as late as the 1850s, keeping cotton production low and corn production high in order to protect the livelihood of the farm family and the
personal independence of its patriarch.[42]

The introduction of railroads disturbed this pattern in the backcountry
but did not fully displace it until after the Civil War. The need for a cash
income to repair the damage and neglect of wartime seems then to have
tempted large numbers of farmers to abandon the practice of safety-first agriculture and to expand their cotton production dramatically. As folk wisdom
had predicted, however, the new generation of market producers was hit by
the massive deflation of the later nineteenth century, and millions of formerly
landowning families were impoverished and swept into tenancy.[43]

Market revolution therefore came differently to the South's dual economy
than to the free labor environment of New England, though some forms of
change were inescapable in both regions. As David Weiman has shown, a
decision by the more prosperous or ambitious members of a backcountry
community to seek greater market involvement inevitably disrupted the pattern of noncash exchanges that sustained the community as a whole and
gradually forced all local residents into a commercialized way of life. The

balance between the market-oriented plantation and the isolated world of the yeoman farmer was inherently unstable, for the slow entry of railroads, plank roads, and stores into upland counties was the first step toward heavier production of staples, greater reliance on slaves, and a serious erosion in status and wealth for those who could not make a successful transition to market conditions.[44] Paul Escott has shown the beginning stages of this process in an analysis of the response of North Carolina Piedmont farmers to the completion of the North Carolina Railroad in 1856.[45] Divergent reactions to this process of change disturbed the structures of southern society and politics, laying the basis for political partisanship and steadily escalating sectionalism.

Signs of difficulty appeared in the Upper South as early as the late eighteenth century. Tobacco planters in Virginia, Maryland, and North Carolina complained bitterly of stagnant profits, eroded fields, collapsed land values, and declining private fortunes.[46] Some addressed the problem by shifting from tobacco to wheat. Over the next generation, others decided to leave the exhausted soils of the Chesapeake for the seemingly bottomless topsoil of the Alabama and Mississippi black belts, and a major surge of southwestern migration gathered force soon after General Andrew Jackson had dispatched the menace of Indian attacks by his exploits in the War of 1812.

For some distressed plantation owners, migration was not the answer. Observing the stir for new technology that invigorated England and the northern states, they called for transportation improvements that would cut the costs of land and water carriage and bring the staple producer closer to his markets. These improvements would naturally have noneconomic benefits as well. The youthful John C. Calhoun of South Carolina spoke for many of his generation by linking the economic, political, and military benefits of better roads together. "We are great, and rapidly, [I] was about to say fearfully, growing," he warned the House of Representatives in 1817. To surmount the long-recognized difficulties of a distended republic, as well as to facilitate the movement of troops and supplies in wartime, Calhoun hoped to integrate all sections of the country into a common commercial network. "The more enlarged the sphere of commercial circulation," as he put it, "the more strongly are we bound to together. . . . Let us then . . . bind the Republic together with a perfect system of roads and canals. Let us conquer space."[47]

Not all of Calhoun's neighbors shared his enthusiasm. Older and more cautious leaders growled dissent. Led by Virginia's John Randolph and North Carolina's Nathaniel Macon, the so-called Old Republican faction had already emerged to criticize federal actions of this kind as unrecognized by the Constitution and therefore hazardous to slavery. Speaking the thoughts of this group, Macon mocked Calhoun's "fashionable expression 'to conquer space,' " and asked, "if Congress can establish banks, make roads and canals, whether they cannot free all the slaves in the U.S.?"[48]

Ultimately, John C. Calhoun would come to share the strict constructionist leanings of his more wary colleagues, and opposition to federal financing of internal improvements became a hallmark of the South's Jacksonian Democratic party. Even so, the needs articulated by the younger Calhoun did not vanish merely because the South Carolina statesman began to see the constitutional dangers lurking in his earlier tolerance for broad construction. As time went by, more and more planter-politicians saw the need for improved access to distant markets.

The root problem continued to be their perception of southern economic decline in comparison to the growing and modernizing states of the North. Cliometric historians have pointed out that the antebellum South was actually quite wealthy in comparison to other contemporary societies in continental Europe.[49] If true, however, the point is irrelevant. The South was not locked into political or cultural competition with France or Germany; by the only standards that seemed to matter, the South was dangerously behind. In particular, lagging prosperity meant lagging population, as native southerners moved away in search of greener pastures, and newcomers failed to take their places. Political power in Washington depended directly on the region's numbers, and southern politicians were well aware that stalled growth at home could mean weakened power to defend the region's interests in the national government.

The danger was not imaginary. When the Constitution had been ratified, the states south of Pennsylvania had been allotted 30 out of 65, or 46 percent, of the seats in the House of Representatives. By 1830, even with the advantage offered by the three-fifths clause, the slave states' share of congressmen had fallen to 100 out of 242, or 41 percent, and by 1860 the ratio would fall to 85 out of 243, or 35 percent. Following the Compromise of 1850, even the balance between free states and slave states in the Senate disappeared. If the economic health of the plantation South and the political security of the slave system itself were to be protected, something had to be done.

In South Carolina, low-country hotspurs of the early 1830s came to blame the federal tariff for their problems and launched the nullification crusade to save themselves and their institutions, as they thought, from certain destruction.[50] Faced with similar decline, combined with the deadly example of Nat Turner's rebellion, Virginia and Maryland legislators actually contemplated emancipation in 1831 and 1832, only to flinch at the prospect of such a massive social revolution.[51] Elsewhere, cooler heads were just as concerned about the economic health of slavery and the plantation system, but reasoned that a judicious measure of modern technology would be more productive than social or political adventurism. Coming together in the ranks of the emerging Whig party, they called for greater efforts to build state systems of internal improvements, deepen and broaden the South's commitment to market society, and import the blessings of nineteenth-century progress. Pounding away at these themes, they repeated their message unceasingly from the 1820s to the 1850s.

Taken as a whole, the reformers' pronouncements reveal a bitter struggle on the part of proslavery "progressives" to "modernize" the South by bringing its yeoman population under the sway of commercial agriculture and the bourgeois values of hard work and self-improvement. Internal improvements were a key to the process, and so were public schools. Religious conversions could likewise sacralize the cult of hard work and self-improvement while helping to attack superstition and whetting the thirst for literacy. If successful, southern reformers would have abolished the dual economy, recruited the yeomanry to wider slave ownership and greater commercial production, and ultimately pushed the plantation system into the South's remotest corners. The yeomanry's ambivalent resistance to this crusade was the primary political component of the South's internal struggle with the market revolution.

During the 1830s and 1840s, the struggle to reform the southern yeomanry and eliminate the dual economy was institutionalized in the second party system. Like all successful political parties in the United States, southern Whigs and Democrats each formed a diverse coalition, and virtually no generalization can be made about their membership that cannot be contradicted by a counterexample. Taken as a whole, however, the Democrats tended to attract voters whose attitude toward the market revolution ranged from indifferent to hostile, particularly when state or federal powers were being expanded to promote the growth of commerce. Continuing in the Old Republican path mapped out by Nathaniel Macon and John Randolph, for example, tidewater planters of Virginia and North Carolina tended to sympathize with the Democrats, once they recovered from their alarm over Andrew Jackson's reckless pronouncements in the nullification crisis. Lower South Democrats tended to come from the most isolated hill country of Alabama and Mississippi and the backwater parishes of Louisiana. Whigs, by contrast, found their supporters among those who longed for greater commercial progress and favored public investments in banks and internal improvements. They might include farsighted planters who saw no way to sustain the slave-based economy without the advantages of advanced commercial institutions, and also a reasonable number of ambitious farmers who felt that the advantages of commercial progress were worth the risks. The great Whig centers of the Lower South were thus the black belt counties of Georgia, Alabama, Mississippi, and Louisiana, while the Whigs of the Upper South were more likely to come from the regions of Virginia, North Carolina, and Tennessee most in need of transportation improvements.[52]

The political party structure of the antebellum South thus emerged in the context of a long debate over how the South might be saved. Proponents of the market revolution urged repeatedly that internal improvements at public expense were the only means available to rescue a perishing society. As early as 1815, Archibald D. Murphey of North Carolina articulated a standard theme of Upper South orators. "It is mortifying to witness the fact," he mourned, "that thousands of our wealthy and respectable citizens are annually moving to the west in quest of that wealth which a rich soil and a commodious navigation never fail to create in a free state; and that thousands of our poorer citizens follow them, being literally driven away by the prospect of poverty." He concluded: "In this state of things, agriculture is at a stand."[53]

Joseph Eggleston Segar of Virginia struck the same refrain in 1838. "A generous system of internal improvement and the glory and prosperity of Virginia are 'one, inseparable, and indivisible,' " he told his colleagues in the House of Delegates. Why was the Old Dominion in trouble? Because, according to Segar, "Her sons, neglected by an unparental government, are wending their way by thousands upon thousands, from the land of their fathers—that land, to make it a paradise wanting nothing but a market—to bury their bones in the land of strangers." Internal improvements, Segar insisted, were "the 'only way under heaven,' whereby this sinking commonwealth can be saved."[54]

Segar and his colleagues did not speak for a generic, apolitical version of modernization that would make all societies more like each other and gradually eliminate the issues that divided the South from the North. He spoke instead for a specifically proslavery form of improvement, which would fortify the peculiar institution against its critics. "The opening of one line of communication between the James River and the Ohio, will do more to check the progress of abolition in the free states of the west," he predicted, "than all the appeals which eloquence can make, and all the arguments that ingenuity can urge."[55]

Support for southern reform originated among Whigs but eventually crossed party lines. As Mills Thornton, Marc Kruman, and Michael Holt have shown, the 1850s were a period of booming prosperity that drew many Democrats to the support of Whiggish measures like bank charters, internal improvements projects, charitable institutions, and the like. A growing political consensus eroded party identity and contributed to the destruction of the second party system.[56] As parties declined, the immanent sectional conflict they had long disguised became more serious. In the process, the crusade to open the backcountry and uplift the yeomanry increasingly took the form of a nonpartisan or bipartisan campaign for the future security of a slave-based society.

Proslavery arguments were often at the heart of Democratic appeals for internal improvements in the 1850s. "The Southern States have common institutions which distinguish them from the other states of the union, and from the rest of the world," warned Leroy Walker of Alabama in 1854. The future secretary of war for the Confederacy pointed eloquently to the menace of New England, even as he urged his state to imitate the hated Yankees' example. "If we will but put forth our energies and cope with the North in works of public improvement and the encouragement of domestic industry, we shall place ourselves on an equal platform with her in power, and thus render as impotent as it is vile and vindictive, the incendiary agitation which threatens our altars and firesides."[57] Democratic editor William W. Holden of North Carolina agreed. "The South must . . . look more and more to the development of her resources, and to building up seaports and markets within her own limits," he declared. "To this end, systems of internal improvement should be pushed forward, and agriculture, mining, manufactures, and the arts generally promoted and encouraged . . . else when 'the evil day' comes it will find us divided and defenseless before our enemies."[58]

By the eve of secession, B. M. Jones of Virginia had taken the argument a step farther, reasoning that railroads linking the mountain regions of North Carolina and Virginia would cement the loyalties of southerners whose fidelity to the slave system was not completely reliable. "The building of these roads will serve to bind more closely to us a sister Southern state," he claimed, "one identified with us in feeling and interest, and ready to stand *shoulder to shoulder* whenever, if ever, 'the irrepressible conflict' or any similar disaster may burst upon us." If war or slave revolt should come, Jones predicted, "the *mountain rifles* of the Carolinas and Georgia" would be ready and willing to crush the "traitors of the present day," whom he compared to "*the far less infamous tories* of the revolution."[59]

Who were the opponents of this expansive vision of an improved and modernized slave economy? When improvements were first proposed for western or upland regions, opposition frequently came from tidewater legislators who worried that ambitious westerners would pay for improvements with such heavy taxes on land and slaves that the plantation districts would be bankrupted and slavery imperiled. In Virginia and North Carolina especially, these sentiments lay behind eastern opposition to measures for increasing the power of western counties in the state legislatures. As Abel Upshur put it to the Virginia convention of 1829–30, tidewater slave owners would always demand protection from "oppressive and unequal taxation," for without it, "*our* property . . . is exposed to peculiar impositions, and therefore, to peculiar hazards." Two decades later, an eastern North Carolinian repeated the same idea in a chatty letter to an emigrant to California: "The greatest stew amongst us at this time is state improvements such as Rail Roads, Plank Roads & clearing out rivers and Creeks. I am rather of the opinion that our public men will tax the state till she will not be worth the taxes."[60]

A more pervasive and enduring theme, though, was the reformers' conviction that popular sentiment, rooted in the subsistence economy of the plain folk, was inveterately hostile to the "improvement" of southern society. For decades, speechmakers and pamphleteers directed their heaviest fire against an opposing mentality whose convictions rarely took printed form, except in the parodic paraphrases of its enemies. The problem, reformers agreed, was the same rural lifestyle denounced by Byrd and Olmsted, which drew on hunting, fishing, and a leisurely subsistence agriculture to protect the liberty and independence of its participants. Having no real chance to change their manner of living, and seeing no reason to do so, the white majority steadfastly resisted high taxes for education or internal improvement, and likewise refused to submit to the time-work discipline demanded by middle-class reformers. A Virginia essayist spoke for many when he compared the poor of Maryland, where he claimed there were railroads aplenty, with those of his own state. In Maryland, B. M. Jones complained, "they do not think it beneath the dignity of a white man to earn his living by the sweat of his brow. Let the poor men of Virginia and Carolina have the same inducements held out to them—and many who are not too proud, or rather too lazy to work, and prefer to derive a precarious subsistence from hunting, will commence tilling the earth, and become useful members of society, instead of idlers and vagabonds." Even better, Jones insisted, as poor whites worked harder, their commitment to the South's endangered institutions would increase. As proof, he offered the story of a mountain community where harvesters had once worked for a dollar a day or less, but peppered visitors with questions about how to buy slaves when the arrival of a railroad transformed the local economy.[61]

Like Edward Lee Winslow of the Fayetteville and Western Plank Road Company, reformers struggled endlessly to awaken their countrymen to what they considered to be their own best interests. Some had faith that exhortations would arouse individual self-interest and lead to popular demands for improvements. "The first step towards the accomplishment of any great work," a Virginian pointed out, "is to render the desire of achieving it in the minds of those whose efforts are to bring it about. . . . If we would see the husbandman cast off the lethargy which has hung with leaden weight upon his progress . . . , we must arouse in him a disposition to improve."[62] Others hoped that if only the railroads came first, the desire to use them would follow, and moral and cultural improvements could not be far behind. "The whole country is benefitted," in the view of an Alabama railroad convention, "from the highest to the lowest, from the richest to the poorest, by the spirit of industry, energy, and enterprise, which [a railroad] engrafts upon the business habits of the whole people."[63]

Joseph Caldwell, president of the University of North Carolina from 1804 to 1836, tried both approaches. A transplanted Presbyterian minister from New Jersey, Caldwell struggled to uplift his adopted state with arguments for railroads and public schools, even as he wrestled with the demanding business of building a fledgling college. He began with a premise that blended elements of revolutionary republicanism with the liberal cult of material progress. "The happiness of a people," he wrote, "next to public and private virtue, consists in a perpetual growth into better circumstances."[64] Not surprisingly, he identified internal improvements as crucial to this process, but discovered that popular apathy and opposition were formidable obstacles to his efforts. As a genuine lover of learning, Caldwell's greatest hope for social improvement was the advancement of education in North Carolina, but he came to believe that an expanded market economy was a necessary precondition for the achievement of his dreams. "Excluded as we now are from the markets of the world," Caldwell explained, "the necessity of a rigid economy is urged against every expenditure however small, and the first plea which meets us, when the education of children is pressed upon parents, is their inability to bear the expense. . . . Among all the improvements which we are called to for the benefit of the state, commercial opportunity should be the first."[65]

If only a central railroad could be built through North Carolina, the professor predicted, the goad of self-interest would finally convert North Carolina yeomen to the hardworking, calculating, self-denying, cash-and-carry mentality that Caldwell saw as the key to a culture of progress and self-improvement. His ultimate goals, Caldwell made clear, were at war with the rural "social economy" of shared work, noncash payment of debts, and indefinite credit arrangements that many Tarheel farmers relied on for their sense of personal autonomy. North Carolinians, Caldwell urged, should "adopt system and economy in our modes of farming and living," and waste no time, prosecute our business intently, manure our lands, lay them off for a regular succession of crops, so they shall improve continually and not run to broomgrass; in short, to make a plenty of corn, wheat, cotton, tobacco, cider, brandy, butter, cheese, everything that will bring money; to provide a rail-road that carriage may cost nothing, and all that we raise may bring as much abroad as it does at home; that we may be able to sell as cheap as others, and have a plenty of cash to pay our contracts, be paid punctually by our neighbours who owe us, and who can then do the same thing, and thus have plenty to spare in the domestic treasury.[66]

The now-aging educator was not very confident. "No, never! say these enemies of rail-roads" was the answer he anticipated (and largely received) to his proposals for reform.[67]

In the end, the antebellum southern reformers won no more than partial victories over their region's dual economy. Banks and railroads did extend their range, especially in the 1850s. Most of these new institutions depended on generous public subscriptions to their stock, voted for by state legislators of both parties. Several states even experimented with modest public school programs. The costs of these subsidies and new expenditures were covered by sharply rising taxes.[68] Where transportation costs declined, moreover, local farmers indeed increased their production of market staples, usually cotton, tobacco, or wheat.[69] Even the plank road company of Edward Lee Winslow returned a modest dividend in this decade, indicating that many, if not all, of its customers had reconciled themselves to paying its burdensome tolls.[70]

The penetration of the institutions and culture of the market was still fragile, however, when the 1850s came to a close. Mills Thornton describes convincingly how the rise of banks, railroads, mining, and urban development left many free white Alabamians terrified of their own economic and political enslavement. Lacy Ford finds a similar phenomenon in upcountry South Carolina, and William H. Barney adds local confirmation in his community study of Dallas County, Alabama. The price of yeoman alienation, it seems, was an ever more eager audience for sectionalist fire-eaters and a mounting political pressure for secession.[71]

Ironically, these same marginal communities would be the first to withdraw their support for the Confederacy when the campaign for southern independence brought white nonslaveholders "a rich man's war and a poor man's fight." Confederate common soldiers and their families suffered food shortages and privation in the war, to say nothing of death, mutilation, and disease, and their protests, ranging from food riots to desertion and draft dodging, played a key role in Confederate demoralization and defeat.[72] The values of the self-sufficient yeoman community remained strong well into Reconstruction, moreover, and likewise contributed to popular protest movements of the late nineteenth century, ranging from the overthrow of Reconstruction to the Populist uprising of the 1890s.[73]

In retrospect, however, it is clear that the outcome of the Civil War doomed the societies created by the South's dual economy. Wherever the armies had marched, wartime destruction had spawned urgent needs in the spring of 1865. The land itself remained, and southerners had not forgotten how to farm it, but homes, towns, and railroads had been ruined. Banks had folded, their assets invested in worthless Confederate securities. Livestock had disappeared into the maws of both armies, while barns, fields, and fences had all suffered from four years' neglect. The demand for cash to finance repairs and to put life together again was desperate, and prewar routines would not suffice for the emergency. Meanwhile, the international price of cotton had soared during the years of federal blockade, so planters and yeomen alike turned eagerly to King Cotton for a solution to their cash flow problems.

In the former plantation regions, commitment to staple exports was nothing new, but the terms of involvement were utterly transformed. After a brief period of uncertainty, the former masters emerged with secure ownership of their lands, but the former slaves now held far more bargaining power than they had previously. Newly freed African Americans may have lacked property and formal education, but they knew that the farms of their former masters could not become productive without their labor, and they now held the power to choose employers and to bargain over the terms of employment. After an interval of struggle, the well-known system of sharecropping emerged as the compromise between the planters' desires for a return to some system of forced labor and the freed people's demands for a measure of independence. Large landowners divided their estates into smaller plots and rented them to laboring families, who paid one-half of their crops in return. The chosen crop was usually cotton (but sometimes tobacco), for nothing else would command the ready cash return that landlords demanded as rent. The tenant's half of the crop was almost certainly cotton too, rather than a food crop like corn, not only because landlords and creditors required it, but because market forces decreed that cotton belt tenants could purchase more food from the sale of their staple than they could grow on the small plots available to them. Before the war, most plantations had been self-sufficient in food, but postwar laborers purchased their supplies on credit from a local storekeeper, who demanded a "crop lien" on the tenants' half of the cotton as security. At the end of each growing season, the landlord thus took one-half of the crop and the "furnish merchant" took the other. The balance left over for the sharecropper amounted to little or nothing, so the great bulk of the former slaves remained bound in the direst poverty.[74]

The case was somewhat different for the white yeomen farmers who had clung to semisubsistence and safety-first agriculture before the war. When the fighting ended, these families also needed a cash stake to get started again, though most undoubtedly hoped for an early return to the independence they had previously enjoyed. Tempted by high prices in the late 1860s, white yeomen farmers also took credit from storekeepers and planted more cotton then they had ever done before. Production of cotton boomed, and the extent of cotton cultivation expanded deep into upland areas far beyond the limits of the old plantation belt. In a local variation of the same theme, upland farmers in North Carolina and Virginia plunged into the culture of bright-leaf tobacco, a flashy bonanza crop first used for wrapping plugs and twists of darker chewing tobacco, later the key ingredient of the newly popular cigarette. In cotton and tobacco regions alike, crop liens guaranteed the extension of credit to white farmers as well as black, giving storekeepers a deciding voice in the production and sale of the crops.[75]

The yeomanry's shift into market production was aided by institutional and technological developments and by key state policies. Whether they were dominated by Confederates or carpetbaggers, postwar state governments pinned their hopes on railroad construction as the key to economic recovery. State aid and northern investment sent iron rails all over the countryside and brought upland communities far closer to world market opportunities than ever before. Regional self-sufficiency in food crops came to an end, as southerners specialized in cotton and as rail lines and integrated national markets brought salt pork and cornmeal from the Midwest to exchange for their commodities. Retail stores appeared at every crossroads to supply these goods and to finance the crop lien system. Commercial fertilizers became available and proved essential in extending the range of cotton and tobacco into previously hostile environments. The zeal of Reconstruction governments for free schools and rail construction brought tax increases, and all these changes increased the pressure for cash-cropping within previously isolated communities.[76]

One particularly important turning point in the old safety-first farming communities was a widespread shift in local fencing laws, obliging livestock owners to confine their own animals instead of requiring the cultivators of fields to enclose their crops. This apparently minor reversal provoked fierce controversy in numerous localities from the 1870s to the 1890s, for it meant that tenants or small landowners could no longer keep cattle or hogs roaming at large, freely foraging on the uncultivated woodlands of others. Under the new fence laws, livestock breeding could become more systematic for those who could pay for pasturage and feed, while staple crop producers were relieved of the heavy costs of fencing. The full cultural implications of the new fence policies are still disputed among specialists, but they clearly marked a significant institutional departure from the world of antebellum subsistence and market isolation.[77]

Unfortunately for postbellum farmers who renewed their faith in King Cotton, cultivation of the staple was also expanding in places like Egypt and India, and the growth of world cotton demand did not keep pace with the dramatic increase in its supply. The depression that began in 1873 brought high cotton prices to an end, and prices kept on sinking for decades to come. Credit purchases of fertilizer and other goods became harder and harder to pay for, yet no escape back into self-sufficiency was possible for farmers who were already in debt, since creditors continued to demand payment in the staple crops that brought a ready sale.[78] For black farmers, penury seemed almost inescapable. The number of white sharecroppers also rose steadily, as population pressures made lands increasingly scarce and the exigencies of credit and falling prices made ownership increasingly insecure. By 1880, southern per capita income was only half that of the rest of the country, and by 1900, half of all southern white farmers were tenants.[79] By that time, the South's dual economy had disappeared forever, and a lengthy cycle of poverty, underdevelopment, and one-crop agriculture had taken its place.

To be sure, everything was not static in the market economy of the New South. Towns grew rapidly and merchants acquired a new importance in the countryside. Planter scions who took advantage of these changes could repair the family fortunes in no time and invest the proceeds, if they were shrewd, in the spreading network of cotton mills. These entrepreneurs were a new class, in the sense that the scale of their activities had no regional precedent, but their personal ties to the antebellum elite were so extensive that their success also represented a continuation of the antebellum class structure.[80] White families exhausted by tenancy found ready employment in the new mill towns, laying the basis for the growing urban and industrial South of the twentieth century. Supporters of these changes became the ideologues of the New South, dusting off the maxims of antebellum reformers to urge the adoption of a new regional ethos based on hard work, market incentives, urbanization, industrialization, popular education, and racial segregation.[81] Eventually, the pressures of the Great Depression, World War II, and technological transformation of farm work itself would destroy the tenant system and clear the way for the diversified southern economy of the late twentieth

century. The circumstances of the South's market transformation in the post–
Civil War period, however, would leave a lasting mark in regional inequality,
underdevelopment, and cultural isolation.

The institution of slavery had done much to create and preserve the South's
dual economy, by limiting the market's penetration of the backcountry and by
discouraging slaveholders from experiments in industrialization. The reformers who sought an end to this dual economy—and the dual white society it
fostered—could make no more than limited headway while slavery persisted.
In 1861, however, the reformers understood little of this as they rushed to lend
their energies to an uplifted and improved southern republic, equally dedicated, they hoped, to hard work, self-improvement, market exchange, and human slavery. It would not be until after the war, with slavery left behind, that a
fundamental transition of southern society could take place.

By then, of course, the dynamics of the market revolution had changed
beyond recognition. To a lucky handful of urban southerners, postwar society
brought the expansion of choices and freer lifestyles that echoed the gains
won by prosperous antebellum northerners when commercial society had
flowered in the free states. For a much larger number, however, the triumph
of market-based society came under circumstances of compulsion and con-
straint. White farmers especially, who once boasted of glorious independence
from outside forces, faced a new order bound by chains of credit and declining commodity prices. In effect, the dual economy created by slavery had
isolated them from world market forces until the last possible moment, then
thrust them into staple crop production when the terms for small producers
had reached their worst. For the yeoman landowner reduced to sharecropping, the result was a state of peonage that his Jacksonian ancestors would
not have hesitated to call slavery. By contrast, African Americans won the
inestimable benefit of legal freedom in the new order, but not relief from
inequality, poverty, and exploitation. For both groups, the bonds of slavery's
warped markets would linger long after its more visible chain had broken
at last.

NOTES

1. Proceedings of the Second Annual Meeting of the Fayetteville and Western Plank
Road Company, Fayetteville, N.C., Apr. 11 and 12, 1850, p. 2.

2. Ibid., p. 24.

3. For details on the Winslow family connection, see Harry L. Watson, *Jacksonian Politics and Community Conflict: The Emergence of the Second American Party System in Cumberland County, North Carolina* (Baton Rouge, La., 1981), pp. 41–42, 250–52, and passim.

4. Charles Sellers, *The Market Revolution: Jacksonian America, 1815-1846* (New York, 1991). Cf. George Rogers Taylor, *The Transportation Revolution, 1815–1860* (New York, 1951).

5. Morton Rothstein, "The Antebellum South as a Dual Economy: A Tentative Hypothesis," *Agricultural History* 41 (1967): 373–83.

6. Nancy F. Cott, *The Bonds of Womanhood: "Woman's Sphere" in New England, 1780–1835* (New Haven, Conn., 1977); Paul E. Johnson, *A Shopkeeper's Millennium: Society and Revivals in Rochester, New York, 1815–1837* (New York, 1978); Mary P. Ryan, *Cradle of the Middle Class: The Family in Oneida County, New York, 1790–1865* (Cambridge, Eng., 1983).

7. Sellers, *Market Revolution*. See also Harry L. Watson, *Liberty and Power: The Politics of Jacksonian America* (New York, 1990).

8. This simple comparison of population figures obviously glosses over the degree to which population growth in the North, particularly by foreign immigration, was a result of market change as well as a cause of it.

9. Robert William Fogel, *Without Consent or Contract: The Rise and Fall of American Slavery* (New York, 1989), pp. 84–89. For representative complaints about southern poverty and underdevelopment, see Frederick Law Olmsted, *The Cotton Kingdom*, ed. Arthur M. Schlesinger, Sr., (New York, 1984); Hinton Rowan Helper, *The Impending Crisis of the South: How to Meet It* (New York, 1857); George McDuffie, "Speech . . . at . . . Charleston, May 19, 1831," reprinted in William W. Freehling, ed., *The Nullification Era: A Documentary Record* (New York, 1967), pp. 104–19.

10. For the tensions provoked by market relations in the early plantation system, see T. H. Breen, *Tobacco Culture: The Mentality of the Great Tidewater Planters on the Eve of Revolution* (Princeton, N.J, 1985).

11. The recent study of American backcountry farmers owes much to three now classic articles: Michael Merrill, "Cash Is Good to Eat: Self-Sufficiency and Exchange in the Rural Economy of the United States," *Radical History Review* 4 (1977): 42–71; James A. Henretta, "Families and Farms: *Mentalité* in Pre-Industrial America," *William and Mary Quarterly* 35 (1978): 3–32; and Christopher Clark, "The Household Economy, Market Exchange, and the Rise of Capitalism in the Connecticut Valley, 1800–1860," *Journal of Social History* 13 (1979): 169–90. Accounts of the lives of southern yeomen that rely on similar insights include Forrest McDonald and Grady McWhiney, "The Antebellum Southern Herdsman: A Reinterpretation," *Journal of Southern History* 41 (1975): 147–66; John T. Schlotterbeck, "The 'Social Economy' of an Upper South Community: Orange and Greene Counties, Virginia, 1815–1860," in Orville Vernon Burton and Robert C. McMath, Jr., eds., *Class, Conflict, and Consensus: Antebellum Southern Community Studies* (Westport, Conn., 1982), pp. 29–56; and Steven Hahn, *The Roots of Southern Populism: Yeoman Farmers and the Transformation of the Georgia Upcountry, 1850–1890* (New York, 1983).

12. Rothstein, "The Antebellum South as a Dual Economy." For detailed maps of southern regional variations, see Sam Bowers Hilliard, *Atlas of Antebellum Southern Agriculture* (Baton Rouge, La., 1984).

13. Eugene D. Genovese, *The Political Economy of Slavery* (New York, 1965); Ulrich

Bonnell Phillips, *American Negro Slavery* (reprint, Baton Rouge, La., 1966); Charles Sellers, *The Southerner as American* (Chapel Hill, N.C., 1960); Kenneth M. Stampp, *The Peculiar Institution: Slavery in the Ante-Bellum South* (New York, 1956); Robert W. Fogel and Stanley Engerman, *Time on the Cross: The Economics of American Negro Slavery*, 2 vols. (Boston, 1974); Fogel, *Without Consent or Contract.*

14. Immanuel Wallerstein, *The Modern World-System I: Capitalist Agriculture and the Origins of the European World-Economy in the Sixteenth Century* (New York, 1974), esp. pp. 86–89, 99–100.

15. Winifred Rothenberg, "Markets without Contracts: The Cliometrics of Slavery," *Reviews in American History* 21 (1993): 589.

16. See Eugene D. Genovese, introduction to Phillips, *American Negro Slavery*, p. x.

17. Eric Foner, *Politics and Ideology in the Age of the Civil War* (New York, 1980), p. 4.

18. Genovese, *The Political Economy of Slavery*, p. 8.

19. J. Mills Thornton III, *Politics and Power in a Slave Society: Alabama, 1800–1860* (Baton Rouge, La., 1978); William J. Cooper, Jr., *Liberty and Slavery: Southern Politics to 1860* (New York, 1983). For the northern counterpart to southern obsessions with white men's liberty, cf. Eric Foner, *Free Soil, Free Labor, Free Men: The Ideology of the Republican Party before the Civil War* (New York, 1970).

20. Both sides seem to have moved much closer on this question in recent writings. See James Oakes, *Slavery and Freedom: An Interpretation of the Old South* (New York, 1990); Eugene D. Genovese, *The Slaveholders' Dilemma* (Columbia, S.C., 1991).

21. There is now an extensive literature on the acquisition of property by slaves, much of it explicitly comparative. See Philip D. Morgan, "The Ownership of Property by Slaves in the Mid-Nineteenth-Century Low Country," *Journal of Southern History* 49 (1983): 399–420; Ira Berlin and Philip D. Morgan, eds., *The Slaves' Economy: Independent Production by Slaves in the Americas* (London, 1991); Roderick A. McDonald, *The Economy and Material Culture of Slaves: Goods and Chattels on the Sugar Plantations of Jamaica and Louisiana* (Baton Rouge, La., 1993).

22. Frederic Bancroft, *Slave Trading in the Old South* (New York, 1931); Michael Tadman, *Speculators and Slaves: Masters, Traders, and Slaves in the Old South* (Madison, Wis., 1989); Edmund L. Drago, ed., *Broke by the War* (Columbia, S.C., 1991).

23. Tadman, *Speculators and Slaves*, esp. pp. 21–31.

24. Ibid., p. 45.

25. Drew Gilpin Faust, *A Sacred Circle: The Dilemma of the Intellectual in the Old South, 1840–1860* (Philadelphia, 1977).

26. Edmund S. Morgan, *American Slavery, American Freedom: The Ordeal of Colonial Virginia* (New York, 1975), p. 333.

27. Eugene G. Genovese, *Roll, Jordan, Roll: The World the Slaves Made* (New York, 1974), pp. 535–40.

28. John Campbell, "'As a Kind of Freeman'?: Slaves' Market-Related Activities in the South Carolina Upcountry, 1800–1860," and John T. Schlotterbeck, "The Internal Economy of Slavery in Rural Piedmont Virginia," both in Berlin and Morgan, *Slaves' Economy*, pp. 131–69, 170–81; McDonald, *Economy and Material Culture of Slaves*, pp. 50-91.

29. Quoted in Philip D. Morgan, "Work and Culture: The Task System and the World of Lowcountry Blacks, 1700 to 1880," *William and Mary Quarterly* 39 (1982): 587–88.

30. Quoted in Joseph P. Reidy, *From Slavery to Agrarian Capitalism in the Cotton Plantation South: Central Georgia, 1800–1880* (Chapel Hill, N.C., 1992), p. 61.

31. "To the General Assembly of Virginia," Feb. 16, 1832, Greensville County Legislative Petitions, 1781–1859, Virginia State Library.

32. Quoted in Genovese, *Roll, Jordan, Roll,* p. 539. See also Campbell, "'As a Kind of Freeman'?" in Berlin and Morgan, *Slaves' Economy,* pp. 131–69.

33. Morgan, "Ownership of Property," p. 413.

34. Quoted in Morgan, "Ownership of Property," p. 595.

35. William Byrd II, "History of the Dividing Line," in Louis B. Wright, ed., *The Prose Works of William Byrd of Westover: Narratives of a Colonial Virginian* (Cambridge, Mass., 1966), pp. 204–5.

36. Olmsted, *The Cotton Kingdom,* pp. 146–47.

37. Ibid., p. 148.

38. Fogel and Engerman, *Time on the Cross,* 1:191–209.

39. A different picture of the Appalachian South emerged from Robert D. Mitchell's *Commercialism and Frontier: Perspectives on the Early Shenandoah Valley* (Charlottesville, Va., 1977). Mitchell found that the economy of this key valley was highly commercialized by the end of the eighteenth century. A subsequent volume of essays seems to suggest that Mitchell's earlier generalizations were overdrawn, perhaps because the Shenandoah was a major artery of north-south migration from its earliest days of settlement. See Robert D. Mitchell, ed., *Appalachian Frontiers: Settlement, Society, and Development in the Preindustrial Era* (Lexington, Ky., 1991).

40. Christopher Clark, *The Roots of Rural Capitalism: Western Massachusetts, 1780–1860* (Ithaca, N.Y., 1990).

41. Gavin Wright, *The Political Economy of the Cotton South* (New York, 1978); Fred Bateman and Thomas Weiss, *A Deplorable Scarcity: The Failure of Industrialization in the Slave Economy* (Chapel Hill, N.C., 1981).

42. Gavin Wright and Howard Kunreuther, "Cotton, Corn, and Risk in the Nineteenth Century," *Journal of Economic History* 35 (1975): 526–51; Wright and Kunreuther, "Cotton, Corn, and Risk in the Nineteenth Century: A Reply," *Explorations in Economic History* 14 (1977): 183–95; Wright, *Political Economy,* pp. 62–74.

43. Gavin Wright, *Old South, New South: Revolutions in the Southern Economy since the Civil War* (New York, 1986); Forrest McDonald and Grady McWhiney, "The South from Self-Sufficiency to Peonage: An Interpretation," *American Historical Review* 85 (1980): 1095–1118.

44. David Weiman, "Petty Commodity Production in the Cotton South: Upcountry Farmers in the Georgia Cotton Economy, 1840 to 1880" (Ph.D. diss., Stanford University, 1983).

45. Paul D. Escott, "Yeoman Independence and the Market: Social Status and Economic Development in Antebellum North Carolina," *North Carolina Historical Review* 66 (1989): 275–300.

46. Lewis Cecil Gray, *History of Agriculture in the Southern United States to 1860,* 2 vols. (Washington, D.C., 1932), 1:166–69.

47. John C. Calhoun, "Speech on Internal Improvements," February 4, 1817," in Robert L. Meriwether, ed., *The Papers of John C. Calhoun,* 21 vols. (Columbia, S.C., 1959–), 1:401.

48. Edwin Mood Wilson, "The Congressional Career of Nathaniel Macon," *James Sprunt Historical Monographs*, no. 2 (Chapel Hill, N.C., 1900), p. 48. See also Harry L. Watson, "Squire Oldway and His Friends: Opposition to Internal Improvements in Antebellum North Carolina," *North Carolina Historical Review* 54 (1977): 105–19.

49. Fogel and Engerman, *Time on the Cross* 1:249.

50. William W. Freehling, *Prelude to Civil War: The Nullification Controversy in South Carolina, 1816–1836* (New York, 1965).

51. Alison Goodyear Freehling, *Drift toward Dissolution: The Virginia Slavery Debate of 1831–1832* (Baton Rouge, La., 1982); William W. Freehling, *The Road to Disunion: Secessionists at Bay, 1776–1854* (New York, 1990), pp. 178–210.

52. Charles Grier Sellers, Jr., "Who Were the Southern Whigs?" *American Historical Review* 59 (1954): 335–46; Watson, *Jacksonian Politics and Community Conflict*; Thornton, *Politics and Power*; Arthur Charles Cole, *The Whig Party in the South* (Washington, D.C., 1913).

53. Archibald D. Murphey, "Report of the Committee on Inland Navigation," North Carolina Senate, 1815, in William Henry Hoyt, ed., *The Papers of Archibald D. Murphey*, 2 vols. (Raleigh, N.C., 1914), 2:20–21.

54. Joseph Eggleston Segar, "Speech of Mr. Segar of Northampton, on the Subject of a General System of Internal Improvements," House of Delegates, Feb. 12 and 14, 1838 (Richmond, Va.), p. 3.

55. Ibid., p. 26.

56. Thornton, *Politics and Power*, pp. 267–342; Michael F. Holt, *The Political Crisis of the 1850s* (New York, 1978), pp. 101–38; Marc W. Kruman, *Parties and Politics in North Carolina, 1836–1865* (Baton Rouge, La., 1983), pp. 140–58.

57. Leroy P. Walker, "Speech of . . . Leroy P. Walker on Internal Improvements, Delivered in the House of Representatives on the 30th of November, 1853" (Montgomery, Ala., 1854), pp. 13–14.

58. *North Carolina Standard*, May 24, 1854.

59. B. M. Jones, *Railroads: Considered in Regard to Their Effects upon the Value of Land, in Increasing Production, Cheapening Transportation, Preventing Emigration, and as Investments for Capital* (Richmond, Va., 1860), p. 71.

60. Abel Upshur, quoted in Alison Goodyear Freehling, *Drift toward Dissolution*, pp. 53–54; Dempsey Harrell to Thomas Oliver Larkin, Jan. 20, 1850, in Robert J. Parker and David Leroy Corbit, "California's Larkin Settles Old Debts: A View of North Carolina, 1847–1856," *North Carolina Historical Review* 17 (1940): 338.

61. Jones, *Railroads*, p. 43.

62. Franklin Minor, "Address Delivered before the Agricultural Society of Albemarle, Saturday, November 1st, 1845," (Charlottesville, Va., 1846), p. 14.

63. "Memorial to the Legislature of Alabama in relation to the Alabama Central Railroad, Adopted by a Convention held in Decatur on the 30th of November, 1853" (Montgomery, Ala., 1854).

64. Joseph Caldwell, *The Numbers of Carleton, Addressed to the People of North Carolina on the Subject of a Central Railroad* through the State (New York, 1828), p. 152.

65. Joseph Caldwell, *Letters on Popular Education, Addressed to the People of North Carolina* (Hillsborough, N.C., 1832), p. 4.

66. Caldwell, *Numbers of Carleton,* p. 108.

67. Ibid.

68. Peter Wallenstein, *From Slave South to New South: Public Policy in Nineteenth-Century Georgia* (Chapel Hill, N.C., 1987).

69. Escott, "Yeoman Independence," pp. 275–300; Lacy K. Ford, Jr., *Origins of Southern Radicalism: The South Carolina Upcountry, 1800–1860* (New York, 1988), pp. 244–63.

70. Robert B. Starling, "The Plank Road Movement in North Carolina," *North Carolina Historical Review* 16, no. 1–2 (1939): 1–22, 147–73.

71. Thornton, *Politics and Power,* pp. 267–342; J. Mills Thornton III, "The Ethic of Subsistence and the Origins of Southern Secession," *Tennessee Historical Quarterly* 48 (Summer 1989): 67–85; Ford, *Origins of Southern Radicalism,* pp. 308–37; William L. Barney, "Towards the Civil War: The Dynamics of Change in a Black Belt County," in Burton and McMath, *Class, Conflict, and Consensus,* pp. 146–72.

72. Eric Foner, *Reconstruction: America's Unfinished Revolution, 1863–1877* (New York, 1988), pp. 15–18.

73. J. Mills Thornton III, "Fiscal Policy and the Failure of Radical Reconstruction in the Lower South," in J. Morgan Kousser and James M. McPherson, eds., *Region, Race, and Reconstruction: Essays in Honor of C. Vann Woodward* (New York, 1982), pp. 349–94; Lawrence Goodwyn, *Democratic Promise: The Populist Moment in America* (New York, 1976).

74. Roger L. Ransom and Richard Sutch, *One Kind of Freedom: The Economic Consequences of Emancipating* (Cambridge, Eng., 1977), pp. 56–105.

75. Wright, *Political Economy,* pp. 164–76.

76. Wright, *Old South, New South,* pp. 39–43; Thornton, "Fiscal Policy"; Robert C. McMath, Jr., *American Populism: A Social History, 1877–1898* (New York, 1993), pp. 34, 37.

77. Hahn, *Roots of Southern Populism,* pp. 239–68. Hahn argues that the defenders of the older, open range policy were still dedicated to an economy of common rights and "habits of mutuality" which characterized the antebellum yeoman community, and were therefore averse to the values of market-oriented society. For the dispute over this interpretation, see Shawn Everett Kantor and J. Morgan Kousser, "Common Sense or Commonwealth? The Fence Law and Institutional Change in the Postbellum South," *Journal of Southern History* 59 (1993): 201–42; Steven Hahn, "A Response: Common Cents or Historical Sense?" ibid., pp. 243–58; Shawn Everett Kantor and J. Morgan Kousser, "A Rejoinder: Two Visions of History," ibid., pp. 259–66.

78. Wright, *Political Economy,* pp. 172–76; Wright, *Old South, New South,* pp. 107–15.

79. Roger L. Ransom, *Conflict and Compromise: The Political Economy of Slavery, Emancipation, and the American Civil War* (Cambridge, Eng., 1989), p. 241; Wright, *Old South, New South,* p. 107.

80. The debate over "planter persistence" is too extensive to summarize here. My own view of the question owes much to the analysis presented in Wright, *Old South, New South,* pp. 17–50.

81. Wright, *Old South, New South,* pp. 124–55; Paul M. Gaston, *The New South Creed: A Study in Southern Mythmaking* (New York, 1970).

3

Home Life and the Morality of the Market

AMY DRU STANLEY

W HAT WE KNOW AS THE MARKET REVOLUTION posed a momentous moral problem that contemporaries, in the first instance, understood as a problem of gender. In America the ascendance of
free market society coincided with the consolidation of an antagonistic regime of chattel slavery in the South. Thus the two discussions were insepa-
rably bound together: gender provided the categories, the common ideological framework, both for taking stock of the transformations wrought by a
burgeoning market culture and for contrasting freedom and bondage. But
gender is an anachronistic term. In the nineteenth century those who de-
bated the virtues of market freedom and chattel slavery characteristically
spoke of home life, of marriage and family bonds, of male and female natures,
of sexual spheres. How, asked the Reverend Henry Ward Beecher at the end
of the Civil War, should the North "carry the Yankee ideas, and colonize them
at the South?" Beecher, who had a knack for giving voice to Yankee gospel,
wove together the themes of free labor, manhood, and home life in arguing
that the imperial sway of the free market would transcend differences not
only of region but of race. "The reform," he declared, "is to make . . . the
workman a man. . . . The slave is a man and he will respond to human influences. Although a black man may never be a Yankee, he will follow hard
after. Why should he, an ill-compensated and bewhipt drudge work willingly?
Give him the prospect of a home, a family that is not marketable, and he
will work."[1] In the Yankee worldview the essential difference between the
economy of the free market and that of slavery was home life—the promise
of a family "not marketable."

Beecher's themes are the themes of this essay. My intent is to show that the
representations of gender invoked by a wide range of contemporaries to bestow legitimacy on market society also figured critically in the symbolism of
antislavery, which depicted North and South as polar opposites and thereby
contributed to valorizing the free market as the arbiter of human relations. It
is conventional, however, for historians to treat the relationship between the
market revolution and constructions of gender in the North as a topic uncon-

nected to the ideological contest over slavery. There is an abundant literature tying the efflorescence of the idea of separate sexual spheres to the flourishing of capitalism and the growth of industrialization. It is also well documented that abolitionism had a great deal to do with sustaining the cultural hegemony of capitalist social relations. But these are separate fields of inquiry. How the two distinct systems of binary symbolism—of sexual difference and of freedom and slavery—joined in legitimating free market relations has not drawn much attention. In this essay I argue that the ideology of separate spheres coalesced with the logic of antislavery to define the moral nature of market society in terms of the right to a family unscathed by the market's calculus.

Given the capaciousness of the term *market* (variously denoting a place, an economic system, an ethos, a form of human relationship), I should indicate at the outset the sense in which I am using it. I am not concerned here with the formation of a national market network for commodities, or with the inanimate instruments of finance, price, production, transport, and law involved in the emergence of a market economy in the early American republic. Nor is my principal interest the changing quality of exchange relations as the market ceased to be bounded in space and time. Rather, I am mainly concerned with the implications of what C. B. Macpherson called "market society"—one that reached its zenith in the nineteenth century and that was characterized specifically by traffic in human labor power, rather than simply by the marketing of land, money, and other goods. According to Macpherson's classic description of this social order, "where labour has become a market commodity, market relations so shape and permeate all social relations that it may properly be called a market society, not merely a market economy." In this essay the market revolution is taken to constitute a problem by reason of the relations spawned by the making of free labor into an impersonal market commodity. And in seeing the market's dominion as problematic—as opposed to being a historical catalyst solely of liberty and humanitarianism—I am influenced by the work of many besides Macpherson who have brought to light the moral dilemmas and social contradictions generated by commodity relations. This critical tradition is over a century old. But only recently have historians recognized that gender relations and representations of sexual difference lie at the heart of the problems posed by market society.[2]

That insight remains to be yoked to the perspectives on gender afforded by the slavery debate, the task I undertake in this essay. Such a double vantage point illuminates in new ways how contemporaries deployed the idea of

"separate spheres" to contain the contradictions and ambiguities of market
society. The counterpoint between market freedom and the dependencies of
home life, I argue, bears further reflection.[3]

The standard story of the effect of capitalist transformation on women's lives
is the one told by Charles Sellers in *The Market Revolution*. Sellers presents a
schematic model of social and cultural change, in which work was redirected
from subsistence toward market needs, productive labor moved from the
household to the workplace, and social existence split into separate sexual
spheres. Capitalism, he writes, "created a male public world of competitive
production sundered from a female domestic world of altruistic reproduction." In other words, the ascendance of market relations gave rise to the
fundamental polarities of private and public, home and work, family and
market—all of which rested on the difference between women and men. As
the "traditional patriarchy" of the household economy collapsed, Sellers further notes, women gained new power at home, which was enshrined in a cult
of domesticity. And these economic and cultural changes coincided with
bourgeois moralists' new insistence on erotic repression as part of the broad
effort to shore up the authority of their class. Sellers elucidates with dispatch
what he terms the "radical redefinition of gender" embedded in the antebellum market revolution.[4]

    This focal point is nowhere to be found in much of the classic literature
on market thought and practice. For example, Karl Polanyi's account of the
convulsive transformation brought by the market economy and Macpherson's study of possessive individualism still guide current scholarship, and
justifiably so. But both of these highly influential books are blind to the organization and imagery of sex difference. To be sure, the writings of Marx
and Engels—the sociological portraits, the historical analyses, the moral in-
dictments of market society—take account of capitalism's tendency to reor-
der gender relations. But even some of the most sophisticated of contemporary historians of emergent market culture, who are explicitly influenced by
Marx as well as by Polanyi and Macpherson, give little attention to issues of
gender. Thus, for example, *The Culture of the Market: Historical Essays,* an
anthology published in 1993 containing essays on diverse themes by writers
with differing interpretative orientations, does not include a single piece
framed around gender as a central analytic category.[5]

    Yet, a generation of historians of women has devoted a great deal of print
to discovering the links between market transformation and changing relations between men and women. Sellers's synthesis is a welcome contribution,
though it does not break new ground in reckoning with gender. In fact, its

approach is by now outdated. He reiterates an account of separate spheres that was clearly the first fruits—not the last word—of an effort to rethink the social and cultural problems posed by the spread of free market relations.

Roughly two decades ago, when the first studies were published linking the code of separate spheres to market expansion, they were truly pathbreaking. In *The Bonds of Womanhood,* Nancy Cott located the social origins of antebellum "woman's sphere" in "economic modernization": the shift to "market-oriented production," the cleavage between "the household and the business of society," the "separation of workplaces from the home." The canon of domesticity, its ideological complexities notwithstanding, was rooted in real "material change," she argued, that rendered the "two spheres" of the market and the home "the separate domains of the two sexes." Likewise, Mary Ryan's *Cradle of the Middle Class* interpreted the doctrine of sexual spheres as bearing "some resemblance to social reality" and related its cultural power both to the process of middle-class formation and to structural economic changes—namely, the transition from a rudimentary exchange economy to a pervasive market system—that gave rise to the stark oppositions of home and work, private and public, female and male. With these tremendously influential studies the interpretive paradigm was established.[6]

This paradigm is a common aspect of landmark pieces of scholarship that otherwise differ markedly in subject matter and analytical perspective. So, for instance, it forms the unquestioned premise of Carroll Smith-Rosenberg's vision of gender relations in Victorian America. The outcome of market expansion in Jacksonian America, she writes in *Disorderly Conduct,* was to engender a familiar set of "binary opposites": home and marketplace had formerly been one, but now men followed work into the "agora" and women stayed home in "isolated domesticity." Still more noteworthy is the way the paradigm has swept across the Mason-Dixon line, defining, by negation, what was distinctive about the slave society of the Old South. The essence of the southern household was that it combined relations of production and reproduction, argue Elizabeth Fox-Genovese and Eugene Genovese. In the South there were no separate spheres; under the slave system, dependent labor was absorbed within the household. By contrast, in the North, where market relations prevailed, maintains Eugene Genovese, "the household itself became a separate sphere oriented toward consumption." This interpretation is fully elaborated in Fox-Genovese's *Within the Plantation Household.* She ascribes the differences between southern and northern gender relations to the antinomies of slavery and free market relations, arguing that "developing capitalism" tended to confine women to the home, which was isolated from production. "The separation of home and work . . . constituted the material

embodiment of northeastern men's and women's separate spheres." Ironically, in arguing that Yankee women's history does not fit the world of slaveholders and slaves—in insisting on the distinctiveness of the southern social
formation—Fox-Genovese tightens the interpretive equation between the
market's dominion and the rise of a gender system based on the reality of
separate spheres.[7]

Clearly, then, there is good precedent for the kind of argument Sellers
advances about the market's impact on antebellum women. Although those
who first propounded this argument carefully limited it to the northern
middle classes, it quickly became a tidy shorthand for summing up the entire
history of women and gender from the early national era through the Gilded
Age. More recent accounts, however, make this interpretation less convincing
than it once may have appeared. The way that the development of market
society shaped gender relations and vice versa was more complicated, less
linear, less dichotomous than the model of separate spheres allows.

In myriad ways the deepening intrusion of market relations into family
economies involved all sorts of different women in selling commodities, making commodities, buying commodities, turning parts of their homes into
commodities, disposing of their time and skill as commodities. Even for the
middle class, the idea is no longer tenable that the world of most women was
remote from the market, that their labor had no cash value, that their homes
were not also places of work, both paid and unpaid.

Certainly, the expansion of the market did not deter women of the laboring poor from engaging in a motley range of very public marketing activities,
just as their forbears had done in the past. Quite the contrary. What Henry
Mayhew in his famous survey of Victorian London termed the "Ancient Calling of Costermongers" hardly disappeared among poor women in America
any more than in the Old World. On city streets, in stalls set up in market-
places, by the docks, they hawked fruit and fish and other wares. Street ped-
dling in particular was the work of black women and the very poor, a way to
earn the cash that was becoming increasingly crucial to family survival as
men's wages regularly dropped below subsistence. Pawning too was women's
work; if not in countinghouses, then in pawnshops, many women grew
skilled at driving hard bargains. From the work of Christine Stansell and others we now know that women along with their menfolk were enmeshed in
the spreading cash and credit relations of market society.[8]

Not only did poor women in cities continue to follow traditional marketing pursuits outside their homes; more middling sorts in rural areas as well
as urban working-class women hastened to turn their traditional, sex-

specific, productive labors to new account, making the valuable goods exchanged in the widening national market. For them, there was no sharp divide between home and work; home was instead the site of commodity production. Toiling at their churns, for instance, farm women in the Philadelphia countryside were petty, independent producers, engaged in a cottage butter industry that was not only attuned to the market but central to commercial development in the Middle Atlantic region. They actively shaped economic growth and worked in every facet of the business, from milking and churning to selling the butter from the curbs of city market streets. Through outwork in a variety of consumer industries—such as shoemaking, hatmaking, and weaving—many other farm women earned wages as the social relations of domestic crafts were transformed by thriving merchant capitalism and heightened market dependency in the countryside as well as the city. For these women, the home was a place of dependent commodity production. As one Vermont wife, who braided palm-leaf hats in the 1830s, explained why she engaged in market relations: "money is so very scarce and we must have some." Similar need drove working-class women to enter the metropolitan outwork system, which flourished especially in the needle and clothing trades and which merged with sweated labor. The tenement sweatshop was the most infamous embodiment of the fusing of home and work, family and market. Or, more precisely, it was the most infamous in free society. The slave system was premised on the fusion of household and market, a fusion blatantly epitomized in the marketing of slave family members.[9]

Just as women's commodity production inside the home blurred the supposed distinction between spheres, so too did the sale of their labor outside it further belie the notion that women were cloistered away from competitive economic relations. As scrubwomen, domestic servants, and factory hands, women entered the widening market for free labor. Female wage earning was most common in the households of blacks, immigrants, and the laboring poor, the renowned case of Yankee farm girls employed at the Lowell mills notwithstanding. Alternatively, women found a market for both their domestic space and their household services by taking in boarders and lodgers. Less well known is the fact that the altruistic ladies who administered the vast benevolent empire of the antebellum era sometimes earned wages for charity work. That empire was said to be coextensive with "women's sphere." In truth, there was marked "affinity between benevolent activity and business enterprises," writes Lori Ginzberg in a striking discovery. Not only were charitable women of the middle class altruists; they were paid for saving orphans, widows, and other misfortunates. For all the ethos of altruism untainted by professionalism or profit, female benevolent societies operated at the cutting edge of the market economy. The affluent women who ran them entered into a matrix of complex economic relations: they raised huge sums of money, made shrewd investment decisions, and disbursed funds. They even secured corporate charters, thereby gaining the legal and financial benefits of incorporation. The canon of domesticity held that women acted purely from motives of the heart. But female benevolence, Ginzberg discloses, was a *business*—anything but "distant from society's crass commercialism." Notions of sexual difference, as codified in the doctrine of spheres, masked "the fact that benevolence and money went hand in hand."[10]

Paradoxically, too, money was closely wed to housework—that most paradigmatically female and private of all benevolent callings. Domestic labor was unwaged service that a woman owed her husband as his dependent by law and custom. But as the market dependency of northern households deepened dramatically in the early nineteenth century, domestic economy became ever more intimately joined to the market economy's cash nexus. In sustaining their families, women of all classes became more and more busy with spending money, saving money, banking money, and negotiating credit. To varying degrees, the domestic manufacture of some family necessaries declined. Housework was transformed, as Jeanne Boydston argues, by the new "complexity of household economies" in a market economy. It took on "a more 'modern' function: that of mediating between the demands of the cash market and the often-quite-different imperatives of family survival." But that does not mean housework became unproductive. Its product, Boydston says, was "the household itself." This is a subtle and intricate argument, joined to a larger theoretical debate over the meaning of value and the labor of social reproduction, to which I cannot fully do justice here. But, bluntly stated, the point of Boydston's *Home and Work* is that housework—though unpaid—produced economic value, a value denied by market society's esteem for money as the sole index of all value. And rather than simply being altered by economic change, female domestic labor played a "constitutive economic role" in the forging of capitalism and wage relations. Not only did unpaid housework merge with women's money-generating labor; its "invisible" value helped create the surplus value that was the lifeblood of capital accumulation by enabling employers to set wages below subsistence.[11]

More visible were changes in the law that registered women's presence in the market and simultaneously redefined the property relations of men and women. The married women's property laws of the nineteenth century entitled wives to own and dispose first of real and personal property and later of wages earned through their labor. Enacted in piecemeal fashion beginning in the 1830s, the laws undercut the traditional marriage rule of coverture, which submerged the legal and economic identity of women in that of their husbands on the theory that men provided support and protection for their dependent wives and thereby had exclusive right to own all household property as well as their wives' labor and its proceeds. According to the prevailing wisdom, the crucial legal changes that underwrote the market revolution—foremost among them the rise of contract law—had nothing to do with gender. Yet, by the Civil War, some married women's laws explicitly or by implication gave wives the right to contract. Thus the law set its imprimatur on a relationship between women and the marketplace unmediated by husbands. Not only did the legislation clarify the rights and liabilities of wives involved in commodity relations; it fostered the indiscriminate liquidity of property and labor essential to a market economy. As the reformer Wendell Phillips dryly remarked, the laws suited the "bank interest" as much as the cause of women's rights.[12]

Evidence therefore abounds that runs contrary to the model of separate spheres. It is clear that as a way of representing the nature of gender relations and the changing circumstances of women in the market society of nineteenth-century America this model is overly simple. In the eyes of some historians, it is plainly wrong. Elizabeth Blackmar states this flatly in *Manhattan for Rent, 1785–1850,* a study of housing's transformation into a commodity. "Far from being 'removed' from the marketplace, the home stood at the heart of new property and labor relations," she writes. Neither the dualism of home and work nor of private and public described "social reality." In a sense the entire project of Boydston's history of housework is deconstructing the simple story of sexual spheres—demystifying the idea that a female domestic realm stood apart from and in contrast to the capitalist market economy of men. As Linda Kerber puts it, "to use the language of separate spheres is to deny the reciprocity between gender and society, and to impose a static model on dynamic relationships."[13]

Such scholarship contributes considerably to the inquiry called for a decade ago by the theorist Nancy Fraser into the interlocking character of family economy and the market economy, and the gender identities presumed by both. By questioning the objective truth of the idea of sexual spheres, it lays bare the cultural dimensions of the idea's past use. It compels attention to separate spheres as a belief system, a rhetoric, "a metaphor for complex power relations"—an ideology that managed, and often obscured, the social and cultural contradictions of market society.[14]

In turn, the ideological analysis of separate spheres casts doubt on another, corollary, dualism: the difference between Yankee homes and southern households. If, contrary to the Genoveses' argument, homes in the antebellum North were indeed units of production as well as of consumption, then households in the Old South do not appear so distinctive after all. The theory of southern distinctiveness does not simply presuppose the questionable link between free market society and separate spheres; it takes proslavery apologetics about family life both too seriously and not seriously enough. Too seriously, in promoting the notion of the peculiar organicism and paternalism of slave-owning households. Not seriously enough, in treating as mainly polemical the slaveholders' analogy between the domestic relations of slavery and marriage.[15]

What is evident, however, is that the unity of production and reproduction based on dependent labor within the household ought to be seen as characteristic of *both* free and slave society—once it is recognized that the work of wives at home (with all its ambiguities) was, as slaveholders said, a form of dependent labor in some ways like, though hardly identical with, chattel slavery. What then of the undeniable difference between slavery and freedom? Or, to put the problem another way, what difference did the market make in home life? This question lay at the heart of the argument between free and slave society, an argument in which the ideology of separate sexual spheres played no small part.

When the proslavery writer George Fitzhugh assailed the "political economy" of free society as erosive of moral sentiment, he was voicing fears that haunted the North itself. The "moral code" of market society, Fitzhugh wrote with customary irony in 1854, was "at war with morality." Laments on the theme of the market's blasphemy had filled jeremiads delivered from New England pulpits since colonial times. And for all the tributes to competitive individualism, uneasiness about market values lasted into the antebellum era (and beyond) in the North as well as the South. No set of symbols had greater cultural force in expressing and resolving the moral problem of the market than images of gender. If, as Fitzhugh put it, the spirit of the market was summed up in the adage "Every man for himself, and devil take the hindmost," then the countervailing doctrine of gender might have been stated aphoristically as, Every woman for somebody else, which keeps the devil away. This symbolism of sex difference, however, was imbricated with the debate over slavery. Which is not to say it was insignificant in its own right. But it is impossible to understand how free market society was vindicated through gender representations without also taking into account how it was assailed by defenders of slavery.[16]

It is well established that the Victorian concept of gender spheres did a great deal of the ideological work of legitimating market relations. Supposedly, the home sphere of women was the antidote to the selfish materialism of the economic domain of men, a sphere that embodied the virtues of compassion and self-denial, a hallowed place of refuge and regeneration, a sanctuary that would redeem and recuperate the competitive marketplace. According to J. G. A. Pocock, there has been in "every phase of Western tradition" a sense of virtue being threatened by "the spread of exchange relations." In the eighteenth century the dominant intellectual framework for dealing with that apprehension was Enlightenment philosophy, with its validation of rational egoism and its conversion of passions into interests. But in the nineteenth century the arid assurances of Common Sense gave way to the romantic cult of sensibility and the doctrine of sexual spheres. Even classical political economy espoused the view that the home supplied the moral counterweight to the insensitivity and brutality of the free market. It is in this sense that separate spheres has been understood as an ideology.[17]

In antebellum America an astonishingly broad range of contemporaries found reassurance in the ideology of spheres. Worries about spreading market relations pervaded differing languages of reform and literary works of many different genres. But for Americans otherwise divided—poor and rich, slave and free, black and white, women and men—the home represented the prospect of "human relations unqualified by a price." The effect of this ideology was to consolidate bourgeois authority by promising a boundary to the inhumanity of market relations, by locating morality in female nature, and by obscuring relations of hierarchy other than those domestic in form. Thus in 1834 a ladies magazine celebrated the "bliss of home," where every man was a master and every woman an angel. "Enviably happy," its writers claimed, "the man who is lord of such a paradise. . . . Should he meet . . . storms abroad, yet sunshine and peace await him at home; and when his proud heart would resent the language of petty tyrants . . . from whom he receives the scanty remuneration for his daily labors, the thought that she perhaps may suffer thereby, will calm the tumult of his passions, and bid him struggle on, and find his reward in her sweet tones, and soothing kindness." The same gender ideology underlay confident postbellum predictions such as Henry Ward Beecher's that freedmen would enthusiastically embrace market incentives.[18]

Not only did the image of spheres provide a boundary to corrosive market values, it also reestablished with stark clarity the boundary between masculine and feminine attributes, a boundary that had been blurred by transformations in the understanding of human psychology that accompanied the triumph of market relations. Sexual difference palliated the market's problematical meaning; but it also constituted part of the problem. Many of the traits associated with "economic man," the Promethean individual of the nineteenth century, had been traditionally stigmatized as female. In the eighteenth century, to engage in speculative exchange relations, to be buffeted by fortune, was to be dependent—the fate of women. The emergence of a new "marketing psychology" entailed valorizing impulse, passion, fantasy, and appetite. That meant reconceiving as inherent in men's nature the very propensities that had been equated shamefully with female hysteria, slavish dependence, and social disorder.[19]

Here, too, separate spheres did critical ideological work. The fixed spatial representation of sexual difference offset slippage and confusion in gender identity. Insight into the crisis of identity caused by "an increasingly placeless and timeless market process" is amply provided by Jean-Christophe Agnew's *Worlds Apart*, a study of the theatricality of early market culture. The problem of gender, though, does not take center stage. Yet the spherical system of sexual difference was absolutely fundamental to the search for a stable self— the "desire to purify, clarify, and restore lost boundaries" that Agnew shows was at the core of the "complex problematic of market exchange."[20]

The desire to clarify boundaries between men and women took on new urgency when the problem at stake was not simply the spread of exchange relations but rather the relentless conversion of human labor into a commodity. The ascendance of a market in free labor transformed the texture of social relations in ways that the swelling commerce in inanimate goods had not. At issue was not merely the degree of consumption or the enigmas of exchange introduced by money values, but rather profound change in relationships of authority and submission—in the rights and obligations of those who owned property and of the growing masses who did not. As Thomas Holt has written, "the commodification of labor power . . . required a decisive and problematic rupture in how humans traditionally related to each other." Or in Polanyi's words, which echo the terms of American slave owners' critique of free society: "To separate labor from other activities of life and to subject it to the laws of the market was to annihilate all organic forms of existence and to replace them by . . . an atomistic and individualistic one." The distinctive moral problem posed by market society was how to impart legitimacy to the traffic in free labor that constituted its defining characteristic.[21]

Like the birth of "economic man," the conversion of his labor into a commodity confused traditional understandings of sexual difference, blurring the boundary between women and men. It was an axiom of Enlightenment political thought that persons who sold their labor—however voluntarily—

were dependent, and therefore not fully autonomous or capable of exercising the virtue required of citizens. Wage labor was associated with the hierarchies of the household. Indeed, in Anglo-American law through the nineteenth century it was categorized together with marriage and slavery as a "domestic relation" explicitly based on dominion and subordination. The hireling's legal status paralleled the wife's. The spread of wage labor, then, threatened to make men more like women, throwing gender identity into question. Though virtually unnoted in the scholarly literature on the market, ambiguities of sexual difference were a troubling aspect of labor's commodification. So, when Jacksonian journeymen protested their dependence and spoke of their rights, they feared for their identity both as republican citizens and as men. It has become clear that notions of racial difference were essential to white workingmen's sense of class identity and framed their response to their dependent status. The same was true of notions of sex difference, symbolized by separate spheres.[22]

To reconstruct the ideological meaning of wage labor was by no means a simple or uncontested endeavor for capitalism's proponents. Just as legitimating commerce had involved translating unruly female passion into rational male interest, so legitimating the commerce in labor involved redefining the hireling as independent. Among other things, that meant subverting the cultural association of wage labor with the household and domestic dependency—disrupting the analogy between wives and hired men. Separate spheres fulfilled this ideological purpose. The counterposing of home and work sharply distinguished women's dependent household labor from men's independent wage labor. As a market commodity, male labor was valorized both literally and figuratively by contrast with female housework, which allegedly produced nothing and had no value. Much has recently been written about how ideas of sexual difference can make other relations of subordination appear natural, as southerners invoked marriage to do for slavery. But in the North, gender ideology had the opposite effect. Instead of giving nature's cast to the inequalities of class and the asymmetries of power created by wage relations, it tended to deny them. Supposedly, the formal freedom and equality of contracting parties in the marketplace stood in opposition to the hierarchies of gender that were thought to be uniquely defensible because uniquely derived from nature—from bodily differences presumed to be immutable. In free market society the difference between the sexes did not represent a model for the social order outside the home, but rather its antithesis.[23]

Such an interpretation of the ideology of spheres inverts the usual scholarly understanding of its dualistic logic. The home has been taken to represent the benign and redemptive place that would hedge the corrosive thrust of acquisitive market relations. However, the boundary between the spheres also worked the other way: to fence in the dependencies of the home, to stop them from permeating and contaminating the marketplace where labor power was bought and sold. The home may have been the market's anodyne, but along with female virtue it also embodied inequality. Only as wage labor lost the taint of domestic subordination, removed from the household's shadow into a putatively separate sphere, could exponents of the free labor system pronounce hirelings fully independent.

Thus could the antislavery leader William Lloyd Garrison contrast the condition of the wage laborer to that of "a domestic animal." Was the hireling not a "free agent?" asked Garrison. "Are his movements dependent on the will and pleasure of another?" Notably, the unfortunate domestic beast could have been a metaphor for either the wife or the chattel slave.[24]

In the debate over slavery, no issue carried greater ideological weight than the relationship between the market and home life. However much slaveholders and abolitionists differed over the merits of freedom and bondage as systems of production and reproduction, they agreed that these elements of the social order were inexorably joined—that relations of labor could not be dissociated from family relations. Defenders of slavery contended that the free labor system destroyed "domestic affection"; abolitionists held that slavery's "worst abuse" was its "outrage upon the family."[25] Domesticity supplied a language for sectional controversy, and the family a measure for the moral consequences of opposing systems of political economy. The question boiled down to which form of commodity relationship constituted the bedrock of home life: the market in free labor or the market in slaves?

Proslavery theorists maintained that free society was at war with organic family ties and blunted all altruistic feeling. As Fitzhugh wrote, freedom's defining social exchange was "hard dealing," an exchange that incited "rivalries, jealousies and hatreds on all hands" and made a virtue out of "avarice." The hireling might have been a free agent, but he lived in a world devoid of "domestic affection," excluded from the "holy and charmed circle" of the family that surrounded the slave in its protective web. Condemning the materialistic and competitive ethos of the free market, Fitzhugh averred that "domestic affection cannot be calculated in dollars and cents." The notion that the slave system—in contrast to free labor—created an extended biracial household was essential to the slaveholders' worldview. In the words of one southern minister, God had "included slavery as an organizing element in that family order which lies at the very foundation of Church and State." In proslavery thought, slavery and marriage stood together as the pillars of a well-ordered society.[26]

Proponents of slavery did not simply argue that free market society eroded the affective ties between master and servant; they held that it imperiled marriage and the family. Only the slave system, founded on dependence and protection, secured the household intact, slaveholders insisted. "We shall not sully our sheet with descriptions of the marriage relation as it often presents itself . . . in free America," Fitzhugh sniffed. Yet he cataloged wrongs in the North ranging from the murder of wives as "holiday pastime" to the sufferings of widowed needlewomen to rampant divorce and prostitution. Fitzhugh admitted that the domestic slave trade cruelly severed family ties; but he countered that delicate Yankee women were forced by brutal necessity to "quit the domestic hearth . . . to seek a living among strangers," a topic so painful that "delicacy" forbade its further discussion. Expressing a belief widely shared in the Old South, he maintained that women—like slaves— were fit only for a condition of dependency. And dependency was the social prerequisite of human affection and moral virtue. "A state of dependence is the only condition in which reciprocal affection can exist among human beings," Fitzhugh postulated, "in which the war of competition ceases." A social theory exalting domestic reciprocity based on the hierarchies of subordination and protection underpinned southerners' insistence on the analogy between marriage and slavery. Fitzhugh emphasized the "intimate connexion" between these two domestic relations. Ominously, he warned, "Marriage is too much like slavery not to be involved in its fate." In the proslavery view, therefore, the triumph of free market society ultimately meant the downfall of the home.[27]

But that was precisely what abolitionists argued about slavery. They tirelessly polemicized that treating slaves as market commodities desecrated the much-vaunted southern family, black and white. Frederick Douglass thundered against the defense of slavery as a "domestic institution." The use of this "soft and innocent term," he declared, hid the fact that the reality of slavery was "to sunder families for the convenience of purchasers" and to subject female slaves to the "barbarous work" of debauched slave masters. Another former slave, William Wells Brown, sought to bring home to free men the meaning of the traffic in slaves: "Go into a southern market and see men and women sold in lots. . . . Place your wife, daughter or child in their position, to be struck off to the highest bidder." Abolitionists strove to show that the slave system polluted and destroyed the "domestic society" of both masters and slaves. As one writer argued in 1837, "no part of the dark and hidden iniquities of slavery" demanded exposure more than its "odious lusts" and violation of the "nuptial covenant." It was not freedom but slavery, declared the African Methodist Episcopal Church, that was synonymous with "fornication, adultery, concubinage." No abolitionist argument proved more compelling than that testifying to the conflict between slavery and domesticity, as demonstrated by Harriet Beecher Stowe's best-selling 1852 melodrama *Uncle Tom's Cabin*.[28]

From its inception in the early 1830s, the radical abolition movement claimed that all the wrongs of slavery accrued from converting human beings into "marketable commodities," holding them as "piece[s] of merchandise." Abolitionists repeatedly used market terminology—buying, selling, leasing, mortgaging—to condemn slave relations, and contrasted the divinity of the human spirit to crass money values. The goal of abolition, wrote Angelina Grimké in 1836, was "no longer to barter the *image of God* in human shambles for corruptible things such as silver and gold." The slave auction was the primary symbol of market corruption—above all, as the site where slave households were forcibly sundered by sale. There, wrote Frances Ellen Watkins Harper, the most famous black poet of her day,

> mothers stood, with streaming eyes,
> And saw their dearest children sold
> . . . tyrants barter'd them for gold.
> And woman, with her love and truth . . .
> Gaz'd on the husband of her youth,
> With anguish none may paint or tell.

An unmistakable strain of ambivalence, even abhorrence, toward the market ran through antislavery propaganda. And it was most pronounced in abolitionist claims that commodity relations were at odds with family bonds.[29]

The intent of abolitionists was hardly to discredit all forms of market exchange, but rather to isolate the trade in slaves as singularly unacceptable. Yet all the discussion about the evils of setting a price on human faculties and body parts—"blood and nerves," "bodies and souls"—had implications beyond the issue of chattel slavery. At the very moment abolitionists were attacking the South for its commerce in unfree persons, the North was being transformed by the commerce in free labor. The antislavery outcry against turning human life into cash value thereby resonated with potential, if unintended, meaning for free persons grappling with the upheaval caused by the rise of wage labor and market society. As is well known, however, abolitionists generally endorsed the wage system. Thus the antislavery argument was complicated by the problem of containing its own diatribe against commodity relations, especially as it pitted the market against the sanctity of the family. For this predicament the recourse lay in thoroughly conventional gender doctrine, even though abolitionists were accused of harboring sexual beliefs as blasphemous as their views of slavery.[30]

By the lights of abolitionists, a free man differed from a slave not only because he was a "free agent" and the sovereign of himself, but because he possessed an inalienable right to his family. Denouncing the theory that the free market could breed "wages slavery," they constantly contrasted the domestic circumstances of hirelings to those of bondsmen. As Garrison asked with regard to the condition of "the most degraded and dependant free laborer, . . . Can any power take from him wife and his children?" The wretched hireling was "still a freeman . . . still the owner of his own body . . . still a husband." In the eyes of the black abolitionist Uriah Boston, no slave was "better off than the free colored people" in the North. For slaves had "no legal right to wife or children," or any of "the rights pertaining thereto."[31] Abolitionists readily granted that market norms of competitive individualism ran counter to the paternalistic principles of both slavery and the family. Nevertheless, they held that only a free market in labor, as in other commodities, ensured that the household would remain inviolate—a sphere of domestic entitlement insulated from competing claims.

That theory had been handed down from none other than Adam Smith, the progenitor of classical economics. According to Smith, the market in free labor was entirely congruent with the customary dependencies of the household. He emphasized that hirelings toiling at the most brutish drudgery were elevated far above the slave's "miserable life," for they had a right to the "liberty of marriage" as well as to wages. Indeed, he posited that the wage bought men their liberty as husbands: contrary to the idea that commodity relations and domestic bonds were in conflict, the wage, like other forms of property ownership, formed the material basis of a man's rights as master of a household. "Especially in the lower ranks," wrote Smith, the wife owed her "maintenance . . . intirely to her husband, and from this dependence it is that she is thought to be bound to be faithfull and constant to him." Conversely, even if a male slave cohabited with a female slave, he had no claim to her labor or sexuality, for she was maintained not by the bondsman but by her master, who had an exclusive right to her person. Smith elucidated the economic connection between wage labor and domestic rights in a theory that associated male freedom and female dependency while obscuring the value of housework to family maintenance.[32]

Well versed in liberal political economy and legal doctrine, most abolitionists argued that it was as much the birthright of free men to claim property in their wives as in themselves. As they saw it, the right of a man to have a family carried with it a corollary right of dominion and proprietorship. Despite the commitment of many abolitionists to the woman movement, they contrasted freedom to slavery through inventories implying that a man's right to his family was equivalent to his title to material things: "As a free man, his earnings would be his . . . his furniture, his comforts would be his—his wife, his children would be his."[33] The paternal form of power and property that abolitionists would have stripped from slave masters, therefore, they were more than willing to grant all free men in relation to their presumably dependent wives and children. And only free market relations, they argued tenaciously, would guarantee these fundamental rights of possessive domesticity denied to the slave.

It has been established that the symbol of the slave historically has defined, by negation, the meaning of freedom.[34] Thus in antebellum America the free market was thought by most northerners to safeguard the domestic ties destroyed by the market in slaves, to keep separate the spheres of kin and commerce so notoriously merged by slavery, to give material substance to the formal right of every man to be master of a family, which no slave could claim. As Henry Ward Beecher said so plainly in the wake of emancipation, it was "the prospect of a home, a family that is not marketable" that distinguished wage labor from bondage. Home life marked the crucial difference between the commodity relations of freedom and slavery.

Gender ideals based on the split between market and household were central, then, to the negative representations of the South that helped to affirm the legitimacy of free market society. The role played by this symbolism of sex difference in validating the emergent wage economy was inseparable from its role in highlighting the evils of slavery. Separate spheres figured so powerfully as a legitimating ideology in antebellum America precisely because it marked the boundary not only between women and men, but also between the sale of slaves and of free labor. Yet the debate over slavery lent a new cast to the ideology of spheres. In the antislavery version of this ideology, the market had redeeming value for the home, as well as the reverse. By virtue of the contrast with the slave system, the home stood as a sign of the fundamental morality of the market in free labor. Unlike the bondsman, the hireling could count himself free because the sale of his labor ensured his property in his domestic dependents.[35]

By the turn of the century the market in free labor had become considerably less free, at least according to classical liberal definitions. A framework of protective labor laws was being set in place that interfered with the right of buyers and sellers of labor power to reach whatever bargains they saw fit. Long opposed as a threat to free laborers' independence, this system of state regulation was central to the social and legal reforms of the Progressive Era.

At the heart of the ideological shift that ushered in the regulatory state lay a perception that the spheres of home and market were overlapping in a way that endangered what contemporaries called "the future of the race." Reformers cried out that the conditions of industrial labor had put the family in crisis. They pointed to a host of problems—wages below subsistence, long hours, tenement sweatshops, the wage work of women and children—and argued that the unregulated market had contaminated the household and disrupted proper gender roles. As Florence Kelley argued in 1905, the pathology of the working-class home justified "ethical gains through legislation." The idea that law should impose a moral dimension otherwise absent from commodity relations first won support mainly as a theory of sex-specific labor law, when the strife of the market, in the words of the United States Supreme Court, clashed with the "burdens of motherhood." Alarm not only about the household's integrity but especially about the increasing presence of ostensibly dependent women in the workplace provided the opening wedge for protective law.[36]

In the name of the family, therefore, the market in labor began to be regulated by the state. Ironically, the notion of separate spheres that had once served to legitimate the free market had now come to challenge it.[37] All the reasons why this was so cannot be explored here. But with the downfall of slavery may well have come a heightened sense that the dangers to home life existed not just outside free market society but within it.

NOTES

1. *National Freedman,* Nov. 1865, p. 332.

2. C. B. Macpherson, *The Political Theory of Possessive Individualism: Hobbes to Locke* (Oxford, 1962), pp. 48, 272. On the market as a catalyst of humanitarian and emancipatory reform, see Thomas L. Haskell, "Capitalism and the Origins of the Humanitarian Sensibility," parts 1 and 2, *American Historical Review* 90 (1985): 339–61, 547–66. Examples of

influential works addressing the problematical meaning of free market relations that take little or no account of gender as a central analytical category include Karl Polanyi, *The Great Transformation: The Political and Economic Origins of Our Time* (Boston, 1944); Jean-Christophe Agnew, *Worlds Apart: The Market and the Theater in Anglo-American Thought, 1550–1750* (New York, 1986); David Brion Davis, *The Problem of Slavery in the Age of Revolution, 1770–1823* (Ithaca, N.Y., 1975); Sean Wilentz, *Chants Democratic: New York City and the Rise of the American Working Class* (New York, 1984); Steven Hahn, *The Roots of Southern Populism: Yeoman Farmers and the Transformation of the Georgia Upcountry, 1850–1890* (New York, 1983); Eric Foner, *Reconstruction: America's Unfinished Revolution 1863–1877* (New York, 1988). A recent, less critical assessment of the market revolution that is also inattentive to the problem of gender is Winifred Barr Rothenberg, *From Market-Places to a Market Economy: The Transformation of Rural Massachusetts, 1750–1850* (Chicago, 1992). For a skeptical assessment of the notion of wrenching cultural transformation caused by the rise of the market economy, see Gordon Wood, "Inventing American Capitalism," *New York Review of Books,* June 9, 1994, pp. 44–49.

3. For an analysis of the intersection of antislavery and Victorian gender ideology in England, see Catherine Hall, *White, Male and Middle Class: Explorations in Feminism and History* (New York, 1992), pp. 205–54; Persis Charles, "The Name of the Father: Women, Paternity, and British Rule in Nineteenth-Century Jamaica," *International Labor and Working-Class History* 41 (1992): 4–22, and responses by Catherine Hall, Thomas C. Holt, and Dale Tomich in the same issue, pp. 23–41.

4. Charles Sellers, *The Market Revolution: Jacksonian America 1815–1846* (New York, 1991), pp. 242, 245–6, 242. For a critique of this model, see, in addition to the books discussed below in the text and notes at notes 12 and 13, Joan W. Scott, "The Woman Worker," in Georges Duby and Michelle Perrot, eds., *Histoire des Femmes en Occident,* 4 vols. (Paris, 1991), 4:399–426.

5. Polanyi, *The Great Transformation;* Macpherson, *Political Theory of Possessive Individualism;* Thomas L. Haskell and Richard F. Teichgraeber III, eds., *The Culture of the Market: Historical Essays* (New York, 1993). On the significance of the work of Polanyi and Macpherson, see the introduction in *The Culture of the Market.*

6. Nancy F. Cott, *The Bonds of Womanhood: 'Woman's Sphere' in New England, 1780–1835* (New Haven, Conn., 1977), pp. 40, 25, 59, 66, 67; Mary P. Ryan, *Cradle of the Middle Class: The Family in Oneida County, New York, 1790–1865* (New York, 1981), p. 191. On the career of the concept of separate spheres in the field of women's history, see Linda Kerber, "Separate Spheres, Female Worlds, Woman's Place: The Rhetoric of Women's History," *Journal of American History* 75 (1988) 9–39.

7. Carroll Smith-Rosenberg, *Disorderly Conduct: Visions of Gender in Victorian America* (New York, 1985), pp. 85, 86; Eugene Genovese, "'Our Family, White and Black': Family and Household in the Southern Slaveholders' World View," in Carol Bleser, ed., *In Joy and In Sorrow: Women, Family, and Marriage in the Victorian South, 1830–1900* (New York, 1991), p. 72; Elizabeth Fox-Genovese, *Within the Plantation Household: Black and White Women of the Old South* (Chapel Hill, N.C., 1988), chap. 1, esp. pp. 59–79, quotes at pp. 59, 61.

8. Henry Mayhew, *London Labour and the London Poor,* 4 vols. (1861–62; reprint, New

York, 1968), vol. 1; Christine Stansell, *City of Women: Sex and Class in New York, 1789–1860* (New York, 1986).

9. Joan M. Jensen, *Loosening the Bonds: Mid-Atlantic Farm Women, 1750–1850* (New Haven, Conn., 1986), esp. pp. 79–89; Nancy Grey Osterud, *Bonds of Community: The Lives of Farm Women in Nineteenth-Century New York* (Ithaca, N.Y., 1991); Thomas Dublin, "Women and Outwork in a Nineteenth-Century New England Town: Fitzwilliam, New Hampshire, 1830–1850," in Steven Hahn and Jonathan Prude, eds., *The Countryside in the Age of Capitalist Transformation: Essays in the Social History of Rural America* (Chapel Hill, N.C., 1985), p. 64. On urban outwork and sweating, see Stansell, *City of Women*, pp. 105–19; Elizabeth Blackmar, *Manhattan for Rent, 1785–1850* (New York, 1989), pp. 124–26.

10. Lori D. Ginzberg, *Women and the Work of Benevolence: Morality, Politics, and Class in the Nineteenth-Century United States* (New Haven, Conn., 1990), pp. 59, 53, 42. On women's varied waged employments and income earning through taking in boarders and lodgers, see Stansell, *City of Women*, pp. 12–18, 45, 120–29; Blackmar, *Manhattan for Rent*, pp. 61–67; Jeanne Boydston, *Home and Work: Housework, Wages, and the Ideology of Labor in the Early Republic* (New York, 1990), pp. 36–37.

11. Boydston, *Home and Work*, pp. 124, 125, 122, 137. And see Nancy Folbre, "The Unproductive Housewife: Her Evolution in Nineteenth-Century Economic Thought," *Signs* 16 (1991): 463–84. On the economic value of women's labor in the late eighteenth century, see Laurel Thatcher Ulrich, *A Midwife's Tale: The Life of Martha Ballard, Based on Her Diary, 1785–1812* (New York, 1990).

12. Phillips quoted in Amy Dru Stanley, *The Bonds of Contract: Wage Labor and Marriage in the Age of Slave Emancipation* (Cambridge, Eng., forthcoming). The leading account of the legal history of market development (an account followed in Sellers's book) is Morton Horwitz, *The Transformation of American Law, 1780–1860* (Cambridge, Mass., 1977). Sellers's account of legal developments includes no reference to gender issues; see pp. 47–59. On the married women's laws, see Amy Dru Stanley, "Conjugal Bonds and Wage Labor: Rights of Contract in the Age of Emancipation," *Journal of American History* 75 (1988): 471–500; Kerber, "Separate Spheres," pp. 21–22; Norma Basch, *In the Eyes of the Law: Women, Marriage, and Property in Nineteenth-Century New York* (Ithaca, N.Y., 1982).

13. Blackmar, *Manhattan for Rent*, pp. 112, 126; Kerber, "Separate Spheres," p. 38.

14. Nancy Fraser, "What's Critical about Critical Theory? The Case of Habermas and Gender," *New German Critique* 35 (1985): 97–131. The quote is from Kerber, "Separate Spheres," p. 28; also see Mary Poovey, *Uneven Developments: The Ideological Work of Gender in Mid-Victorian England* (Chicago, 1988), pp. 1–23; Leonore Davidoff and Catherine Hall, *Family Fortunes: Men and Women of the English Middle Class, 1780–1850* (Chicago, 1987); Boydston, *Home and Work*, pp. 142–47; Blackmar, *Manhattan for Rent*, p. 126; Frances E. Olsen, "The Family and the Market: A Study of Ideology and Legal Reform," *Harvard Law Review* 96 (1983): 1497–1578.

15. On proslavery apologetics, see George Fitzhugh, *Sociology for the South, or The Failure of Free Society* (1854; reprint, New York, 1965); Michael P. Johnson, "Planters and Patriarchy: Charleston, 1800–1860," *Journal of Southern History* 46 (1980): 45–72; Gen-

ovese, "Our Family, White and Black"; Elizabeth Fox-Genovese, "Family and Female Identity in the Antebellum South: Sarah Gayle and Her Family," in Bleser, *In Joy and In Sorrow*, pp. 15–31; Stephanie McCurry, "The Two Faces of Republicanism: Gender and Proslavery Politics in Antebellum South Carolina," *Journal of American History* 78 (1992): 1245–64.

16. Fitzhugh, *Sociology for the South*, pp. 200, 51; Edmund S. Morgan, *The Challenge of the American Revolution* (New York, 1976), pp. 90–95; Toby L. Ditz, "Shipwrecked; or, Masculinity Imperiled: Mercantile Representations of Failure and the Gendered Self in Eighteenth-Century Philadelphia," *Journal of American History* 81 (1994): 51–80; Steven Watts, "Masks, Morals, and the Market: American Literature and Early Capitalist Culture, 1790–1820," *Journal of the Early Republic* 6 (1986): 127–49; Karen Haltunnen, *Confidence Men and Painted Women: A Study of Middle-Class Culture in America, 1830–1870* (New Haven, Conn., 1982), pp. xvi, 18–55. To underscore anxiety about market relations is not to discount evidence of Americans' enthusiastic consumption of commercial goods in the eighteenth and nineteenth centuries; see Carole Shammas, *The Pre-Industrial Consumer in England and America* (New York, 1990); T. H. Breen, "Narrative of Commercial Life: Consumption, Ideology, and Community on the Eve of the American Revolution," *William and Mary Quarterly* 50 (1993): 471–501.

17. J. G. A. Pocock, *Virtue, Commerce, and History: Essays on Political Thought and History, Chiefly in the Eighteenth Century* (New York, 1985), pp. 104, 113; Albert O. Hirschman, *The Passions and the Interests: Political Arguments for Capitalism before Its Triumph* (Princeton, N.J., 1977); Agnew, *Worlds Apart*, pp. 174–75, 188; Davidoff and Hall, *Family Fortunes*, p. 185; David Brion Davis, "Reflections on Abolitionism and Ideological Hegemony," *American Historical Review* 92 (1987): 812; Cott, *Bonds of Womanhood*, pp. 63–74.

18. Blackmar, *Manhattan for Rent*, p. 126; Cott, *Bonds of Womanhood*, pp. 69–70. On antebellum anxiety about market relations, see Wilentz, *Chants Democratic*. On the links between this anxiety, the theory of women as innately moral, and the ideological effect of separate spheres, see, in addition to the works cited in notes 14 and 17, Gillian Brown, *Domestic Individualism: Imagining Self in Nineteenth-Century America* (Berkeley, Calif., 1990), pp. 3–38; Ronald G. Walters, "The Family and Ante-bellum Reform: An Interpretation," *Societas* 3 (1973): 221–32; Ginzberg, *Women and the Work of Benevolence*, pp. 11–35; John Ashworth, "The Relationship between Capitalism and Humanitarianism," *American Historical Review* 92 (1987): 813–28; Ruth H. Bloch, "The Gendered Meanings of Virtue in Revolutionary America," *Signs* 13 (1987): 37–58; Nancy F. Cott, "Passionlessness: An Interpretation of Victorian Sexual Ideology, 1790–1850," *Signs* 4 (1978): 219–36; Poovey, *Uneven Developments*, pp. 9–12, 18; Denise Riley, *"Am I That Name?": Feminism and the Category of "Women" in History* (Minneapolis, 1988), pp. 45–48; Ryan, *Cradle of the Middle Class;* Stansell, *City of Women*, p. xii.

19. Pocock, *Virtue, Commerce, and History*, pp. 113–15, 99. The term "market psychology" is Polanyi's, though he does not address its gender implications (*The Great Transformation*, p. 44); and see Ditz, "Shipwrecked."

20. Agnew, *Worlds Apart*, pp. x, 104.

21. Thomas C. Holt, "Explaining Abolition," *Journal of Social History* 24 (1990): 372; Polanyi, *The Great Transformation*, p. 163; Davis, *Problem of Slavery;* Ashworth, "Capitalism and Humanitarianism." On consumption and the rise of a market economy, see

Christopher Clark, "Household Economy, Market Exchange, and the Rise of Capitalism in the Connecticut Valley, 1800–1860," *Journal of Social History* 13 (1979): 169–89. On money and enigmatic exchange relations, see Agnew, *Worlds Apart.*

22. Stanley *Bonds of Contract*, chap. 1; Christopher Tomlins, "Subordination, Authority, Law: Subjects in Labor History," *International Labor and Working-Class History*, no. 47 (1995): 56–90; David R. Roediger, *The Wages of Whiteness: Race and the Making of the American Working Class* (London, 1991); Joan W. Scott, *Gender and the Politics of History* (New York, 1988), pp. 53–67. And on the market and ambiguities of racial identity, see Michael O'Malley, "Specie and Species: Race and the Money Question in Nineteenth-Century America," *American Historical Review* 99 (1994): 369–95.

23. Boydston, *Home and Work;* Joan W. Scott, "Gender: A Useful Category of Historical Analysis," *American Historical Review* 91 (1986): 1053–75; Scott, *Gender and the Politics of History*, pp. 55–65; McCurry, "The Two Faces of Republicanism"; E. J. Hobsbawm, *The Age of Capital, 1848–1875* (New York, 1975), pp. 237–40.

24. *Liberator*, Oct. 1, 1847.

25. Fitzhugh, *Sociology for the South*, p. 105; Harriet Beecher Stowe, *The Key to Uncle Tom's Cabin* (Boston, 1853), p. 257.

26. Fitzhugh, *Sociology for the South*, pp. 38, 106; Genovese, "Our Family, White and Black," p. 70. See Johnson, "Planters and Patriarchy."

27. Fitzhugh, *Sociology for the South*, pp. 195, 84, 213, 216, 250, 230, 246, 206, 205.

28. Frederick Douglass, "The Address of Southern Delegates in Congress to their Constituents; or, The Address of John C. Calhoun and Forty Other Thieves," *North Star*, Feb. 9, 1849, reprinted in Philip S. Foner, ed., *The Life and Writings of Frederick Douglass*, 4 vols. (New York, 1950–55), 1:358, 360; Frederick Douglass, *My Bondage and My Freedom* (1855; reprint, New York, 1969), p. 87; C. Peter Ripley, ed., *The Black Abolitionist Papers*, vol. 4, *The United States, 1847–1858* (Chapel Hill, N.C., 1991), p. 247; George Bourne, *Slavery Illustrated in Its Effects upon Woman and Domestic Society* (1837; reprint, Freeport, N.Y., 1972), pp. 13, 31, 29; *Black Abolitionist Papers* 4:196; Harriet Beecher Stowe, *Uncle Tom's Cabin: Or, Life among the Lowly* (1852; reprint, New York, 1952). See Stanley, *Bonds of Contract*. chap. 1.

29. William H. Pease and Jane H. Pease, eds., *The Antislavery Argument* (New York, 1965), p. 67; Angelina E. Grimké, *Appeal to the Christian Women of the South* (New York, 1836), p. 26; Frances Ellen Watkins [Harper], "The Slave Auction," *Frederick Douglass' Paper*, Sept. 22, 1854, p. 4. See Brown, *Domestic Individualism*, pp. 1–60; Ashworth, "Capitalism and Humanitarianism."

30. William Wells Brown, "The American Slave-Trade," *Liberty Bell* (1848): 231, 235–36. On abolitionists' defense of free wage labor, see Davis, *Problem of Slavery;* Eric Foner, *Politics and Ideology in the Age of the Civil War* (New York, 1980), pp. 34–53; Jonathan A. Glickstein, "'Poverty Is Not Slavery': American Abolitionists and the Competitive Labor Market," in Lewis Perry and Michael Fellman, eds., *Antislavery Reconsidered: New Perspectives on the Abolitionists* (Baton Rouge, La., 1979), pp. 195–218. My analysis of the complexities of antislavery arguments about the market is indebted to and parallels that of David Brion Davis regarding abolitionists' simultaneous critique of the coercive physical discipline of slavery and endorsement of new, more subtle, forms of work discipline characteristic of industrial wage labor. On the complexities of abolitionists' gender beliefs,

see Kristin Hoganson, "Garrisonian Abolitionists and the Rhetoric of Gender, 1850–1860," *American Quarterly* 45 (1993): 556–95; Jean Fagan Yellin, *Women and Sisters: The Antislavery Feminists in American Culture* (New Haven, Conn., 1989); Karen Sanchez-Eppler, "Bodily Bonds: The Intersecting Rhetorics of Feminism and Abolitionism," *Representations* 24 (1988): 28–59.

31. *Liberator,* Oct. 1, 1847, and Dec. 24, 1841; *Black Abolitionist Papers* 4:323. See David Roediger, *Wages of Whiteness,* p. 83.

32. See Stanley, *Bonds of Contract,* chap. 1.

33. *Emancipator,* Aug. 1835. See Stanley, "Conjugal Bonds and Wage Labor," 480; Stanley, *Bonds of Contract,* chap. 1; Carole Pateman, *The Sexual Contract* (Stanford, Calif., 1988); Johnson, "Planters and Patriarchy"; Eric Foner, "The Meaning of Freedom in the Age of Emancipation," *Journal of American History* 81 (1994): 435–60, esp. 455.

34. Davis, *Problem of Slavery;* Orlando Patterson, *Freedom,* vol. 1, *Freedom in the Making of Western Culture* (New York, 1991); Thomas C. Holt, *The Problem of Freedom: Race, Labor, and Politics in Jamaica and Britain, 1832–1938* (Baltimore, 1992), pp. 25–26.

35. This aspect of the antislavery ideology of spheres has gone largely unnoted by scholars, who stress the standard logic of the family-market antithesis; see Brown, *Domestic Individualism,* pp. 13–38; Ashworth, "Capitalism and Humanitarianism."

36. Florence Kelley, *Some Ethical Gains through Legislation* (1905; reprint, New York, 1969); *Muller v. Oregon,* 208 U.S. 412 (1908), at 421; Eileen Boris, *Home to Work: Motherhood and the Politics of Industrial Homework in the United States* (New York, 1994).

37. See Alice Kessler-Harris, *A Woman's Wage: Historical Meanings and Social Consequences* (Lexington, Ky., 1990), p. 40.

PART II

Political Ideology

4

Free Labor and Nineteenth-Century Political Ideology

ERIC FONER

I T IS A DISCOMFITING THOUGHT—for the author at least—that a quarter of a century has passed since the publication of my first book, *Free Soil, Free Labor, Free Men*. That the book remains in print and is still assigned in history courses in the United States is extremely gratifying, although I must admit that its initial impact derived in part from the good fortune of appearing at the very moment when American historians were rediscovering the concept of ideology. The book argued, in brief, that the Republican party before the Civil War was united by a commitment to a "free labor ideology" grounded in the precepts that free labor was economically and socially superior to slave labor and that the distinctive quality of northern society was the opportunity it offered wage earners to rise to property-owning independence. From this creed flowed Republicans' determination to arrest the expansion of slavery and place the institution on what Lincoln called the road to "ultimate extinction."[1]

Twenty-five years establishes enough distance to allow one to reflect not only on a book's longevity, but also on its limitations. On rereading, it is clear that *Free Soil, Free Labor, Free Men* took the free labor ideology as a given, making little effort to trace its ideological origins, social roots, or evolution over time. Free labor, moreover, was presented as a straightforward, unitary concept, with little sense of how different Americans might have infused it with substantially different meanings.

My purpose here, however, is not to review my own book, but to suggest how the transformation of historical scholarship during the past quarter-century enables us to better understand the idea of free labor and the society in which it flourished. Written, as it were, on the threshold separating two generations of historical scholarship, *Free Soil, Free Labor, Free Men* lacked the benefit of the "new histories" that have matured since 1969, along with the new concepts and methodologies that scholars have applied to the study of labor, gender, the law, and political language itself. These make it possible to take a fresh look at the idea of free labor, describing the idea in all its complexity and situating it more fully in nineteenth-century American history.

When *Free Soil* was published, historians were just emerging from what in retrospect appears to have been a fairly sterile debate over whether consensus or conflict characterized the American past. It is now clear that, if nineteenth-century Americans shared a common language of politics, the very universality of that rhetoric camouflaged a host of divergent connotations and emphases. Concepts central to the era's political culture—independence, equality, citizenship, freedom—were subject to constant challenge and redefinition, their substance changing over time as different groups sought to redraw their boundaries and reshape their meanings. Such concepts, moreover, were generally defined and redefined through the construction of sharp binary oppositions that ordered Americans' understanding of social reality, simultaneously illuminating some parts of that reality and obscuring or glossing over others.[2] Just as freedom and slavery were joined in the actual development of the New World, so the definition of free labor depended on juxtaposition with its ideological opposite, slave labor. Under the rubric of free labor, northerners of diverse backgrounds and interests could rally in defense of the superiority of their own society, even as other voices questioned whether the contrast with slavery did not disguise the forms of compulsion to which free laborers were themselves subjected. The dichotomy between slave and free labor masked the fact that *free labor* itself referred to two distinct economic conditions—the wage laborer seeking employment in the marketplace and the property-owning small producer enjoying a modicum of economic independence. Despite large differences in their economic status, people in these groups had in common the fact that they were not slaves, that the economic relationships into which they entered were understood as voluntary rather than arising from personal dependence.

Thinking of free labor as coexisting in ideological tension with slave labor (real or imagined, contemporary or, after the Civil War, remembered) suggests that the free labor ideology could not develop without a sharpening of the actual dichotomy between slavery and freedom. It is sometimes forgotten how many varieties of partial freedom coexisted in colonial America, including that of indentured servants, apprentices, domestic laborers paid largely in kind, sailors impressed into service in the British navy, and, in a few areas, tenant farmers. (I leave to one side, for the moment, the quasi-free status of colonial women, whose labor legally belonged to their fathers or husbands.) Indentured servitude, a form of voluntary unfreedom, comprised a major part of the nonslave labor force throughout the colonial era. As late as the early 1770s, nearly half the immigrants who arrived in America from England

and Scotland had entered into contracts for a fixed period of labor in exchange for passage. Although not slaves, indentured servants could be bought
and sold, they were subject to corporal punishment, and their obligation to
fulfill their duties (*specific performance* in legal terminology) was enforced by
the courts. They occupied, a Pennsylvania judge remarked in 1793, "a middle
rank between slaves and freemen."[3]

Of the two kinds of free labor—wage work and independent proprietorship—the latter predominated in colonial America. By the time of the Revolution, the majority of the nonslave population were farmers who owned
their own land and worked it by family labor, supplemented in many areas
by the labor of indentured servants and slaves. Recourse to wage labor on the
farm was quite rare, and hired workers tended to be youths who could expect
to acquire property in the future. In colonial cities, wage labor was more
prevalent, although the unfree formed a crucial part of the labor force, even
outside the South. Until at least 1750, large numbers of artisans and merchants, North as well as South, owned slaves and employed indentured servants and apprentices. After 1750, the ranks of wage earners began to grow,
their numbers augmented by population growth, declining access to land in
rural areas, and the completion of the terms of indentured servants. The economic depression of the 1760s seems to have persuaded many employers that
the flexibility of using wage laborers, who could be hired and fired at will,
made it economically preferable to investing in slaves or servants.[4]

If colonial Americans were familiar with a broad range of degrees of unfreedom, they viewed dependence itself as degrading. It was an axiom of
eighteenth-century political thought that dependents lacked a will of their
own, and thus did not deserve a role in public affairs. "Freedom and dependence," wrote James Wilson, were "opposite and irreconcilable terms," and
Thomas Jefferson insisted in his *Notes on the State of Virginia* that dependence "begets subservience and venality, suffocates the germ of virtue, and
prepares fit tools for the designs of ambition." Representative government
could rest only on a citizenry that enjoyed the personal autonomy that arose
from ownership of productive property, and was thus able to subordinate
self-interest to the public good. Not only personal dependence, as in the case
of a domestic servant, but working for wages itself, was widely viewed as
disreputable. This belief had a long lineage. In seventeenth-century England,
wage labor had been associated with servility and loss of freedom. Wage laborers (especially sailors, perhaps the largest group of wage earners in port
cities) were deemed a volatile, dangerous group in the Atlantic world of the
eighteenth century.[5]

The abhorrence of the consequences of personal dependence, and the equation of political identity with economic autonomy, have been taken to illustrate the influence of republican thought on American political culture. These beliefs sank deep roots in eighteenth- and nineteenth-century America, however, not simply as part of an ideological inheritance, but because they accorded with the wide distribution of productive property that made a modicum of economic autonomy part of the lived experience of millions. From the earliest days of settlement, migrants from Europe held the promise of the New World to be liberation from the economic inequalities and widespread economic dependence of the Old World. John Smith had barely landed at Jamestown when he observed that in America "every man may be master and owner of his owne labour and land." Throughout the nineteenth century, the "small producer ideology," resting on such tenets as equal citizenship, pride in craft, and the benefits of economic autonomy, underpinned a widespread hostility to wage labor, as well as to "nonproducers" who prospered from the labor of others. The ideology of free labor would emerge, in part, from this vision of America as a producer's republic.[6]

In the generation after the American Revolution, with the rapid decline of indentured servitude and apprenticeship, the disappearance of journeymen residing in their employers' homes, and the identification of domestic service as an occupation for blacks and white females, the contrast between free and slave labor grew ever sharper. The growing availability of wage earners, the sense that servitude of any kind was incompatible with revolutionary ideology, and the actions of servants and apprentices themselves (many of whom took advantage of the turmoil of the Revolution to abscond from their masters), hastened the decline of the halfway houses between slavery and freedom. The waning of indentured servitude transformed the very meaning of the word *servant*. In the North, deemed an affront to personal liberty, it fell into disuse (superseded, for domestic workers, by *help*); in the South, no longer applied to bound white labor, *servant* became a euphemism for slave. At the same time, the abolition of slavery in the North drew a geographical line across the country, separating slave and free states. Thus, the stage was set for the development of an ideology that identified the North as the home of free labor.[7]

These changes were only a small harbinger of the economic revolution that swept over the United States in the first half of the nineteenth century. Thanks to the work of a generation of social historians, the complex consequences of the market revolution are now familiar. Changes in transportation linked yeoman farmers to national and international markets and, at least in the North, made them major consumers of manufactured goods. Family labor, however, remained the norm, even as the outwork system associated with early industrialization expanded the scope of family labor to include wage work in many rural homes. "Don't hire when you can do the work yourself," read a maxim in an 1830 almanac, and hired agricultural labor remained seasonal and temporary. Not until the 1850s did the decline in the northern birthrate and the increased availability of immigrant labor combine to make wage work on the farm both necessary and available.[8]

Of course, no household could be truly independent in the age of the market revolution. Property-owning small producers, however, retained considerable choice as to the extent of their market participation, and a degree of shelter from the vicissitudes of commerce. In general, they pursued a "safety first" economic strategy that concentrated on providing for family needs and only then took advantage of the benefits of market involvement. So long as yeoman families retained control of productive property and had the realistic prospect of passing it on to their children, the ideal of autonomy retained social authenticity. "Proprietorship," concludes Randolph A. Roth's study of Vermont's Connecticut River Valley, an area fully integrated into the capitalist marketplace by 1860, "remained the ideal and was still a possibility for most citizens." The opening for settlement of land in the West made the goal of farm ownership even more realistic for small farmers and their descendants.[9]

Far different were the consequences of capitalism's development in the nation's commercial and manufacturing cities. Here the increased scale of production, undermining of traditional crafts, and dwindling of opportunities for journeymen to rise to the status of independent master combined to make wage labor rather than ownership of productive property the economic basis of family survival. As the centrality of the household to production waned, many male homeowners were transformed into wage earners; they occupied simultaneously the positions of property owner and dependent employee, even as the spread of outwork mobilized tens of thousands of poor women for paid labor in their own homes. After 1830, the rapid increase of immigration swelled the bottom ranks of the labor force. At midcentury, the number of wage earners in America for the first time exceeded the number of slaves, and ten years later, according to one estimate, wage laborers outnumbered self-employed members of the labor force.[10]

Although nineteenth-century liberalism defined the labor market as inhabiting a private sphere that existed outside the legitimate purview of government, in fact changes in the law and its enforcement helped to institutionalize the wage relationship and legitimize it as an authentic expression of freedom. During the first half of the nineteenth century, American law adopted the definition of wage labor as the product of a voluntary agreement between autonomous individuals. The freedom of free labor arose from the

noncoerced nature of the contract itself, not whether the laborer enjoyed economic autonomy. This legal transformation both reflected and reinforced the
shift in economic power toward entrepreneurs and investors, while in some
ways limiting the actual liberty of wage earners. Court-ordered specific performance of a labor contract fell into abeyance, no longer deemed compatible
with the autonomy of the free laborer; but, by the same token, the legal doctrine of "employment at will" also relieved employers of any obligation to
retain laborers longer than economically necessary. If the right to quit helped
define the difference between the free laborer and the slave, along with it
came lack of recourse against being fired. Although labor itself was not legally
enforceable, the labor contract was held to clothe employers with full authority over the workplace. Thus, work rules that seemed extremely arbitrary to
employees had the force of law behind them, and those who refused to follow
reasonable commands could legally be dismissed without payment of wages
due. Judges deployed the definition of the laborer as an autonomous individual to impede workers, via conspiracy laws, from organizing collectively
to seek higher wages and to prevent them from obtaining compensation from
employers for injuries on the job (as free individuals, they were presumed to
have knowingly assumed the risks of employment). "Free labor" did not, in
other words, contradict severe inequalities of power within either the workplace or the labor market.[11]

The rise of wage labor, and its institutionalization in the law, posed a profound challenge for the ethos that defined economic dependence as incompatible with freedom. The market revolution, Thomas Haskell has argued,
encouraged a humanitarian sensibility by promoting a sense of individual
control over one's own future, and responsibility for the fate of others. But
many Americans experienced the expansion of capitalism not as an enhancement of the power to shape their world, but as a loss of control over their
own lives. Invigorated with a leaven of Ricardian economics, which identified
labor as the source of all wealth and the worker as entitled to the full fruits of
his labor, the ideal of the autonomous small producer reemerged in Jacksonian America as a full-fledged critique of early capitalism and its inexorable
transformation of free labor into a commodity.[12]

The metaphor that crystallized this discontent—"wage slavery"—implicitly challenged the contrast between free and slave labor. There was nothing
new, or uniquely American, in the rhetorical mobilization of chattel slavery
to criticize labor relations under capitalism. In Britain, descriptions of wage
laborers as subject to coercion akin to slavery dated back to the eighteenth
century, and even as the Jacksonian labor movement adopted this rhetoric in

the 1830s and 1840s, the Chartist press was carrying articles on "The White Slaves of Great Britain," and Engels was employing much the same language in his critique of the conditions of the working class. But this vocabulary took on special power in America, where slavery was an immediate reality, not a distant symbol, the small producer still a powerful element in the social order, and the idea widespread that the wage earner was somehow less than fully free.[13]

The metaphor of wage slavery (or, in New England, its first cousin, "factory slavery") drew on immediate grievances, such as low wages, irregular employment, the elaborate and arbitrary work rules of the early factories, and the inadequacy of contract theory to describe the actual workings of the labor market. But at its heart lay a critique of economic dependence. Workers, wrote one labor leader, "do not complain of wages slavery *solely* on account of the poverty it occasions. . . . They oppose it because it holds the laboring classes in a state of abject dependence upon capitalists." In perhaps the most influential statement of the wage slavery argument, Orestes Brownson described wages as "a cunning device of the devil for the benefit of tender consciences who would retain all the advantages of the slave system without the expense, trouble, and odium of being slaveholders." His essay, Brownson later recalled, elicited "one universal scream of horror" from respectable opinion. But the idea that permanent wage labor bore some resemblance to slavery was not confined to labor radicals or disaffected intellectuals. Within the Jacksonian Democratic party, from the colorful Mike Walsh (who told New York workingmen, "You are slaves, and none are better aware of the fact than the heathenish dogs who call you freemen") to less demagogic politicos like Amos Kendall, it remained axiomatic that the ideal citizen was a farmer or independent mechanic and that the factory system and merchant-dominated craft workshop were introducing to America a system of despotism akin to slavery.[14]

Northern laborers and Jacksonian politicians were not alone in deploying the concept of wage slavery as a critique of free labor. Southern defenders of slavery like John C. Calhoun, Thomas R. Dew, and George Fitzhugh insisted that the freedom of the northern wage earner amounted to little more than the opportunity either to be exploited or to starve. The free laborer was "the slave of the *community*," a situation far more oppressive than to be owned by an individual master, shielded from the exploitation of the competitive marketplace. The very idea of free labor, they claimed, was a "brutal fiction" that allowed the propertied classes to escape a sense of responsibility for the well-being of social inferiors. The elevation of free labor depended on slavery, insisted Senator David S. Reid of North Carolina, for slavery liberated white men from the degrading "low, menial" jobs, like factory labor and domestic service, performed by wage laborers in the North.[15]

It has recently been argued that, North as well as South, the rhetoric of wage slavery implicitly rested on a racist underpinning. Slavery was meant for blacks, freedom for whites, and the degrading quality of wage slavery in factories and workshops lay in reducing white men to the same level as African Americans. The obvious elements of exaggeration in the idea of wage slavery (sometimes magnified to the point where northern laborers were said to work in more oppressive conditions than southern slaves) lends credence to this argument, as does the overt racism of Mike Walsh and other Jacksonians who employed wage slavery language. (Walsh and his fellow New York City Democrats linked to the labor movement even supported Calhoun's quixotic quest for the presidency in 1844.) On the other hand, artisans and factory workers were, in general, hardly known as defenders of slavery, and many who employed the language of wage slavery assumed that, as a Lynn, Massachusetts, labor paper put it, "all kinds of slavery" should be "buried . . . forever." However employed, wage slavery, as David Brion Davis has written, was a blunt instrument for describing the range of subtle coercions operating in the capitalist marketplace; indeed, Davis suggests, analogies with chattel slavery may well have "retarded the development of a vocabulary" more appropriate to market society. Yet, at a time when British labor radicalism remained locked within a fundamentally political analysis of the causes of poverty and inequality, the idea of wage slavery provided American labor and its allies with a critique of emerging capitalism in which workplace exploitation, not control of the government by placemen and nonproducers, took center stage. In effect, the idea of wage slavery suggested the superiority of a very different conception of labor relations than that embodied in contract thought. It embodied values deeply rooted in nineteenth-century America—that the nation's destiny was liberation from the inequalities of Europe and that avarice, class conflict, and economic inequality endangered the republic.[16]

I have dwelled on the idea of wage slavery because in many ways the forthright articulation of an ideology of free labor emerged as a response to this critique of Northern wage labor. This is not to say that free labor was cynically calculated as a defense of labor exploitation; rather, in a society of rapidly expanding capitalism, the analogy between free worker and slave inevitably called forth a response celebrating the benefits of the marketplace and the laborer's juridical freedom. One source of the free labor ideology lay in the effort of antebellum economists to reconcile belief in economic progress with the rise of a large number of wage earners. To do so, they turned to Adam Smith and other exponents of eighteenth-century liberalism, who had insisted that slavery was a far more costly and inefficient means of obtaining labor than the payment of wages, since it prevented the laborer's self-interest from being harnessed to the public good. "No conclusion seems more certain than this," Smith's compatriot John Millar had written in 1771, "that men will commonly exert more activity when they work for their own benefit than when they are compelled to labor for another." The ever-expanding wants stimulated by participation in the marketplace offered the most effective incentive for productive labor. While lamenting the effects of the division of labor on workmen consigned to mindless, repetitive tasks, Smith nonetheless insisted that in a commercial society wage laborers were genuinely "independent," since the impersonal law of supply and demand rather than the decision of a paternalistic master determined their remuneration, and they could dispose of their earnings as they saw fit.

In the 1850s, the Republican party would hammer home Smith's antislavery message: freedom meant prosperity, and slavery retarded economic growth. A generation earlier, however, it was not Smith's hostility to slavery that appealed to defenders of Northern labor relations as much as his contention that the transformation of labor into a marketable commodity did not contradict the autonomy of free labor. But Smith's American disciples added a new wrinkle to the argument, one in keeping with the vitality of small producer ideals in America. Smith had seen intractable class divisions as an inevitable consequence of economic development; American economists sought to reconcile wage labor with the idea of the New World as a classless utopia by insisting that in the United States industrious and frugal laborers could save money, purchase their own homes, and eventually acquire a farm or shop, thereby escaping the status of wage laborers and assimilating into the republic of property holders.[17]

This effort to counteract labor's gloomy portrait of the conditions of the wage laborer overlapped and reinforced another source of the free labor ideology—the effort of craft employers and factory owners to reaffirm the harmony of interests of all engaged in productive enterprise. Just as the master artisan had claimed to embody the interests of the entire craft, including those of his journeymen and apprentices as craftsmen of the future, so capitalist entrepreneurs professed a common interest with wage laborers in promoting the economic progress that would enable employees to become proprietors themselves. Via the Whig party, this defense of capitalism and entrepreneurship in the name of equal opportunity entered the political discourse of Jacksonian America. The Democrats' rhetoric of class conflict, the

Whigs insisted, was a European import irrelevant to a society of "self-made men" where the vast majority of the population either owned productive property or had a reasonable expectation of acquiring it. In America, wage laborer was a temporary status, and "laborers for hire do not exist as a class."[18]

As an intersectional party, the Whigs were understandably reluctant explicitly to contrast free labor with slavery. That task, so essential to the development of a mature free labor ideology, emerged from a different quarter in Jacksonian America—the crusade against slavery. By and large, the defense of free labor was a minor strand in abolitionists' thought; morality, not economics, was always paramount in their minds. Nonetheless, abolitionists, quite naturally, resented equations of northern labor with southern bondage. In affirming the uniqueness of the evil of slavery, abolitionists helped to popularize the sharp dichotomy between slavery's illegitimate coercions and the condition of labor in the North, and the related concept that freedom was a matter not of the ownership of productive property, but of the property in one's self. Slavery's denial of self-ownership, including ownership of one's labor and the right to dispose of it as one saw fit, differentiated it from freedom. "Self-right is the *foundation* right," insisted Theodore Weld, the basis of all other rights in society.[19]

On those occasions when they sought to imagine a postemancipation world, abolitionists generally envisioned slaves as becoming wage workers, with no stigma attaching to this condition. In 1833, the New England Anti-Slavery Society defined immediate abolition via recognition of blacks' family rights, access to education, and conditions such "that the planters shall employ their slaves as free laborers, and pay them just wages." Abolitionists vociferously rejected the idea that Northern laborers could accurately be described as wage slaves, a terminology, they insisted, that deflected moral attention from the singular evil of bondage. There was no analogy between the status of laborer in the North and the status of laborer in the South, insisted Edmund Quincy, because the free laborer had the right to "choose his employer," "contract for wages," and leave his job if he became dissatisfied. To black abolitionists, the wage slavery analogy seemed particularly spurious. When Frederick Douglass, soon after escaping from slavery, took his first paying job in New Bedford, he did not consider himself a wage slave; instead, the wage seemed an emblem of freedom: "I was now my own master . . . [in] a state of independence." Thus, by sharpening the ideological contrast between free labor and slave labor, the abolitionist movement helped to legitimize the wage relationship even as it was coming under bitter attack.

Wage slavery, wrote William Lloyd Garrison, was an "abuse of language." "We cannot see that it is wrong to give or receive wages."[20]

Despite the widespread popularity of the rhetoric of wage slavery, it would be wrong to assume that the emerging ideology of free labor had no appeal among Northern workers. Indeed, another root of the free labor ideology lay in the divided mind of labor itself, which celebrated the independence and equal rights of working men even as they insisted they were reduced to wage slavery if forced to market their labor as a commodity. Ironically, the very struggles to incorporate propertyless men into political democracy reinforced the market definition of self-ownership as the foundation of freedom. Beginning with demands for the right to vote by lesser artisans, journeymen, and wage laborers during the American Revolution, insistent pressure from below for an expansion of the suffrage did much to democratize American society. Political enfranchisement, however, subtly contradicted the rhetorical image of the worker as a wage slave and greatly expanded the traditional definition of personal independence. Every man had a property in his own labor. Political virtue was not confined to property holders, said one delegate to the Massachusetts Constitutional Convention of 1820, for men who supported their families "with their daily earnings" had as much "regard for country" as the wealthiest entrepreneur.[21]

The decades after the Revolution witnessed what Gordon Wood has called a transvaluation of labor in which idleness, not manual labor, came to be viewed as disreputable (except in the South). The glorification of labor of all kinds as dignified and not degraded—a standard element of political rhetoric by the 1830s—had its appeal to working people. Earning an honest living could appear as part of the definition of social independence, setting Northern laborers apart from both southern slaves and aristocratic nonproducers. Many journeymen and apprentices may well have found the wage relationship—and the definition of worker and employer as equals in the eyes of both law and marketplace—liberating when contrasted with the traditional hierarchy of the artisan shop and the stigma of subservience that had long attached to manual labor. Indeed, at a time of wide and rapid economic fluctuations, a good wage might offer more genuine independence than the uncertain prospects of operating one's own business, especially in those forms of artisanal and early industrial labor where skilled employees retained considerable control over the work process. The contrast between the slave bound to an owner and the free worker able to leave his job was more than mere rhetoric; it defined a central reality of social life in antebellum America. "No one who enters the factory," said a Waltham worker, "thinks of remain-

ing there his whole life-time." Turnover rates were extremely high, and for
many laborers physical mobility—"freedom to move"—served as a means
of obtaining leverage in the labor market, an essential element of strategies
for survival and possible advancement in a market society.[22]

One further element flowed into the free labor ideology as it emerged in
mature form in the 1850s. This was the movement for free soil that emerged
in the aftermath of the depression of 1837–42, which identified access to land
as the route to economic independence. Of course, Americans' ideas about
freedom have long been tied up with the promise of the West. At the Constitutional Convention, Madison had suggested that territorial expansion would
enable the republic to avoid the dangerous rise of a large class of permanently
poor citizens. For years, the Democratic party had advocated a policy of easy
access to government land, "to afford every American citizen of enterprise,"
as President Andrew Jackson put it, "the opportunity of securing an independent freehold." But in the 1840s, it was veterans of the Jacksonian labor
movement, like newspaper editor George Henry Evans, and the iconoclastic
Horace Greeley, a Whig who was sympathetic, at this point, to communitarian socialism, who popularized the idea that free homesteads in the West
provided the antidote to wage slavery. "Freedom of the soil," Evans insisted,
offered the only alternative to permanent dependence for laboring Americans. Indeed, he added, in a preview of Reconstruction debates, if not combined with access to land, the abolition of slavery would leave blacks with no
alternative but to be "ground down by the competition in the labor market."
Land reform was a persistent, if still neglected, strand in nineteenth-century
reform politics, its lineage running from Tom Paine's *Agrarian Justice* through
Evans and Greeley and on to demands for land distribution during Reconstruction, Henry George, the Knights of Labor, and Populism. As the nation's
political system began to dissolve under the impact of the question of the
expansion of slavery, the idea of free labor was yoked ever more tightly to free
soil, as access to western land came to be seen as the necessary condition for
avoiding the further growth of wage slavery in the North.[23]

Thus, numerous ideological currents came together in the free labor ideology of the 1850s. The glue was provided by the Republican party's condemnation of the slave society of the South and glorification of the progress, opportunity, and individual freedom embodied in the "free society" of the
North. In constructing the rhetorical image of slave society as the antithesis
of free society, Republicans consolidated the free labor ideology and gave it
its deepest meaning. Republicans were far more sympathetic than most abolitionists had been to the aspirations of Northern laborers to independence,
but they identified slavery and the threat of its expansion, not the inner logic

of capitalism, as the force that threatened Northern workers' right to the fruits of their toil. The two definitions of free labor that had emerged in the first half of the nineteenth century—one that characterized the laborer as small producer and the other that cast him as freely contracting wage earner—coexisted in uneasy tension within the free labor ideology, only partly reconciled by the insistence that free society offered every industrious wage earner the opportunity to achieve economic independence. Nowhere was the broad appeal of the free labor ideology more apparent, or its internal tensions more evident, than in the speeches and writings of Abraham Lincoln, whose own life embodied the opportunities Northern society ostensibly offered to all laboring men. Even though, by the 1850s, he lived in a society firmly in the grasp of the market revolution (and he himself served as attorney for the Illinois Central Railroad, one of the nation's largest corporations), Lincoln's America was the world of the small producer. Lincoln was fascinated and disturbed by the writings of proslavery ideologues like George Fitzhugh. The southern critique of wage slavery catalyzed in Lincoln a defense of free society. Most Northerners, he insisted, were "neither *hirers* nor *hired,*" but worked "for themselves, on their farms, in their houses, and in their shops, taking the whole product to themselves, and asking no favors of capital on the one hand, nor hirelings or slaves on the other." Wage earners were generally young "beginners" hired "by their own consent"; contrary to southern charges, they were not "fatally fixed in that condition for life." For Lincoln, unlike his Whig predecessors a generation earlier, this vision of Northern society led inexorably to an indictment of slavery. The slave, quite simply, was an individual illegitimately deprived of the fruits of his labor, and denied the social opportunity that should be the right of all Americans. Yet even Lincoln's eloquent exposition could not escape free labor's inherent ambiguities. Was wage labor a normal, acceptable part of the Northern social order, or a temporary aberration, still associated with lack of genuine freedom? To some extent, the answer depended on which laborers one was talking about.[24]

For Lincoln, as for most Republicans in the 1850s, the idea of free labor rested on universalistic assumptions. Human nature itself, which responded more favorably to incentive than coercion, explained why free society outstripped slave society in economic progress. When, in his debates with Stephen A. Douglas, Lincoln insisted that the right to the fruits of one's labor was a natural right, not confined to any particular set of persons, he drove home the point by choosing as his example a black woman. Like any ideology, however, free labor was defined, in part, by boundaries, lines of exclusion understood as arising from the natural order of things and therefore not really seen as exclusions at all. Lincoln himself hinted at these boundaries when he remarked that only those with a "dependent nature" did not take advantage of the opportunity to escape the status of wage earner.[25] Who were those dependent by nature and hence outside the boundaries of free labor thought? The answer was provided by the course of development of American society itself. In a nation in which slavery was a recent memory in the North and an overwhelming presence in the South, whose westward expansion (the guarantee of equal opportunity) required the removal of Indians and the conquest of lands held by Mexicans, it was inevitable that the language of politics—such concepts as citizenship, democracy, and free labor itself—would come to be defined in racial terms. And in an economy where labor increasingly meant work that produced monetary value, it became increasingly difficult to think of free labor as encompassing anyone but men.

Despite its universalistic vocabulary, the idea of free labor had little bearing on the actual conditions of nonwhites in nineteenth-century America. Four million African Americans, of course, toiled as slaves; in addition, neither free blacks nor members of other racial minorities could easily be assimilated into the rigid compartmentalization of labor systems as either free or slave. Among them, the halfway houses of semifree labor, which disappeared for whites by the early nineteenth century, endured. The West, imagined (and often experienced) by white laborers as a land of economic independence, simultaneously harbored indentured Indian labor, Mexican-American peonage, and labor under long-term contracts for Chinese immigrants. These labor systems persisted well past midcentury; indeed, they were reinvigorated by the expansion into the West of highly market-oriented, labor-intensive enterprises in mining, manufacturing, and commercial agriculture. In the older states, free blacks were the last group to experience indentured servitude, for emancipation generally required children of slave mothers to labor for their owners for a number of years before being freed (twenty-eight years in Pennsylvania, far longer than had been customary for white indentured servants). Indeed, the growing identification of indentured servitude with blacks made it all the more offensive a status in the eyes of whites.[26]

If any group in American society could be identified as wage slaves, it was free blacks in the antebellum North. Until the onset of large-scale immigration, African Americans formed a significant portion of the region's wage-earning proletariat. While the free labor ideology celebrated social advancement, blacks' actual experience was downward mobility. At the time of abolition, because of widespread slave ownership among eighteenth-century artisans, a considerable number of Northern blacks were skilled craft workers. While many artisans were critics of southern slavery, however, few viewed the free black as anything but a low-wage competitor, and some sought to bar him from skilled employment. "They are leaders in the cause of equal rights for themselves," a black editor commented of New York City's radical artisans in the 1830s. Hostility from white craftsmen, however, was only one among many obstacles that kept blacks confined to the lowest ranks of the labor market, for white employers refused to hire them and white customers did not wish to be served by them. The result was a rapid decline in economic status until, by midcentury, the vast majority of Northern blacks labored for wages in unskilled jobs and personal service. The goal of economic independence held as much appeal to free blacks as to white Americans. But in fact it was almost unimaginably remote. Excluded from the twin definitions of American identity in the antebellum North—free labor and citizenship (for almost none could vote by the 1830s)—free blacks found the rigid dichotomy between freedom and slavery inadequate to describe their circumstances.[27]

Women were another group whose "nature" ostensibly excluded them from the opportunities of free society. For men, control over a household of family dependents offered visible testimony to their own independence. For women, opportunities for independence barely existed. Women could not compete freely for employment, since only a few low-paying jobs were available to them. Nor could they be considered freely contracting wage workers. According to common law, married women could not sign independent contracts, and not until after the Civil War did the states accord them control over the wages they earned. Even then, a husband retained a proprietary claim to his wife's person and domestic labor. Thus, just as the republican citizen was indisputably male, so, too, was the ideologically constructed free laborer in antebellum America.[28] The prevailing definition of the proper roles of men and women, known to historians as the ideology of separate spheres, defined women as existing outside the labor market altogether. Domesticity described women's place; working for wages was not simply demeaning, as for men, but fundamentally alien to their nature. The proper woman entered the market as a consumer, not a laborer. A reflection of the growing separation of productive labor from the household (at least in the North), the ideology of separate spheres never described the actual lives of most American women. But by identifying the workplace as the world outside the home, it had the effect of rendering women's actual labor virtually invisible. As early as the 1790s, one supporter of Alexander Hamilton's program of economic development insisted that factory work would benefit women, "who otherwise would have little or nothing to do."[29]

It hardly seems necessary to point out that women, in fact, had a great deal to do. The widely accepted distinction between productive and domestic work was ideological rather than economic (far more accurate was the time-honored adage, "woman's work is never done.") On small farms, North and South, men's work ebbed and flowed with the seasons; women's—including labor in the fields, child rearing, cleaning, cooking, and laundering, producing clothing and other items for use at home and others for sale—was constant. By reducing the need to turn to the marketplace for the necessities of life, the production of food and clothing at home by women was essential to the independence of the yeoman household. Early industrialization enhanced the importance of women's work in the North, as the spread of the putting-out system in such industries as shoemaking, hatmaking, and clothing manufacture allowed women working at home to contribute to family income even as they retained responsibility for domestic chores. At the same time, the early factories offered new employment opportunities for the young daughters of farm families. In either case, the vaunted independence of the yeoman household depended in considerable measure on the labor of women—whether unremunerated within the household, or paid wages at home or outside. So, too, did the free time that enabled men to participate as citizens in the public arena. Thus, free labor embodied a contradiction akin in some ways to slavery's: since no one could remain independent without enlisting uncompensated labor, free labor for some rested on dependent labor for others.[30]

The idealization of the home as a refuge from the marketplace was, of course, a middle-class ideology, and the "idle" housewife, supported by her husband, a token of bourgeois respectability. Even for the middle class, the cult of domesticity concealed the fact that the home was, in fact, a place of work. Not only did middle-class women have many arduous domestic tasks, but, through servants—the largest employment category for women in the nineteenth century and a ubiquitous emblem of the bourgeois standard of living—wage labor itself entered the middle-class home (even though relations with servants were generally understood as problems in morality and discipline rather than labor relations). There were 32,000 women working as domestics in New York City in 1855, but this labor, too, was essentially invisible when contemporaries spoke of the rights and wrongs of free labor.[31]

Among urban artisans and wage laborers, women's work often spelled the difference between independence and dependence, and even outright survival. Their homes, too, sheltered paid labor by women—especially the sweated labor of outworkers toiling at subsistence wages. Like domestic servants, the army of female outworkers was rarely mentioned when contemporaries spoke of free labor, except as another indication of how the spread of capitalism was degrading men. The idea that the male head of household

should command a "family wage" enabling him to support his wife and children had as powerful a hold on working-class culture as on middle-class up-
holders of the domestic ideal. Capitalism, said labor leader P. J. McGuire in
the 1870s, "tore the woman from her true duties as mother and nurse of the
human race," subjecting her to wage slavery while undermining the natural
order of the household and the independence and authority of its male head.
The fight for a family wage mobilized successive generations of labor organizations, embodying not only a call for substantive justice for wage earners,
and resistance to employers' assuming control over important aspects of a
family's life, but the ideal of a social order in which men supported their
families and women remained at home. Male laborers before the Civil War
sometimes supported the demands for higher wages and better working conditions of factory girls and urban seamstresses (often members of the same
families as unionists), but their organizations excluded women from membership and they generally viewed women workers as threats to craft skills
and male wages. Women workers were dependents to be protected, not independent free laborers. Indeed, the contrast between a "family wage" or a
"man's wage" (increasingly a badge of honor) and a "woman's wage" (a term
of opprobrium) helped to legitimate the idea that wage laborer was an appropriate status for an American man if he was equitably rewarded.[32]

Work outside the home was, of course, the province of relatively few
women in nineteenth-century America. Taking the female population as a
whole, less than 15 percent could be found in the wage labor force at any one
time. Only at the end of the century did significant numbers of married
women enter the paid labor market outside the home. In a certain sense,
women workers seem to have achieved the free labor ideal of making wage
labor a temporary status; however, they left the labor market not for independence, but for the dependence of life and work in the home.[33]

Not all women workers, however, agreed that wage labor was inherently
oppressive, or that a woman's dignity arose from her status in the family
rather than the ability to earn a living. If blacks saw wage labor as a definite
improvement over slavery, many nineteenth-century women found in working for wages an escape from the paternalistic bonds and personal dependence of the household. As Harriet Hanson Robinson later reminisced about
her time in the Lowell mills, working for wages offered women autonomy:
for the first time, "they could earn money, and spend it as they pleased. . . .
For the first time in this country a woman's labor had a money value." Equal
opportunity to enter the labor market was a persistent demand of the early
movement for women's rights, which utterly rejected the domestic ideology's
celebration of the "idle" housewife. Women isolated within the home, cut off

from the opportunity to earn wages, and economically dependent, argued nineteenth-century feminists from Susan B. Anthony to Charlotte Perkins Gilman, could make no significant contribution to society. None rejected the identification of true womanhood with freedom from work more powerfully than Sojourner Truth, in her famous 1851 speech, which alluded to a lifelong experience of physical labor, then asked, "And ain't I a woman?" Preferring the metaphor the *slavery of sex* rather than *wage slavery*, early feminists identified the slave woman as an emblem for all women, since all were subject to arbitrary authority and denied the fruits of their labor. Women, wrote Pauline Davis in 1853, "must go *to work*" to emancipate themselves from "bondage."[34]

The triumph of a party dedicated to the ideology of free labor, of course, precipitated southern secession and the onset of the Civil War. And the destruction of slavery posed in the most concrete way the issue of how Americans would henceforth understand free labor. Having written a book of over 600 pages on the era of Reconstruction, I have no desire here to explore these debates in any detail. I do want to emphasize, however, that northern Republicans to a large extent viewed the transition from slavery to freedom through the prism of free labor. The sheer drama of the triumph of the Union and the destruction of slavery fixed the free labor ideology in the popular mind even more firmly than before the Civil War. Efforts by white southerners to restrict the freedom of the former slaves in ways that violated fundamental free labor premises had much to do with the unraveling of President Andrew Johnson's postwar policies and the coming of Radical Reconstruction. The Reconstruction period saw the embodiment of free labor principles in federal law, and a redrawing of the boundaries of these principles to encompass black Americans (although women remained outside its purview). Yet even as the war vindicated the free labor ideology, it strengthened tendencies that inexorably transformed the society of small producers from which that ideology had sprung. At the very moment of its triumph were revealed more fully than ever the contradictions inherent in the concept of free labor.[35]

The Civil War, wrote Republican leader and textile manufacturer Edward Atkinson of Massachusetts, was "a war for the establishment of free labor, call it by whatever name you will." In the vision of a reconstructed South that emerged from the war, blacks were absorbed into the definition of universal human nature at the heart of free labor thought. Enjoying the same opportunities as northern workers, motivated by the same quest for self-improvement, and capable of the same market discipline, they would labor more productively than as slaves. Meanwhile, northern capital and immigrants would energize the economy, and eventually the South would come to resemble the free labor image of the North—a society of small towns and independent producers. Unified on the basis of free labor, proclaimed Carl Schurz, America would become "a republic, greater, more populous, freer, more prosperous, and more powerful, than any state history tells us of." Free labor, in sum, was central to the vision of a triumphant national state that emerged from the war.[36]

Proclaiming the superiority of free labor was easy; implementing that vision proved more troublesome. Even as the war drew to a close, the Republican Congress, in debates over the Thirteenth Amendment, struggled to define precisely the repercussions of the destruction of slavery. All agreed that property rights in man must be abrogated, contractual relations substituted for the discipline of the lash, and the master's patriarchal authority over the lives of the former slaves abolished. The phrase most often repeated in the debates—the *right to the fruits of his labor*—was thought to embody the distinction between slavery and freedom. These debates also made clear what was not implied by emancipation. Several congressmen expressed concern that the amendment's abolition of "involuntary servitude" might be construed to apply to relations within the family. "A husband has a right of property in the service of his wife," said one congressman. But the Thirteenth Amendment was hardly intended to touch power relations within the family. Indeed, slavery's destruction of family life (including the husband's role as patriarch and breadwinner) had been one of abolitionism's most devastating criticisms of the peculiar institution. Republicans assumed emancipation would restore to blacks the natural right to family life, with women assuming the roles of daughters, wives, and mothers within the domestic sphere. Thus, even as they rejected the racialized definition of free labor that had emerged in the first half of the nineteenth century (an accomplishment whose importance ought not to be underestimated), Republicans still clung to the sentiment that the female laborer was an anomaly, not really a free laborer at all.[37]

Southern whites, particularly the planter class devastated by wartime destruction and the loss of their slave property, had, of course, a very different definition of a free labor South. Before the Civil War, white southerners had condemned free labor as a disguised form of the general servitude of work. After the war, they responded to emancipation by attempting to impose on the former slaves an updated form of general servitude, insisting that blacks remain a dependent plantation labor force, subject to strict discipline from their employers and deprived of the opportunities to acquire property and advance in the marketplace. The destiny of the former slaves, said a southern newspaper, was "subordination to the white race." To enforce this understanding of free labor, the governments of Presidential Reconstruction enacted the notorious black codes, seeking, through mandatory yearlong contracts, vagrancy laws, coercive apprenticeship regulations, and criminal penalties for breach of contract, to force the former slaves back to work on plantations. Resurrecting forms of labor coercion familiar in the eighteenth century but which had subsequently fallen into disuse, these measures seemed to make a mockery of essential free labor values: contracts should be free and voluntary agreements, arrived at by mutual consent; workers should be able to choose their employment and leave at will; and the state should not enforce specific performance of contractual obligations to labor.[38]

The Civil Rights Act of 1866, in part a response to southern black codes that severely limited the liberty of the former slaves, enshrined free labor values as part of the definition of American citizenship. Contract was central to the bill: no state could deprive any citizen of the right to make contracts, bring lawsuits, or enjoy equal protection of the rights of the security of person and property. The law, one congressman declared, proposed "to secure to a poor, weak class of laborers the right to make contracts for their labor, the power to enforce the payment of their wages, and the means of holding and enjoying the proceeds of their toil." One year later, the Peonage Act outlawed "voluntary or involuntary servitude" throughout the country, and barred states from criminally punishing breaches of labor contracts, another embodiment of free labor ideas in federal law.[39]

Thus, Reconstruction legislation rejected efforts to reimpose a system of legal coercion of labor in the postwar South. But what of the coercions embedded in the free labor market itself? Ostensibly, it was the opportunity to escape wage labor altogether that provided free labor's answer. But, as the radical New Orleans *Tribune* repeatedly pointed out, the realities confronting the former slaves rendered this free labor assumption utterly unrealistic. Lacking land, and encountering not social harmony but unrelenting hostility on the part of the white community, they "cannot rise . . . they must be servants to others, with no hope of bettering their conditions." When General William T. Sherman met with a group of black ministers in the famous Colloquy of January 1865, their spokesman, Garrison Frazier, offered a pithy definition of slavery and freedom as defined by those who had known bondage. Slavery, he said, was "receiving . . . the work of another man, and not by his consent." Freedom meant "placing us where we could reap the fruit of our own labor." For most former slaves, this meant ownership of land. In their own way, the freed people reaffirmed the small producer ideal that equated free labor with ownership of productive property.[40]

As is well known, efforts to give the former slaves land, rather than establishing the conditions that would enable them to acquire it after working for wages, failed to receive congressional approval. "The system of labor for wages," Congressman William D. Kelley said, is not the freedom of which he [Thaddeus Stevens, the prime advocate of land distribution] . . . dreamed." Failure to redistribute land, warned another Radical, George W. Julian, would reduce the freed people to "a system of wages slavery . . . more galling than slavery itself." Most Republicans, however, believed such "gifts" of land would deaden the very spirit of enterprise and ambition for material advancement that animated free labor, white or black.[41]

In retrospect, Reconstruction may be seen as a decisive moment in fixing the dominant understanding of free labor as freedom of contract in the labor market rather than ownership of productive property. Even as the overthrow of slavery reinforced the definition of the contract as the very opposite of the master-slave relationship, the policy of awarding black men the right to vote while denying them the benefits of land reform powerfully fortified the idea that the free citizen could be a dependent laborer.

The massive economic changes that followed Reconstruction, as the United States matured into an industrial economy and the "labor question" replaced the struggle over slavery as the dominant focus of public life, further undermined the vision of the small producers' republic. By the late nineteenth century, it became increasingly difficult to maintain that wage labor was a temporary condition on the road to economic independence, or to deny that what *The Nation* called "the great curse of the Old World—the division of society into classes" had become a permanent feature of American life. Increasingly, the contract definition of free labor was enshrined in orthodox economic thought and the emerging social sciences. Severed from empathy for the aspirations of the upwardly mobile poor, this understanding of free labor became part of a doctrinaire laissez-faire ideology. The man born a laborer, announced economist David A. Wells in 1877, would "never be anything but a laborer," and government could do nothing to alter this situation. To liberal thinkers, the right to the fruits of one's labor and the promise of upward mobility seemed quaint anachronisms, irrelevant at a time when the modern corporation had replaced the independent producer as the driving force of economic progress.[42]

The identification of freedom of labor with freedom of contract was enshrined in successive decisions of state and federal courts, which struck down state laws regulating economic enterprise as an interference with the right of the free laborer to choose his employment and agree to whatever working conditions he saw fit. This line of thinking was pioneered by Justice Stephen J. Field's famous 1873 dissent in the *Slaughterhouse Cases,* which insisted that a butchering monopoly established by Louisiana violated "the right of free labor" now enshrined in federal law. Essentially, according to Field, this right encompassed the ability to pursue any lawful employment without state interference, and to enjoy the fruits of one's labor. *Slaughterhouse,* of course, formed a key step in the Supreme Court's abandonment of Reconstruction. But Field's dissent also pointed the way to subsequent decisions that would offer entrepreneurs (if not former slaves) federal protection for the rights secured by the Civil War. "Liberty of contract," not equal protection of the laws for blacks, came to be defined as the essence of the Fourteenth Amendment. By the 1880s, the Court consistently ruled that state regulation of business enterprise, including laws establishing maximum hours of work or ensuring safe working conditions, were a remnant of older paternalism, which deprived the worker of the right to freely dispose of his labor. (Field's belief that freedom involved the right to the fruits of one's labor was by now lost sight of.) Free labor, declared the West Virginia Supreme Court in 1889, meant "not only freedom from servitude . . . but the right of one . . . to pursue any lawful trade or avocation," and no state law could restrict this liberty. Although this court often used the gender-neutral term *one,* this principle still did not apply to women. They were not independent free laborers, and the Supreme Court proved willing to sanction restrictions on their choice of occupation (upholding, for example, in *Bradwell v. Illinois,* a state law barring women from practicing law).[43]

The dichotomy between free labor and the ghost of slavery continued to shape discourse on American labor relations to the turn of the century and beyond. Like former slaves, many wage laborers in the Gilded Age contested the definition of free labor as personal liberty to sign labor contracts. Even as the courts and middle-class opinion invoked the struggle against slavery to clothe the interests of capitalist entrepreneurs with the mantle of free labor, the labor movement responded that coercion was as inherent in industrial capitalism as it had been in slavery. "Slavery declared to be liberty" was one labor journal's pithy response to the 1885 decision of the New York Court of Appeals striking down a state law prohibiting cigar making in tenement houses as a violation of freedom of contract. Reaching back across the divide of the Civil War, labor defined employers as a new "slave power," called for the "emancipation and enfranchisement of all who labor," and resurrected for one last time the metaphor of wage slavery as a critique of the plight of workers in the Gilded Age. Through the 1880s, "the abolition of the wage system" remained the stated goal of labor organizations. So widespread, on both sides of the Atlantic, was the rhetoric of wage slavery in the late nineteenth century that when he published his *History of Slavery and Serfdom* in 1895, the English economic historian John K. Ingram felt compelled to include an appendix on the "lax" uses of the word *slavery* among his contemporaries.[44]

Only with the rise of the American Federation of Labor in the 1890s did the dominant organization among American workers frankly accept the fact that class divisions and the wage labor system were intrinsic to capitalism. Free labor was wage labor, insisted Samuel Gompers, and should organize as such, seeking security of employment and favorable wages and working conditions, not the utopian dream of economic autonomy. Independence for the worker meant not self-employment, but a degree of control over the work process—a control still enjoyed by considerable numbers of skilled industrial workers among whom the AF of L organized.[45]

By the twentieth century, as the promise of economic abundance blunted hostility to the wage system, slave wages replaced wage slavery as a mark of servitude, and a family's level of consumption—the so-called American standards of living—came to define the essence of the American dream. The free American was the citizen able to consume some of the cornucopia of goods created by industrial capitalism. Here we enter the realm of twentieth-century consumer culture, in which the focus of life shifted over time from work to leisure, production to consumption.[46] Elements of free labor language endure to this day—for example, in antiunion legislation known, in a throwback to the 1880s, as "right-to-work" laws, or in demands of professional athletes (perhaps the last group denied the right to change employers at will) for "free agency." But these are shards of an ideology that has long since lost its social relevance. For historians of the nineteenth century, however, free labor, despite its contradictions and ambiguities, blind spots and exclusions, continues to offer a valuable window on the consequences of capitalism's expansion, and the divergent ways Americans responded to them.

NOTES

1. Eric Foner, *Free Soil, Free Labor, Free Men: The Ideology of the Republican Party before the Civil War* (New York, 1970).

2. See Leon Fink, "Labor, Liberty, and the Law: Trade Unionism and the Problem of the American Constitutional Order," *Journal of American History* 74 (1987): 907; Joan W. Scott, *Gender and the Politics of History* (New York, 1988), pp. 5–7.

3. Robert J. Steinfeld, *The Invention of Free Labor: The Employment Relation in English and American Law and Culture, 1350–1870* (Chapel Hill, N.C., 1991), pp. 3–5, 46, 101–2;

Linda G. DePauw, "Land of the Unfree: Legal Limitations on Liberty in Pre-revolutionary America," *Maryland Historical Magazine* 68 (1973): 355–68; Elizabeth Blackmar, *Manhattan for Rent, 1785–1850* (Ithaca, N.Y., 1989), p. 5; Bernard Bailyn, *Voyagers to the West: A Passage in the Peopling of America on the Eve of the Revolution* (New York, 1986), p. 166; Gordon S. Wood, *The Radicalism of the American Revolution* (New York, 1992), pp. 51–55.

4. Allan Kulikoff, *The Agrarian Origins of American Capitalism* (Charlottesville, Va., 1992), p. 7; John L. Brooke, *The Heart of the Commonwealth: Society and Political Culture in Worcester County, Massachusetts, 1713–1861* (New York, 1989), pp. 42–44; Stephen L. Innes, ed., *Work and Labor in Early America* (Chapel Hill, N.C., 1988), pp. 18–32; David W. Galenson, "Labor Market Behavior in Colonial America: Servitude, Slavery, and Free Labor," in David W. Galenson, ed., *Markets in History: Economic Studies of the Past* (New York, 1989), pp. 84–93; Sharon W. Salinger, *"To Serve Well and Faithfully": Labor and Indentured Servants in Pennsylvania, 1682–1800* (New York, 1987), pp. 15–17, 62–69, 137–38, 156–70.

5. Wood, *Radicalism*, p. 56; Thomas Jefferson, *Notes on the State of Virginia* (New York, 1964), p. 157; Richard L. Bushman, " 'This New Man': Dependence and Independence, 1776," in Richard L. Bushman, Neil Harris, David Rothman, Barbara Miller Solomon, and Stephen Thernstrom, eds., *Uprooted Americans: Essays to Honor Oscar Handlin* (Boston, 1979), pp. 77–96; Christopher Hill, *Change and Continuity in Seventeenth-Century England* (London, 1974), pp. 219–24; Peter Linebaugh, "All the Atlantic Mountains Shook," *Labour/Le Travailleur* 10 (1982): 87–121.

6. Philip L. Barbour, ed., *The Complete Works of Captain John Smith (1530–1631)*, 3 vols. (Chapel Hill, N.C., 1986), 1:332; Ronald Schultz, *The Republic of Labor: Philadelphia Artisans and the Politics of Class, 1720–1830* (New York, 1993), pp. 4–13, 154–58; Christopher Clark, *The Roots of Rural Capitalism: Western Massachusetts, 1780–1860* (Ithaca, N.Y., 1990), pp. 16, 22–23.

7. Salinger, *"To Serve,"* pp. 142–53; Shane White, *Somewhat More Independent: The End of Slavery in New York City, 1770–1810* (Athens, Ga., 1991), pp. 25–36; Bernard Elbaum, "Why Apprenticeship Persisted in Britain But Not in the United States," *Journal of Economic History* 49 (1989): 346; Steinfeld, *Free Labor*, pp. 122–33; Albert Matthews, "Hired Man and Help," *Publications of the Colonial Society of Massachusetts* 5 (1898): 225–56.

8. Clark, *Roots*, pp. 16–17, 105, 194–95, 252–60, 305; Jeremy Atack and Fred Bateman, *To Their Own Soil: Agriculture in the Antebellum North* (Ames, Iowa, 1987), p. 186; John M. Faragher, "History from the Inside Out: Writing the History of Women in Rural America," *American Quarterly* 33 (1981): 546.

9. Lacy K. Ford, *Origins of Southern Radicalism: The South Carolina Upcountry 1800–1860* (New York, 1988), p. 56; Kulikoff, *Agrarian Origins*, pp. 27–29, 35–47; Jonathan Prude, "Town-Country Conflicts in Antebellum Rural Massachusetts," and John M. Faragher, "Open-Country Community," in Steven Hahn and Jonathan Prude, eds., *The Countryside in the Age of Capitalist Transformation: Essays in the Social History of Rural America* (Chapel Hill, N.C., 1985), pp. 75–76, 245–47; Randolph A. Roth, *The Democratic Dilemma: Religion, Reform, and the Social Order in the Connecticut River Valley of Vermont, 1791–1850* (New York, 1987), p. 297.

10. Sean Wilentz, "The Rise of the American Working Class, 1776–1877," in J. Carroll Moody and Alice Kessler-Harris, eds., *Perspectives on American Labor History* (De Kalb, Ill., 1989), pp. 83–151; Blackmar, *Manhattan*, p. 125; Amy Bridges, *A City in the Republic: Antebellum New York and the Origins of Machine Politics* (New York, 1984), pp. 46–58; U. S. Department of Commerce, Bureau of the Census, *Historical Statistics of the United States*, 2 vols. (Washington, D.C., 1975), 1:139; Stanley Lebergott, "The Pattern of Employment Since 1800," in Seymour E. Harris, ed., *American Economic History* (New York, 1961), pp. 290–91.

11. Christopher L. Tomlins, *Labor, Law, and Ideology in the Early American Republic* (New York, 1993); Steinfeld, *Free Labor*, pp. 144–60; Jay M. Feinman, "The Development of the Employment at Will Rule," *American Journal of Legal History* 20 (1976): 118–35.

12. Thomas L. Haskell, "Capitalism and the Origins of the Humanitarian Sensibility," *American Historical Review* 90 (1985): 339–61, 547–66; Sean Wilentz, *Chants Democratic: New York City and the Rise of the American Working Class, 1788–1850* (New York, 1984), pp. 63–103; Schultz, *Republic of Labor*, pp. 206–29.

13. David B. Davis, *The Problem of Slavery in the Age of Revolution, 1770–1823* (Ithaca, N.Y., 1975), p. 462; David Turley, *The Culture of English Antislavery, 1780–1860* (London, 1991), pp. 182–84.

14. Barry Goldberg, "Slavery, Race and the Languages of Class: 'Wage Slaves' and White 'Niggers,' " *New Politics*, n.s., 3 (1991): 64–70; *Liberator*, Sept. 25, 1846; David A. Zonderman, *Aspirations and Anxieties: New England Workers and the Mechanized Factory System 1815–1850* (New York, 1992), pp. 113–15; Joseph L. Blau, ed., *Social Theories of Jacksonian Democracy* (Indianapolis, 1954), pp. 306–10; Christopher Lasch, *The True and Only Heaven: Progress and Its Critics* (New York, 1991), p. 191 n.; John Ashworth, *"Agrarians" and "Aristocrats": Party Political Ideology in the United States, 1837–1846* (London, 1983), p. 31.

15. Marcus Cunliffe, *Chattel Slavery and Wage Slavery: The Anglo-American Contest 1830–1860* (Athens, Ga., 1979), pp. 4–7; Eugene D. Genovese, *The Slaveholders' Dilemma: Freedom and Progress in Southern Conservative Thought* (Columbia, S.C., 1992), pp. 33–34, 48; Jonathan A. Glickstein, *Concepts of Free Labor in Antebellum America* (New Haven, Conn., 1991), pp. 35–37, 154–56.

16. David A. Roediger, *The Wages of Whiteness: Race and the Making of the American Working Class* (New York, 1991), pp. 7–14, 68–77; Michael A. Bernstein, "Northern Labor Finds a Southern Champion: A Note on the Radical Democracy, 1833–1849," in William Pencak and Conrad E. Wright, eds., *New York and the Rise of American Capitalism: Economic Development and the Social and Political History of an American State, 1780–1870* (New York, 1989), pp. 147–67; Teresa A. Murphy, *Ten Hours Labor: Religion, Reform, and Gender in Early New England* (Ithaca, N.Y., 1992), p. 183; Thomas Bender. ed., *The Antislavery Debate* (Berkeley, Calif., 1992), p. 175; Zonderman, *Aspirations and Anxieties*, p. 116; Bridges, *City in the Republic*, pp. 121–23; Gareth Stedman Jones, *Languages of Class: Studies in English Working Class History 1832–1982* (Cambridge, Eng., 1983), pp. 90–178.

17. Robin Blackburn, *The Overthrow of Colonial Slavery 1776–1848* (London, 1988), pp. 51–52; Istvan Hont and Michael Ignatieff, "Needs and Justice in the *Wealth of Nations*: An Introductory Essay," in Istvan Hont and Michael Ignatieff, eds., *Wealth and Virtue:*

The Shaping of Political Economy of the Scottish Enlightenment (Cambridge, Eng., 1983), pp. 13–15; William B. Scott, *In Pursuit of Happiness: American Conceptions of Property from the Seventeenth to the Twentieth Century* (Bloomington, Ind., 1977), pp. 87–93.

18. Wilentz, *Chants Democratic,* pp. 271–86, 303–304; Sean Wilentz, "Many Democracies: On Tocqueville and Jacksonian America," in Abraham S. Eisenstadt, ed., *Reconsidering Tocqueville's "Democracy in America"* (New Brunswick, N.J., 1988), pp. 218–19; Ashworth, *"Agrarians" and "Aristocrats,"* p. 68.

19. Eric Foner, *Politics and Ideology in the Age of the Civil War* (New York, 1980), p. 65; Jonathan A. Glickstein, "'Poverty is Not Slavery': American Abolitionists and the Competitive Labor Market," and Ronald G. Walters, "The Boundaries of Abolitionism," in Lewis Perry and Michael Fellman, eds., *New Perspectives on the Abolitionists* (Baton Rouge, La., 1979), pp. 207–11, 9.

20. William H. Pease and Jane H. Pease, ed., *The Antislavery Argument* (Indianapolis, 1965), p. 61; *Liberator,* Oct. 1, 1847; Judith N. Shklar, *American Citizenship: The Quest for Inclusion* (Cambridge, Mass., 1991), p. 83; Foner, *Politics and Ideology,* pp. 70–71.

21. Robert J. Steinfeld, "Property and Suffrage in the Early American Republic," *Stanford Law Review* 41 (1989): 335–76; Rowland Berthoff, "Independence and Attachment, Virtue and Interest: From Republican Citizen to Free Enterpriser, 1787–1837," in Bushman et al., *Uprooted Americans,* pp. 115–16.

22. Wood, *Radicalism,* p. 277; *(New York) Tribune,* Nov. 11, 1857; Shklar, *American Citizenship,* pp. 64–67; Gary J. Kornblith, "The Artisanal Response to Capitalist Transformation," *Journal of the Early Republic* 10 (1990): 318–20; Zonderman, *Aspirations and Anxieties,* p. 288; Charles Stephenson, "'There's Plenty Waitin' at the Gates': Mobility, Opportunity, and the American Worker," in Charles Stephenson and Robert Asher, eds., *Life and Labor: Dimensions of American Working-Class History* (Albany, N.Y., 1986), pp. 72–91; Jonathan Prude, *The Coming of Industrial Order: Town and Factory Life in Rural Massachusetts, 1810–1860* (New York, 1983), pp. 114–15; Clark, *Roots,* p. 313.

23. Peter S. Onuf, "Liberty, Development, and Union: Visions of the West in the 1780s," *William and Mary Quarterly* 43 (1986): 202–3; Drew R. McCoy, *The Elusive Republic: Political Economy in Jeffersonian America* (Chapel Hill, N.C., 1980), pp. 203–4, 237; Scott, *In Pursuit,* p. 59; Bernard Mandel, *Labor: Free and Slave* (New York, 1955), p. 85; Foner, *Politics and Ideology,* p. 70.

24. Foner, *Free Soil,* pp. 11–39; Yehoshua Arieli, *Individualism and Nationalism in American Ideology* (Cambridge, Mass., 1964), pp. 315–17; Roy F. Basler, ed., *The Collected Works of Abraham Lincoln,* 9 vols. (New Brunswick, N.J., 1953–55), 2:405, 3:462, 477–79.

25. Basler, ed., *Lincoln Works,* 2:405, 3:479; Uday S. Mehta, "Liberal Strategies of Exclusion," *Politics and Society* 18 (1990): 427–30.

26. Howard Lamar, "From Bondage to Contract: Ethnic Labor in the American West," in Hahn and Prude, eds., *The Countryside,* pp. 293–326; Alexander Saxton, *The Indispensable Enemy: Labor and the Anti-Chinese Movement in California* (Berkeley, Calif., 1971), pp. 3–8; Gary B. Nash and Jean R. Sonderlund, *Freedom by Degrees: Emancipation in Pennsylvania and its Aftermath* (New York, 1991), pp. 173–77.

27. Gary B. Nash, *Forging Freedom: The Formation of Philadelphia's Black Community 1720–1840* (Cambridge, Mass., 1988), p. 146; Graham R. Hodges, *New York City Cartmen, 1667–1850* (New York, 1986), pp. 158–59; Leonard P. Curry, *The Free Black in Urban*

America 1800–1850 (Chicago, 1981), p. 260; *An Address to the Three Thousand Colored Citizens of New-York Who Are the Owners of One Hundred and Twenty Thousand Acres of Land . . .* (New York, 1846), p. 10.

28. Stephanie McCurry, "The Politics of Yeoman Households in South Carolina," in Catherine Clinton and Nina Silber, eds., *Divided Houses: Gender and the Civil War* (New York, 1992), p. 31; Alice Kessler-Harris, *A Woman's Wage: Historical Meanings and Social Consequences* (Lexington, Ky., 1990), p. 36; Norma Basch, *In the Eyes of the Law: Women, Marriage, and Property in Nineteenth-Century New York* (Ithaca, N.Y., 1982), pp. 17–26; Joan R. Gunderson, "Independence, Citizenship, and the American Revolution," *Signs* 13 (1987): 59–77; Amy Stanley, "Conjugal Bonds and Wage Labor: Rights of Contract in the Age of Emancipation," *Journal of American History* 75 (1988): 482–99; Blackmar, *Manhattan*, p. 125.

29. Kessler-Harris, *A Woman's Wage*, pp. 59–63; Linda K. Kerber, Nancy F. Cott, Robert Gross, Lynn Hart, Carroll Smith-Rosenberg, and Christine M. Stansell, "Beyond Roles, Beyond Spheres: Thinking about Gender in the Early Republic," *William and Mary Quarterly* 46 (1989): 565–68; Nancy Osterud, *Bonds of Community: The Lives of Farm Women in Nineteenth-Century New York* (Ithaca, N.Y., 1991), pp. 5–7; Jeanne Boydston, *Home and Work: Housework, Wages, and the Ideology of Labor in the Early Republic* (New York, 1990), pp. 18–27, 45–47; Berthoff, "Independence," p. 124.

30. Stephanie McCurry, *Masters of Small Worlds: Yeoman Households, Gender Relations, and the Political Culture of the Antebellum South Carolina Low Country* (New York, 1995), chap. 2; Clark, *Roots*, pp. 132–46; John M. Faragher, *Sugar Creek: Life on the Illinois Prairie* (New Haven, Conn., 1986), pp. 101–9, 179–80; Mary Blewett, *Men, Women, and Work: Class, Gender, and Protest in the New England Shoe Industry, 1780–1910* (Urbana, Ill., 1988), pp. 14–19, 45–61, 103–10; Thomas Dublin, "Women and Outwork in a Nineteenth-Century New England Town," in Hahn and Prude, eds., *The Countryside*, pp. 51–66; Claudia Goldin and Kenneth Sokoloff, "Women, Children, and Industrialization in the Early Republic: Evidence from the Manufacturing Censuses," *Journal of Economic History* 42 (1982): 741–74; Boydston, *Home and Work*, pp. 40, 59, 76–93.

31. Blackmar, *Manhattan*, pp. 112–21; Nancy Fraser, "What's Critical About Critical Theory? The Case of Habermas and Gender," in Seyla Benhabib and Drucilla Cornell, eds., *Feminism as Critique*, (Minneapolis, 1987), pp. 36–38; Linda K. Kerber, "Separate Spheres, Female Worlds, Woman's Place: The Rhetoric of Women's History," *Journal of American History* 75 (1988): 9–39.

32. Christine Stansell, *City of Women: Sex and Class in New York, 1789–1860* (New York, 1986); Wilentz, *Chants Democratic*, pp. 51, 249; Murphy, *Ten Hours*, pp. 47–49; Blewett, *Men, Women, and Work*, 69–85; Fraser, "What's Critical," pp. 42–43; David N. Lyon, "The World of P. J. McGuire: A Study of the American Labor Movement" (Ph.D. diss., University of Minnesota, 1972), p. 55; Kessler-Harris, *A Woman's Wage*, pp. 3–10.

33. Alice Kessler-Harris, *Out to Work: A History of Wage-earning Women in the United States* (New York, 1982), pp. 46–49, 70–71; David Montgomery, *The Fall of the House of Labor: The Workplace, the State, and American Labor Activism, 1865–1925* (New York, 1987), pp. 136–37.

34. Kessler-Harris, *A Woman's Wage*, pp. 27–28; Blewett, *Men, Women, and Work*, pp. 321–33; Harriet H. Robinson, *Loom and Spindle; or Life among the Early Mill Girls*

(New York, 1898), p. 69; Ellen C. DuBois, "Outgrowing the Compact of the Fathers: Equal Rights, Woman Suffrage, and the United States Constitution, 1820–1920," *Journal of American History* 74 (1987): 847; Daniel T. Rodgers, *The Work Ethic in Industrial America 1850–1920* (Chicago, 1978), pp. 183–90; Jean F. Yellin, *Women and Sisters: The Antislavery Feminists in American Culture* (New Haven, Conn., 1989), pp. 78–80; Jean Matthews, "Race, Sex, and the Dimensions of Liberty in Antebellum America," *Journal of the Early Republic* 6 (1986): 282.

35. Eric Foner, *Reconstruction: America's Unfinished Revolution 1863–1877* (New York, 1988); William E. Forbath, "The Ambiguities of Free Labor: Labor and the Law in the Gilded Age," *Wisconsin Law Review* (1985): 778.

36. Foner, *Reconstruction*, pp. 155–56, 225; Carl Schurz, *For the Great Empire of Liberty, Forward!* (New York, 1864).

37. Lea S. VanderVelde, "The Labor Vision of the Thirteenth Amendment," *University of Pennsylvania Law Review* 138 (1989): 437–504; *Congressional Globe*, 38th Cong., 2d sess., p. 215; Ira Berlin, Thavolia Glymph, Steven F. Miller, Joseph R. Reidy, Leslie S. Rowland, and Julie Saville, eds., *The Wartime Genesis of Free Labor: The Lower South* (New York, 1990), p. 15; Leslie Ann Schwalm, "The Meaning of Freedom: African-American Women and Their Transition from Slavery to Freedom in Lowcountry South Carolina" (Ph.D. diss., University of Wisconsin, 1991), pp. 290–324.

38. Foner, *Reconstruction*, pp. 129–35, 199–201; VanderVelde, "Labor Vision," pp. 487–90.

39. Foner, *Reconstruction*, pp. 243–45; Steinfeld, *Free Labor*, p. 184.

40. Foner, *Reconstruction*, pp. 70, 378–79.

41. Foner, *Reconstruction*, pp. 68, 236–37.

42. *The Nation*, June 27, 1868; Rodgers, *Work Ethic*, p. 35; John G. Sproat, *"The Best Men": Liberal Reformers in the Gilded Age* (New York, 1968), pp. 145–46; James L. Hutson, "The American Revolutionaries, the Political Economy of Aristocracy, and the American Concept of the Distribution of Wealth, 1765–1900," *American Historical Review* 98 (1993): 1103.

43. Forbath, "Ambiguities of Free Labor," pp. 767–817; Charles W. McCurdy, "Justice Field and the Jurisprudence of Government-Business Relations: Some Parameters of Laissez-Faire Constitutionalism, 1863–1897," *Journal of American History* 61 (1975): 970–1005; Kessler-Harris, *A Woman's Wage*, pp. 37–47; Lea S. VanderVelde, "The Gendered Origins of the Lumley Doctrine: Binding Men's Consciences and Women's Fidelity," *Yale Law Review* 101 (1992): 830.

44. Eileen Boris, "'A Man's Dwelling House Is His Castle': Tenement House Cigar-making and the Judicial Imperative," in Ava Baron, ed., *Work Engendered: Toward a New History of American Labor* (Ithaca, N.Y., 1991), pp. 114–41; Christopher L. Tomlins, *The State and the Unions: Labor Relations, Law, and the Organized Labor Movement in America, 1880–1960* (New York, 1985), pp. 49–51; Leon Fink, "Labor, Liberty, and the Law," p. 912; Goldberg, "Slavery, Race and the Languages of Class," pp. 71–77; John K. Ingram, *A History of Slavery and Serfdom* (London, 1895), p. 261.

45. Boris, "Dwelling House," pp. 134–35; Lasch, *True and Only Heaven*, pp. 207–8; Montgomery, *Fall of the House of Labor*, p. 13.

46. Lawrence Glickman, "Inventing the 'American Standard of Living': Gender, Race,

and Working Class Identity, 1880–1925," *Labor History* 34 (1993): 221–35; David Horowitz, "Consumption and Its Discontents: Simon N. Patten, Thorstein Veblen, and George Gunton," *Journal of American History* 67 (1980): 301–17; Lasch, *True and Only Heaven,* p. 302; John Alt, "Beyond Class: The Decline of Industrial Labor and Leisure," *Telos* 28 (1976): 55–80.

5

Free Labor, Wage Labor, and the Slave Power: Republicanism and the Republican Party in the 1850s

JOHN ASHWORTH

ISTORIANS HAVE RECENTLY STARTED once again to place emphasis on economic transformations, in particular on the implications of what is now termed the market revolution that swept over the United States in the decades following the Peace of Ghent. As yet, however, no consensus exists on the chronology of this development or even on its precise character. While an increasing number of Americans were clearly spending more of their working lives engaged in producing for the market, such changes were almost certainly not unique to the mid-nineteenth century. And what actually constitutes a market revolution? How does its impact on a slave society differ from that on a society committed to free labor? How did it affect the cluster of values and ideals that historians now refer to as constituting the ideals of republicanism? These issues—and many others too—are still largely unresolved.[1]

It is little more than a truism that the market revolution had a transforming effect on American politics. One can trace the profound effects of economic change on political ideology in any decade of the antebellum era. By concentrating, however, on a single decade, the 1850s, and a single party, the Republicans, it may nevertheless be possible to refine our understanding of the processes at work, and to shed some light on the political consequences of the market revolution.

What was the Republican party about? This would once have seemed the most futile of questions. If the Civil War had, as James Ford Rhodes once observed, a single cause, slavery, then the role of the Republican party, in seeking to arrest the spread of that institution was clear to all.[2] To be sure, opinions might differ as to the wisdom or the expediency of such a course, and historians might ask in whose interest slavery was being opposed. But if slavery was the key cause of the war, then the Republican party's role was clear. Although not in the 1850s committed to abolition, it was nevertheless an antislavery party.

This interpretation has a long and distinguished history. Most historians of the Civil War have simply assumed that antislavery was at the heart of the Republican appeal. Those with a southern bias have often condemned leading Republicans—and especially Radical Republicans—for their excessive zeal and have found hypocrisy and fanaticism in equal measure. Others, following Rhodes, have emphasized the moral superiority of the antislavery cause (though Rhodes, it should be said, castigated northern radicals for their excessive faith in the capacity of blacks). In either case, however, the links between the Republican party and antislavery remained intact.[3] Indeed, it was perhaps for this very reason that until 1970 no book-length treatment of the ideology of the antebellum Republican party appeared. In that year, however, Eric Foner published his *Free Soil, Free Labor, Free Men* and the modern historiographical controversy over the Republican party began.[4]

Despite its originality, Foner's work did not overturn the traditional view of the Republican party as an organization that derived its vigor from the antislavery crusade. Indeed, he confirmed that this was so. In a sense, his main contribution was actually to strengthen this view by demonstrating that antislavery was not merely a set of negative reference points; instead Republicans, in his view, were driven to oppose slavery because of their full and unreserved commitment to the values of "free labor." The concept of free labor, he declared, "lay at the heart of the Republican ideology," and it was because southern slave society negated so many of the values associated with free labor that the Republicans were impelled to prevent its spread onto the "free soil" of the West. Sectional conflict and ultimately civil war were the consequences.[5]

Despite—or perhaps because of—this forceful restatement of Republican objectives, other historians have since reexamined the Republican appeal and have sought to revise Foner's view in different ways and to different extents. At the risk of oversimplification, I shall suggest that three alternative explanations have been offered. First, in 1978 Michael Holt argued that, while opposition to the extension of slavery was indeed a major goal of Republican policy, it was not the party's "fundamental purpose." Those who followed Foner in asserting that "free-soilism constituted the core of Republicanism" were all too likely to "miss the essence of the Republican appeal." What was that essence? For Holt it was the maintenance of republican values, the cluster of ideas in whose defense political parties had been mobilizing for many decades. Holt spoke of "a deep-seated republican ideology that had suffused

American politics since the time of the Revolution." What were its characteristics? Although taking pains to acknowledge that the republican creed was
neither monolithic nor unchanging, he explained that to most Americans "it
meant . . . government by and for the people, a government whose power
over the people was restrained by law, and whose basic function was to protect the equality and liberty of individuals from aristocratic privilege and concentrations of arbitrary power." Here, then, was the Republican party's mission in the 1850s. Although many within the party were genuinely and
sincerely concerned with the slavery of black Americans, a still larger number
within the party were still more genuinely and sincerely concerned with the
threatened enslavement of white Americans. Enslavement in this context did
not necessarily mean the imposition of chattel status (though some Republicans indeed feared that slaveholders had designs on northern whites); rather
it meant the enslavement that was the necessary effect of submission to rule
by a privileged elite.[6]

At this point Holt's interpretation—emphasizing the danger to republicanism—merges with a second alternative to the Foner view. William E.
Gienapp, author of a monumental study of the origins of the Republican
party, has also dissented from the view that free soil was the essence of the
Republican appeal.[7] Gienapp drew attention to one of the key issues raised
by Foner's work. Foner had not considered—and could scarcely have been
expected to consider—the views of other northerners outside the Republican
party. The most important of these groups was clearly the northern Democrats. But were they not also imbued with the values of free labor? As Gienapp
put it, "the ideology of free labor may have distinguished northerners from
slaveowners, but that it divided Republicans from northern Democrats is
questionable." For "all northerners and not just Republicans, shared a belief
in the values associated with free labor."[8] How, then, could it be appropriate
to claim for these values a distinctively Republican parentage?

Gienapp insisted that at the core of Republicanism was not a commitment
to free labor—a commitment shared by almost all northerners—but instead
a fear of the "slave power" evinced by Republicans,[9] but not by Democrats.
Here for Gienapp was the crucial issue that could mobilize northerners in
defense of traditional republican values. Southern slaveholders and their dependents, Republicans argued, constituted a slave power that was seeking to
trample on the rights and liberties of northern freemen as well as of southern slaves. Issues like "Bleeding Kansas" raised not merely the question of
the spread of slavery, but also even more crucial issues about the purity of the
ballot box (imperiled by the attempt to impose an undemocratic constitution
on Kansans), while issues like "bleeding Sumner" were equally important as

evidence of the desire of the aristocratic slave power to curtail freedom of speech in Congress. By the end of 1856, according to Gienapp, the Republican appeal was clearly defined; at its heart was the emphasis on the southern slave power.

Although Gienapp's conclusion is in no way at odds with Holt's interpretation, the third challenge to the Foner free soil view is radically different. The so-called new political history that emerged in the 1960s and 1970s emphasized the role played in antebellum politics by ethnocultural factors. By this, these historians meant religious and moral values together with the loyalties inspired by ethnic identity. In explaining the political upheaval of 1854, when the Whig party in many northern and southern states disintegrated and the Republican party in some northern states first saw the light of day, the new political history stressed the importance of ethnocultural factors rather than the sectional issues that historians traditionally assumed to have been decisive.[10]

In a sense, this view culminated in an article by Joel Silbey entitled "The Surge of Republican Power."[11] Here Silbey argued not that slavery was unimportant as an issue, but rather that it "was part of the larger matter of cultural hegemony."[12] Silbey deliberately focused upon a question largely neglected by other new political historians: the origins of the Civil War itself. The Republicans, he suggested, were not so much the party of free soil, nor even of opposition to the slave power. Rather they were the party of Yankee cultural imperialism. They wished to impose, by law if necessary, the values of their section.

Some of these values were those of antislavery and of free labor, but others were more closely related to familiar ethnocultural issues—temperance, anti-Catholicism, hostility to immigrants. The Democratic party had traditionally opposed the attempt to impose these values on the nation, and many Democrats continued to view the threat posed by the Republicans in precisely these terms. Silbey quotes one Democratic editor whose views perfectly encapsulate his interpretation of the Republican appeal: "abolitionism is but a small part of their programme and probably the least noxious of their measures." Their mission was to stir up hostility to immigrants, to launch crusades against liquor, to fan the flames of religious discord—as well as to promote antislavery. For Silbey, the slavery issue could and should be subsumed under the larger heading of cultural politics.[13]

How is this controversy to be resolved? Needless to say, some of the evidence is not yet available, and further research is needed before some important questions can be answered. Yet some tentative conclusions are possible. First, it is clear that Foner's critics have raised some damaging questions. In a

sense, the key issue concerns the northern Democrats, or rather the distinctiveness of Republican ideology within the North. Gienapp and others are
surely correct in their observation that northern Democrats in the 1850s believed in free labor. Indeed, one could push this point further. Northern
Democrats and indeed every other significant party in the North since at least
the 1820s had been committed to free labor. By the 1830s, at the very latest, it
was impossible for any northern politician to express the view that slave labor
in northern climes was the equal of free. Even the most "doughfaced" of
northerners did not make this claim—not, at any rate, if they coveted electoral survival. Instead all agreed that free labor was, overall, superior. If this
is so, what was specific to the Republican appeal in the 1850s? This is the logic
upon which Gienapp and others have built their case for the slave power as
the crucial Republican reference point. There is no doubt that this slogan
informed Republican discourse, and it is equally true that it was absent from
the rhetoric of northern Democrats, either in the 1850s or earlier. Thus
Gienapp's view identifies a specifically and distinctively Republican appeal in
a way that Foner's, it would appear, cannot.

Nevertheless, there are major weaknesses in the arguments of Foner's critics. If hostility to the slave power was the key Republican theme, why did it
emerge when it did? Republicans emphasized that their struggle with the
southern aristocracy was essentially defensive; they were seeking to maintain
the rights of white northerners as well as those of black slaves. But historians
who have studied the South have also taken pains to confirm that southerners, too, believed that they were involved in a defensive campaign. Indeed,
all the arguments presented by Silbey confirm that this was so. If both sides
were seeking to defend what they already had, what was the struggle all about?
The danger is of a collapse into old-style revisionism—the claim that the
entire sectional controversy is attributable to the irresponsible activities of
agitators on both sides. More specifically, emphasizing slave power and the
defense of republican values generally risks detaching the sectional conflict
from the processes of economic and social change—the market revolution—
that characterized the era.[14] As Gienapp acknowledges, his emphasis is on
political rather than economic factors. The danger is of severing political history from its social and economic moorings, reducing the processes of political change to the political realm. But is it not axiomatic that the political and
the social are inextricably linked? The Foner view had the great merit of situating Republican thought in its economic context. As Foner argued, the Republicans' confidence in the values of "free labor" was the direct effect of
their experience of a highly buoyant and expansive northern economy.

What of the notion of Republican politics as cultural imperialism? This, too, has its strengths. There is no doubt that many of their opponents insisted that antislavery was only one of the evils with which the Republican party was tainted. Some northerners (but few southerners) also claimed that temperance and nativism were more important than slavery. There is no doubt, either, that these various issues were, as Silbey has emphasized, interlinked. Yet it is claiming too much to suggest that in the nation as a whole, and in the 1850s overall, these other issues were as important as those in which slavery was directly implicated. Moreover, the Republican commitment to temperance, to nativism, and to Sabbatarianism was far more tentative and ambiguous than Silbey allows. Many Republicans—Lincoln and Seward to name only the two most important leaders of the party in the 1850s—would have nothing to do with any of these crusades. And the slavery question was larger than any of them. Although it had important links with some of the ethnocultural issues, it simply cannot be subsumed under the umbrella of cultural politics.

The controversy has thus apparently arrived at an impasse. As is frequently the case with historical debates, the various protagonists can claim success in pointing to the weaknesses in alternative accounts, but are less convincing in the defense of their own interpretations. Nevertheless, it might be suggested that this controversy can be resolved with surprising ease. If the Foner view is given a single modification, it can not only withstand the criticisms leveled against it, but also accommodate all the insights generated by the critics. The modification is a simple one: for *free labor* we should read *wage labor*.

We cannot understand the political universe in which the Republicans flourished without first considering some of the opinions of the patron saint of American democracy, Thomas Jefferson. Jefferson defined the American democratic creed and the values of republicanism in his struggle with the Federalists in the 1790s. Although the Republican party of the 1850s constantly harked back to Jefferson and indeed claimed inspiration from such Jeffersonian triumphs as the Northwest Ordinance of 1787, the Republican victory of 1860 in fact marked the overthrow of the Jeffersonian system. Under the impact of the economic changes associated with the market revolution, the Republicans redefined the American democratic tradition and, in their triumph over the South in the Civil War, destroyed the regime established in 1776 and reconstituted by the Jeffersonian triumph of 1800.

Jefferson's agrarianism, his belief in states' rights, his commitment to limited government—indeed all the major tenets of the Jeffersonian political faith—are all too well known to require any rehearsal here. Nevertheless, it is worth recalling his view of agriculture. This received its most eloquent expression in the *Notes on Virginia,* where Jefferson explained that the farmers' independence and moral purity made them "the chosen people of God, if ever He had a chosen people." [15] In the 1820s the Jeffersonian mantle was picked up by those who rallied to Andrew Jackson. And as the principles of Jacksonian Democracy were defined in the course of Jackson's two administrations, especially under the impact of the struggle with the Bank of the United States, they came increasingly to resemble those of John Taylor of Caroline, high priest of Jeffersonian Democracy. Once again, praise was heaped on agriculture and on the landed interest. Thus, in 1839 the *Democratic Review,* semiofficial magazine of the party, did precisely as Jefferson had done a half-century earlier and compared city and country. The conclusion was a quintessentially Jeffersonian one:

> The farmer is naturally a Democrat—the citizen may be so, but it is in spite of many obstacles. In the country a more healthy moral atmosphere may be said to exist, untainted by the corruptions and contagions of the crowded city, analogous to its purer breezes which the diseased and exhausted denizen of the latter is from time to time compelled to seek for the renovation of his jaded faculties of mind and body. In the city men move in masses. . . . In the country, on the other hand, man enjoys an existence of a healthier and truer happiness, a nobler mental freedom, a higher native dignity—for which a poor equivalent is found in that superficial polish produced by the incessant mutual attrition, and that more intense life, if we may so speak, excited by the perpetual surrounding stimulus that belong to cities. He is thrown more on himself. Most of his labors are comparatively solitary, and of such kind as to leave his mind meanwhile free for reflection. Every thing around him is large, open, free, unartificial, and his mind insensibly, to a greater or less extent, takes a corresponding tone from the general character of the objects and associations in the midst of which he lives and moves and has his being. He is less dependent on the hourly aid of others, in the regular routine of his life, as likewise on their opinions, their example, their influence. The inequalities of social distinctions, the operation of which is attended with equal moral injury to the higher and the lower, affect less his more simple and independent course of life. He is forced more constantly to think and act for himself, with reference to those broad principles of natural right, of which all men alike, when unperverted by artificial circumstances, carry with them a common general understanding. And to live he must labor: all the various modes by which, in great congregations of men, certain classes are ingeniously able to appropriate to themselves the fruits of the general toil of the rest, being to him alike unknown and impracticable. Hence does he better appreciate the true worth and dignity of labor, and knows how to respect, with a more manly and Christian sympathy of universal brotherhood, those oppressed masses of the laboring poor, whose vast bulk constitutes the basis on which alone rests the proud apex of the social

pyramid. In a word, he is a more natural, a more healthy, a more independent, a more genuine *man*,—and hence, as we have said above, the farmer is naturally a democrat; the citizen may be so, but it is in spite of many obstacles. We have here briefly, in passing, alluded to the reasons for our preference of the political support of the country over that of the city; and to the causes of the fact that, as a general rule, the former has always been found to be the true home of American democracy; while in the latter, and in their circum-radiated influence, has usually been found the main strength of that party by which, under one form and name or another, the progress of the democratic principle has, from the outset, been so bitterly and unremittingly opposed.

For Jefferson and the Jacksonians alike, the farmer who was most estimable was not the tenant, but the freeholder. He it was who enjoyed the independence that was so necessary to participation in a democratic government.[16]

One can argue that Jeffersonian and Jacksonian Democracy provided a considerable measure of covert support for slaveholders, whose plantations were, in Democratic rhetoric, smoothly assimilated into the farm.[17] But what this tradition could not easily accommodate was the wage laborer. This is less surprising than might be thought. It is too easily forgotten that for most of human history the status of the wage laborer has been a humble one indeed. Americans were heirs to a long and venerable tradition of hostility to wage labor. From Aristotle to the English revolution and beyond, one prominent political thinker after another stressed that the wage worker was akin to a slave. As Aristotle put it, "No man can practise virtue who is living the life of a mechanic or labourer."[18]

These attitudes survived in Europe for hundreds of years. They were evident in the utterances of the Levellers and the Diggers during the English revolution, for example.[19] And they reemerged in the United States to inform both Jeffersonian and Jacksonian views of wage labor. Not surprisingly, a party that was unhappy with the dependence entailed by tenant farming was unenthusiastic about the relationship between employer and worker. In fact, those who were most implacable in their hostility to the banking system—the key political issue of the 1830s—tended also to be the most distrustful of wage labor. At the furthest reaches of the Democratic party was Orestes Brownson, who, as is well known, in 1840 proposed that the party prohibit the inheritance of property. Less well known, however, is the view of wages that he expressed at the same time. Brownson's goal was to "combine labor and capital in the same individual," and he argued that it was agriculture, more than any other pursuit, that could achieve this. But even in the agricultural sector the situation was deteriorating, since "the distance between the owner of the farm, and the men who cultivate it" was "becoming every day greater and greater." Yet this problem shrank into insignificance when compared with the scene in the towns and manufacturing villages, where "the distinction between the capitalist and the proletary" was "as strongly marked as it is in the old world." For Brownson the ultimate threat to individual autonomy was the wages system. Wages were "the cunning device of the devil," and the wage system had to be eliminated, "or else one half of the human race must forever be the virtual slaves of the other."[20]

Brownson was an unusual Democrat and an erratic partisan. More measured in his utterances was New York Senator Silas Wright, who was known to speak for the Van Burenites, in the late 1830s and early 1840s the dominant group within the party. Wright focused attention on manufacturing and complained of "the great power which the manufacturing capitalist must hold over the employee, and, by necessary consequence, over the living, the comfort, and the independence of the laborer." Similarly, Amos Kendall, one of Andrew Jackson's closest collaborators, urged the sons of farmers to remain on the farm rather than to seek employment in factories.[21]

For Kendall the worthy citizen was either a farmer or an "independent mechanic." Here he perhaps left the way open for a modest amount of wage labor. What did he mean by *independent*? Unfortunately, it is difficult to answer this question. An independent mechanic, according to Kendall, was one who could refuse "to sell his services to any man on other conditions than those of perfect equality—both as citizens and men." Kendall may have meant here the self-employed craftsman, who sold his services not to an employer, but instead to the consumer. Or he may have meant a wage worker, whose terms of employment were not such as to produce large inequalities of wealth, power, and esteem. How were such terms to be attained? Kendall did not specify.[22]

Other Democrats had trouble with wage labor. Like Kendall they believed that independence was essential, and like him they were unsure whether it was compatible with employment for wages. The Washington *Globe* referred approvingly to, in effect, two kinds of mechanic or artisan and had no difficulty in defining the first. He was none other than the self-employed craftsman. But a string of subordinate clauses was necessary to offer even an approximate definition of the second. The newspaper spoke of "the healthy mechanic or artisan, who works for himself at his own shop, or if he goes abroad, returns home to his meals every day, and sleeps under his own roof every night; whose earnings are regulated by the wants of the community at large, not by the discretion of a pernicious master; whose hours of labor depend on universal custom; who, when the sun goes down, is a freeman until he rises again, who can eat his meals in comfort, and sleep as long as nature requires." The problem was that the *Globe,* like Kendall and like other Democrats, did not explain how the conditions necessary for acceptable forms of wage labor were to be obtained.[23]

In these circumstances, it was not surprising that the northern Democrats in the 1850s did not extol the wage labor system of the North. Although they were quite certain that free labor was superior to slave labor, they did not glorify wage labor. From the mid-1840s onward, of course, the nation's economy revived, and the resulting prosperity weakened Democratic radicalism. Some of it, nevertheless, persisted into the 1850s. Thus Theophilus Fisk claimed that free-soilism and abolition distracted northern workers from "their own grievous wrongs and intolerable oppressions." More significant, Fernando Wood, campaigning for Breckinridge in 1860, insisted that "until we have provided and cared for the oppressed laboring man in our own midst, we should not extend our sympathy to the laboring men of other states." As mayor of New York city in 1857, Wood set out a view of the condition of northern labor that both revived Democratic radicalism of previous decades and revealed a jaundiced view of the condition of northern wage workers: "In the days of general prosperity they [the working classes] labor for a mere subsistence whilst other classes accumulate wealth, and in the days of general depression they are the first to feel the change, without the means to avoid or endure reverses. Truly it may be said that in New York those who produce everything get nothing, and those who produce nothing get everything. They labor without income, whilst surrounded by thousands living in affluence and splendor who have income without labor."[24]

These views were distinctly uncommon within the Democratic party in the 1850s. They were more common, however, than the celebrations of wage labor in which Republicans (as we shall see) frequently indulged. A prevalent view was simply to record the condition of the wage worker and to argue that he had no cause for complaint. Unlike that of the Republicans, Democratic rhetoric in no way privileged the role of the wage laborer or the relationship between employer and worker. Such had not been Democratic practice in the past; such was not Democratic practice in the 1850s.

In fact, most Democrats abstained from a close analysis of the northern labor system. Republicans, however, did not. While it is true that their rhetoric emphasized free labor, it is equally true that all who listened knew that Republicans had not merely reconciled themselves to wage labor, but had instead come to view it as a key element in the social order, the cement of the northern social system. Freedom, equality, the Union, American democracy itself—all depended, in Republicans' eyes, on the existence of wage labor. This view distinguished them sharply from northern Democrats; it was this, above all, that separated the two parties in the 1850s.[25]

The importance of wage labor in the thinking of Republicans is implicit or explicit in some of the speeches of Charles Sumner. Prior to the election of 1860, Sumner began to adopt a shorthand phrase to refer to southern slavery. He began to call it "labor without wages," confident, it would seem, that this phrase would convey to his listeners the injustice inherent in the master-slave relation. In June 1860, all the evil effects of slavery were traced to its "single object of compelling men to work without wages." This, he repeated a month later, was its "single motive," its "single object." For the greater part of human history labor has been done without wages, and for much of that time, as we have seen, it would have been grounds for complaint if a system had compelled men to work *with* wages. On the same occasion, Sumner employed a familiar argument against slavery when he claimed that it was contrary to God's intentions for mankind. Less familiar, however, was his assumption about wages. "When God created man in his own image," he declared, "and saw that his work was good, he did not destine his fellow creature for endless ages to labor without wages, compelled by the lash." The rhythm of this sentence seems to require that a heavy emphasis be placed upon "without wages," perhaps as heavy as "compelled by the lash." The implication is surely that God approves of wage labor.[26]

Sumner's attitude was made even more explicit in a rhetorical question that he put to the Senate in 1860. Speaking of "the slaveholder," he asked, "How can he show sensibility for the common rights of fellow citizens who sacrifices daily the most sacred right of others merely to secure *labor without wages?* With him a false standard is necessarily established, bringing with it a blunted moral sense and clouded perceptions, so that, when he does something intrinsically barbarous or mean, he does not blush at the recital." Here, then, is the reason Sumner believed that to refer to slavery as "labor without wages" could convey the enormity of the evil. He seems to have viewed wage labor, properly rewarded, as an anchor of morality. The passage makes no sense unless it is assumed that the wage laborer is worthy of respect or esteem. Gone is the old hostility.[27]

Sumner, of course, was a spokesman for Radical Republicanism and represented Massachusetts, the state with the most developed economy in the Union. By contrast, Lincoln was a moderate and came from a far more agricultural state, albeit one whose economy was advancing rapidly in the 1850s. Although his social thought has often been analyzed,[28] the significance and novelty of his view of wage labor have not been fully appreciated. In one respect, however, his views were entirely traditional: he remained somewhat critical of the worker who remained, for the duration of his working life, a wage earner. As he told a Milwaukee audience in 1859, "If any continue though life in the condition of the hired laborer," it was "because of either a dependent nature which prefers it, or improvidence, folly or singular misfortune." In the same vein, Lincoln tended to repel southern charges of wage slavery not by defending the status of the wage earner as a wage earner, but instead by pointing to his opportunities to cease to work for wages. Thus in 1856 he noted than many southerners were claiming that their slaves were "far better off than northern freemen." Lincoln did not take the modern view and reject the comparison by denying the dependence of the wage earner. Instead he charged southerners with an egregious error: "What a mistaken view do these men have of northern laborers! They think that men are always to remain laborers here—but there is no such class. The man who labored for another last year, this year labors for himself, and next year he will hire others to labor for him." Thus mobility legitimated wage labor. Lincoln also took pleasure in recording how small a proportion of the labor of the North was done for wages. At Cincinnati in 1859, he remarked that the wage system entailed "a relation of which I make no complaint." But, he added, "I do insist that the relation does not embrace more than one-eighth of the labor of the country." Though this estimate was almost certainly far wide of the mark, it may be more important to note Lincoln's defensive tone here. Clearly he was glad that wage earners did not constitute a larger proportion of the northern workforce.[29]

At the same time, however, Lincoln glorified the wage labor—and not merely the free labor—system of the North. We can perhaps best understand this by looking at his view of mobility. More than any previous president, Lincoln emphasized social mobility.[30] As early as 1856, he was attributing American greatness to the fact that in the United States "every man can make himself." For Jefferson and Jackson, freedom and equality had necessitated an agrarian society in which the freeholding farmer would, whether or not he went to the West, remain a freeholding farmer for his entire life, gradually acquiring a "competence" for his old age. Such a society would be characterized by an equality of conditions rather than merely an equality of opportunity. Indeed, inequalities of outcome, while inevitable, would present a danger; they would in no sense be necessary to the functioning of the economy. For Lincoln, however, the citizens of the United States, or at least those of the northern states, were engaged in "a race of life." Unequal outcomes are implicit in—indeed the very purpose of—a race. In 1864 he told an Ohio regiment that they were fighting "to secure such an inestimable jewel" as "equal privileges in the race of life." Lincoln's other favorite metaphor was also one that conveyed the idea of mobility and, more specifically, upward mobility. This involved the image of weights being lifted from shoulders. In February 1861, he told a Philadelphia audience that the unity of the nation had hitherto been maintained by "something in that Declaration [of Independence] giving liberty not alone to the people of this country, but hope to the world for all future time." This was the promise "that in due time the weights should be lifted from the shoulders of all men, and that all should have an equal chance." In his special session message of July 4, 1861 he again used both this image and the race-of-life metaphor to explain the purpose of the struggle. The Union itself was now explicable in terms of social mobility.[31]

Mobility had also subtly narrowed the Jacksonian view of equality and liberty so that both were now understood in terms of equality of opportunity. Addressing another Ohio regiment in 1864, the President declared that "nowhere in the world is presented a government of so much liberty and equality." As if to define his terms, he immediately added, "To the humblest and poorest among us are held out the highest privileges and positions." If opportunities were equal and plentiful, then Americans were free and equal. Little wonder, then, that Lincoln invited Americans to internalize the goal of social mobility, as he himself had done. "I hold [that] the value of life," he once said, is "to improve one's condition."[32]

How was mobility to be secured? Lincoln held that "when one starts poor, as most do in the race of life, free society is such that he knows he can better his condition; he knows that there is no such fixed condition of labor, for his whole life." It was this that distinguished free labor, "which has the inspiration of hope," from slave labor, "which has no hope." For "the power of hope upon human exertion, and happiness, is wonderful." Yet, just as free labor was essential for social mobility, so, for Lincoln, were wages essential to free labor. And just as mobility legitimated wage labor, so was wage labor essential for mobility. In all Lincoln's descriptions of mobility the need for wage labor was either explicit or implicit. On one occasion free labor was actually defined in terms of the individual's progress from the rank of wage laborer to that of employer. Thus at Milwaukee in 1859 he spoke of "the prudent, penniless beginner in the world," who "labors for wages awhile, saves a surplus with which to buy tools or land for himself, then labors on his own account another while, and at length hires another new beginner to help him." The conclusion was significant: "This say its advocates, is *free* labor [emphasis added]—the just and generous and prosperous system, which opens the way for all—gives hope to all, and energy, and progress, and improvement of condition to all." Finally, and even more explicitly, at Cincinnati the same year he announced that the very purpose of American democracy was to facilitate the progress of the wage laborer: "This progress, by which the poor, honest, industrious, and resolute man raises himself, that he may work on his own account, and hire somebody else, is that progress that human nature is entitled to, is that improvement in condition that is intended to be secured by those institutions under which we live, is the great principle for which this government was really formed." Thus, for Lincoln democracy, the Union, freedom, equality, even the Declaration of Independence could not be understood except in terms of mobility, free labor, and wages.[33]

Lincoln was not alone in these opinions. In New York City the *Times,* an exponent of conservative Republican thought, while the economy was in recession in 1857, replied to southern critics of northern society. "Our best answer," it claimed, "is that the majority of those who suffer from a panic here are by the time the next one comes around in a position not to fear it." For "the Northern artisans of 1837 . . . are the merchants, traders, farmers and statesmen of 1856 and 1857." This was thanks to "free labor," which was "our glory and our safeguard." Thus, for the *Times,* the stability of the northern social system depended on free labor and social mobility. And free labor clearly required wage labor.[34]

There was thus a marked difference between Republican and northern Democratic perceptions of the northern social order. While both groups did not doubt that, so far as the North was concerned, free labor was superior to slavery, the Republicans enthused about the relationship between employer and wage earner, while the Democrats did not. In 1859, the *Chicago Times* neatly illustrated this difference when it chided Lincoln after one of his speeches and claimed that he had misrepresented the condition of northern workers, only 10 percent of whom could become employers. The Republicans and the Democrats saw free labor and the contrast with slavery differently. Essentially Republicans saw slavery and free labor (with its foundation in the wages system) as the bases for divergent social systems; northern Democrats perceived them rather as distinct interests.[35]

What does it mean to say that certain values formed the core of a party's beliefs? One possible answer might be that these values were those that the party's spokesmen most often articulated. In this eventuality, it would be possible to determine which were the key Republican values by counting the references made to the slave power, to free labor, and to wage labor. In this

contest it is entirely possible that the slave power would emerge the win-
ner, wage labor a poor third. But such an analysis would be profoundly
unsatisfactory.[36]

It is frequently the case that the various components of an ideology or a
worldview are interdependent, with each reinforcing, and reinforced by,
many of the others. It is also, however, frequently the case that such interdependence is asymmetrical; some components give rise to others, but are less
dependent upon them. So it was with wage labor and the slave power in
Republican thought. Republicans saw a slave power where Democrats did
not, because their faith in the northern social system was so great that they
could explain the success of slavery in the South and even (to some extent)
in the West only by claiming that normal democratic processes had been
subverted or overturned. Since the free labor and wage labor system of the
North was deemed "natural,"[37] it followed that a slave power was required to
explain its failure to take hold in the South and the attempts to spread an
alternative system into the West and even the North.[38] Hence the Republicans' preference for a wage labor system can explain their references to the
slave power. But this interdependence was asymmetrical: in no sense did a
belief in the slave power give rise to Republican perceptions of wage labor.

There is, moreover, additional cause to emphasize the importance of wage
labor. For such an emphasis immediately opens up a connection with the
dominant economic processes of the mid-nineteenth century. In 1800 only
about 10 percent of the American workforce was employed for wages; by 1860
the figure was about 40 percent, heavily concentrated, of course, in the
North.[39] The Democratic party, with its strength increasingly concentrated in
the South, could not develop a wage labor or even a free labor ideology;
indeed, it was all northerners could do to prevent their southern colleagues
from placing a proslavery plank in the party platform. Finally, of course, the
party split in 1860 over precisely this issue. But for some years before this
Democrats in the North had experienced great difficulty in engaging with the
dominant economic processes of their time. Perhaps if the panic of 1857 had
lasted, a revival of the antibank and anticommercial sentiment of the 1830s
and early 1840s might have solved this problem. But it did not. In these circumstances, northern Democrats were impelled to fall back on an appeal to
the ethnocultural values that they had always espoused, but now without the
economic and social underpinning they had previously had. In this sense,
therefore, theirs was an increasingly dislocated ideology.

Here is an additional reason why the Silbey interpretation of Republicanism is unsatisfactory. Not only were the Republicans profoundly divided on
all the ethnocultural questions that did not involve slavery;[40] they knew, as

most southerners knew, that the slavery question transcended issues like rum and Romanism. It raised too many vital questions about the nation's political economy to be treated in the way that the parties had treated the ethnocultural issues. A society's labor system—the question whether it should be based upon slavery or wages—is simply more important than the decision whether to introduce laws on temperance. Most partisans and observers in the 1850s knew that this was so. Of course the northern Democrats would have liked nothing more than to have subsumed slavery under the heading of "cultural politics," since they would then have had a more potent appeal to the electorate. But the history of the 1850s is, in a sense, the history of the frustration of these hopes.

In the longer view, the Republican achievement was momentous. The election of Lincoln and the victory of the North in the Civil War meant that a fundamental—indeed revolutionary—change in American politics had occurred. The American democratic tradition, forged by Jefferson and by Jackson, had given covert support to the slaveholder by assimilating the slaveholding plantation into the farm. The American democratic tradition as reconstituted in the political upheavals of the 1850s and 1860s would instead rest American democracy upon the relationship between employer and employee, between capitalist and worker, a relationship now hailed as a quintessential characteristic of a "free" society. There it remains to this day.

NOTES

1. A key work is Charles Sellers, *The Market Revolution: Jacksonian America, 1815–1846* (New York, 1991). I have been greatly influenced by all Sellers's work on the Jacksonian era.

2. James Ford Rhodes, *Lectures on the American Civil War* (New York, 1913), p. 2; *History of the United States from the Compromise of 1850*, 7 vols. (New York, 1893–1906), 5: 485.

3. On the historiography of the Civil War, Thomas J. Pressly, *Americans Interpret Their Civil War* (rev. ed., New York, 1962) remains the key work.

4. Eric Foner, *Free Soil, Free Labor, Free Men: The Ideology of the Republican Party before the Civil War* (New York, 1970).

5. Foner, *Free Soil*, p. 11.

6. Michael F. Holt, *The Political Crisis of the 1850s* (New York, 1978), pp. 189, 4–5.

7. William E. Gienapp, *The Origins of the Republican Party, 1854–1856* (New York, 1987). The Gienapp interpretation of Republican ideology, however, is most clearly stated

in Gienapp, "The Republican Party and the Slave Power," in Robert H. Abzug and Stephen E. Maizlish, eds., *New Perspectives on Race and Slavery in America* (Lexington, Ky., 1986), pp. 51–78.

8. Gienapp, "Republican Party and Slave Power," p. 58. Gienapp added that "some have argued that these values were not exclusively northern, and that southerners including slaveowners embraced them."

9. Also, one might add, by abolitionists. See John Ashworth, *Slavery, Capitalism, and Politics in the Antebellum Republic*, vol. 1, *Commerce and Compromise, 1820–1850* (New York, 1966).

10. Among the more important examples of the new political history are Paul Kleppner, *The Third Electoral System, 1853–1892: Parties, Voters, and Political Cultures* (Chapel Hill, N.C., 1979) and Ronald P. Formisano, *The Birth of Mass Parties, Michigan, 1827–1861* (Princeton, N.J., 1971). See also Don E. Fehrenbacher, "The New Political History and the Coming of the Civil War," *Pacific Historical Review* 54 (1985): 117–42.

11. Silbey's work is most conveniently consulted in Silbey, *The Partisan Imperative: The Dynamics of American Politics before the Civil War* (New York, 1985). The article "The Surge of Republican Power" is to be found on pp. 166–89.

12. Silbey, "Surge of Republican Power," p. 186.

13. Silbey, "Surge of Republican Power," p. 179.

14. Though it should perhaps be added that Holt's work by no means ignores the economic changes of the 1840s and 1850s. See Holt, *Political Crisis of the 1850s*, esp. pp. 101–38.

15. Thomas Jefferson, *Notes on the State of Virginia* (reprint, New York, 1964), p. 157.

16. *United States Magazine and Democratic Review* 6 (1839): 500–502. For additional evidence of these attitudes, see John Ashworth, *"Agrarians" and "Aristocrats": Party Political Ideology in the United States, 1837–1846* (London, 1983), particularly p. 22.

17. This point cannot be developed here. It is, however, a main theme of Ashworth, *Slavery, Capitalism, and Politics*, vol. 1.

18. Aristotle, *Politics*, Book 3, chap. 5 in Richard McKeon, *Introduction to Aristotle* (New York, 1947), pp. 587–88.

19. Christopher Hill, "Pottage for Freeborn Englishmen: Attitudes to Wage Labour," in his *Change and Continuity in Seventeenth-Century England* (London, 1974), pp. 219–38. It may be worth noting that during Reconstruction freedmen preferred even the smallest landholding to the condition of wage laborer.

20. *Boston Quarterly Review* 3 (1840): 475, 467–71; 3 (1840): 370, 374.

21. Ransom H. Gillet, *The Life and Times of Silas Wright*, 2 vols. (Albany, 1874), 2:1487–88; *Kendall's Expositor*, May 31, 1842, p. 163. See also *Democratic Statesman*, May 10, 1845; *Young Hickory Banner*, Aug. 24, 1844; *Kendall's Expositor*, May 31, 1842, p. 163.

22. *Kendall's Expositor*, May 31, 1842, p. 163.

23. *(Washington) Globe*, Jan. 11, 1842.

24. *The National Crisis* (Washington, D.C., 1860) 1:10, 13; *Speech of Fernando Wood, Delivered before the Meeting of the National Democratic Delegation to the Charleston Convention, at Syracuse, Feb. 7 1860* (New York, n.d.), p. 5. See also Fernando Wood in the *New York Times*, Oct. 23, 1857.

25. A good treatment of the views of northern Democrats in the 1850s is to be found in

Bruce W. Collins, "The Ideology of the Ante-Bellum Northern Democrats," *Journal of American Studies* 11 (1977): 103–21. Those, like Gienapp, who have asserted that northern Democrats and Republicans had the same view of the free (and thus presumably the wage) labor system of the North have cited no evidence for this claim, but instead have referred to Collins. However, Collins provides no evidence for the claim, either. On the northern Democrats see also Jean H. Baker, *Affairs of Party: The Political Culture of Northern Democrats in the Mid–Nineteenth Century* (Ithaca, N.Y., 1983); Roy F. Nichols, *The Democratic Machine* (New York, 1923); Roy F. Nichols, *The Disruption of American Democracy* (New York, 1948); Stephen E. Maizlish, "Race and Politics in the Northern Democracy: 1854–1860," in Abzug and Maizlish, *New Perspectives on Race and Slavery,* pp. 79–90.

It is true that some Republican ideas were anticipated by the Whigs. This question is beyond the scope of the present study. The primary difference between Republican and (northern) Whig ideas on mobility and wages was that the Whigs experienced great difficulty in enthusing about American democracy. An excellent discussion is to be found in Daniel Walker Howe, *The Political Culture of the American Whigs* (Chicago, 1979), esp. pp. 96–112, 138.

26. *The Works of Charles Sumner*, 15 vols. (Boston, 1870–1893), 5:106, 208, 209, 267. A similar implication was present in a statement made ten years earlier by George Julian, later to join Sumner on the radical wing of the Republican party. Julian referred to "that principle of eternal justice, a fair day's wages for a fair day's work." See George W. Julian, *Speeches on Political Questions* (New York, 1872), pp. 7, 10.

27. *Works of Charles Sumner*, 5:267.

28. For example, Gabor S. Boritt, *Lincoln and the Economics of the American Dream* (Memphis, 1978); Bernard Mandel, *Labor Free and Slave: Workingmen and the Anti-Slavery Movement in the United States* (New York, 1955), pp. 56–62; Richard Hofstadter, "Abraham Lincoln and the Self-Made Myth," in his *The American Political Tradition* (reprint, New York, 1973), pp. 118–74.

29. Roy F. Basler, ed., *The Collected Works of Abraham Lincoln*, 8 vols. (New Brunswick, N.J., 1953–1955), 3:478–79; 2:364; 3:459; Basler, ed., *Supplement to the Collected Works of Lincoln* (Westport, Conn., 1974), pp. 43–44.

30. The novelty of Lincoln's position and its break with Democratic tradition have been underestimated because of the tendency to view Jacksonian Democrats as rising entrepreneurs. See Ashworth, *"Agrarians" and "Aristocrats."*

31. Basler, *Works of Lincoln*, 7:512; 4:240, 438.

32. Basler, *Works of Lincoln*, 2:364; 7:528; Boritt, *Lincoln and Economics*, p. 150.

33. Basler, *Works of Lincoln*, 4:24, 462, 478–79; Basler, *Supplement to Works of Lincoln*, 44.

34. *New York Times*, Nov. 18, 1857.

35. *Chicago Times*, in Boritt, *Lincoln and Economics*, p. 179. It is also the case that the northern Democrats and the Republicans viewed slavery differently. Unfortunately this issue is beyond the scope of the present discussion.

36. This kind of "content analysis" might well yield the result that most American political parties were committed to liberty. Such a conclusion would hardly help elucidate a party ideology, still less determine which aspects of it were most critical.

37. It is a general feature of ideology to present as natural what is, in reality, the product of various and specific historical developments.

38. A parallel might be suggested here with the support for McCarthy and the anticommunist crusade of the 1950s. The more confident Americans were that a "free enterprise" system corresponded with the "natural" human longing for liberty and justice, the more susceptible they were to the view that only a conspiracy could explain the success of an alternative system elsewhere. Hence McCarthy's strongest supporters were right-wing Republicans.

39. Unfortunately economic historians have given little attention to the question of the numbers in the antebellum workforce who were wage workers. See, however, Stanley Lebergott, "The Pattern of Employment Since 1800," in Seymour E. Harris, ed., *American Economic History* (New York, 1961), pp. 281–310 (from which my statements on this subject are derived). See also Lebergott, *Manpower in Economic Growth: The American Record Since 1800* (New York, 1964); David Montgomery, *Beyond Equality* (New York, 1967), p. 27.

40. Although they were also divided on the slavery issue, this division was of a different order. The disagreement over slavery was over the *extent* to which they should oppose it. Thus conservatives wanted merely to restore the Missouri line, radicals to effect the entire separation of the federal government from slavery. This was the kind of difference that characterizes *all* mass parties. On the ethnocultural questions, however, there was no agreement even at the most basic level. Republicans could not agree that they were in any way opposed to immigrants, or in favor of temperance legislation.

PART III

Political Expressions of the Market Revolution

6

The Market Revolution and the Transformation
of American Politics, 1801–1837

RICHARD E. ELLIS

THE MARKET REVOLUTION is the key development that explains the transition from what is known as Jeffersonian Democracy to Jacksonian Democracy in United States history.[1] When Thomas Jefferson assumed the presidency in 1801, a substantial portion of Americans, perhaps even a majority, lived in areas far from cities and other commercial centers and lacked access to inexpensive forms of transportation. They were self-sufficient farmers who, at best, had only sporadic and irregular contact with the marketplace. These farmers existed, for the most part, in small-scale local economies, and they bartered for much of what they could not produce for themselves. Only occasionally, and in an unpredictable fashion, did they exchange their goods and services for cash. Most of these people tended to be uneducated, provincial, and unprogressive. They also tended to be democratic and egalitarian, at least where white Protestant males were concerned. Their politicization was a major factor in the Jeffersonian Republican victory in 1800, and it was they whose lives underwent the greatest change as a consequence of the market revolution that took place over the next several decades, driven by changes in transportation and an increased demand for American agricultural products. As a result, the simpler agrarian society of these farmers was replaced by a more complex, progressive and interconnected one in which considerations of the marketplace increasingly took control of their existence.[2] It also changed the way politics operated and was perceived in the United States at that time.

Any attempt to understand the political impact of the market revolution must start with the significance of the Jeffersonian ascendancy between 1801 and 1828.[3] Until fairly recently, the tendency among scholars has been to define the Jeffersonians mainly in terms of the campaign that brought them to power in 1800 and of the agrarian bias of the party. Emphasis is placed upon the 1798–99 Kentucky and Virginia Resolutions, which took direct issue not only with the Alien and Sedition Acts, but also with the extreme nationalism of the Federalist party during the 1790s by offering an alternative view of the origins and nature of the union—one that stressed the importance of states' rights, majority rule, and the decentralization of power. On the basis of the principles espoused in these resolutions, the clear expectation of many people who supported Jefferson in the election of 1800 was that the power of the central government would be dismantled and the United States Constitution altered to undermine the nationalist principles contained in it. The Jeffersonians also assailed the economic system established by Alexander Hamilton, which provided for the funding of the national and state debts, the first Bank of the United States, and a variety of direct taxes. In its place, they promised a government of limited authority and simple economy. Yet, according to this interpretation, the Jeffersonians, once in power and faced with the practical exigencies of ruling the nation, were forced to abandon the principles upon which they were elected, and out-Federalized the Federalists. If anything, through the Louisiana Purchase Treaty (1803) and the adoption and enforcement of the Embargo Acts of 1807–1809, they increased the power of the national government.[4]

There is much that is of value in this interpretation, especially in its treatment of the election of 1800. For in that campaign the Jeffersonians, in reaching out for agrarian and Old Republican support, did adopt a position of extreme opposition to the Federalist policies of the 1790s, and did seem to indicate that if they were victorious, root and branch reform would follow. But this interpretation misses the point of what the Jeffersonians, once in power, were trying to do. For in recent years a growing number of scholars have come to recognize that the victorious Jeffersonian Republican party of 1800 was not made up simply of small farmers and Old Republicans. It contained a powerful and dynamic commercial wing made up of planters and other market-oriented farmers, lawyers, merchants, and skilled artisans who had been alienated by the economic policies of the Federalists and by their general pro-English bias, and who had their own vision for the economic development of the United States.[5]

When Jefferson assumed the presidency in 1801, these two groups almost immediately came into conflict. The Old Republicans favored going back to the original principles of the American Revolution, which, as they saw it, had been fought against the distant and tyrannical central government of Great Britain. They believed the central government created by the United States Constitution had proved equally dangerous during the 1790s when its vast power had come under the control of Hamilton and his followers. Specifically, they wanted to see Hamilton's financial program repealed, the powers of the president and the federal courts limited, and the prerogatives of the federal government to raise and spend money reduced. Many of the leaders of this group had been Antifederalists or were sympathetic to the concerns expressed by the opponents of the Constitution in the great debate of 1787– 88. By the first decade of the nineteenth century, the most prominent members of this group included John Taylor, John Randolph, James Monroe, Spencer Roane, George Clinton, Nathaniel Macon, Daniel Tompkins, and Simon Snyder.[6]

Members of the commercial wing of the Jeffersonian Republican party opposed these demands. The leaders of this group had supported the adoption of the Constitution in 1787–88 and had gone into opposition in the 1790s because they were critical of measures adopted during the administrations of George Washington and John Adams. Their major concern, when Jefferson assumed the presidency in 1801, was that he would capitulate to pressure from the agrarian and Old Republican wing of the party and bring about changes in the Constitution and policies that would take the country back to the problems of the Articles of Confederation. What these more moderate or practical Republicans wanted were changes in the policies and personnel of the federal government, but not changes in the government itself.

As president, Jefferson, with some ambivalence, sided with the commercial, national, and more moderate wing of his party. He appreciated the dangers that would occur if every time the out party came into power, as his party had in 1801, there were major changes in the structure of the government. Jefferson placed a premium on constitutional stability, and he adopted a policy of moderation and reconciliation toward the Federalists. He refused to go along with substantive amendments to the Constitution or to repeal Hamilton's financial system. He did not support the attempt of the more extreme members of his party to attack the federal judiciary by broadly defining the impeachment process in the trial of Associate Supreme Court Justice Samuel Chase. Refusing to impose party regularity, he allowed enough Republican senators to vote not guilty to put an end to the attack on the federal judiciary. Changes did take place, to be sure. Jefferson reduced the size of the army and the navy, repealed all internal taxes, established a program to try to pay off the national debt, and instituted policies to encourage orderly settlement of the national domain. All this was done, however, within the framework of the strong national government created by the United States Constitution.[7]

The commercial and national wing of the Jeffersonian Republican party won another major victory when James Madison, despite the opposition of the Old Republicans, became president in 1809. His most important allies included Albert Gallatin, Robert R. Livingston, Wilson Cary Nicholas, Alexander J. Dallas, James Sullivan, John Jacob Astor, Stephen Girard, and, for a while, Robert and Samuel Smith. During his first term in office Madison's strong nationalist principles quickly became apparent. When Governor Snyder of Pennsylvania, with the approval of his legislature, tried to prevent the enforcement of the United States Supreme Court decision in *United States v. Peters* (1809), Madison established the supremacy of the federal government by threatening to use force to apply the decision, thereby compelling the state to back down. He also appointed Joseph Story, an extreme nationalist, to the Supreme Court. It is no accident that the most important economic and constitutional decisions of the Supreme Court under the leadership of Chief Justice John Marshall occurred after Madison became president.

Despite these accomplishments, Madison's presidency was marked by an inordinate number of disappointments, problems and failures. He and his secretary of the treasury, Gallatin, endorsed the rechartering of the first Bank of the United States in 1811, but the measure did not pass. His first administration was torn up by various personality and policy conflicts within his cabinet. Drift and confusion characterized his foreign policy. He was barely reelected in 1812. The war against England that began in that year did not go very well. The country was unprepared militarily, and the war effort was marked by chaos and inefficiency.[8]

Yet, despite all this, Madison endured and persevered. The events leading up to the War of 1812 may have been muddled and confused and the war itself ineptly handled, but the results, at least for Madison and his followers, were clear and glorious: a spirit of nationalism pervaded most parts of the United States. It was aided and magnified, of course, by Andrew Jackson's belated but impressive victory at New Orleans. As Gallatin observed in 1816: "The War has been productive of evil and good, but I think the good preponderates. . . . The war has renewed and reinstated the national feelings and character which the Revolution had given and which was daily lessened. The people have now more general objects of attachment with which their pride and political opinion are connected. They are more American; they feel and act more as a nation; and I hope that the permanency of the Union is thereby better secured."[9]

On a more concrete level, an important result of the War of 1812 was that Madison, for the last two years of his second administration, was extremely popular and powerful.[10] For fifteen years he had been fending off the opposition and dealing with the obstructionist tactics of the Federalists and Old Republicans. Both groups were now in disrepute. The Federalists would no longer be a force in national politics. The Old Republicans were in disarray and divided between those who had opposed the war (Taylor and Randolph) and those who had given their allegiance to Madison and the government (Monroe and Roane). Effective control of the government thus fell into the hands of the national republican wing of the Jeffersonian party. Particularly important at this point in time was an emerging younger generation that included Henry Clay, John C. Calhoun, John Quincy Adams, William Lowndes, Langdon Cheves, Nicholas Biddle, and Story. Although they might occasionally differ on specific policies, they generally shared a common desire to encourage the economic development of the United States, a nationalist interpretation of the Constitution, and an elitist view of how the political process should operate.

The significance of national republican hegemony at the end of the War of 1812 quickly became apparent. They created a second Bank of the United States and adopted a protective tariff, and passed a bill for a federal program of internal improvements, which was vetoed by Madison for constitutional, not policy, reasons. Other measures contemplated by them were a national university and educational system, an expansion of the power of the federal courts, and the maintenance of an extensive military establishment.[11]

National Republican policies also stressed the settlement and development of the West. The Federalists during the 1790s were not very enthusiastic about the movement of settlers into the Old West after the Revolution. This attitude was understandable, since the three states—Vermont, Kentucky, and Tennessee—that entered the Union during the 1790s were overwhelmingly Republican. Federalist policy, therefore, did not encourage western settlement: it sold land in large lots and at high prices, mainly to speculators, and did not push the Spanish very hard to open the Mississippi River and the port of New Orleans to American navigation. In contrast, Jeffersonian land policy encouraged the settlement and development of the West: it reduced the size of the tracts of land needed for a minimum purchase and, until 1820, sold much of the national domain on credit. The Jeffersonians also adopted a policy of intimidation toward the Indians east of the Mississippi, forcing them to cede their lands to the national government, and acted aggressively against French and Spanish possessions in the New World, which led to the Louisiana Purchase in 1803 and the acquisition of Florida in 1819.

Jeffersonian land policy tried to bring about a settled and orderly development of the West; this was the central philosophy behind the rectangular land system that had been borrowed from New England and adopted by the Continental Congress under Jefferson's leadership during the 1780s. Jeffersonian land policy also encouraged a spirit of business enterprise in the West. It emphasized the importance of contiguous settlement, and those sections of the national domain conducive to commercial development were the first to be surveyed and put up for public sale. Squatters who randomly settled on the public domain, often in areas outside the market economy, were treated harshly. These unauthorized settlers suffered financial penalties and occasionally were removed by the military.[12] As Richard Rush, secretary of the treasury under John Quincy Adams, put it, "It is a proposition too plain to require elucidation, that the creation of capital is retarded, rather than accelerated, by the diffusion of a thin population over a great surface of soil. Anything that may serve to hold back this tendency to diffusion from racing too far, and too long, into an extreme, can scarcely prove otherwise than salutary."[13]

To ensure the commercial development of the country and especially the West, many Jeffersonians favored a nationally financed system of internal improvements, broadly defined to include not only river clearance and the building of roads and canals but also various educational, scientific, and literary institutions. Jefferson declared in his sixth annual message to Congress that as a consequence of this policy "new channels of communication will be opened between the states, the lines of separation will disappear, their interests will be identified and their union cemented by new and indissoluble ties." Not only would a national system of internal improvements bind the country together; it would provide opportunities for growing numbers of people to participate in the market economy. The ensuing spirit of enterprise, it was believed, would have an uplifting effect on the morals and behavior of individuals who, because of inadequate transportation and other circumstances, had not been able to engage extensively in commerce. People outside the market economy, Peter B. Porter believed, did not work hard enough, and this had "the most disastrous effects, not only on the industry but upon the morals of the inhabitants." It created "idleness and dissipation." Simply put, many Jeffersonians believed the spread of commerce was good for the people.[14]

The attempt to implement a federal program of internal improvements began in Jefferson's first administration. The Ohio Enabling Act of 1802, by which the state entered the union, provided for the federal government to retain title to all ungranted tracts within the state's boundaries. It set aside one section in each township for educational purposes and provided that 5 percent of the proceeds from the sale of its public lands were to be used to build roads to connect the state with the east. A short time later, a national road was started, stretching from Maryland into Pennsylvania and through western Virginia into the Old Northwest. In 1808, Gallatin presented an elaborate plan for a national system of internal improvements that provided for a complex of roads and canals to link the different parts of the country together. Strong support for these developments came from Joel Barlow,

Robert Fulton, Henry Gilpin, Porter, and eventually Henry Clay, John C. Calhoun, and John Quincy Adams.

These policies raised a variety of political and constitutional problems. How were the different sites and routes to be chosen? Who would control or maintain them—the states or the federal government? Should the state have a veto power over the decisions of the federal government that affected their lands and citizens? Jefferson denied that the "general welfare" clause of the Constitution, as some argued, gave the federal government the authority to act without consulting the state in these matters. He, therefore, requested an amendment to the Constitution to clarify the issues involved. As it turned out, the difficulties in foreign affairs and the economic hard times that dominated the end of Jefferson's second administration forced the matter to be postponed. It was not taken up again until after the War of 1812, by which time Jefferson had retired from politics. But his successors, James Madison and James Monroe, both followed Jefferson's admonition and insisted upon a constitutional amendment. When Congress refused to go along with this, and tried to establish a federally controlled system of improvements, they vetoed the measures. In spite of this, the building of roads and canals went on apace, undertaken by the state governments and by private enterprise.[15]

The encouragement and protection of industry was another important facet of the Jeffersonian program for American economic development. During the 1790s the artisans and skilled laborers who made up the manufacturing sector of the American economy had become increasing disillusioned with Hamilton's financial system, which did little to further their interests and even encouraged people to satisfy their demands for manufactured products through imports from Great Britain. By 1800, the artisans and skilled laborers in the urban areas south of New England had become an important part of the victorious Jeffersonian coalition. After 1806, with the adoption of the Embargo and Nonintercourse Acts, and during the War of 1812, when trade with Great Britain was suspended, American manufacturers began to play an increasingly important role in the domestic economy. But, after the end of the War of 1812, the manufacturing sector of the American economy found itself in serious trouble because the British, whose industry was far more advanced and who could produce goods that were cheaper and of higher quality, actually began to sell their goods at a loss in America in order to put their emerging rivals out of business.

The tariff of 1816 placed a duty of 25 percent on most woolen, cotton, and iron manufactured goods imported into the country. Opposition came from New England, which was dominated by its commercial interests. The strongest support for the tariff came from the Middle Atlantic states and the Northwest, where American manufacturing interests were most firmly established. The South was divided. Most southerners wanted to keep the cost of manufactured goods as low as possible, and therefore voted against the measure. But enough southerners adopted a spirit of generous nationalism and supported the measure because, even though it was not in their direct interest to do so, they believed it was in the country's interest to develop a more balanced economy.[16]

Banking was another important issue for the Jeffersonians. Critical of Federalist control of the banking system during the 1790s, enterprise-oriented Jeffersonians greatly expanded the number of banks during the first two decades of the nineteenth century. In 1791, there were only three state-chartered banks; by 1800 their number had increased to twenty-nine. Serving mainly commercial interests, they were conservatively run operations making loans mainly to merchants for short periods of time: 30 to 120 days. During the Jeffersonian ascendancy, the number of these state-chartered banks increased to 90 by 1811 and to almost 250 by 1816. By 1820, they exceeded 300 in number. These banks did much more to service the agricultural sector of the economy than did their Federalist counterparts, for they made loans for longer periods of time—often two to five years—which facilitated the purchase of land and slaves and the planting of crops.

To be sure, the growth of state banking under the Jeffersonians created problems. Many of the banks were inadequately capitalized and overextended their loans. The result was inflation, and a large number of state banks suspended specie payment on their notes during the War of 1812. Despite this, the expansion in the number of state banks contributed in an important way to the spread of the market economy. These banks provided a medium of exchange that allowed an increasing number of people to buy and sell goods, to purchase land, to raise crops for sale, and to develop and expand new and existing commercial centers. Older urban areas like New York, Philadelphia, Baltimore, and New Orleans grew rapidly during the first two decades of the nineteenth century, and boom towns like Pittsburgh, Lexington, Louisville, Cincinnati, St. Louis, Rochester, Nashville, Huntsville, and Milledgeville quickly emerged as a result of the capital state banks provided.[17]

Taken as a whole, the Jeffersonian scheme of political economy became known as the American System. Its purpose was to establish prosperity, promote employment, create wealth, and further the commercial development of the United States. It stressed the need for a diversified economy that balanced agriculture, manufactures, and commerce. Its aim was to create an internal economy that would make the United States economically independent of Europe, and especially of Great Britain. Each section of the country would make its contribution in areas to which it was best suited: the South would specialize in staple exports like cotton, tobacco, and sugar; the West and Middle Atlantic area in grains, meat products, and manufactures; and the Northeast in various commercial and financial services and manufactures. The economy of the entire country would become "a world within itself."[18] The complementary nature of the national economy thus created would defuse sectional tensions. And class tensions would be reduced as prosperity, opportunity, and commercial development leaked down to all levels of society through the spread of the market.

The "Era of Good Feelings" was the political side of the Jeffersonian program promulgated by the party's triumphant commercial wing. It was made possible by the disappearance, after the War of 1812, of the Federalists as a political force on the national level, which in effect created a period of one-party rule. Moreover, Madison and his most important followers were never advocates of the various democratic devices—including rotation in office, a broad suffrage, annual elections, the popular selection of judges, legislative supremacy, and the diffusing of political power through decentralization—that had become popular at the time of the Revolution and that (it was believed) would encourage broad participation in the political process. Instead, they believed politics should be left to elites. They believed in rule by the natural "aristocracy" of the country—people who had earned their positions through merit and achievement, who were wise and virtuous, and who would rule on behalf of the public interest.

The congressional caucus was an important manifestation of the political theory of the Madison-led wing of the Jeffersonian Republican party. Under this system, the Republican members of Congress met as a separate body, a caucus, to determine who would be the party's candidate for president of the United States. This nomination was by far the most significant step in a presidential race, since selection by the Republican caucus was tantamount to election during the first two decades of the nineteenth century. The struggle in the caucus could at times be very sharp, as in 1808, when the Old Republicans failed to deny Madison the nomination, and as in 1816, when James Monroe was selected over William H. Crawford by a mere eleven votes. But once the caucus made its decision, the politicking would stop. No attempt was to be made by the defeated candidates to take their cause to the public.[19] An exception to this occurred in 1812, when DeWitt Clinton, an important Jeffersonian Republican from New York, aligned himself openly with a number of Federalists and other discontented Republicans in order to oppose Madison's re-election. It was a very close election, but Madison won. From that point on, Clinton, who remained a major force in New York politics, was totally proscribed from the national arena. In fact, Madison and Monroe used their control of the federal patronage to strengthen Clinton's opponents in New York.[20] For understandable reasons, therefore, Crawford supported Monroe in 1816, accepted the appointment as secretary of the treasury in his cabinet, and expected to receive the caucus nomination for president in 1824 after Monroe had served his two terms in office.

On the state level, politics was similar in substance if not in form. Local elites controlled the selection of candidates for the state legislature, and personal connections, family ties, and the public's perception of who constituted the natural aristocracy determined who would get the nod. Elections were often uncontested, and even when there was more than one candidate, contests were usually one-sided. The various local oligarchies that came together in the state legislature determined how patronage would be distributed and who would get the land grants, bank charters, and other special privileges associated with the creation of corporations. Open debate took place on occasion, but for the most part the key decisions were made behind the scenes, frequently by way of compromises consciously fashioned to avoid going to the electorate to determine their outcome. That was the way politics operated in most of the states. New York and Pennsylvania were often exceptions because they were large and heterogeneous, with a variety of interests that often were irreconcilable. As a consequence, politics in those states was much more volatile and occasionally led to sharply contested elections.

But New York and Pennsylvania *were* exceptions. Politics during the short-lived Era of Good Feelings between 1815 and 1819 generally operated, on both the national and state levels, in a way sanctioned by Jeffersonian theory: political leaders were chosen because of their demonstrated superiority in education, experience, and accomplishments, and, once in office, they made public policy decisions for the people on the basis of their superior knowledge and discernment. This approach to politics stressed consensus, compromise, and—at least outwardly—a harmony of interests. It also stressed a separation between the making of public policy, which was the job of elites, and participation in the market economy by the mass of the people, which was the object of the American System. This dichotomy worked, at least for a while, but it required prosperity and a preoccupation on the part of most people with getting ahead.

The second decade of the nineteenth century was a period of intense economic development for the United States. During these ten years, and especially during the second half of the decade, the market economy not only took off but also came to dominate the lives of most Americans. The decade opened and closed with hard times, but there was a major difference between the United States' economy in 1810 and in 1820. In 1810, the United States consisted of numerous disconnected local or regional economies. The British Orders in Council, Napoleon's Continental System, and Jefferson and Madison's response to them created hard times in many parts of the United States. But there were also major pockets of prosperity. Such conditions were possible because the economic development of one part of the United States was not linked to the situation in other areas of the country. By the end of the decade, when the panic of 1819 occurred, it is clear that, though the impact of the panic varied across the United States, the entire country experienced the financial crisis and the depression that followed. A truly national economy had been created by the end of the second decade of the nineteenth century, so that hard times in one section of the country had a major impact upon the economic development of other sections.

The intense economic lurch forward that the United States experienced between 1810 and 1820 was the result of a number of separate but converging developments. American shippers had made high profits from the neutral carrying trade during the Napoleonic wars, and this created investment capital. The demand for American manufactured goods grew as a consequence of the reduction of trade with Great Britain after 1806. The economy was further stimulated by government spending on the military during the War of 1812. The extensive military campaigns in the Old Southwest and Northwest and along the Niagara frontier in western New York created an extensive demand for food, clothes, and supplies, triggering the economic transformation of those regions.

Even more significant was what happened after the end of the War of 1812. The defeat of the Indians encouraged western migration. The population west of the Appalachian mountains doubled between 1810 and 1820, and five new states entered the Union: Indiana in 1816, Mississippi in 1817, Illinois in 1818, Alabama in 1819, and Missouri in 1821. Jeffersonian land policy facilitated this development, but the major stimulus was an increase in European demand for American agricultural products. Denied access to American cotton during the war, the British textile industry had built up an insatiable demand. Cotton production spread into the Old Southwest as prices soared. At the same time Europe, devastated by the Napoleonic wars, a series of crop failures, and inclement weather, was having trouble feeding itself. Demand increased and prices rose for American pork, beef, wheat, flour, and other grain products.

Improvements in transportation also played an integral role in the market revolution that swept the United States during the second decade of the nineteenth century. A series of toll roads or turnpikes linked major cities like New York, Philadelphia, and Baltimore to their hinterlands, encouraging small farmers to produce dairy products, vegetables, fruits, and poultry for sale. The introduction of the steamboat after 1815 on the Ohio River complex and its tributaries was another significant factor in America's economic development. It reduced the costs and increased the speed of shipping goods, and allowed commerce to operate in both directions on the rivers. At the same time, the currency and credit needed to facilitate the rapid increase in commercial transactions between 1810 and 1820 was provided in abundance by the proliferation of state banks following Congress's decision not to recharter the first Bank of the United States in 1811.

The spread of commerce and prosperity was more dramatic in some parts of the United States than in others. The economies of Ohio, Kentucky, Tennessee, Alabama, Mississippi, Louisiana, and backcountry South Carolina and central Georgia were totally transformed by the agricultural prosperity that developed after 1815. Much of New York, Pennsylvania, New Jersey, and the areas around Baltimore in Maryland were centers of feverish economic activity. Some growth took place in parts of New England, Virginia, North Carolina, and eastern Georgia and South Carolina, but it was not as spectacular. Other areas such as northern New England, the southern tier and northern parts of New York, the northern tier of Pennsylvania, western North Carolina and eastern Tennessee, and most of Indiana, Illinois, and Missouri (with the exception of St. Louis) were only marginally affected by the market revolution.[21]

Overall, there is no question that the United States went through a period of rapidly accelerating economic growth in the years immediately following the end of the War of 1812. This boom period, driven by rising agricultural prices that lasted until the middle of 1818, was in many ways the practical fulfillment of Jeffersonian economic theory. The penetration of the market economy not only created widespread economic opportunity, but also coincided for the most part with a sharp decline of public interest in the political process. Most people were simply too preoccupied with making money, getting ahead, and reaping the tangible benefits of their success to be concerned with the making of public policy.

Most people did not want to rock the boat. A good example of this mood was the prevailing attitude toward the operation of the state-chartered banks created during the second decade of the nineteenth century. It was widely recognized that these banks lacked adequate capital and specie reserves to back up the numerous loans and the currency they issued. But very few people were prepared to make an issue of it, and those who did were ignored. Condy Raguet, a Pennsylvania state senator and expert on banking, explained the situation in his state to the British political economist David Ricardo in the following manner: "The whole of our population are either stockholders of banks or in debt to them. It is not the *interest* of the first to press the bank, and the rest are *afraid*. This is the whole secret. An independent man, who was neither a stockholder or debtor, who would have ventured the banks to do justice, would have been persecuted as an enemy of society." [22]

The economic boom of 1815–18 was the high point of Jeffersonian hegemony, and it produced a major transformation of the American economy. It was during those years that the spirit of enterprise and commerce became a mass phenomenon in the United States. But the period also had a darker side; it was a time of widespread speculation and rampant inflation. The second Bank of the United States was created in 1816 to deal with the failure of the state banks to provide adequate specie reserves to back up their notes, but instead of adopting a deflationary course, it gave in to the demands of the aggressive and speculative members of its Board of Directors and Stockholders to embrace the opportunities offered by the boom of 1815 to increase loans and profits. The policies adopted by the Bank contributed further both to inflation and to the expansion of the American economy. [23]

The postwar boom had other inadvertent results that created problems in their own right, undercutting the significance of the Jeffersonian success. To begin with, the market revolution turned slavery into a dynamic and profitable institution. The Jeffersonians had never been prepared to deal directly with the slavery issue and how it related to the egalitarian impulses the Revolution had unleashed. For the most part, they considered slavery to be a local problem, to be dealt with on the state level. Although the Jeffersonians did abolish the foreign slave trade in 1808, their other efforts to deal with the problem of slavery were ineffective. Some prominent Jeffersonians were members of the American Colonization Society, founded in 1818 as an attempt to encourage the freeing of slaves by underwriting their transportation back to Africa. Its purpose was to alleviate the racial fears of white slaveholders, who feared retribution from the freed slaves. The society's efforts proved useless, because it did not even keep up with the natural increase of slaves and because those blacks returned to Africa usually came from the ranks of those already freed. There were a few antislavery societies even in the Upper South, but they did not accomplish very much. Many Jeffersonians also believed in the diffusion argument, which claimed that the development of the West would lead to the spread of slavery and thus make it easier to liberate slaves in the future, since the great majority would no longer be so dangerously concentrated in a small part of the country.

The market revolution totally undercut the Jeffersonian position on slavery, such as it was. The increased demand for American staple products led to the spread but not the diffusion of slavery. Slavery became an entrenched and dynamic institution in much of Tennessee, Mississippi, Alabama, and Louisiana. By 1820 it was even threatening to spread into the southern parts of Ohio, Indiana, and Illinois, where it was outlawed. At the same time, a brisk and profitable interstate slave trade developed between Maryland and Virginia, which became breeding states, and the Lower South, where there was a rising demand for cheap labor. By the 1820s, antislavery sentiment in the South was limited to the mountainous regions of the Upper South, to the Quakers, and to various German religious sects found in North Carolina and Tennessee. The peculiar institution was thriving.[24]

Another unforeseen consequence of the market revolution was a growing disparity of wealth, for an equality of opportunity did not produce an equality of result. Despite the existence of much fluidity in the American class system, especially as compared with the European, and the fact that many people increased their standard of living and made significant gains in income, there were many others who either lacked the skills and ability to get ahead or were simply unlucky. Those who were already wealthy, educated, knowledgeable, and experienced in commerce were usually the most successful. In commercial farming areas, there were not only slaves who owned nothing, but also many white farmers who, for whatever reason, did not own their own land and were forced to work for others. And throughout the country, but especially in the cities, growing numbers of skilled journeymen laborers, in addition to the unskilled, were finding themselves permanently relegated to wage-earner status rather than becoming masters of their own shops.[25]

Actually, many of these developments were not new. A disparity of wealth had begun to appear by the second half of the eighteenth century. The greatest opportunities to make money in post-Revolutionary America existed in urban or commercial farming areas, but these same areas were also marked by the greatest social and economic distinctions. In them the wealthiest and the poorest people in the United States coexisted, not always peacefully, together. In social and economic terms, it was in agrarian backcountry and subsistence farming areas that wealth was most evenly distributed and the social structure was most egalitarian.[26] The growth of the market economy in the early nineteenth century increased the number of people living in the inegalitarian commercial areas at the expense of the more egalitarian subsistence farming areas. The resentment and envy created by these developments were held in check by the prosperity that engulfed the country between 1815 and 1818. But they were never far below the surface, and the coming of hard times in the 1820s quickly uncovered them.

A final unexpected result of the market revolution was that, while it certainly led to a growth in the importance of the internal economy as compared with the foreign sector, that growth did not make the United States economically independent from Europe, as many had hoped. If anything, the opposite was true. As a consequence of the market revolution, the American economy became more finely tuned and, therefore, more sensitive to the vicissitudes of the international marketplace. This led, among other things, to the United States being swept into the boom-and-bust cycle that was to characterize economic development in the nineteenth century. It meant the United States economy regularly would undergo periods of intense prosperity and expansion followed by panic and depression. It meant a pursuit of enterprise that caused an increasing number of Americans to be vulnerable to economic forces they could neither understand nor control.[27]

These problems began to emerge by the end of the second decade of the nineteenth century. The panic of 1819 led to the first truly national depression in United States history. It lasted for almost a decade, undermined the Jeffersonian economic and political system, and created the movement known as Jacksonian Democracy.

The causes of the panic can be traced back to changes on the international scene. By 1818 Europe had begun to feed itself, cutting the demand for American food products. English manufacturers, unhappy over escalating cotton prices, looked to India for a new source of supply. Although in the long run Indian cotton did not prove to be a substitute for the tougher fiber grown in the United States, it did, in the short run, lead to the collapse of the American cotton market. About this time, also, eastern Europe went on to the gold standard, and this led to a major drain on specie reserves throughout the world.

The impact of the panic of 1819 in the United States was intensified by the easy credit that had been offered by numerous banks, which now had to call in their loans and demand payment in specie. Beginning in the late summer of 1818, commodity prices declined, businesses failed, unemployment rose, creditors moved against debtors, and there were widespread foreclosures on lands bought with loans that could no longer be paid. The panic of 1819, and the depression that followed, hit hardest in those areas of the country that had undergone the greatest expansion in the 1815–1818 period.[28]

The consequences of the panic of 1819 went far beyond its impact on the economy. It had major psychological, ideological, and political ramifications. Many Americans became convinced that their wild pursuit of wealth, their overconfident optimism, and their uncritical equation of change with progress during the immediate years after the War of 1812 had created an extravagant, corrupt, and immoral society and that the promise of the American Revolution had been betrayed.[29] Widespread unrest and dissatisfaction with the entrenched Jeffersonian leadership quickly became apparent, although in the beginning it was unclear in what direction it would take the country. John Quincy Adams described a conversation he had with John C. Calhoun in May 1820 on "politics, past, present and future," in which the South Carolinian observed: "There has been within these two years an immense revolution of fortunes in every part of the Union; enormous numbers of persons utterly ruined. Multitudes in deep distress; and a general mass of disattention to the Government, not concentrated in any particular direction, but ready to seize upon any event and looking out anywhere for a leader. . . . It was a vague but widespread discontent, caused by the disordered circumstances of individuals, but resulting in a general impression that there was something radically wrong in the administration of government." Adams concurred, noting that "these observations are undoubtedly well founded."[30]

The 1820s saw a growth of interest in politics on the part of enfranchised white males. The older Jeffersonian view, which separated economics and politics and left the making of key public policy decisions in the hands of a wise and virtuous elite, was no longer acceptable. Widespread hostility emerged toward those who had used political influence to gain economic privilege, for there was a growing recognition that government policies could have unequal effects and, therefore, had to be carefully monitored. On the national level, the tariff, public land policy, the need for a general bankruptcy law, and the role of the second Bank of the United States quickly became hotly contested issues.

Some of the bitterest fights took place on the state level. Popular hostility toward bankers and banking corporations were especially intense. A number of banks failed as a result of the panic of 1819, and the ensuing investigations revealed the political machinations and corrupt practices that had led to the granting of their charters. Many other banks suspended specie payments on their notes, causing them to depreciate sharply and leaving those holding them to deal with the losses involved, while at the same time they foreclosed on the property of debtors who could not pay, paid dividends to their stockholders, and gave special dispensations to their officers and members of their boards of directors and political allies who owed them money. Much time was spent adopting legislation to regulate such activities. There was also a widespread demand for stay and replevin acts and for the creation of loan offices to help debtors out, while for their part creditors were equally vociferous in denouncing such measures. Candidates for office were forced to take stands on these issues if they wanted to be elected. They had to know and even pander to the feelings of their constituents. The Jeffersonian scheme of politics was being torn apart.[31]

The 1820s also saw a rebirth of states' rights thought. Much of it came in opposition to decisions of the United States Supreme Court, handed down during the second decade of the nineteenth century, that were both probusiness and extremely nationalistic. These included *United States v. Peters* (1809), *Fletcher v. Peck* (1810), *Martin v. Hunters Lessee* (1816), *McCulloch v. Maryland* (1819), *Dartmouth College v. Woodward* (1819), *Sturges v. Crowninshield* (1819), *Cohens v. Virginia* (1821), and *Osborn v. Bank of the United States* (1824). Major attempts, ultimately unsuccessful, were made to repeal section 25 of the Judiciary Act of 1789, which allowed the Supreme Court to hear appeals of state court decisions involving the Constitution, laws of Congress, or treaties of the United States. Amendments were proposed to the Constitution to limit the powers of the federal judiciary and to make sure the states, rather than the Supreme Court, were the final arbiters in disputes between the states and the federal government. Another proposal authorized the United States Senate to act as a final court of appeals to determine disputes between the states and the nation. There was also growing opposition to a federal program of internal improvements during the 1820s. Ironically, John Quincy Adams's controversial election to the presidency in 1824–1825 finally brought into the White House a National Republican who not only favored such a program on policy grounds, but actually believed it did not require an amendment to the Constitution. But, by this time, support for such a program was so diminished in Congress that it was possible to get only a few minor measures adopted, and these only by means of a clever log-rolling system.[32]

The Missouri controversy of 1819–1821 was another manifestation of the breakdown of Jeffersonian unity and control. Missouri's request for admission to the Union as a state in which slavery would be permitted touched off a long and bitter debate that revealed the concern developing among many Americans over the expansion of slavery. The debate itself uncovered the bankruptcy of Jeffersonian policy on the slavery issue, and to a certain extent was a precursor to the great debate that would slowly come to dominate American politics in the 1840–1860 period. The outcome of the debate, the Missouri Compromise, is also significant because it is a key to understanding the battles over the expansion of slavery into the territories that followed in the wake of the Mexican-American War, the Kansas-Nebraska Act, and the Dred Scott case.

What is much more difficult to assess is the role the Missouri Compromise played in the political revolution of the 1820s. The attempt to prevent Missouri from entering the Union as a slave state was led primarily by James

Tallmadge and John Taylor of New York, who were political allies of DeWitt Clinton at the time, and leading Federalists like Rufus King. These people were critical of, among other things, Virginia's domination of the presidency and the advantage that the three-fifths clause of the Constitution gave the South in the House of Representatives. By highlighting the slavery issue, they hoped to restructure American politics on a sectional basis and come into power. It was the fear of this development that led northern and southern Jeffersonians to compromise their differences and to bury the slavery issue effectively for the rest of the 1820s.[33]

The antislavery forces on the Missouri question were also bucking the resurgent states' rights tide of the 1820s. Advocates of restriction adopted a nationalist position when they argued that Congress had the power to restrict slavery in a new state; this was hardly the dominant or popular position at the time. The antislavery movement, with its strong nationalist overtones was, therefore, an anomaly in the 1820s. For example, antislavery sentiment could be found in Pennsylvania and Ohio, especially among Quakers, but the clamor for states' rights and the hostility to the second Bank of the Unites States was even stronger in these two states. Pennsylvania proposed an amendment to the United States Constitution restricting the headquarters of the Bank of the United States to Washington, D.C., and prohibiting it from establishing branches in any state unless granted permission by that state. Ohio politics during the time of the Missouri controversy was dominated by the state's aggressive action against the Bank of the United States and its hostility to the United States Supreme Court. Disregarding the decision in *McCulloch v. Maryland,* it forcibly collected a fifty-thousand-dollar state tax on each of the branches in Cincinnati and Chillicothe, which effectively made the Bank close down its operations in the state. Even William Pinkney, the great constitutional lawyer, orator, and senator from Maryland, who had so brilliantly espoused the nationalist position on behalf of the Bank in *McCulloch v. Maryland* in 1819, had by the time of the Missouri debates less than a year later switched to a states' rights position. He was now one of the leaders of the southern antirestrictionist position on the Missouri question and argued that new states had the same right as the original thirteen to choose slavery if they so wished. Granted that sectional politics did exist in the 1820s, however, it is important to recall that the East-West division on internal improvements and public land policy was at least as significant as the North-South division over slavery and the tariff.[34]

Of vital importance in any attempt to understand the general thrust of American politics during the 1820s is the presidential election of 1824. By that year, the general broadening of popular interest in politics had discredited the role of the congressional caucus in selecting the Jeffersonian presidential candidate. Although the caucus did meet and selected Crawford of Georgia (at that time secretary of the treasury), it did not mean much, since only 66 out of a possible 216 congressmen attended the meeting. By this time, also, an overwhelming majority of the states chose presidential electors by popular vote instead of by state legislature, further diminishing the influence of entrenched politicians. The other candidates in the election, all of whom denounced the role of the caucus and appealed for popular support, were John C. Calhoun (secretary of war), Henry Clay (speaker of the House of Representatives), and John Quincy Adams (secretary of state). However, the great surprise of the election of 1824 was the emergence of Andrew Jackson.

Well known as an Indian fighter who had won a number of important victories in the Old Southwest and had crushed the Seminoles in Florida in 1818, not to mention as the military hero who had defeated the British at New Orleans, Jackson was a famous but not a political figure. At first, his more established rivals did not take his candidacy very seriously. But his popularity with the voters soon became clear, and his supporters overwhelmed their opponents in every section of the country except New England. In effect, Jackson's supporters ran the first grassroots campaign in the history of American presidential elections. Although no one really knew where Jackson stood on specific issues, his followers pointed out that he had never been part of the established Jeffersonian leadership with which the public had become so disenchanted, and that as a decisive and successful military leader only he was capable of bringing the country back to the original principles of the American Revolution. Roger Brooke Taney of Maryland explained his support for Jackson in 1824 in these terms: "He is honest, he is independent, is not brought forth by any class of publicians, or any sectional interest. He is not one of the Secretaries. He is taken up spontaneously by the people, and if he is elected will owe obligations to no particular persons. . . . I am sick of all Secretary candidates, and would be glad to see it understood that a man must be elected without the patronage of the President . . . or the power of members of Congress, or a combination of mercenary presses, or local interests.[35]

Jackson won a plurality of the popular and the electoral votes in 1824. Because he did not receive a majority of the latter, the Constitution required that the election be decided by the House of Representatives, where John Quincy Adams was selected on the first ballot. This outcome was mainly Clay's doing. He feared Jackson as a formidable rival for western support, and he did not believe Jackson had either the experience or the temperament to be a good president. He also correctly believed that Jackson was no friend of the American System. Following the announcement of Clay's appointment by Adams as secretary of state, angry and disappointed Jacksonians raised the cry of "Bargain and Corruption" throughout the country, claiming that the people's will had been denied—a potent accusation. Jackson's supporters immediately launched their campaign to capture the presidency in 1828.

The important presidential election of 1828 operated on several different levels. First, the Jacksonians broadened even further their popular support. They developed various committees on the local, county, and state levels to direct and coordinate their activities. These committees, in turn, organized numerous parades, rallies, barbecues, militia musters, and other forms of entertainment to mobilize the electorate. In contrast, Adams, despite the appeals of a number of his advisors, did very little to try to attract the votes to his side. He remained very much a Jeffersonian politician, reluctant to engage in campaigning and other partisan activities. He did not even use his extensive patronage powers to further his cause. In fact, early in his presidency, when pushing his unpopular legislative program, Adams urged Congress not "to be Palsied by [the] will of our Constituents." Adams never really understood the political changes that had occurred during the 1820s or that America had become, as one contemporary put it, "a nation . . . agitated with political strife."[36]

Substantive issues, too, were involved in the election of 1828. Adams organized his whole administration and ran for reelection on a platform of the American System. This included not only a protective tariff and the establishment of a second Bank of the United States, but also an ambitious and broadly conceived program of internal improvements that would lead both to the extension of commerce and to the "moral, political, and intellectual" uplifting of the country. The Jacksonians, on the other hand, increasingly advocated limited government, economy, and states' rights. Jackson received strong support in the South, the Old West, and the Middle Atlantic states from people who had strong emotional and ideological ties to Antifederalism and Old Republicanism. This group, which included Thomas Hart Benton, Amos Kendall, Francis Preston Blair, Martin Van Buren, Thomas Ritchie, John Randolph, and Nathaniel Macon, was strongly committed to the view of the origins and nature of the Union that had been articulated in the Kentucky and Virginia Resolutions of 1798–99—a view they believed had been validated by the people in the election of 1800 and then abandoned with the emergence to power of the Madisonian platform and the New Republicans during the first two decades of the nineteenth century.

The desire to reverse this trend and to return the country to plain republican principles, which its supporters justified by invoking what became known as the "spirit of '98," became apparent early in the 1820s. Virginia led the way in denouncing the Supreme Court decisions in *McCulloch v. Maryland* and *Cohens v. Virginia.*[37] But the movement was prominent in other states. The Ohio Legislature in 1820 argued that, by way of the Kentucky and Virginia Resolutions and the election of 1800, the question "whether the federal courts are the sole expositors of the Constitution of the United States in the last resort, or whether the states . . . have an equal right to interpret that Constitution, for themselves . . . [had] been decided against the pretension of the federal judges, by the people themselves, the final source of all legitimate powers."[38]

By the late 1820s, Old Republicanism of the "spirit of '98" kind was the driving ideological force behind the Jacksonian movement. Francis Preston Blair, an important participant in the Kentucky relief struggle of the 1820s who was soon to become editor of the *Washington Globe,* the semi-official Jackson administration newspaper, broke his political alliance with Henry Clay in 1827, giving as his reason that "I never deserted your banner until the questions on which you and I so frequently differed in private discussion— (state rights, the Bank, the power of the judiciary, etc.)—became the criterions to distinguish the parties, and had actually renewed in their practical effects, the great divisions which marked the era of 1798."[39]

Blair was not the only one who switched sides as a consequence of the political changes that occurred in the 1820s. It is well known that Daniel Webster was a Federalist spokesman for the shipping interests of New England at the time of the War of 1812. He opposed a protective tariff and favored states' rights. By 1828, he was a National Republican, a leading advocate of the emerging industrial interests of New England, a proponent of protection, and a particularly articulate spokesman of the nationalist view of the origin and nature of the Union. Also well known is that John C. Calhoun had converted, by 1828, from nationalist and advocate of the American System to nullifier and opponent of protection. But there were also others who changed. Of especial importance was Jackson himself. He was essentially an apolitical figure during and immediately after the War of 1812. His likes and dislikes of people were almost always determined by personal considerations. By 1824, he was fully immersed in the political process and was mending old personal feuds to gain political allies. Before the panic of 1819, Thomas Hart Benton was a wild speculator in the Missouri fur trade; by the late 1820s he had become a proponent of hard money and opposed all banks. Amos Kendall, who became a speechwriter for President Jackson and one of his most important

advisers, followed a course similar to Blair's in the 1820s: he was closely associated with Clay until the issues became much more clearly defined, where-
upon he switched his allegiance to Jackson.

Beyond the specific issues, Adams and Jackson projected very different
images in 1828. Adams's supporters presented him as a well-educated, knowledgeable, and experienced public servant. But his opponents portrayed him
as the privileged son of an unsuccessful ex-president who was Harvard educated and who had spent too much time soaking up the decadent culture of
Europe. They also condemned him for never having had a private career and
for having spent his whole life feeding at the public trough. He was simply
too refined and too urbane, they believed, to deal with the very real and
fundamental problems engulfing the United States in the 1820s. Jackson's enemies viewed him as unfit by temperament, experience, and education for the
highest office in the land. Further, he was a rash, bloody-minded military
man, dangerously inclined to use force to get his way, and thus one who—
perhaps like Julius Caesar—posed a threat to the very existence of the republic. However, Jackson's supporters effectively turned this argument around
and presented him as a natural and virtuous man, a true American who was
born and raised in the South and North Carolina backcountry and who, with
God's blessing, had made his fortune on the Tennessee frontier. Given the
overwhelmingly rural nature of American society in the early nineteenth century, it is no surprise that Jackson easily won the hearts of the American
people in 1828.[40]

Jackson's victory brought an end to the era of Jeffersonian Democracy. The
era of Jacksonian Democracy now began. Moreover, it was the Old Republican value system, which had been pushed aside by the entrepreneurial wing
of the Jeffersonian party in the first two decades of the nineteenth century,
that had reemerged by the late 1820s as the dominant ideological force behind
the Jackson movement.

Once in office, Jackson quickly dismantled the American System and
moved to confront the nationalist interpretation of the Constitution and of
the origins and nature of the Union upon which it was based. He made clear
his opposition to a federal program of internal improvements on both constitutional and policy grounds. He vetoed the rechartering of the second Bank
of the United States. Moreover, in exercising this veto, and in implementing
his Indian policy, he took direct issue with the nationalist claim that the Supreme Court was the exclusive or final arbiter in disputes between the federal
and state governments. Although Jackson played politics with the tariff for a
while, eventually he not only lowered it but also abandoned any commitment
to protection. Jacksonian land policy also tended to be much more favorable

to squatters than had been that of the Jeffersonians. The one question on which the Jacksonians essentially adopted Jeffersonian policy was that of slavery. They viewed it as mainly a local issue over which the federal government lacked jurisdiction. They did not care for the emerging proslavery forces, but they disliked the abolitionists even more. For Jackson and his followers, slavery was a dangerous political issue—one to be avoided.[41]

Despite their numerous political successes, the Jacksonians were never adequately able to come to terms with the market revolution itself. Their philosophy of government was essentially a negative one. It is summed up in such shibboleths as "That government is best, which governs least," and "The world is too much governed." The Jacksonians articulated the darker side of the market economy and, for a while at least, they severed the Jeffersonian-built connection between the federal government and special interest groups, but they never effectively implemented a positive program to change things. They certainly did not return the country to the simpler agrarian economy of the early republic, as many Jacksonians had hoped. It was too late for that. The market revolution had turned the American economy into a much more complex, interconnected, and dynamic one, with a life of its own. It was now an independent variable, no longer dependent upon government support. By the 1830s, the American economy transcended the political process. It was in many ways beyond government control.[42]

It is the inability of the Jacksonians to come to terms with the market revolution itself that perhaps best explains the various paradoxes of the movement. This inability explains why the causes and results of Jacksonian Democracy were so different. It explains why Jackson came into the presidency an advocate of the principle of rotation of office for federal officeholders, only to see that principle transformed into the spoils system. It explains why Jackson's destruction of the second Bank of the United States, which he hoped would lead to the adoption of a hard-money policy, led instead to a proliferation of state banks and an increasing dependence on paper money during the mid-1830s. It explains why Jackson came into power advocating states' rights as a means to achieve majority rule, only to see the argument captured by Calhoun and the proslavery forces during the nullification crisis and converted into a device to protect minority interests. It explains why Jackson tried to stabilize the American economy, only to see it continue to be caught up in an uncontrollable boom-and-bust cycle.[43]

Because the Jacksonians were no more successful than the Jeffersonians in controlling the American economy, the early and mid-1830s proved to be a period of rising prosperity, wild speculation, and inflation. This culminated in the panic of 1837 (whose immediate causes were to be found in Europe), which in turn worsened into a major depression lasting—in the United States—until the mid-1840s. The results of this depression were different from those caused by the panic of 1819, when economic issues had been brought to the forefront of the political process. By the 1840s, the two major attempts to come to terms with the market revolution—the American System and the Jacksonian response—had both become proven failures. The two major political parties, the Whigs, who continued the national republican advocacy of the virtues of the American System, and the Jacksonian Democrats, who were preoccupied with the darker side of the market revolution, continued to debate the leading economic issues of the day: banking and currency problems, a federal program of internal improvements, land policy, and the need for a protective tariff. But this debate lacked the intensity and urgency that it had had during the 1820s and early 1830s and, for many voters, rang hollow as growing numbers of people became disillusioned at the inability of government to come to terms with the changes that had been unleashed by the market revolution or to control the economy. The debate between Whigs and Democrats over economic issues in the 1840s brought a kind of superficial stability to the political process, but below the surface, and especially on the local level, a new set of political issues had begun to emerge. These new issues were social and moral. They included education, temperance and prohibition, women's rights, peace, religious reform, anti-Catholicism, and, of course, slavery. A new phase in American politics had begun.

NOTES

1. The seminal work on this topic is Charles Sellers, *The Market Revolution: Jacksonian America, 1815–1846* (New York, 1991). For an important earlier version see Charles Sellers and Henry May, *A Synopsis of American History* (Chicago, 1963), chaps. 9–11. Also of value are Sean Wilentz, "Society, Politics and the Market Revolution, 1815–1848," in Eric Foner, ed., *The New American History* (Philadelphia, 1990), pp. 51–72; and Harry L. Watson, *Liberty and Power: The Politics of Jacksonian America* (New York, 1990). Both authors place considerable emphasis on "The republican synthesis."

2. Among the more important works that deal with this are: James Henretta, "Families and Farms: *Mentalité* in Pre-Industrial America," *William and Mary Quarterly* 35 (1978): 3–32; Michael Merrill, "Cash Is Good to Eat: Self-Sufficiency and Exchange in the Rural Economy of the United States," *Radical History Review* 3 (1977): 42–71; Christopher Clark,

The Roots of Rural Capitalism: Western Massachusetts, 1780–1860 (Ithaca, N.Y., 1990); Daniel Vickers, "Competency and Competition: Economic Culture in Early America," *William and Mary Quarterly* 47 (1990): 3–29; Allan Kulikoff, *The Agrarian Origins of American Capitalism* (Charlottesville, Va., 1992). For a different interpretation of rural America, see James T. Lemon, *The Best Poor Man's Country: A Geographical Study of Early Southeastern Pennsylvania* (Baltimore, 1972); Robert D. Mitchell, *Commercialism and Frontier: Perspective on the Early Shenandoah Valley* (Charlottesville, Va., 1977); Bettye Hobbs Pruitt, "Self-Sufficiency and the Agricultural Economy of Eighteenth-Century Massachusetts," *William and Mary Quarterly* 41 (1984): 333–64; Winifred Barr Rothenberg, *From Market-Places to a Market Economy: The Transformation of Rural Massachusetts, 1750–1850* (Chicago, 1992).

3. Leonard White, *The Jeffersonians: A Study in Administrative History, 1801–1829* (New York, 1951).

4. Henry Adams, *John Randolph* (New York, 1882) and *History of the United States of America during the Administrations of Thomas Jefferson and James Madison, 1801–1816*, 9 vols. (New York, 1891–96).

5. Joyce Appleby, *Capitalism and a New Social Order: The Republican Vision of the 1790's* (New York, 1983); John R. Nelson, *Liberty and Property: Political Economy and Policymaking in the New Nation, 1789–1812* (Baltimore, 1987); Steven Walts, *The Republic Reborn: War and the Making of Liberal America* (Baltimore, 1987); Paul Goodman, *The Democratic-Republicans of Massachusetts: Politics in a Young Republic* (Cambridge, Mass., 1964); Richard E. Ellis, "The Political Economy of Thomas Jefferson," in Lally Weymouth, ed., *Thomas Jefferson: The Man, His World, His Influence* (London, 1973), pp. 81–95. For a different point of view, see Drew R. McCoy, *The Elusive Republic: Political Economy in Jeffersonian America* (Chapel Hill, N.C., 1980). McCoy stresses the importance of "the republican synthesis" for explaining Jeffersonian attitudes toward economic development. He does not deal adequately, in my opinion, with such key issues as federal land policy, internal improvements, and the expansion of state banking. Important critiques of "the republican synthesis" may be found in the following works: Joyce Appleby, "The Social Origins of American Revolutionary Ideology," *Journal of American History* 64 (1978): 935–58; Jack P. Greene, *The Intellectual Heritage of the Constitutional Era* (Philadelphia, 1983); Isaac Kramnick, "Revisionism Revisited," *American Historical Review* 87 (1982): 629–64; David Lundberg and Henry May, "The Enlightened Reader in America," *American Quarterly* 27 (1976): 262–71; Donald Lutz, "The Relative Influence of European Writers on Late Eighteenth Century American Political Thought," *American Political Science Review* 78 (1984): 189–97; James T. Kloppenberg, "The Virtue of Liberalism: Christianity, Republicanism and Ethics in Early Discourse," *Journal of American History* 74 (1987): 9–33; Daniel T. Rodgers, "Republicanism: The Career of a Concept," *Journal of American History* 79 (1992): 24–31.

6. Richard E. Ellis, "The Persistence of Antifederalism after 1789," in Richard Beeman, Stephen Botein, and Edmund C. Carter II, eds., *Beyond Confederation: Origins of the Constitution and American National Identity* (Chapel Hill, N.C., 1987), pp. 295–314.

7. Richard E. Ellis, *The Jeffersonian Crisis: Courts and Politics in the Young Republic* (New York, 1971).

8. H. C. A. Stagg, *Mr. Madison's War: Politics, Diplomacy, and Warfare in the Early*

American Republic, 1783–1830 (Princeton, N.J., 1983); Donald R. Hickey, *The War of 1812: A Forgotten Conflict* (Urbana, Ill., 1989).

9. Albert Gallatin to Matthew Lyon, May 7, 1816, in Henry Adams, ed., *The Writings of Albert Gallatin*, 3 vols. (Philadelphia, 1879), 1:700.

10. Drew R. McCoy, *The Last of the Fathers: James Madison and the Republican Legacy* (New York, 1989), pp. 9–83.

11. See especially Joseph Story to Nathaniel Williams, Feb. 22, 1815, in W. W. Story, ed., *Life and Letters of Joseph Story*, 2 vols. (Boston, 1851), 1:253–54.

12. Paul W. Gates, *History of Public Land Law Development* (Washington, D.C., 1968); Daniel Feller, *The Public Lands in Jacksonian Politics* (Madison, 1984); Payson Jackson Treat, *The National Land System, 1785–1820* (New York, 1967); Malcolm Rohrbough, *The Land Office Business: The Settlement and Administration of American Public Lands, 1789–1837* (New York, 1968); Benjamin Horace Hibbard, *A History of the Public Land Policies* (New York, 1927); Roy M. Robbins, *Our Landed Heritage: The Public Domain 1776–1936* (Princeton, N.J., 1942).

13. Quoted in Merrill D. Peterson, *The Great Triumvirate: Webster, Clay and Calhoun* (New York, 1987), p. 85.

14. *Debates and Proceedings in the Congress of the United States*, 19 vols. (Washington, D.C., 1834–53), 11:1388–1404.

15. John L. Larson, "'Bind the Republic Together': The National Union and the Struggle for a System of Internal Improvements," *Journal of American History* 74 (1987): 363–87; Joseph H. Harrison, Jr., "Sic et non: Thomas Jefferson and Internal Improvement[s]," *Journal of the Early Republic* 7 (1987): 335–49, and "The Internal Improvements Issue in the Politics of the Union, 1783–1825" (Ph.D. diss., University of Virginia, 1954); Carter Goodrich, *Government Promotion of American Canals and Railroads, 1800–1890* (New York, 1960).

16. Norris W. Preyer, "Southern Support of the Tariff of 1816: A Reappraisal," *Journal of Southern History* 25 (1959): 306–22.

17. J. Van Fenstermaker, *The Development of American Commercial Banking: 1782–1837* (Kent, Ohio, 1965); Bray Hammond, *Banks and Politics in America: From the Revolution to the Civil War* (Princeton, N.J., 1957).

18. Peterson, *The Great Triumvirate*, pp. 71, 501 n. 9.

19. George Dangerfield, *The Era of Good Feelings* (New York, 1952), and *The Awakening of American Nationalism, 1815–1828* (New York, 1965); William G. Morgan, "The Congressional Nominating Caucus of 1816: The Struggle against the Virginia Dynasty," *Virginia Magazine of History and Biography* 80 (1972): 461–75; Charles S. Sydnor, "The One Party Period of American History, *American Historical Review* 51 (1946): 439–51.

20. Craig R. Hanyan, "DeWitt Clinton and Partisanship: The Development of Clintonianism from 1811 to 1820," *New York Historical Society Quarterly* 57 (1973): 309–25; Solomon Nadler, "The Green Bag: James Monroe and the Fall of DeWitt Clinton," *New York Historical Society Quarterly* 59 (1975): 202–25.

21. George Rogers Taylor, *The Transportation Revolution, 1815–1860* (New York, 1951); Douglass C. North, *The Economic Growth of the United States, 1790–1860* (New York, 1961); Stuart Bruckey, *The Roots of American Economic Growth, 1601–1861* (New York, 1965); Diane Lindstrom, *Economic Development in the Philadelphia Region, 1810–1850*

(New York, 1978); Erik F. Haites, James Mak, and Gary M. Walton, *Western River Transportation: The Era of Early Internal Improvement Development, 1810–1860* (Baltimore, 1975).

22. Quoted in Murray N. Rothbard, *The Panic of 1819* (New York, 1962), pp. 10–11.

23. Ralph C. H. Catterall, *The Second Bank of the United States* (Chicago, 1903); Walter B. Smith, *Economic Aspects of the Second Bank of the United States* (Cambridge, Mass., 1953); Hammond, *Banks and Politics.*

24. William W. Freehling, *The Road to Disunion: Secessionists at Bay, 1776–1854* (New York, 1994), pp. 121–43; David Brion Davis, *The Problem of Slavery in the Age of Revolution* (Ithaca, N.Y., 1975); George M. Frederickson, *The Black Image in the White Mind: The Debate on Afro-American Character and Destiny, 1817–1914* (New York, 1971); Frederic Bancroft, *Slave Trading in the Old South* (Baltimore, 1931); P. J. Staudenraus, *The African Colonization Movement, 1816–1865* (New York, 1961); Gordon E. Finnie, "The Antislavery Movement in the Upper South before 1840," *Journal of Southern History* 35 (1969): 319–42; Alice D. Adams, *The Neglected Period of Antislavery in America, 1808–1831* (Boston, 1908); James Oakes, *The Ruling Race: A History of American Slaveholders* (New York, 1982).

25. Jeffrey G. Williamson and Peter Lindert, *American Inequality: A Macroeconomic History* (New York, 1980); Edward Pessen, *Riches, Classes, and Power before the Civil War* (Lexington, Mass., 1973); Douglass C. Miller, *Jacksonian Aristocracy: Class and Democracy in New York, 1830–1860* (New York, 1967).

26. Jackson T. Main, *The Social Structure of Revolutionary America* (Princeton, N.J., 1965).

27. Rothbard, *The Panic of 1819;* William Buckingham Smith and Arthur Harrison Cole, *Fluctuations in American Business, 1790–1860* (Cambridge, Mass., 1935); Reginald C. McGrane, *The Panic of 1837: Some Financial Problems of the Jacksonian Era* (Chicago, 1924); Peter Temin, *The Jacksonian Economy* (New York, 1969).

28. Rothbard, *The Panic of 1819*, pp. 1–23.

29. Sellers, *Market Revolution*, pp. 103–201.

30. Entry of May 20, 1820, in C. F. Adams, ed., *Memoirs of John Quincy Adams*, 12 vols. (Philadelphia, 1874–77), 5:128.

31. Charles G. Sellers, "Banking and Politics in Jackson's Tennessee, 1817–1827," *Mississippi Valley Historical Review* 41 (1954): 61–84; Kim T. Phillips, "The Pennsylvania Origins of the Jackson Movement," *Political Science Quarterly* 91 (1976): 489–508; Donald J. Ratcliffe, "The Role of Voters and Issues in Party Formation: Ohio, 1824," *Journal of American History* 59 (1973): 847–70; Ruth Ketring Nuemberger, "The 'Royal Party' in Early Alabama Politics," *Alabama Review* 6 (1953): 81–98, 198–212; Frank F. Mathias, "The Relief and Court Struggle: Half-Way Home to Populism," *Register, Kentucky Historical Society* 71 (1973): 154–76; Arndt M. Stickles, *The Critical Court Struggle in Kentucky, 1819–1829* (Bloomington, Ind., 1829).

32. Charles Warren, "Legislative and Judicial Attacks on the Supreme Court of the United States—A History of the Twenty-fifth Section of the Judiciary Act," *American Law Review* 47 (1913): 1–34, 161–89; Charles Warren, *The Supreme Court in United States History*, 2 vols. (Boston, 1926); Charles G. Haines, *The Role of the Supreme Court in American Government and Politics, 1789–1835* (New York, 1960); G. Edward White, *The Marshall Court and Cultural Change, 1816–1835* (New York, 1988); R. Kent Newmyer, *Supreme Court*

Justice Joseph Story, Statesman of the Old Republic (Chapel Hill, N.C, 1985); Samuel Flagg Bemis, *John Quincy Adams and the Union* (New York, 1956), pp. 55–97.

33. Glover Moore, *The Missouri Controversy, 1819–1821* (Lexington, Ky., 1953).

34. Herman V. Ames, ed., *State Documents on Federal Relations: The States and the United States* (New York, 1970), pp. 89–90, 93–101; Frederick Jackson Turner, *Rise of the New West* (New York, 1905), pp. 206–14; Paul W. Gates, "Tenants of the Log Cabin," *Mississippi Valley Historical Review* 49 (1962): 3–31.

35. Quoted in Carl Brent Swisher, *Roger B. Taney* (New York, 1936), pp. 121–22.

36. *Niles' Weekly Register* 33 (1827): 241; Robert V. Remini, *The Election of Andrew Jackson* (Philadelphia, 1963); Richard Latner, *The Presidency of Andrew Jackson: White House Politics, 1829–1837* (Athens, Ga., 1979).

37. Richard E. Ellis, "The Path Not Taken: Virginia and the Supreme Court, 1789–1821," in A. E. Dick Howard and Melvin I. Urofsky, eds., *Virginia and the Constitution* (Charlottesville, Va., 1992), pp. 24–52; Gerald Gunther, ed., *John Marshall's Defense of McCulloch v. Maryland* (Stanford, Calif., 1969); "Judge Spencer Roane of Virginia: Champion of States' Rights—Foe of John Marshall," *Harvard Law Review* 66 (1953): 1242–59.

38. "Report of the Joint Committee of Both Houses of the General Assembly of the State of Ohio on the Communication of the Auditor of the State upon the Subject of the Proceedings of the Bank of the United States against the Officers of the State in the United States Circuit Court," *Annals of Congress,* 16th Cong., 2d sess., 1820–21, 1685–1714.

39. Francis P. Blair to Henry Clay, Oct. 3, 1827, in James F. Hopkins et al., eds., *The Papers of Henry Clay* (Lexington, Ky., 1959) 6:1106–7.

40. John William Ward, *Andrew Jackson: Symbol for an Age* (New York, 1955).

41. Latner, *Presidency of Andrew Jackson;* Donald B. Cole, *The Presidency of Andrew Jackson* (Lawrence, Kans., 1993).

42. Temin, *The Jacksonian Economy.*

43. Leonard White, *The Jacksonians: A Study in Administrative History, 1829–1861* (New York, 1954), pp. 300–46; Sellers, *Market Revolution,* pp. 333–48, 355–59; Richard E. Ellis, *The Union at Risk: Jacksonian Democracy, States' Rights, and the Nullification Crisis* (New York, 1987); Temin, *The Jacksonian Economy.*

7

The Crisis of Commercialization: National Political Alignments and the Market Revolution, 1819–1844

DONALD J. RATCLIFFE

I F THE MARKET REVOLUTION is to work as an organizing idea for the Jacksonian era, it must be able to explain the politics. On the face of things, this is no great problem: the centrality of the Bank War and the constant arguments over financial and economic issues can easily be related in general terms to the contemporary experience of economic change.[1] The problem is that the leading exponents of the market revolution thesis apply the idea to politics in such broad terms that it runs foul of detailed evidence that it cannot explain. Their syntheses misinterpret some key episodes, and their interpretations often proceed with scant regard for the known facts of electoral behavior. Charles Sellers in particular writes on occasion as if Lee Benson had never issued his call to make political history more scientific, and his somewhat romanticized account at times bears close resemblance to the bald generalizations of Arthur M. Schlesinger, Jr., about the nature of the Jacksonians' electoral support.[2]

In practice, the detailed evidence of voter behavior does not obviously reflect a socioeconomic division between the advantaged and the disadvantaged, between the commercial classes and the agrarian masses. Countering Schlesinger four decades ago, William Sullivan, Edward Pessen, and others demonstrated the difficulties of determining the political preferences of the working classes.[3] Benson subsequently taught us not to presume the priority of socioeconomic divisions, and his disciples have generally concluded that voters were little influenced by the financial and economic issues that preoccupied national politicians.[4] Some historians, including Roger Sharp, have nevertheless endeavored to show that the issues of the Jacksonian era did divide the electorate along socioeconomic lines, with the more economically advanced constituencies favoring the Whigs and the more backward the Democrats, but their accounts have stumbled over exceptions and contradictions—over the problem of men with similar interests voting different ways, of highly commercial counties producing Democratic rather than Whig majorities.[5] And already the critics have pointed to the lack of electoral evidence to sustain either Harry Watson's or Charles Sellers's version of the market revolution thesis.[6]

The fact is that the American political system only imperfectly reflects the development of the society it governs; not all problems and experiences enter politics or are regarded as appropriate matters for government. Conversely, the political system itself conjures up experiences and allegiances and operating pressures that can act as independent variables, influencing the progress of politics almost regardless of external social realities. For this reason many influences affected the pattern of political conflict in the Jacksonian era that are only indirectly expressions of the market revolution, and so it is highly misleading to describe all that happened in that period as a response to the economic changes of the age.

Yet there is one highly significant—indeed, central—political development of this period that can be explained satisfactorily only in terms of the market revolution. The mid-1830s saw a crisis in the Anglo-American economy that had a disruptive effect on political alignments throughout North America: in Upper and Lower Canada it produced armed agrarian rebellion; in the United States it provoked significant political realignments, which varied according to the existing structure of political loyalties.[7] The main trouble with the market revolution interpretation as we currently have it is that it serves to obscure the colossal impact that the acute commercial crisis of the 1830s had on the pattern of American political conflict. By comparison, it is in many ways a distraction to waste the term *market revolution* on national political developments before 1833, when many varied influences operated to create the confusing pattern of partisan conflict that marked the early stages of the second party system.

After the breakdown of the Republican party in 1819–21, the gradual formation of two competing political combinations had generated, by the end of 1828, a set of loyalties that burned far deeper and proved far more resilient than most recent historians have been willing to allow. In many states— broadly speaking, the Middle Atlantic states, the older half of the Old Northwest, most border states, and Louisiana—the voter formations that sustained the second party system had been largely created by 1828, and the Whig party in those areas was little more than the National Republican party under another name.[8] Even in those northern states where the Antimasons became a significant force between 1830 and 1834, the basic pattern of party loyalties was not disrupted by the insurgency: contrary to fashionable assumption, Antimasonry did not markedly or permanently increase voter participation, nor did it strengthen the opposition to Jacksonianism. Indeed, like the Workingmen's party in New York, the Antimasons tended to drop their independent action as soon as they were faced by a national election that recalled voters to their prior commitments to national parties.[9]

Throughout this formative period, real arguments over the virtues of increasing commercialization appeared in the local politics of many states. The panic of 1819 and the depression that followed had stimulated popular discontent and created demands for redress that had a marked impact on politics at the local and state levels; many states experienced popular rebellions that challenged the position of political and business elites.[10] Yet these rebellions had relatively little influence on the formation of national political alignments in the 1820s, because too many other varied influences affected political behavior.

Critically, the many-sided crisis of 1819–21 had transformed national politics into a contest of sectional interests. On the one hand, the Missouri crisis raised the question of slavery so bruisingly that northern and southern politicians found it difficult immediately thereafter to accept the prospect of the other's leadership. On the other hand, the economic issues that dominated Congress's proceedings after 1821 produced a clear voting alignment that divided East from West: the more heavily populated areas closely connected with the Atlantic in both the Southeast and New England opposed the combined ambitions of the rapidly expanding Middle Atlantic and western states and of interior areas of the Southeast.[11] That cross-cutting cleavage—North versus South and East versus West—explains the basic pattern of the confusing 1824 presidential election. The four-way sectional split was greatly complicated, however, by the peculiar internal political complexities of the Middle Atlantic states, by the multiplication of candidates representing the slaveholding and internal-improvement outlook of the southwestern and Piedmont areas, and by the lack of a viable candidate who could appeal to those who were both antagonistic to slavery and ardent for the American System.[12]

In these circumstances, it is a great mistake to make the central theme of the early 1820s Andrew Jackson's rise as the champion of popular discontents stemming from the market revolution. In 1823–24, Jackson's immediate successes were limited essentially to the Southwest and Pennsylvania. Once brought forward as a local maneuver in Tennessee, he outbid Henry Clay in the new southwestern states because of the clear differences in their records on the Indian question: in 1822, Clay had seemed the obvious candidate for that region until men remembered his criticism of Jackson's single-minded and unrestrained pursuit of the enemy during the Seminole War of 1818.[13] In Pennsylvania, the initial movement in Jackson's favor came from small-time, virtually unknown politicians in the Scotch-Irish areas around Pittsburgh,

and both former Federalists like James Buchanan and Old School Democrats
in Philadelphia jumped on the bandwagon as a means of breaking the allegiance of the Scotch-Irish (and Germans) to the New School Family party
that dominated the state.[14] Though he attracted some support late in the day
in his own right in the southeastern states, Jackson also inherited Calhoun's
strength there when Calhoun threw in his hand after the Pennsylvania de-
bacle. He won North Carolina on a "People's Ticket" that was dedicated to
giving the state's electoral college vote to any candidate who could beat William Henry Crawford—and owed its success partly to the support of Adams
men who had little enthusiasm for an ill-governed general.[15]

Moreover, it is far from clear that Jackson was indeed the most popular
candidate in the country in 1824. His vote in the electoral college owed more
than that of any other candidate to minority votes picked up in states using
the district system, and to votes purloined in shady legislative deals, notably
in Louisiana and Illinois. Some contemporaries tried to calculate what the
nationwide popular vote would have been had every state used the general-
ticket system, assuming that the electoral college votes cast by legislatures had,
in the end, accurately reflected local public opinion. By a perfectly reasonable
counterfactual calculation, these early cliometricians demonstrated that a
more universally democratic system would have given John Quincy Adams a
plurality of the popular vote and made him the leading candidate in the electoral college, with Henry Clay in third place.[16] That result, of course, reflects
the outcome of the popular uprising in New York led by the state's People's
party. This expression of discontent with a ruling group that refused to allow
the people a say in the choice of presidential electors was not primarily an
effort to vindicate DeWitt Clinton (who ran some 16,000 votes behind his
running mate for lieutenant governor, the anti-Clintonian James Tallmadge),
but rather was an attempt by dissident Bucktails to prevent the election as
president of yet another southern slaveholder. And the beneficiary of this
undoubted democratic uprising was not Andrew Jackson but John Quincy
Adams.[17]

Similarly, after 1824 the dominant feature of the newly emerging partisanship was not some nebulous democratic impulse arising from the market
revolution, but a contest for sectional advantage. The need to elect a president
brought the northeastern, northwestern, and border states together behind
Adams in 1825, while the various strands of opposition in the South had
drawn together by the end of 1827. Jackson's presidential claims were irresistible throughout most of the South, especially the Deep South, and his supporters soon began to make significant congressional gains even in Kentucky,

Missouri, and Louisiana. Adams was equally unstoppable in areas settled by New Englanders. In Congress, contests over land policy and internal improvements still produced East-West divisions, but increasingly the growing saliency of the tariff issue and the South's anxieties about its ability to determine the future of its racial minorities ensured that the basic cleavage would be between "negro states and yankees."[18] As John C. Calhoun remarked, the sectional "feeling on the Tariff on both sides" was "much stronger" than over the presidential contest, where the internal divisions within the North made it possible for the candidate of southern political revanchism to win.[19]

Jacksonian successes were scored even in advance of the looming presidential election. In the congressional elections of 1826–27, the Jacksonians began to gain seats in New York, northern New England, and the newer parts of the Old Northwest, a success they expanded upon in the congressional elections of 1828. At the same time, Jackson retained his support in Pennsylvania and some older parts of the Northwest, despite the deep commitment to the American System in those areas.[20] This partisan success derived in part from ethnocultural tensions that encouraged certain distinctive groups to support a Scotch-Irish conqueror of the British, and it undoubtedly expressed a popular resentment of established politicians that had been fostered by socioeconomic tensions and distressful memories of the depression. Curiously perhaps, the local divisions generated by the economic crisis of the early 1820s had more impact on voting alignments in 1828 than they had had four years before. But Jacksonian success also owed more than is usually allowed to the survival in New York and New England of intense party feelings derived from memories of the first party system. Martin Van Buren's contribution to Jackson's triumph was to combine "Genl. Jackson's personal popularity with the portion of old party feeling yet surviving," especially in New York, and so carry a significant bloc of northern voters into alliance with the South in the face of sectional antagonisms.[21]

Of course, each of these influences on party formation in the 1820s may be explained as a response to the market revolution. Differences over slavery have been ascribed to a burgeoning capitalist bourgeois ideology; pressures for Indian removal reflected the demand for the extension of cotton cultivation to satisfy world demand; arguments over internal improvements, the tariff, and land policy obviously concerned issues at the heart of the market revolution; mounting socioeconomic and ethnocultural tensions were a consequence of socioeconomic dislocations brought about by the extension of market relationships. Equally, nostalgia for the old Republican party can be seen as a response to the destruction of the traditional republican value system by market forces. The market revolution obviously provides a binding thread between these phenomena, since each inevitably reflected the major changes of the day.

Yet these responses were widely different in kind and character; and the market revolution concept does not explain why the response took differing forms in different places, among different peoples, at different times. To explain both ardent Jacksonism and insistent Adamsism as reactions against capitalist advance is to produce an explanation that does not explain.[22] The "market revolutionaries" run the risk of explaining so much in terms of the market revolution that the concept comes to be largely meaningless.

The plain fact is that, before 1833, allegiances in national politics in many states could not reflect internal and local conflicts over the virtues of the market revolution because of the preeminence of sectional considerations. As a result, arguments over economic development commonly took the form of disagreement between factions within the dominant party. Thus, in Pennsylvania, in Tennessee, in Georgia, and in much of the Deep South, the Jackson party embraced all sides of the argument over the market revolution.[23] Conversely, in New England, hostility to Jackson as an irresponsible, slaveholding "Napoleon of the Woods" overwhelmed the many local disagreements—including the marked tensions between Calvinists and Unitarians—that would later find expression in contests over Antimasonry.[24] As a consequence, there could be no tie-up there between local conflicts and national party alignments at that time.

Even in cities that had experienced a pronounced social conflict, the early Jackson party was not purely an expression of lower-class discontent. Cincinnati is commonly cited as the prime example of a city where pronounced popular distress and insurgency against a ruling elite after the panic of 1819 contributed to a vigorous and impassioned commitment to Jackson in 1824.[25] Yet so obvious was Jackson's appeal in Cincinnati that politicians of many kinds joined the cause, including long-established members of the city's business elite, and tensions over municipal policy on loans and development continued to divide the party in local elections. By 1827, it was clear that the local party had lost whatever radicalism had once inspired some of its early supporters, and the best-known radical of the early 1820s, James Gazlay, left the party's ranks in February 1828, publicly denouncing its subservience to the "old bankocracy of Porkopolis."[26]

Certainly Jackson himself was not identified as hostile to the market revolution in 1828. Admittedly, he was portrayed in campaign literature as an old Republican hero who stood above the selfishnesses of contemporary America, but no policy statement identified him as antagonistic to the advance of commercialism. The image was perhaps implicitly ambivalent, but so too were many local electoral appeals of the time that extolled Jeffersonian principles of weak, cheap government and yet demanded an ambitious program of internal improvements. Moreover, his attitude toward federal sponsorship of economic development was deliberately shrouded in mystery: his northern supporters presented him as a committed supporter of American System policies, even while southerners trusted that he would repeal what they saw as an abominable and iniquitous system. And what lay at the root of the South's dissatisfaction was not so much antagonism toward the market revolution as the reluctance of thoroughly commercialized planters to contribute to the commercial development of other parts of the country.

The ambiguities of Jackson's position in 1828 ensured that his first administration would not be essentially concerned with the rights and wrongs of the market system or with working out any popular desire to restrain the excesses of commercialization. The new president's primary object was to settle the sectional crisis that troubled the country—and that involved conciliating the South without destroying northern support. Since the president could not safely—or effectively—challenge the protectionist majority in Congress, a major concern had to be to isolate South Carolina, whose anti-tariff demands his advisers knew they could not satisfy. Hence, in December 1829, the only policy Jackson committed himself to was Indian removal, which could tie to the federal government those states most eager to remove their Indians, notably Georgia, which had up to that point been making even more menacing noises than South Carolina.

Similarly, the famous vetoes of 1830 and 1832 were primarily directed at establishing a states' rights basis for the federal government, thus appeasing the Crawfordite "Radicals" of the Southeast. According to the Bank veto message, this restriction of federal power to its "legitimate objects" was the only policy that could hope to avoid "the dangers which impend over our Union." Certainly it is a mistake to construe the Maysville Road veto of May 1830 as an effort to slow down economic development, for Jackson's famous message expressed his "zeal in the cause of internal improvements," accepted the need for government assistance at some level, and looked forward to the day, after the national debt had been paid, when "an accumulating surplus fund . . . may be beneficially applied to some well-digested system of improvement."[27]

Thus, Jackson's masterpiece in his first three years was the maintenance of a balance between competing sectional interests. While effectively cutting back on new federal internal improvement projects, he maintained a markedly "judicious" stance on the tariff issue. He advocated "a fair protection to our own labor," and used his influence to secure a settlement in 1832 that reduced the fiscal burden of the tariff but maintained the principle of discrimination in favor of those products believed to deserve protection. Under the pressure of the nullification crisis, admittedly, Jackson cast away (in Adams's words) "all the neutrality which he had heretofore maintained upon the conflicting interests and opinions of the different sections of the country," and in December 1832 advocated the adoption of a low-tariff policy. But when Congress refused to adopt such a measure, he had little difficulty in accepting the compromise measure engineered by Clay, Calhoun, and John M. Clayton. Far from marking a blow against urbanization and industrialization, the Compromise Tariff of 1833 "save[d] the manufacturers for the time" by maintaining most of the benefits of the 1832 tariff for nine years and ensuring that thereafter even a flat-rate tariff would offer a measure of protection.[28]

At a time when a president had gained power by straddling a variety of issues, it was in the nature of things that his congressional supporters did not vote as a party on such questions—except on the one issue on which Jackson staked his prestige, namely the Indian removal bill.[29] Votes followed sectional interest, and Jackson's policy during his first term did nothing to challenge the consensual view that market development was a good thing. Even the 1832 Bank veto was ambivalent: while rhetorically arguing for the maintenance of old republican values and raising questions about the skimming off of profits by eastern capitalists and overseas investors, the message complained that the Bank bill confined the opportunity to make money to too narrow a group of businessmen—and it specifically expressed the president's willingness to approve a national bank organized on slightly different principles from Biddle's Bank. Hence the election of 1832 could become essentially a vote of confidence by those who had supported Jackson in 1828, without having any sense that these new Democrats were inherently and inevitably hostile to the progress of the market revolution.[30]

But if national political alignments were complex and ambiguous down to 1832, by 1840 the picture had changed considerably. Sectionalism was overwhelmed, for the time being. Abolitionism was brushed aside with the reassurances on slavery agreed upon by Congress in 1835–37. Third parties temporarily disappeared, until the Liberty party raised its futile head in 1840. The South divided within itself, and enjoyed a vigorous internal party conflict through the 1840s. The national party system took on an unusual ideological intensity until at least 1846, and party voting became more common in legislative roll calls. Local and state politics began to be fought along lines dictated by national partisan alignments, and the formations that appeared drew on such depths of loyalty that they survived for nearly two decades, despite the distractions of the territorial issue after 1846. Many historians have recognized that something happened in the 1830s to transform the American party system—though they are not always entirely certain how to account for the transformation.[31]

The best explanation of the phenomenon is that suddenly, as never before, American voters were being asked to approve or disapprove stands taken by national and state leaders on policies relating to economic growth and its concomitant social effects, and these issues related directly to the immediate personal experience of voters. As Harry Watson demonstrated for Cumberland County, North Carolina, such issues had caused deep divisions within the local community before 1832 but had never become the staple of organized party politics; now the conflict in the community was directly and dramatically related to the national party conflict, and the local community divided politically along the preexisting social fault line.[32]

These issues were brought forward to public attention by President Jackson's removal of the federal government's deposits from the Bank of the United States in September 1833, which, to all appearances, irresponsibly plunged the country into recession during the winter months of 1834. The opposition's denunciation of this extraordinary assertion of executive power aroused public awareness and revealed Jackson's doubts about the virtues of contemporary economic institutions and their works. By the beginning of 1834, the president's position was seen to have changed from opposition to Biddle's Bank to hostility to any national bank,[33] and his determination had far-reaching implications for business and for state policy. The immediate consequence in 1834 was a marked swing against the administration in virtually every great commercial city in the nation, and especially in those where the Jacksonians had been strong earlier—notably Philadelphia, Baltimore, Pittsburgh, Cincinnati, New Orleans, and even Albany.[34] The administration's subsequent attempts to tighten control over monetary issues during 1834–36 further alienated many conservative Democrats and provoked a significant internal debate within many of the state parties. Finally, the financial collapse of April 1837 brought on a crisis that demanded government action, but President Van Buren's advocacy of laissez-faire and the separation of government from banking saw the party adopting an increasingly antibank line that completed the polarization of attitudes. The Sub-Treasury proposal became the defining issue of party difference in Congress, and, as Michael Holt has demonstrated, economic influences were the major determinants of election results from 1837 through 1840.[35]

State politics, moreover, now came into line with national politics. In many ways, Jackson's policies had served to decentralize issues and shift the responsibility for furthering the market revolution onto the states. In several states, as in New York and Ohio between 1834 and 1837, the Democratic party agonized over how far it should encourage state monopolies to fill the void created by the demise of the national bank, and in the end the panic persuaded most state parties to prefer the Locofoco position of aborting governmental support of commercial expansion.[36] After 1837, as Roger Sharp has shown, the banking issue dominated state politics, while issues of state debts and the future of state canal and road projects troubled many state governments. In many states, Democrats argued for slowing down developments that used taxpayers' money to benefit the few.[37] Issues that had previously been sectional now became partisan. In Congress, proposals on internal improvements, on land policy, and on the distribution of the proceeds of public-land sales had always raised questions of local interest, but the votes on these issues now increasingly followed party lines. More significantly, perhaps, when the tariff issue raised its head once more in the 1840s, it came to divide Congress along essentially partisan lines: most northern Democrats carried through the logic of their laissez-faire doctrines, while many southern Whigs increasingly appreciated the argument that the protection of industry was an essential part of any governmental program designed to strengthen the national economy.[38] By the early 1840s, the market revolution had conspicuously become central to national as well as state politics.

The centrality of economic issues to political conflict by 1840 is most easily demonstrable in those southern states in which the Jacksonians had been virtually unassailable before 1834. Certainly it is true that extreme states' rights politicians and nullifiers had played a significant role in organizing the rebellion against Jackson in the South; but they proved the least reliable of the Democrats' opponents, as Calhoun and his followers rejected Whig nationalism and turned back to the Democrats as early as 1837. The slavery issue also played a prominent part in the initial campaign of this new oppositional grouping in 1835–36, but Democrats locally and nationally had no trouble demonstrating their own willingness to defend southern institutions. Even before the concessions gained from Congress in 1836, Calhoun was sufficiently reassured to argue that, with consensus on slavery in the South, "we may divide on ordinary political subjects without any great injury to the Country."[39]

These ordinary subjects were the mundane but penetrating issues raised by Jackson concerning the mechanisms of the market revolution. Whatever the nature of the arguments discussed publicly in 1835–36, those southerners

who became Whigs were essentially men alienated by Jackson's financial policies—which they could convincingly blame on the evil influence of his vice
president and nominated successor, Martin Van Buren. As Professor Sellers
pointed out long ago, the southern congressmen who became Whigs were
those who had voted in favor of the Bank of the United States in 1832 and
1834—and disagreements over financial policy continued to disenchant the
more conservative of Jackson's southern supporters in 1835–36.[40] In Tennessee, which, ironically, was to become the strongest Whig state in the nation
by 1839, the alignment in state politics changed from the factional cleavages
of the 1820s: the business elite initially associated with Jackson, including
early presidential advisers as important as Major William B. Lewis and
John H. Eaton, by 1840 had turned to the Whigs. The future policy of the new
opposition in Tennessee may have been cloaked in obscurity in 1835 and 1836,
but once it came to power in 1837, it immediately introduced a state bank and
implemented a program of internal improvements. The natural consequence,
as even William J. Cooper has acknowledged, was the dominance of economic issues in southern politics in the early 1840s.[41]

This conclusion is confirmed by the pattern of voter support evident in
the South by the 1840s. Most students of southern politics now more or less
accept the view proposed by Charles Sellers forty years ago in the *American
Historical Review:* the southern Whigs are commonly seen as more urban and
commercial and "cosmopolitan," the Democrats more rural, isolated, self-
sufficient, and "provincial" in their outlook. Though subsequent historians
of Alabama have rejected Sellers's emphasis on class differences, they have
generally agreed that, by the 1840s, individual voters, regardless of their economic status, were "more likely to be Whigs if they lived in well-developed
economic communities rather than in frontier, or isolated, or more nearly
self-sufficient communities."[42] In Mississippi, Roger Sharp found that the
property valuations of constituencies—which to some extent reflected their
commercial location—correlated impressively with their voting behavior in
1836 and 1844.[43]

Such differences often gave a distinct regional cast to the party division: in
North Carolina, for example, the Democrats did well in older areas that had
no desire for increased government expenditures to promote development,
while the Whigs dominated the market towns and the counties that looked
forward eagerly to state-sponsored internal improvements. On Virginia's
southside, too, William G. Shade discovered that, among voters as a whole,
there were "clear economic differences" between the Whigs and the Democrats. "As elsewhere in the South," he observed, "these differences depended

on the orientation toward the commercial economy implicit in the forms of economic activity rather than the relative accumulation of wealth—what they did rather than how much they owned."[44]

Students of voting behavior in the North, however, have found no such simple correlation with economic character. On the whole, they have been far more impressed by the power of ethnocultural influences, which were undoubtedly all-important for non-British groups, especially in New York and Michigan where those groups faced an influx of New Englanders.[45] With regard to the overwhelming majority of the electorate that was of traditional British background, the ethnoculturalists have demonstrated that large numbers were influenced by their religious orientation. These discoveries, of course, do not contradict the market revolution interpretation, since the voters' ethnocultural outlook could well determine how they reacted to the experience of economic change and how they perceived financial policies proposed by politicians. In particular, many voters aroused by the evangelical revival of the age were understandably attracted by the search for order, social harmony, progress, and improvement that underlay the Whig economic program.[46] Yet most of the evidence for ethnocultural influences on voting is drawn from the 1840s rather than the 1830s; and doubts must exist about the power of evangelical religion over large sections of the electorate, since probably less than half the population were connected with a religious society, and of these a clear majority were women, not to mention minors.[47] So what considerations influenced the others—the majority of the northern electorate?

Their response to the issues of the 1830s is obscured in the election returns because of the complex electoral context in the northern states. In the Deep South, where there had been an overwhelming commitment to the Jacksonians down to 1832, the process of division in 1835–36 reflected fairly fully and accurately the tensions generated by the market revolution. In the New England states, where memories of the old party fight of Jeffersonian days lingered on and Yankee loyalty to National Republicanism had been powerful in the 1820s, the changes in the voting pattern in the 1830s were complicated by a shift of old Jeffersonian Republicans to the Democratic camp.[48] But in the Middle Atlantic states, the border states, and the older parts of the Northwest, a strongly established two-party division existed that had already drawn a large proportion of the electorate into the electoral process. This circumstance ensured that most voters in these states would respond to the financial issues of the 1830s along the lines that their partisan allegiances dictated. Hence the voting returns for most northern states continued to reflect patterns of allegiance established in earlier elections rather than the immediate impact of the Bank War—and so the ethnocultural patterns evident in the returns reflect loyalties created in the 1820s rather than the 1830s crisis of the market revolution.

If the impact of contemporary issues is to be detected in a firmly established two-party system, it can be done—as V. O. Key suggested for the twentieth century[49]—only by examining the slight changes taking place in the voting pattern. These changes may be presumed to reflect, in aggregate, the departure of some voters, the arrival at the ballot box of new voters, and the net result of voters changing sides. When this approach is applied to a large and fairly representative northern state like Ohio, an interesting light may be cast on voter responses to the policy crisis of the 1830s.[50]

The voting returns for presidential elections in Ohio in the 1830s and 1840s primarily reflect the distribution of party support established in 1828. As a result, many highly commercialized counties, like those of southwestern Ohio close to Cincinnati, appear among the Democrats' banner counties. But, already in 1832, minor shifts were appearing in the distribution of support that became even more pronounced in 1836; the overall effect in 1836 was to reduce the Democratic vote by 3.17 percent and so make Ohio a Whig state in national elections until 1848. The same pattern of change reappeared in 1840, despite the unusual excitements that make that campaign appear aberrant. In the 1840s, by contrast, the distribution of votes began to change in other ways, as ethnocultural tensions perceptibly heightened in 1844 and growing concerns over the expansion of slavery disrupted party loyalties thereafter.

These changes in party support reveal several influences on voting between 1832 and 1840 besides the impress of established loyalties. Notably, new immigrants from abroad preferred the Democrats almost regardless of other considerations, but their impact was restricted to a handful of constituencies at this period. Otherwise, one consistent pattern of change appears in the presidential elections of 1832–1840 that had not appeared in 1828 and would not reappear in 1844 or after: as in the southern states, the more isolated counties were returning larger and larger majorities for the Democrats, while the more commercialized counties were showing increasing favor for their opponents.

Every measure suggests that growing involvement in the market system was the common characteristic of Ohio constituencies that swung toward the Whigs. The counties with the largest amount of capital invested in retail dry-goods, grocery, and other stores, those with county towns containing more than twenty-five hundred people, those that possessed banks by 1835, those with significant numbers of men involved in manufacturing, and those in which merchants' capital had increased markedly during the 1830s, all moved consistently away from the Democrats throughout these years. The greatest proportionate growth in the Whig vote came on the open prairies east of the Scioto Valley, where increasingly large herds of cattle were raised for sale in the markets of Detroit, Philadelphia, and Baltimore. Most significantly, all the counties where the character of rural life was revolutionized by new transportation routes—those lying on the canals built by the state between 1825 and 1833 (with one exception where large numbers of German-speaking immigrants were moving in) and those on the National Road, built across Ohio between 1825 and 1840—swung decisively toward the Whigs. A new system of tax valuation had been introduced in 1825 to ensure that those counties that benefited from the state's canal system paid an increasing proportion of the tax bill: wherever valuations increased through the 1830s, so too did preference for the Whigs.[51]

The constituencies that increasingly favored the Democrats, by contrast, either contained increasing numbers of immigrants, notably Germans, or were located in the more backward areas of the state. Several counties in the southeastern hill country, where it was very expensive to make roads, did not share in commercial advance and remained "much out of the world." The northwestern counties, which had been opened to settlement only since 1818, remained a distinctly frontier region, with some counties "mostly all a wilderness" still in 1846. The north-central counties settled more rapidly, but the settlers, according to the *Ohio Gazetteer* in 1837, "being distant from any of the public improvements of the day . . . seem to be behind the age in enterprise and public spirit." This region not only swung toward the Jacksonians in the 1830s, but became the heartland of the irreconcilable "butternut" Democrats later immortalized by Petroleum V. Nasby. In all these areas, rural life continued to operate on the basis of community and reciprocity prevalent before the market revolution.[52]

The discontents of rural industrial workers made little contribution to Democratic strength in Ohio, because the state lacked the new industrial systems of the more advanced parts of the North. Even the putting-out system of organizing domestic manufactures was largely unknown in the state, except within the Cincinnati textile industry.[53] Long hailed as the Queen City of the West, Cincinnati had become by 1840 the sixth-largest city in the nation, and yet its economic life still retained something of a traditional, personal quality, unlike eastern industrial centers such as Lynn, Philadelphia, and New York. Although some factory industry was developing and some old craft industries were being transformed by capitalist methods, most Cincinnati workers were employed in small, unmechanized workshops and remained

close to their employers. Admittedly, labor organizations appeared there between 1827 and 1836 and organized strikes, and worker discontent emerged
again in the bank riots and Working Men's Party of 1842, revealing lower-class
doubts about the benefits of contemporary economic change. Yet the voting
figures suggest that, after 1832, most workers and artisans in Cincinnati
blamed growing poverty and dependency upon Democratic hostility to the
commercial system.[54] Local antipathy to the Bank of the United States had
diminished as the inhabitants came to appreciate the contribution of the
Bank's local branch to the city's recovery and growth after 1825, and the 1832
election saw the city give a majority against Jackson for the first time, though
he still carried the county. Thereafter Cincinnati remained a Whig city until
after 1844, when the continuing influx of German Catholics changed its political character.[55]

By contrast with Ohio, the northern states where the Jacksonian Democrats conspicuously strengthened their position often possessed large numbers who were experiencing the new industrial systems. In southern Massachusetts, northern Rhode Island, and northeastern Connecticut, many
discontented industrial workers had supported the local Antimasonic party;
whereas most New England Antimasons became Whigs, this worker element
in the third party's support—including the shoe-workers of Lynn—appears
to have shifted to the Democrats. This minority among the Antimasons justified their preference partly in terms of old party loyalties, but also on the
grounds that the Antimasonic principle of equal rights logically involved mis-
trust of the chartered privileges of banks, which were inflicting such evident
evils on contemporary society.[56] Similarly, supporters of the Workingmen's
parties of New York, Pennsylvania, and Massachusetts divided between the
main parties, but in New York City those who were most conscious of the
growing clash of class interests suspected Whig mutualism and tended to
favor the Democrats.[57]

This association of the more militant former Workingmen with the Democracy after 1837 did not represent a betrayal of radical principles. Undeniably the Democrats expressed laissez-faire views, but that did not mean they
were essentially entrepreneurial in outlook. What have appeared to historians
as the classic dogmas of liberal capitalism had very different implications for
an essentially undeveloped society. Businessmen knew that what America
needed was improved infrastructure and that a transportation system could
not be created by private enterprise alone, if only because the financial returns
were at best long distant and, in reality, unlikely to materialize. Developmen-
tal capital could be acquired only by using the power of government to confer
special advantages and guarantee loans. Hence to propose the separation of

government and business was to advocate leaving economic development to natural processes in a situation where the factors of production operated to inhibit improvements and the building of commercial institutions. If the implicit threat of radical Democracy to the progress of the market revolution is appreciated, then it becomes easier to accept the logic of the more militant supporters of the "Workie" movements of 1829–1836 who found a political home in the Democratic party of Martin Van Buren.[58]

But market revolutionaries need to do more than simply reconcile the distribution of partisan support with their interpretation. They must also explain the processes by which the policy issues of the market revolution came to dictate the character of party politics. Somehow the Jacksonian Democratic party changed from the pre-1833 ambiguous catch-all coalition with a sectionalist element at its heart to the more ideologically driven political vehicle of the early 1840s. It might be argued that the party, from the start, included elements that were always antagonistic to banks and the credit system, as undoubtedly were those Jacksonians who had previously supported the Kentucky New Court party or the Pennsylvania Old School Democrats,[59] but we still need to understand why that element could win out over the other political groupings in the party that were more sympathetic to the economic changes of the day.

To a remarkable degree, the dynamics of this process have been ignored by political historians. Instead, their approach to the period has remained essentially biographical, revealing only a tentative sense of the precise nature of the pressures operating on politicians at the time. The works of Professor Remini, in particular, maintain the picture of an old-fashioned morality play which the leading market revolutionaries at times accept almost uncritically. The main fault of this Reminiscent tradition is that it focuses essentially on the presidents of the day and on the great orators in the Senate, without analyzing the workings of Congress and the building of legislative majorities in the House.[60]

As Charles Sellers has acknowledged, we need to know far more about the relationship between congressmen and their constituents.[61] After all, at each stage in the evolution of Jacksonian policy, congressmen had to return to their constituencies to secure endorsement for their record: how did the stand taken by a politician in Congress affect his standing at home? In what circumstances could a congressman sustain a voting record contrary to that of his president? If a Jacksonian congressman followed the firm lead of his eccentric and strong-willed president, what processes back home helped to secure that congressman's reelection? How far was the growing radicalism of the Democrats a result of a favorable response from the grass roots that encouraged national leaders to proceed further with their hostility to the corruptions of the banking system and the iniquities of government economic sponsorship? How far, in other words, did biennial decisions within the congressional districts, and indeed within state parties, help to determine the future policy position of the national party?

The Democratic party in Ohio, for example, was deeply divided in 1831–32 over the issue of the Bank of the United States. Many Jacksonian newspapers and state party leaders were favorable to the Bank, appreciating its services to Ohio's recent economic recovery and growth. At the state convention in January 1832, the leadership tried, through control of the resolutions committee, to write approval of the impending recharter bill into the party's platform. However, one member of the committee, the robustly principled old Jeffersonian Benjamin Tappan, summoned up a floor revolt that amended the resolution into a condemnation of the recharter bid. This indication of grassroots feeling was confirmed after the president vetoed the recharter bill in June. Those Democratic newspapers that disapproved of the veto rapidly came into line, under the pressure of party patrons and a readership that approved of anything the president did. And when those Democratic politicians who felt that the veto was a disaster—themselves mainly residents of market towns—went out to canvass the backcountry, they reported, with some surprise, that "the honest yeomanry of the country" had not only read but been persuaded by the veto message. Only those "under the immediate fangs of the Bank" were deserting the cause. This enthusiastic grassroots support effectively made up for the anticipated loss of support in more commercialized areas and convinced many local party leaders of the wisdom of the president's policy.[62]

This situation determined the fate of the Jacksonian congressmen who returned home to Ohio to face reelection after dividing on the recharter issue. In each district there were struggles over the nomination, with most district conventions approving only those incumbents who had voted against overriding the president's veto. In some places, however, dissident Jacksonian incumbents who failed to secure renomination campaigned against the official candidate, and in four marginal districts, incumbents who had opposed Jackson's policies but were still nominally Jacksonians won with the support of the National Republican opposition. In general, the elections in Ohio were a disaster for the official party line, but at least only those clearly earmarked as loyal supporters of the president's policies had won in most of the traditionally strong Jacksonian districts. Similar contests must have taken place in many states in 1832, since the new house, according to Van Buren, had a Democratic majority "which, tho' not half so large as in the previous Congress, was believed to be not only composed of better stuff in general but especially reliable upon [the bank] question."[63]

In the "panic session" of 1833–34, the executive cracked its whip in unprecedented fashion to keep Jacksonian congressmen in line and so prevent the restoration of the deposits and the rechartering of a national bank. When Jacksonian congressmen from the great commercial cities looked for some compromise that might satisfy the economic needs of their constituents, they were bluntly warned off by the White House. Robert Lytle, the Cincinnati congressman, found himself in a cleft stick: on the one hand he was besieged by letters and petitions from constituents demanding a reversal of the president's policy, while the other hand was being wrenched up his back by the president himself. Persuaded to remain loyal to the administration's policy, Lytle returned home to face popular rejection in the local "revolution" that gave the Cincinnati district to the Whigs for the next decade.[64] But if the national party suffered in the great commercial centers in 1834, it also purified itself: of the fourteen Democratic congressmen who had persisted in opposing Jackson over the removal of the deposits in 1834, eleven failed to reappear in the next session.[65]

This evidence suggests that the force of personal loyalty to Jackson played a powerful role in committing his followers to his policies. As a consequence, when the question of a successor came up in 1834, those Ohio Democrats who thought the president's policies politically and economically foolish looked around for a new vehicle acceptable to moderate and sensible men on all sides. They soon discovered, however, that their followers were reluctant to desert a political cause that was seen as involving more than mere loyalty to Jackson. As a consequence, some dissident conservative Democrats who operated in constituencies with overwhelming Democratic majorities were soon scurrying back into the only camp that could offer them a political future.

Most notable among this group was Thomas L. Hamer, who had won his seat in Congress in 1832 in a struggle that offered the voters three different versions of Jacksonism. The incumbent, William Russell, ran as an original Jacksonian whose disillusionment with Jackson's vetoes had made him a National Republican; the official candidate, Thomas Morris, campaigned as a "whole hog" Jacksonian, eagerly supportive of all the president had done; Hamer ran as a loyal Jacksonian who still supported the American System and favored a national bank. Though defeated, Morris was rewarded by the state party with election to the United States Senate, where he vigorously defended Jackson's financial policies.[66] Congressman Hamer, by contrast, became a leading conservative Democrat, constantly out of tune with his party's policies but sustained by an overwhelmingly Jacksonian district that was integrated into the market system and showed increasing favor for the Whig party and its policies. This ability to continue winning seats in the more commercialized areas was vital to the electoral prospects of the Democratic party, but it put conservative Democrats into positions from which they could undermine the policies demanded by the majority of the party. It is mistaken, however, to suggest, as Professor Sellers has done, that the dynamics of the party system served to frustrate the will of the agrarian masses; rather, it was the inertial force of party loyalty that gave the radical Democrats the opportunity to put forward policies that did not necessarily command majority approval in a rapidly commercializing democracy.[67]

Any analysis of the relationship between the market revolution and the pattern of political conflict in Jacksonian America must recognize that the political system possesses internal dynamics of its own that can influence its development almost regardless of external social pressures. The need to put together majorities, the force of party loyalties (sometimes of ancient standing), loyalty to individual associates and leaders, all have to be isolated before the impact of the electorate's current social experiences can be measured. Once that calculation is made, however, a stronger case can be made for the view that differing responses to the market revolution among the electorate had a profound effect on the structure and character of political conflict in the middle and late 1830s. That sudden and decisive impact transformed a party system that primarily reflected sectional antagonisms, with only the middle ground seriously contested between the parties, into a genuinely national contest that saw almost every state internally divided. This broader and deeper party struggle was of great significance for the survival of the nation through the next twenty years, and it was brought about in the mid-1830s by an experience of drastic economic and social change that affected ordinary Americans everywhere in Jacksonian America.

NOTES

1. Daniel Feller, "Politics and Society: Towards A Jacksonian Synthesis," *Journal of the Early Republic* 10 (1990): 135–61, esp. 154–61; Sean Wilentz, "Society, Politics, and the Market Revolution," in Eric Foner, ed., *The New American History* (Philadelphia, 1990); Harry L. Watson, *Liberty and Power: The Politics of Jacksonian America* (New York, 1990);

and Charles Sellers, *The Market Revolution: Jacksonian America, 1815–1846* (New York, 1991). The basic idea behind the thesis may be found in earlier works; for example, Michael F. Holt, "The Democratic Party," in Arthur M. Schlesinger, Jr., ed., *The History of U.S. Political Parties,* 4 vols. (New York, 1973), 1:497–536.

2. Arthur M. Schlesinger, Jr., *The Age of Jackson* (Boston, 1945); Lee Benson, *The Concept of Jacksonian Democracy: New York as a Test Case* (Princeton, N.J., 1961)

3. William A. Sullivan, "Did Labor Support Jackson?" *Political Science Quarterly* 62 (1947): 569–80, and *The Industrial Worker in Pennsylvania, 1800–1840* (Harrisburg, Pa., 1955), esp. pp. 159–207; Edward Pessen, "Did Labor Support Jackson?: The Boston Story," *Political Science Quarterly* 64 (1949): 262–74; Robert T. Bower, "Note on 'Did Labor Support Jackson?: The Boston Story,'" *Political Science Quarterly* 65 (1950): 441–44.

4. Benson, *Concept of Jacksonian Democracy;* Ronald P. Formisano, *The Birth of Mass Political Parties: Michigan, 1837–1861* (Princeton, N.J., 1971); Stephen C. Fox, "The Group Bases of Ohio Political Behavior, 1803–1848" (Ph.D. diss., Cincinnati University, 1973), which has been reprinted in the Garland series of *Dissertations on Nineteenth-Century American Political and Social History* (New York, 1989).

5. For criticisms of James R. Sharp, *The Jacksonians versus the Banks: Politics in the States after the Panic of 1837* (New York, 1970), see the reviews by Michael F. Holt in *American Historical Review* 76 (1971): 1601–2, and James D. Norris in *Journal of Interdisciplinary History* 3 (1972): 367–69, as well as Stephen C. Fox, "Politicians, Issues, and Voter Preference in Jacksonian Ohio: A Critique of an Interpretation," *Ohio History* 86 (1977): 156–63, 165.

6. See the reviews of Watson by Lawrence F. Kohl in *Reviews in American History* 19 (1991): 188–93, and of Sellers by Ronald P. Formisano in *Labor History* 34 (1993): 550–52.

7. Donald J. Ratcliffe, "Responses to British Hegemony: Jacksonian Democracy and the Canadian Rebellions of 1837," paper presented to the annual meeting of the Society for Historians of the Early American Republic, York University, Toronto, Aug. 1990.

8. Charles Sellers, "Who Were the Southern Whigs?" *American Historical Review* 59 (1954): 335–46; Richard P. McCormick, *The Second American Party System: Party Formation in the Jacksonian Era* (Chapel Hill, N.C., 1966).

9. Donald J. Ratcliffe, "Antimasonry and Partisanship in Greater New England, 1826–1836," *Journal of the Early Republic* 15 (1995): 197–237; Jerome Mushkat, *Tammany: The Evolution of a Political Machine* (Syracuse, N.Y., 1971), pp. 121–27; Walter Hugins, *Jacksonian Democracy and the Working Class: A Study of the New York Workingmen's Movement, 1829–1837* (Stanford, Calif., 1960), pp. 3–48; Sean Wilentz, *Chants Democratic: New York City and the Rise of the American Working Class, 1788–1850* (New York, 1984), pp. 201–16, 226–40, 293–94.

10. See, for example, Arndt M. Stickles, *The Critical Court Struggle in Kentucky, 1819–1829* (Bloomington, Ind., 1929); Charles Sellers, "Banking and Politics in Jackson's Tennessee, 1817–1827," *Mississippi Valley Historical Review* 41 (1954): 61–84; Andrew R. L. Cayton, "The Fragmentation of 'a Great Family': The Panic of 1819 and the Rise of the Middling Interest in Boston, 1819–1822," *Journal of the Early Republic* 2 (1982): 143–67; Craig Hanyan with Mary Hanyan, "DeWitt Clinton and the People's Men: Leadership and Purpose in an Early American Reform Movement, 1822–1826," *Mid-America* 73 (1991): 87–114.

11. For voting patterns in Congress in 1824, see *Niles' Weekly Register* 25 (1824): 387; 26 (1824): 113–14, 137, 172–73.

12. Donald J. Ratcliffe, "The Role of Voters and Issues in Party Formation: Ohio, 1824," *Journal of American History* 59 (1973): 847–70.

13. Charles Sellers, "Jackson Men with Feet of Clay," *American Historical Review* 62 (1957): 537–51, delineates the murky origins of Jackson's candidacy, but does not provide clear evidence explaining why the candidacy attracted such popular support in the Southwest. See the letters of local politicians in James F. Hopkins and Mary W. M. Hargreaves, eds., *The Papers of Henry Clay* (Lexington, Ky., 1963) 3:243, 265, 284, 360–61, 427–28, 460, 490–91.

14. Philip S. Klein, *Pennsylvania Politics, 1817–1832: A Game without Rules* (Philadelphia, 1940), pp. 117, 119–20, 249–368; James A. Kehl, *Ill Feeling in the Era of Good Feeling: Western Pennsylvania Political Battles, 1815–1825* (Pittsburgh, 1956), pp. 211–34. For an alternative (but reconcilable) explanation, see Kim T. Phillips, "The Pennsylvania Origins of the Jackson Party," *Political Science Quarterly* 91 (1976): 489–508.

15. Albert R. Newsome, *The Presidential Election of 1824 in North Carolina* (Chapel Hill, N.C., 1939).

16. *Wooster Ohio Oracle*, Aug. 4 and Sept. 8, 1826; *Speech of Mr. John C. Wright, on the Subject of Retrenchment, Delivered in the House of Representatives, Feb. 6, 1828* (Washington, D.C., 1828).

17. The events in New York in 1823–24 are commonly misinterpreted, e.g., in Watson, *Liberty and Power*, p. 80, and in Sellers, *Market Revolution*, pp. 194–97. For a corrective, see Jabez D. Hammond, *The History of Political Parties in the State of New York*, 2 vols. (Albany, 1842), vol. 2, esp. pp. 127, 131, 163, 165, 172–74; Harriet A. Weed and Thurlow Weed Barnes, eds., *The Life of Thurlow Weed Including His Autobiography and a Memoir*, 2 vols. (Boston, 1883–84), vol. 1, esp. pp. 105, 108–14, 117–21, 165–67; William H. Seward, *An Autobiography, from 1801 to 1834, with a Memoir of His Life, and Selections from His Letters, 1831–1846*, ed. Frederick W. Seward (New York, 1891), esp. vol. 1, pp. 60–62; C. H. Rammelkamp, "The Election of 1824 in New York," *Annual Report of the American Historical Association for 1904* (Washington, D.C., 1905), pp. 177–201; Mushkat, *Tammany*, pp. 78–92, 95.

18. John H. Marable to Andrew Jackson, Washington, D.C., Apr. 3, 1826, in John S. Bassett, ed., *The Correspondence of Andrew Jackson* (Washington, D.C., 1926–35) 3:299. See also Kenneth C. Martis, *The Historical Atlas of Political Parties in the United States Congress, 1789–1989* (New York, 1989), pp. 88–91; Daniel Feller, *The Public Lands in Jacksonian Politics* (Madison, Wis., 1984).

19. John C. Calhoun to John McLean, Oct. 4, 1828, in Clyde N. Wilson and W. Edwin Hemphill, eds., *The Papers of John C. Calhoun* (Columbia, S.C., 1977) 10:426.

20. Martis, *Historical Atlas of Political Parties*, pp. 88–89.

21. Martin Van Buren to Thomas Ritchie, Jan. 13, 1827, in Robert V. Remini, ed., *The Age of Jackson* (New York, 1972), pp. 3–7. See also Van Buren to Jackson, Albany, Sept. 14, 1827, in Bassett, ed., *Correspondence of Andrew Jackson* 3:381–82; John C. Fitzpatrick, ed., *The Autobiography of Martin Van Buren* (1920; reprint, New York, 1973) 1:196; Richard H. Brown, "The Missouri Crisis, Slavery, and the Politics of Jacksonianism," *South Atlantic Review* 65 (1966): 55–72.

22. Sellers, *Market Revolution*, pp. 202–300.

23. Klein, *Pennsylvania Politics*; Charles Sellers, "Banking and Politics."

24. Ratcliffe, "Antimasonry and Partisanship."

25. Harry R. Stevens, *The Early Jackson Party in Ohio* (Durham, N.C., 1957), pp. 3–28, 43–47; Ratcliffe, "Voters and Issues," pp. 857–61; Sharp, *Jacksonians versus Banks*, pp. 177–78; Sellers, *Market Revolution*, pp. 167–68.

26. *Cincinnati Western Tiller*, 1826–27, and Feb. 22, 1828. The point is elaborated in Donald J. Ratcliffe, *The Politics of Long Division: Origins of the Second Party System in Ohio* (under final revision), chap. 7.

27. The Bank veto message is conveniently reprinted in George Rogers Taylor, ed., *Jackson vs. Biddle's Bank: the Struggle over the Second Bank of the United States* (Lexington, Mass., 1972), pp. 10–29 (quotation on p. 28). The Maysville veto is reprinted in Remini, ed., *Age of Jackson*, pp. 51–58 (quotation on p. 54).

28. Jackson to Van Buren, Washington, Dec. 17, 1831, in Bassett, ed., *Correspondence of Andrew Jackson* 4:383; Charles Francis Adams, ed., *Memoirs of John Quincy Adams* (1874–77; reprint, Freeport, N.Y., 1969) 8:503, entry for Dec. 5, 1832; Reverdy Johnson to Clay, Baltimore, Feb. 13, 1833, in Robert Seager II and Melba Porter Hay, eds., *The Papers of Henry Clay* (Lexington, Ky., 1984) 8:622. Also see Thomas H. Benton, *Thirty Years' View* (New York, 1859) 1:344–47.

29. David J. Russo, "The Major Political Issues of the Jacksonian Period and the Development of Party Loyalty in Congress, 1830–1840," *Transactions of the American Philosophical Society* 62 (1972): 14; William G. Shade, "Political Pluralism and Party Development: The Creation of a Modern Party System, 1815–1852," in Paul Kleppner et al., eds., *The Evolution of American Electoral Systems* (Westport, Conn., 1981), pp. 93–95.

30. Taylor, ed., *Jackson vs. Biddle's Bank*, pp. 10–29, esp. p. 26. The returns show a high level of correlation between the results of 1828 and those of 1832, despite the intervention of a third party in some states. Shade, "Political Pluralism and Party Development," pp. 83–88.

31. Shade, "Political Pluralism and Party Development," pp. 77–111; Joel H. Silbey, "The Election of 1836," in Arthur M. Schlesinger, Jr., and Fred J. Israel, eds., *The History of American Presidential Elections, 1789–1968* (New York, 1971) 1:577–640; Joel H. Silbey, *The American Political Nation, 1838–1893* (Stanford, Calif., 1991), pp. 16–32; Herbert Ershkowitz and William G. Shade, "Consensus or Conflict? Political Behavior in the State Legislatures during the Jacksonian Era," *Journal of American History* 58 (1971): 591–621; Peter D. Levine, *The Behavior of State Legislative Parties in the Jacksonian Era: New Jersey, 1829–1844* (Cranbury, N.J., 1977).

32. Harry L. Watson, *Community Conflict and Jacksonian Politics* (Baton Rouge, La., 1981).

33. Michel Chevalier, *Society, Manners and Politics in the United States* (1839; reprint, Ithaca, N.Y., 1961), pp. 53, 57, letter of Jan. 11, 1834.

34. *Niles' Weekly Register* 46 (1834): 190, 242, 379, 399–400; 47 (1834–35): 52, 81–85. See also Sullivan, *Industrial Worker*, pp. 195–205; William H. Adams, *The Whig Party of Louisiana* (Lafayette, La., 1973). In some of these cities the swing had first become apparent in 1832; in New York, by contrast, the Whigs won control of the city council for the first time in April 1834, but the Democrats promptly regained control until 1837.

35. Russo, "Major Political Issues," pp. 37–47; Michael F. Holt, "The Election of 1840, Voter Mobilization, and the Emergence of the Second American Party System," in William J. Cooper, Jr., Michael F. Holt, and John McCardell, eds., *A Master's Due: Essays in Honor of David Herbert Donald* (Baton Rouge, La., 1985), pp. 16–58.

36. For New York, see William Trimble, "Diverging Tendencies in New York Democracy in the Period of the Locofocos," *American Historical Review* 24 (1919): 396–421; Ivor D. Spencer, "William D. Marcy Goes Conservative," *Mississippi Valley Historical Review* 31 (1944): 205–24; John A. Garraty, *Silas Wright* (New York, 1949); Mushkat, *Tammany*, pp. 128–84.

37. Sharp, *Jacksonians versus Banks;* Reginald C. McGrane, *Foreign Bondholders and American State Debts* (New York, 1935); John Ashworth, *"Agrarians" and "Aristocrats": Party Political Ideology in the United States, 1837–1846* (London, 1983).

38. Feller, *Public Lands;* Russo, "Major Political Issues"; Thomas B. Alexander, *Sectional Stress and Party Strength* (Nashville, 1967); Joel H. Silbey, *Shrine of Party: Congressional Voting Behavior, 1841–1852* (Pittsburgh, 1967).

39. Calhoun to F. Carter, Fort Hill, Nov. 26, 1835, in J. Franklin Jameson, ed., "Correspondence of John C. Calhoun," in *Annual Report of the American Historical Association for the Year 1899* (Washington, D.C., 1900) 2:358. Richard E. Ellis, *The Union at Risk: Jacksonian Democracy, States' Rights, and the Nullification Crisis* (New York, 1987), points out that in some parts of the South, states' rights arguments appealed in 1832–33 most powerfully to wealthy slaveholders, who rebelled against the Democrats in 1833–34 and presumably found the opposition's economic outlook acceptable thereafter.

40. Sellers, "Southern Whigs," 339–40, and *James K. Polk, Jacksonian, 1795–1843* (Princeton, N.J., 1957).

41. Sellers, "Banking and Politics," 82–83; Paul H. Bergeron, *Antebellum Politics in Tennessee* (Lexington, Ky., 1982). William J. Cooper, *The South and the Politics of Slavery, 1828–1856* (Baton Rouge, La., 1978), considers the slavery issue central to the party division in the South but regards the early 1840s as "The Great Aberration" (pp. 149–81).

42. Sellers, "Southern Whigs"; Thomas B. Alexander, Peggy Duckworth Elmore, Frank M. Lowrey, and Mary Jane Pickens Skinner, "The Basis of Alabama's Ante-Bellum Two-Party System," *The Alabama Review* 19 (1966): 243–76 (quotation on p. 266).

43. The Spearman rank-order correlation was +.771. Sharp, *Jacksonians versus Banks*, pp. 89–109, 334.

44. Marc W. Kruman, *Parties and Politics in North Carolina, 1836–1860* (Baton Rouge, La., 1983), pp. 6–18; William G. Shade, "Society and Politics in Antebellum Virginia's Southside," *Journal of Southern History* 53 (1987): 178.

45. Benson, *Concept of Jacksonian Democracy;* Formisano, *Birth of Mass Political Parties.*

46. William G. Shade, *Banks or No Banks: The Money Issue in Western Politics, 1832–1865* (Detroit, 1972); Daniel Walker Howe, *The Political Culture of the American Whigs* (Chicago, 1979), and "The Evangelical Movement and Political Culture in the North during the Second Party System," *Journal of American History* 77 (1991): 1216–39. Also see Watson, *Liberty and Power*, pp. 177–87.

47. Charles C. Cole, *The Social Ideas of Northern Evangelicals* (New York, 1954), pp. 13–14, estimates that in 1835 one person in eight was a church member (presumably about

one in four of the adult population). In 1842, just under half of those old enough to attend church did so in the town of Hamilton, Ohio, according to one contemporary calculation: *A History and Biographical Cyclopaedia of Butler County, Ohio* (Cincinnati, 1882), p. 336. Richard Carwardine, *Evangelicals and Politics in Antebellum America* (New Haven, Conn., 1993), pp. 43–44, argues that "about 40 percent of the total population" were "in close sympathy with evangelical Christianity" in the mid-1850s. I have expressed my doubts about the ethnocultural interpretation more fully in "Politics in Jacksonian Ohio: Reflections on the Ethnocultural Interpretation," *Ohio History* 88 (1979): 5–36.

48. Donald B. Cole, *Jacksonian Democracy in New Hampshire, 1800–1851* (Cambridge, Mass., 1970); John Niven, *Gideon Welles, Lincoln's Secretary of the Navy* (New York, 1973), pp. 21–149; Paul Goodman, *Towards a Christian Republic: Antimasonry and the Great Transition in New England, 1826–1836* (New York, 1988), pp. 109, 114–15, 117–18, 272.

49. V. O. Key, Jr., *The Responsible Electorate* (Cambridge, Mass., 1966).

50. The evidence for the following paragraphs is presented more fully in Donald. J. Ratcliffe, "The Market Revolution and Party Alignments in Ohio, 1828–1840," in Jeffrey P. Brown and Andrew R. L. Cayton, eds., *The Pursuit of Public Power: Political Culture in Ohio, 1787–1861* (Kent, Ohio, 1994), pp. 98–115.

51. The Spearman rank-order correlation between the new tax valuations and increasing voter preference for the Whigs was +.4703. This is especially impressive in view of the fact that the counties of southeastern Ohio where coal and iron resources were being exploited by 1840—which were all moving strongly toward the Whigs—were poorly endowed with the sorts of agricultural property assessed for tax purposes at the time (ibid.).

52. Henry Howe, *Historical Collections of Ohio* (Cincinnati, 1896) 2:268, 358; 1:956; Warren Jenkins, *The Ohio Gazetteer, and Traveller's Guide* (Columbus, Ohio, 1839), pp. 254, 379–80, 476.

53. Morgan Neville's report, Apr. 20, 1832, in Secretary of the Treasury [Louis McLane], *Documents Relative to the Manufactures in the United States* (1833; reprint, New York, 1969) 2:860–72; Raymond Borycza and Lorin Lee Cary, *No Strength without Union: An Illustrated History of Ohio Workers, 1803–1980* (Columbus, Ohio, 1982), pp. 2–24. Historians should beware of generalizing the striking developments in southern New England, eastern Pennsylvania, and New York City to the remainder of the agricultural North; cf. Watson, *Liberty and Power*, esp. pp. 30, 84.

54. Steven J. Ross, *Workers on the Edge: Work, Leisure, and Politics in Industrializing Cincinnati, 1788–1890* (New York, 1985), pp. 25–63; Borycza and Cary, *No Strength without Union*, pp. 10–11, 15–27.

55. Jean Wilburn, *Biddle's Bank: The Crucial Years* (New York, 1967), pp. 36, 47, 63; Daniel Aaron, "Cincinnati, 1818–1838: A Study of Attitudes in the Urban West" (Ph.D. diss., Harvard University, 1942), pp. 20, 43–44; *Cincinnati Advertiser*, Nov. 7, 1832.

56. Goodman, *Towards a Christian Republic*; Ratcliffe, "Antimasonry and Partisanship."

57. Amy Bridges, *A City in the Republic: Antebellum New York and the Origins of Machine Politics* (Cambridge, Eng., 1984), pp. 22–24, 62–63, 68–70, 103–24. Sullivan, *Industrial Worker*, esp. pp. 199–207, insists that workingmen in general backed the Whigs, especially in major cities; Ronald P. Formisano, *The Transformation of Political Culture:*

Massachusetts Parties, 1790s–1840s (New York, 1983), emphasizes the contribution of the Workingmen's party to the Massachusetts Democratic party. See also Paul Goodman, "The Social Basis of New England Politics in Jacksonian America," *Journal of the Early Republic* 6 (1986): 23–58, esp. 43–47.

58. William G. Carleton, "Political Aspects of the Van Buren Era," *South Atlantic Quarterly* 50 (1951): 167–85. Some historians of the Jacksonian labor movement insist that the Democratic party had little sympathy with social radicalism; see, e.g., Edward Pessen, *Most Uncommon Jacksonians: The Radical Leaders of the Early Labor Movement* (Homewood, Ill., 1969), and Wilentz, *Chants Democratic,* pp. 172–359.

59. Richard Latner, "A New Look at Jacksonian Politics," *Journal of American History* 61 (1975): 943–69; Phillips, "Pennsylvania Origins."

60. See esp. Robert V. Remini, *Andrew Jackson,* 3 vols. (New York, 1977–84), and *Henry Clay: Statesman for the Union* (New York, 1991).

61. Sellers, *Market Revolution,* p. 437.

62. *Columbus Sentinel,* Jan. 17, and 24 and Mar. 15, 1832; Joseph H. Larwill to Amos Kendall, Bucyrus, Sept. 15, 1832, Larwill Family Papers, Ohio Historical Society. This and succeeding paragraphs draw heavily from Ratcliffe, *Politics of Long Division,* chap. 10.

63. Fitzpatrick, ed., *Autobiography of Van Buren,* p. 636.

64. "A. J. D." [Donelson] to Robert Lytle, with postscript from "A. J.," Feb. 26, 1834, and letters from Hamilton County to Lytle, Jan.–June 1834, Robert Todd Lytle Correspondence, Lytle Family Papers, Cincinnati Historical Society; Edward D. Mansfield, *Personal Memories, Social, Political, and Literary, 1803–1843* (Cincinnati, 1879), p. 165. See also Robert V. Remini, *Andrew Jackson and the Bank War* (New York, 1967).

65. Similarly, those Democrats who voted against the Independent Treasury in 1837–38 either failed of reelection or gained election as Whigs. Russo, "Major Political Issues," 34, 43.

66. *Georgetown (Ohio) Castigator,* July 31–Oct. 16, 1832; Benjamin F. Morris, *The Life of Thomas Morris* (Cincinnati, 1856), pp. 60–61, 345–58, 364–85.

67. Sharp, *Jacksonians versus Banks,* pp. 123–59; Sellers, *Market Revolution,* pp. 348–63.

8

Slavery, Antislavery, and Jacksonian Democracy

SEAN WILENTZ

LTHOUGH THE TIME IS FAST GROWING DISTANT, it was once relatively simple to admire the Jacksonian Democrats. Indeed, over the
first half of the twentieth century, the Jacksonians' reputation rose to
levels that few political parties in our history have ever enjoyed. Progressive-
era academics and intellectuals, in rebellion against the genteel tradition,
praised Jackson and his party as pioneers of a democratic agrarianism that
had gone on to give the country some of its better moments. Historians who
came of age in the 1920s read of the Jacksonians as the intrepid foes of American plutocracy, as described in the influential works of Charles and Mary
Beard and of Vernon L. Parrington.[1]

After the crash of 1929, the Jacksonians' standing soared even higher.
Amid the turmoil of the Great Depression and the New Deal, the Jacksonian
Democrats began to look like the spiritual forerunners of the modern reformist Democratic party—the party, supposedly, of the forgotten, down-
trodden farmer and workingman. Historians of diverse temperaments and
backgrounds—Yankee patricians, big-city cosmopolitans, southern liberals,
midwestern neo-Populists—all found reasons to honor the Jacksonian heritage. As if to make matters official, President Roosevelt joined in the eulo-
gies, gratefully looking back to Jackson's presidency—"the struggles he went
through, the enemies he encountered, the defeats he suffered and the victories
he won"—for inspiration and guidance.[2]

The second half of this century has been far less kind to Jackson's legacy. Soon after the publication in 1945 of the celebratory *Age of Jackson* by
Arthur M. Schlesinger, Jr., the Jacksonians began falling victim to what
C. Vann Woodward later described as a "disenchantment of the intellectual
with the masses"—a disenchantment, Woodward added, that was already
"well under way in the forties."[3] The devastation wrought by German Na-
zism and Soviet Communism undermined what had once been a reflexive
identification by liberal intellectuals with mass-based political movements.
The worrisome rampages of Senator Joseph McCarthy in the early 1950s only
deepened intellectuals' misgivings about democratic excesses. By the early
1960s, the Jacksonians were appearing in history books as unheroic ances-

tors of the demagogues of modern times—as rabble-rousing, self-interested, backward-looking pols whose populist rhetoric was just so much claptrap. By contrast, the Whigs, cast by earlier historians as conservative, monied manipulators, began receiving sympathetic treatment as the high-minded, activist, positive liberals of their day.

The later 1960s and 1970s brought yet another turn in historiographical fashion, but little in the way of a reprieve for the Jacksonians.[4] The rise of the civil rights movement and the agitation against the war in Vietnam shattered the ironic liberal consensus mood of the postwar years, particularly among younger scholars. A spirit of revolution, cultural and political, gripped the campuses and produced fresh enthusiasm for the history of popular movements and the oppressed—workers, slaves, American Indians, women. People once dismissed as marginal to American history suddenly became the new historians' major preoccupations. The result might be described (following Woodward) as a reenchantment of the intellectual with the masses.

Unlike their Progressive and New Deal predecessors, however, the new social and radical historians tended to regard the traditional Democratic party with suspicion, even contempt. Outrage at the Johnson administration's Vietnam policies contributed to the anti-Democratic mood. Thereafter, the final breakup of the one-party Democratic South and the subsequent sectional realignment of American politics reminded historians that the Democracy of F.D.R. had been the party of southern segregation as well as the party of liberal reform. And looking further back in time, Jackson's Democratic party appeared to have been the party of slavery, white racism, and imperial-minded manifest destiny—hardly something to inspire up-and-coming young historians. Ever since, the Jacksonians' reputation has languished, mainly because of their record on slavery and race. Today, even those historians who are inclined to sympathize with the Jacksonian Democrats feel compelled to confess, as Harry L. Watson has written, that "racism and support for slavery were . . . logical aspects of Democratic Party ideology."[5]

Recent revisionist scholarship has not completely repudiated the Jacksonian heritage. One of the harsher studies, for example, allows that Jackson and his supporters "asserted the political, civil and moral equality of white male citizens" and "rejected the concept of class hierarchy as applicable to the American nation"—all praiseworthy goals.[6] But the key qualifying words in these assessments are *white* and *male*. Interpreted within the revisionist grid of race, gender, and class, the Jacksonians were at best only one-third admirable—and regarding race, they were repugnant. Jacksonian Democrats, recent works observe, consistently opposed political efforts to tamper with southern slavery and led legislative and judicial efforts to restrict northern free blacks' political and legal rights. Even more than the Whigs (who, overall, were not exactly enlightened on racial matters), the Democrats appealed to the voters with racist slurs, portraying blacks as the subhuman enemies of white men's equal rights and as allies of the crypto-aristocratic money power. To the extent that the Jacksonians were democrats, we are told, they were herrenvolk (that is, master race) democrats whose flattery of the white male masses was explicitly anti-Negro and often explicitly proslavery.[7]

Some of the anti-Jacksonian studies have concentrated on Old Hickory's elevated political standing in the South and on the Democratic party's emergence as a sentinel of the slaveholders' interests. Progressive-era historians, following Frederick Jackson Turner, described Jacksonianism as basically a western frontier movement; New Deal historians, led by Schlesinger, reinterpreted it as a class movement shaped by eastern workers and radicals; today, it is more common to see Jacksonianism portrayed as a southern movement that protected and accelerated the spread of the South's peculiar institution. According to an influential article by Richard H. Brown, the Jacksonian Democratic party was conceived in the aftermath of the Missouri crisis as a guarantor of slaveholders' rights. Building on Brown's contentions, Michael Paul Rogin has described Jackson as a symbol of a "southern majority" position in national affairs, fusing nationalism and support for territorial expansion with support for slavery.[8]

Over the past few years, critics attuned to multiculturalism have expanded this line of argument by shifting attention northward, chastising northern Jacksonians and workers for their racist, proslavery views and asserting that racial identity politics allied the northern and southern wings of the Democratic party. David Roediger, for example, has claimed that white racism permeated the emerging northern working class of the Jacksonian era. With their denunciations of wage labor as "white slavery," Roediger believes, pro-Jacksonian workers and labor leaders drew upon racial as well as class antagonisms, fashioning an ideology of "whiteness" that "at times strongly supported the slavery of Blacks." In a broader consideration of the period, Alexander Saxton has claimed that both the party managers and the rank and file of the northern Democracy were committed to white supremacy and to the preservation of southern slavery—remaining firm in their conviction "that plantation slavery provided the only sure means for quarantining Africans in America."[9]

No fair-minded assessment of Jacksonian politics can dismiss these interpretations out of hand. Democratic aversion to abolitionists and blacks, the insistence by party leaders that the slavery issue be kept out of national affairs, the proslavery leanings of some Jacksonian labor leaders—these matters were all well established in the historical record long before the latest round of academic revisionism began.[10] At times, to be sure, the revisionists may be too quick to detect proslavery motives in every effort by northern Jacksonians to accommodate the South. As John McFaul has pointed out, fear for the fate of the Union—and for the fate of the Democratic party—was the chief factor behind most northern Jacksonian pronouncements about slavery, not active support for slavery as an institution.[11] But in retrospect, whether it was predicated on principle or expediency, the Jacksonian leadership's record on slavery and on attendant racial issues was shabby at best and shameful at worst.

The danger, however, is that, in correcting the pro-Jacksonian writings of earlier generations, current historians have gone too far in the other direction. The old image of the Jacksonians may have exaggerated their liberal egalitarianism; the new image, however, threatens to turn white supremacy into an essential feature of Jacksonian politics, as if racism and proslavery were inevitable ingredients of early nineteenth-century American democratic thought.[12] In what has become a trend toward seeing much of American political history in racial terms, the Jacksonians as a group may well come to be seen as the precursors not of Franklin Roosevelt, but of George C. Wallace and David Duke. Such a jaundiced view, however, not only confuses the expediency of some Jacksonian leaders with race hatred. It also slights those Jacksonians who, as early as the 1830s, took principled stands against slavery and against the racism that justified slavery. It ignores the vital contributions these antislavery Jacksonians made toward enlarging the antislavery cause. It suggests that the Jacksonians left behind a single odious legacy on slavery and race, when in fact their legacy was much more complex.

Part of the problem stems from a common tendency to blur the differences between the Democratic party and the Jacksonian Democracy. It is quite true that, in the 1850s, the party that Jackson helped to found became the primary national political instrument of what its opponents labeled the slave power. Southern defections to the Democrats had created what came to be known as the solid South; and in the North, a long string of doughface presidents and would-be presidents, from Franklin Pierce to Stephen A. Douglas, boasted of their impeccable Jacksonian credentials. In the 1830s and 1840s, however, Jacksonian attitudes toward slavery were less uniform. Southern planters, for example, gravitated to the Whigs, not the Democrats, in the mid-1830s. And over the next twenty years, as the planters switched their allegiances to the Democrats, many once-stalwart northern Jacksonians rejected the party, repelled by its increasingly prosouthern, proslavery stance. "All democracy left the democratic party," the veteran Massachusetts labor Jacksonian Frederick

Robinson later recalled, "and every true democrat that was too intelligent to be cheated by a name, deserted its ranks."[13] As early as 1846, sectional antagonisms had fractured the original Jacksonian coalition; by the time of the massive defections that accompanied the Kansas-Nebraska controversy, Jacksonian Democracy was dead and buried.

With a few exceptions, notably Richard Sewell, current scholars have tried to explain away these events (and sustain the herrenvolk view of Jacksonianism) by attacking the antislavery Democrats as racists. Unlike the sincere abolitionists (so the argument goes), antislavery Jacksonians had no intention of interfering with slavery where it already existed. Indeed, as far as *southern* slavery was concerned, the supposedly antislavery Jacksonians were actually *proslavery* men who feared that emancipation would cause untold thousands of undesirable blacks to emigrate to the North. The dissidents (it is alleged) were chiefly interested in barring blacks from the western territories and in restricting blacks' rights in the free states. Accordingly, beginning in the mid-1840s, they undertook political efforts to halt slavery's spread. At all costs, Alexander Saxton writes, the antislavery Jacksonians insisted "that the entry of Africans, slave or free, into the promised land of the West had to be prevented."[14] Securing that aim required breaking with those Democrats who favored or who tolerated slavery's westward expansion.

There is an ample supply of quotations from antislavery Jacksonians that lend plausibility to these contentions. The Democratic antislavery leader David Wilmot, a favorite target of recent historians, often remarked that he undertook his antislavery efforts on behalf of the white man, not the black man, in order to "preserve to free white labor a fair country, a rich inheritance" in the West. (Wilmot was even more direct in private: "By God, sir," he exclaimed to one associate, "men born and nursed by white women are not going to be ruled by men who were brought up on the milk of some damn Negro wench!") Other antislavery Democrats, wary of appearing overly solicitous of blacks, carefully framed their rhetoric in self-interested terms, claiming that "the question is not, whether black men are to be made free, but whether we white men are to remain free." Some antislavery Democrats, notably the leading lights of New York's Barnburner faction, joined with conservative Democrats in efforts to restrict northern blacks' political and civil rights. And overall, antislavery Democrats were much more prone to resort to racist appeals than antislavery Whigs.[15]

Still, even a brief review of the political and ideological origins of Jacksonian antislavery shows that the racialist interpretation is greatly exaggerated. It was, of course, perfectly possible for antislavery Democrats also to be racists. (Most of them, like most white Americans of the early nineteenth cen-

tury, almost certainly were, to one degree or another.) But it does not necessarily follow that dissident Democrats opposed slavery *because* they were
racists. Although racial anxieties and territorial ambitions swayed some Jacksonian dissidents, other concerns—economic, political, and constitutional—
loomed much larger in the antislavery Jacksonians' writings and speeches.
These concerns were rooted in egalitarian Jacksonian principles about political democracy and economic justice, not in doctrines of white supremacy.
Out of their Jacksonianism, the dissident Democrats forged a democratic antislavery appeal that, at bottom, opposed the perpetuation of slavery in any
form, and in any part of the country. That democratic appeal proved of
crucial importance to the rise of antislavery as a northern mass political
movement.

Jacksonian dissent over slavery began in the 1830s, not the 1840s, and it grew
from controversies over abolitionism, not over slavery in the territories. As
soon as the American Antislavery Society and its allies began agitating for
immediatist abolitionism, mainstream Jacksonian leaders, North and South,
opposed them bitterly—by supporting a ban on abolitionist mailings to the
South, by applauding mob attacks on abolitionist meetings and newspaper
offices, and by voting for the gag rule that tabled abolitionist petitions to the
House of Representatives. The abolition movement, Jacksonian leaders proclaimed, amounted to a conservative plot designed to distract attention from
the crucial banking and currency questions and to drive a wedge between
northern and southern Democrats. Worse, some northern labor Jacksonians
claimed, the abolitionists wanted to free the slaves in order to dispatch them
to the North, where their presence would depress the wages and the status of
white workingmen.[16]

The Jacksonians (it is important to note) were not alone in condemning
the abolition movement. Among the most outspoken, violent, and negrophobic of the antiabolitionists were some leading northern Whigs and ultra-
conservative Democrats. In New York City, it was not the Jacksonians, but
the antiadministration editors James Watson Webb and William Leete Stone
who whipped up racist mobs to attack abolitionist meetings and black neighborhoods. Whig gentlemen of property and standing stirred antiabolitionist
violence in other cities as well. And still elsewhere, individual Whig politicians joined with Democrats in promoting the repression. The "hard" antiabolitionist racism that Saxton has ascribed to the Jacksonians was also ubiquitous among their Whig opponents.[17]

Northern Jacksonians, meanwhile, did not universally support their party
leaders' antiabolitionist campaign. Some of the more prominent dissenting

Democrats endorsed abolitionism outright, among them Amasa Walker, James G. Birney, and (in time) William Leggett. (Likewise, some of the abolitionists, notably Gamaliel Bailey, held strongly pro-Jacksonian views on issues other than slavery.) Other dissident Democrats limited themselves to attacks on slavery, the antiabolitionists, or both. Collectively, however, they established the political and intellectual basis for what would become an irrepressible antislavery division in northern Democratic ranks.

In Massachusetts, the future governor Marcus Morton pronounced slavery "the greatest curse and most portentous evil which a righteous God ever inflicted upon a nation." In New York City, hard-money, prolabor Jacksonian radicals led by Leggett and George Henry Evans lambasted the antiabolitionist mobs and (in Leggett's case) broke with the Jackson and Van Buren administrations over their antiabolitionist policies. In Ohio, the Democratic lawyer and ex-slaveholder Birney began contacting friends about the possibility of forming an independent antislavery political party. In Washington, D.C., Birney's fellow Ohioan, the hard-money Democrat Thomas Morris, took the floor of the U.S. Senate to defend the abolitionists and attack the gag rule—the only senator, of either party, who did so.[18]

Studies of the abolitionist rank and file of the 1830s suggest that these early antislavery Jacksonians helped gain the movement a significant portion of its support. But, lacking anything resembling an independent institutional vehicle, the Democratic dissidents were vulnerable to reprisals from national and state party managers, and the crackdowns quickly followed. Leggett, cut off from party patronage in 1835, was narrowly defeated three years later in a bid for a Democratic congressional nomination, largely because of his antislavery views. Party chieftains castigated other dissenting Democratic editors and lauded mob assaults against them as (in Silas Wright's words) "evidences of the correct state of public opinion." In 1838, Ohio's Democratic legislators denied Thomas Morris reelection to the United States Senate, despite an overwhelming show of support for Morris at the polls. Antislavery, it seemed, was Jacksonian heresy, at least as far as the party's leadership was concerned.[19]

Had the antislavery Democrats and Democratic sympathizers stopped there (or had they converted to the Whig party), they might deserve to be remembered as some historians have described them—as scattered minor exceptions who proved the rule about prosouthern herrenvolk Jacksonianism. Instead, they stuck by both their antislavery politics and their Jacksonian principles, echoing Leggett's remarks that antislavery was "a glorious, and necessary part of democracy" and charging that it was the party regulars, not themselves, who had "deserted the democratic party."[20] The most determined of them became schismatics, joining with abolitionists and antislavery Whigs in the Liberty party in the hope that independent political action might force the Democracy to come to its senses.

Until 1845, the Jacksonian breakaways managed to convince only a tiny sliver of the northern Democratic electorate to abandon its party loyalties. Still, their efforts sustained a fledgling political antislavery movement with marked Jacksonian accents. In Ohio, the hard-money abolitionist Gamaliel Bailey overcame his suspicions of third-party politics, endorsed the Liberty party (and its presidential candidate, his old associate Birney), and went on to become perhaps the most influential antislavery advocate in the West. Thomas Morris also joined the party (and ran for vice president on the Liberty ticket in 1844). In time, the ex-Whig and Democratic sympathizer Salmon P. Chase—who became more closely attached to radical Jacksonian economic ideas the more that he agitated against slavery—emerged as another party stalwart. William Leggett's untimely death in 1839 robbed northeastern antislavery Democrats of their most eloquent voice, but other dissident editors, including William Chaplain of Albany, attempted to fill the void.[21]

Throughout the North (but especially in the western states), antislavery men appealed directly to Jacksonian Democrats, charging that slavery had created "an overwhelming political monopoly"—an insidious force that, in league with the Yankee "aristocracy," had "mobbed, cheated, and gagged" its critics and intended to reduce the "white laborers of the North and South . . . to the condition of serfs." Liberty party campaigners announced that they intended to create a "True Democratic Party," dedicated to the proposition (as one party newspaper exclaimed) that "no man can be a democrat, who is not an abolitionist." And although much remains to be learned about the party's slender political base, studies of western New York and Massachusetts suggest that the Liberty men were especially effective in attracting votes from pockets of antislavery artisans, workers, and nominal Democrats.[22]

Antislavery rumblings emanated from other concerned northern Jacksonians as well, mainly from the radical antimonopoly, antibank wing of the party—men who, for the moment, stuck by the Democracy, but feared that the party had become treacherously hypocritical about slavery. Leggett's old associate Theodore Sedgwick, Jr., was particularly pointed in his observations. "Give us the real issue," Sedgwick demanded in the Democratic New York *Evening Post* in 1840, *"Is Slavery a good or an evil to the free citizens of these states?"* The answer to the question was plain (as Sedgwick went on to elaborate over the next few years). Slavery inevitably "plunged the laboring class into degradation, and made labor itself dishonorable" while it enriched a small slaveholding interest. "The northern man," Sedgwick concluded, "must be false to his education, and blind to his interests, who does not, inch by inch, and hand to hand, resist the extension of the slaveholding power."[23]

Thereafter, amid the political struggles over Texas annexation and the Mexican War, many more Democrats reached the same conclusion—and the antislavery Jacksonians vastly augmented their following. In 1845, when New Hampshire's Democratic managers attempted to read the antiannexationist John P. Hale out of the party, an alliance of so-called Independent Democrats, Liberty men, and antislavery Whigs reelected Hale to Congress and captured control of the state government. Along with the simmering battles between the antislavery Barnburners and the conservative Hunkers in New York, the Hale insurgency persuaded some antislavery leaders that the Democratic party could at last be turned into a national union of antislavery forces. "By taking the name Democrats which justly belongs to us," an excited Salmon Chase wrote to Hale, "& uniting for Liberty for all as the consequence of Democratic principles, we can compel the whole body of the existing Democracy except such parts as are incurably servile to come upon our ground." These predictions proved far-fetched, mainly because there were more "incurably servile" northern Democrats than Chase allowed himself to acknowledge. But the Jacksonian influence in antislavery politics remained strong; and it emerged even stronger in the late 1840s, first during the debates over the Wilmot Proviso, and then during the Van Buren Free Soil campaign of 1848, which gained upwards of 60 percent of its support from nominal Democrats and presaged the utter collapse of the Jacksonian party system.[24]

Without question, the extended political crisis of the 1840s over slavery in the territories marked a turning point in the mobilization of antislavery Democratic opinion. And those debates had unmistakable racialist overtones, touching on the fears of many northern whites that the West would be opened to large numbers of blacks. Yet racial prejudice was not chiefly responsible for the rapid enlargement of the antislavery Jacksonians' political base. Even after 1845, as Sewell has noted, antislavery Democrats "responded primarily to the menace of slavery and the 'Slave Power' and only fitfully and secondarily to the 'curse' of degraded blacks."[25] These responses amplified complaints that the earliest Jacksonian dissenters had begun raising during the fights over abolitionism. (Indeed, one of the remarkable features of antislavery Jacksonianism was the consistency of its main political arguments from the mid-1830s through the late 1840s.) The crisis over the territories did not make racism the central theme of Jacksonian antislavery politics; rather it dramatized the urgency of other themes that antislavery Jacksonians had been proclaiming for more than a decade.

Compared with the radicalism of the immediatist abolitionists and their sympathizers, Jacksonian antislavery ideas were, from the start, decidedly moderate. The anarchist strand that historians have located in the most radical currents of abolitionist thought had no place in the antislavery Jacksonian mind. Dissident Democrats, as pragmatic politicians and principled American democrats, took a dim view of Garrisonian-style attacks on the U.S. Constitution as a satanic pact with slavery. Nor did antislavery Jacksonians (with some important exceptions) propound the sort of racial egalitarianism that inspired many evangelical Protestant antislavery partisans. At times, the antislavery Jacksonians' concern about slavery's effects on whites appeared to outdistance (or even to preclude) any concern for the slaves. "I am not now contending for the rights of the negro," Thomas Morris bluntly stated in 1838, "I am contending for the rights of the free person in the free States." The theme resurfaced in antislavery rhetoric through the 1840s—in David Wilmot's speeches, in the Free Soilers' studied circumspection on racial issues. Yet from the 1830s onward, antislavery Democrats also rejected the racist arguments that justified black *enslavement*—arguments that more conservative Democrats were prepared to accept. Instead, armed with their Jacksonian critique of social and political inequality, they assaulted slavery itself and took steps toward its eradication—all in line with Morris's proclamation, "That all may be safe, I conclude that the NEGRO will yet be set *free*." [26]

At the heart of the Democrats' antislavery beliefs was their fear and resentment of the "slave power"—a term that Morris and other antislavery Jacksonians helped to popularize nearly twenty years before it became a rhetorical staple of the Republican party. Especially to radical, hard-money Democrats, the Jacksonians' raison d'être had been to resist the money power—the interlocking set of monied individuals and institutions, exemplified by the second Bank of the United States, that supposedly exploited the nation's honorable farmers and workingmen. By the mid-1830s, hard-money Jacksonians were sure that Jackson and his administration had the money power on the run—only to discover, Morris observed, that another enemy, slavery, was in league with the Yankee plutocrats. "The slave power of the South and the banking power of the North . . . are now uniting to rule the country," Morris told the Senate. "The cotton bale and the bank note have formed an alliance; the credit system with slave labor. These two congenial spirits have at last met and embraced each other, both looking to the same object—to live upon the unrequited labor of others—and have now erected for themselves a common platform . . . on which they can meet, and bid defiance, as they hope, to free principles and free labor." Whereas orthodox Jacksonians described the slaveholding planters as honorable producers, antislavery Jacksonians ranked the slaveholders among the oppressive aristocrats who had scant respect for ordinary men's rights and liberties. Tied as they were to their southern creditors, northern capitalists would allow no interference with slavery's prosperity and expansion; southern slaveholders, in turn, would undercut *all* workingmen's dignity and equal rights by attempting to stigmatize labor as an estate fit only for slaves.[27]

Part of the Democratic attack on the slave power focused on slavery's damaging economic effects on both the South and the nation at large. Like many of the immediatist abolitionists, antislavery Democrats regarded slavery as a backward system that dishonored work, indulged aristocratic luxury, and retarded commercial development. "Slavery withers what it touches," William Leggett observed, and had sunk the South into a "deadening lethargy." Worse still, slaveholders kept themselves afloat by borrowing and buying on credit from northern financiers and merchants, who had gained their own profits by plundering the wealth of northern farmers and workingmen. In order to preserve the balance of power between the blighted South and the industrious North, the dissidents held, the slave power set its sights on "crippling the energies of the latter."[28]

To achieve these economic ends (antislavery Jacksonians argued), the slave power had to secure command of the nation's politics. And, much as orthodox Jacksonians saw political corruption at the root of the money power's ascendancy, so the dissenting Democrats believed that the slave power's success required curtailing the equal rights of white freemen. The slaveholders' antidemocratic machinations were, to be sure, nothing new: at the nation's inception in Philadelphia in 1787, antislavery Democrats alleged, the southern delegates had successfully united to fend off attacks on slavery and insert the three-fifths clause in the United States Constitution. Gradually, the force of these proslavery protections had weakened as the free state populations grew and as northern criticism of slavery mounted. Undaunted southern slaveholders, however, had managed to win control of federal patronage and to gain the upper hand in Congress, and when these measures failed to silence their critics, the slaveholders and their northern friends fought back with mobs, gag rules, and other assaults on the citizenry's democratic privileges. Foreshadowing later antisouthern arguments, Leggett suspected that these excesses stemmed from a peculiar southern truculence that was rooted in slavery. ("Whence comes the hot and imperious temper of southern statesmen," he asked his readers in 1837, "but from their unlimited dominion over other men?") More often, antislavery Democrats simply claimed that the slaveholders and their allies would stop at nothing to preserve and extend the peculiar institution—including limiting the freedoms of speech and debate in ways, one Michigan paper charged, that "tyrannically subverted the constitutional liberties of more than 12,000,000 of nominal American freemen."[29]

Had they stuck only to their attacks on slavery's backwardness and political perfidies, the dissenting Democrats might have avoided any moral reckoning with slavery. Yet, even as they declaimed in favor of white men's equal rights, they made it clear that their basic objection was to the institution of slavery and not merely to its effects on nonslaves. "The oppression which our fathers suffered from Great Britain," Leggett asserted, "was nothing in comparison with that which the negroes experience at the hands of the slaveholders." Slavery, he continued, defied "the great fundamental maxim of democratic faith . . . the natural equality of mankind." Morris, the self-proclaimed champion of white men's rights, was no less insistent about slavery's moral wrongs. "Who has said that slavery is not an evil?" he asked.

> Who has said that it does not tarnish the fair fame of our country? Who has said it does not bring dissipation and feebleness to one race, and poverty and wretchedness to another, in its train? Who has said it is not unjust to the slave and injurious to the happiness and best interest of the master? Who has said it does not break the bonds of human affection, by separating the wife from the husband, and children from their parents? In fine, who has said it is not a blot upon our country's honor, and a deep and foul stain upon her institutions? Few, very few, perhaps none but him who lives upon its labor, regardless of its misery.

Through the late 1840s, antislavery Democrats repeated unambiguously that they were fighting slavery as well as the slave power—that the buying and selling of human beings was, as one Barnburner paper put it, "a great moral and political evil." "We hold that slavery is an evil, a deep, detestable, and damnable evil, an evil in all its aspects," the Democratic Cleveland *Plain Dealer* declared in 1848, "an evil to the blacks and an evil to the whites . . . an evil that stares you in the face from uncultivated fields, and howls in your ears with its horrid din of clanking chains and fetters, and the groans of wretched bondsmen."[30]

Opposing Negro slavery did not, by any means, imply support for making either freeborn blacks or ex-slaves the social and political equals of whites. Yet, as early as the 1830s, at least some influential dissenting Jacksonians did support black equality as well as black freedom, and they took issue with their negrophobic antislavery allies. Leggett, for example, argued that the United States would be truly democratic only when the "enfranchised spirit" of the ex-slave could "roam on the illimitable plain of equal liberty." Ten years later, the Jacksonian sympathizer Gamaliel Bailey declared that the Free Soilers, in fighting for the True Democracy, were "opposed to the spirit of caste, whether its elemental idea be a difference of color, birth, or conditions." Although the intellectual center of gravity among antislavery Democrats was more conservative on racial matters, at least some of them believed that "the antipathy of race" and "the prejudices of color" (along with "the tyranny of capital" and "the pride of birth") were aristocratic enormities.[31]

But wherever they found themselves along the spectrum of racialist thinking, antislavery Democrats insisted on the basic humanity of blacks and rejected racist arguments justifying slavery. In doing so, they also turned Jacksonian principles regarding labor's rights into a central feature of their antislavery arguments. As numerous historians have noted, prolabor Jacksonians viewed politics (and much of human history) as an eternal battle between the many and the few, the producers and the nonproducers. "All wealth is the product of labor and belongs of right to him who produces it," one Massachusetts Jacksonian succinctly explained, "and yet how small a part of the products of its labor falls to the laboring class!" The institution of slavery, however, raised difficult questions about where to draw the line between the few and the many. If, as proslavery men and orthodox Jacksonians believed, the slaveholders were producers (much like the head of any family farm), then the slaves did not count as part of the exploited many. But if, as the antislavery Jacksonians declared, the slaveholders were nonproducing aristocrats, how did the slaves figure in?[32]

Some pro-Jackson northern labor leaders (as David Roediger has argued) may have dismissed these questions on racist grounds, viewing blacks as inferior creatures who merited slavery. The Jacksonian antislavery dissidents, however, saw matters very differently. To be sure, they often dwelled on slavery's damaging effects on white workers and on how the slaveholders aimed to degrade free white labor. (The Free Soiler Walt Whitman's famous remark that the issue was between "*the grand body of white workingmen* . . . and the aristocratic owners of slaves" was, in this connection, typical of Jacksonian antislavery writings.) Yet the antislavery Democrats also insisted, on familiar Jacksonian grounds, that neither blacks nor whites should be *slaves*, unrequited for their labor. While asserting that slavery threatened to reduce white workingmen to the level of slaves, they upheld a universalist view of producers' rights, not a racialist one.[33]

Thomas Morris, a hard-money Jacksonian on economic issues but hardly a radical in his racial thinking, was among the first to formulate the main dissident Jacksonian arguments on slavery and labor. "Human laws, I contend, cannot make human beings property," he began, "[even] if human force can do it. If it is *competent* for our legislatures to make a black man *property* it is competent for them to make a white man the same. . . . To free a slave is to take from usurpation that which it made property and given to another, and bestow it upon its rightful owner." Just as all persons merited freedom, Morris maintained, so all free persons deserved to be treated equally with respect to their labor, regardless of their color. ("Has not the free black person the same right to the use of his hands as the white person," he asked, "the same right to contract for labor for what price he pleases?") The slave power, however, violated this principle twice over: first, by leaving "one man subjected to the will and power of another, and the laws affording him [that is, the slave] no protection" and second, by viewing labor as the lot of a supposedly "servile race." Subsequent antislavery Democrats repeated the argument, attacking slavery for robbing human beings of "the rights which are [their] natural inheritence," including the right to their labor's product—based on what Free Soiler Benjamin F. Butler called the "great foundation truth" of all men's equal rights to the pursuit of happiness.[34]

Putting these principles into practice, the antislavery Democrats concentrated on limiting slavery's expansion—an aim early dissidents articulated years before the struggles over Texas annexation and the Wilmot Proviso. These efforts were always entangled with widespread apprehensions about the presence of free blacks in the North and the West. (Morris, for example, tried to counter orthodox Jacksonians and allay white racial anxieties by fancifully asserting that, after slavery's demise, northern blacks would migrate to the South, where the climate was "more congenial to their natures."[35]) But the antiexpansionist argument did not signal indifference about slavery where it already existed. Nor did it originate in a desire to keep blacks out of the North and the West. A more powerful set of constitutional concerns led antislavery Jacksonians to become antiextensionists; and it was these concerns that dominated their pronouncements on the subject through the late 1840s.

As good Jacksonians, the antislavery Democrats believed in strict construction of the United States Constitution. By any such construction, the federal government had no power to interfere with slavery in those states where slavery already existed. Yet this did not render the Constitution a proslavery document in the dissident Democrats' eyes (as it did for both Garrisonian abolitionists and proslavery partisans). The founding fathers, Leggett argued, considered slavery "the direst curse inflicted upon our country," and hoped that it would one day be erased "and the poor bondsman restored to the condition of equal freedom for which God and nature designed him." And although the delegates at Philadelphia had wound up giving covert recognition to slavery in the Constitution, it was a "great mistake" to assume that they left "the power of the southern states over slavery *and all its incidents* undiminished."[36]

Combing through the Constitution, Leggett and others found specific provisions that limited slavery's national protections. Article 1, section 4, they charged, gave Congress the authority to abolish slavery in the District of Columbia without compensation to the district's slaveholders—a key abolitionist demand. Article 1, section 9, on the importation of slaves, clearly reduced the states' authority over slavery. Above all, according to antislavery interpretations, the Constitution rendered slavery's legal character purely local in character. National recognition of slavery extended only so far as it applied to certain rights of masters under state laws; otherwise, in Leggett's words, the Constitution "nowhere gives any countenence to the idea that slaves are considered *property* in the meaning of the term as used in the fifth article of the amendments."[37]

The claim that slavery had no legitimacy outside of local and state jurisdictions swiftly became one of the antislavery movement's most effective political weapons. In the 1840s, it inspired even more expansive antislavery constitutional arguments—preeminently those developed by Salmon P. Chase and the Liberty party—that the Constitution was *essentially* an antislavery document, that the Fifth Amendment had been designed to prevent the federal government from establishing slavery within its exclusive jurisdiction (including the territories), and that any slave who departed from a slave state immediately became free. The Free Soil party platform of 1848 proclaimed that "Congress has no more power to make a slave than to make a king," and then called on Congress to fulfill its constitutional duty and ban slavery from all United States territories. A few antislavery radicals took such constitutional arguments to the point of saying that Congress actually *did* have the power to abolish southern slavery by direct legislation. Antislavery Jacksonians did not go that far. But, by insisting that the Constitution did not guarantee slavery, the dissident Democrats also implied that Congress could hedge in the institution and deprive it of federal favors—the same assertion that, as adapted by the Republican party, would inflame the politics of the 1850s.[38]

As for slavery's future, antislavery Jacksonians (including the most racially prejudiced among them) were agreed: limiting its expansion would mark the first important step toward slavery's complete eradication. Few Americans at the time doubted that slavery needed to spread to new lands if it was to survive economically. "What does the past teach us?" Gamaliel Bailey's *National Era* asked in 1847. "That slavery lives by *expansion.*" Depriving the slaveholders of fresh territory would throw them back on depleted soils and seal slavery's eventual doom—all while adhering strictly to the United States Constitution. Even such negrophobic Democratic dissidents as David Wilmot recognized this constitutionist logic, and approved of its outcome. It was clear, Wilmot declared in 1847, that restriction would help to "insure the redemption, at an early day, of the negro from his bondage and chains." Rank-and-file dissidents agreed. "To localize slavery," one New York antislavery Democrat wrote to Martin Van Buren in 1848, would be "the first, heavy blow it received before tottering to its Fall." Restrictionism was not an alternative to abolishing slavery; nor was it an evasion to ensure the safety of Southern slavery and the "quarantining" of blacks. Rather it was, as its proponents saw it, a powerful and perfectly constitutional tool for securing slavery's demise.[39]

As it happened, of course, no such tranquil constitutional emancipation was forthcoming. It took southern secession, civil war, and the ratification of the Thirteenth Amendment to free the slaves. Yet the antislavery Democrats, by helping to force the slavery issue to the center of politics, certainly played an important part in bringing about these revolutionary events. They did so in line with what they thought was their unswerving devotion to Jacksonian principles—opposition to the money power and its slave power ally, protection of white men's equal political rights, support for the rights of all producers (black and white) to the fruits of their toil, strict construction of the Constitution, and adherence to the founding fathers' antislavery intentions. And, although the political storms of the 1850s quickly shattered their original moderate hopes, the dissident Jacksonians adjusted to changing circumstances. Most joined the Republican party—and then heartily endorsed the Union effort that crushed both the slaveholders' rebellion and slavery.[40]

The antislavery Jacksonians' achievements hardly vindicate the entire Jacksonian movement, or even most of it. Nor, looking back, were the antislavery Jacksonians always admirable, especially on the question of black political rights (although some important figures, like William Leggett, were more admirable than others). Nevertheless, it is important to recognize that the antislavery Democrats provided an alternative view of where Jacksonians ought to stand regarding slavery and the racism that justified slavery. That alternative eventually caused the vast majority of antislavery men to abandon the Democratic party—but not to abandon their Jacksonian ideals. It was the Democracy, the antislavery leader Preston King later remarked, that had "changed its members, its principles, its purposes, its character."[41] Antislavery Jacksonians, by their own lights, had kept the faith.

These developments, in turn, had a profound impact on the development of the antislavery movement. Historians have, with justice, emphasized the importance of evangelical Christian morality and humanitarian ethics to

the rise of antislavery and abolitionism in the Atlantic world. In the case of
the United States, the impact of the Second Great Awakening and the emergence of the Whiggish, middle-class benevolent empire of reform have figured (especially in recent accounts) as the major forces that drove white
Americans to oppose black bondage.[42] Yet, powerful as they were, these forces
were unable to capture the support of anything approaching a majority of
northern citizens over the decades before the Civil War. As Eric Foner has
remarked about the troubled connections between the labor movement and
the abolitionists, the evangelical antislavery outlook, with its ethic of self-
control and industriousness, and its apparent indifference to the class inequalities that divided northern whites, spoke past the concerns of most Jacksonian Democrats.[43] Without some other antislavery impulse alongside that
of the evangelical reformers, it is hard to imagine that northern antislavery
would have grown as rapidly as it did between 1830 and 1860.

The antislavery Jacksonians were the main suppliers of that democratic
impulse. As early as the 1830s, they established an antislavery minority among
Jacksonian loyalists; in the 1840s and 1850s, they developed their appeal to
embrace a much larger Democratic minority that had little use for Whiggish
evangelical moralism. And their appeal had little in common with the herrenvolk caricatures drawn by recent historians. It renounced the racism that
would make one class of human beings the slaves of another class; it attacked
the enslavement of blacks as a threat to the well-being of the vast majority of
Americans; it insisted, as a matter of first principles, that no democracy could
permit a small combination of men to deny anyone his labor's product.

In the 1850s and 1860s, these ideas became mainstays of the Republican
party coalition. Among their most powerful advocates was Abraham Lincoln—a former Whig who had a low regard for Andrew Jackson, but who
also had a healthy respect for the Democratic strain in American politics.
Lincoln, more than most ex-Whig Republicans, was keenly aware of how
much the antislavery Jacksonians had enriched the political thinking of the
antislavery cause and expanded the cause's following. In 1858, reflecting on
local political conditions in Illinois, he offered as a broader "general rule"
that "much of the plain old democracy is with us, while nearly all of the old
exclusive silk-stocking whiggery is against us"—all of which made perfect
sense to him.[44] The antislavery politics of that "plain old democracy" dated
back to the days of William Leggett and Thomas Morris—a Jacksonian legacy
that helped arouse northerners to repudiate slavery and that, in time, helped
bring slavery to its knees.

NOTES

Personal matters prevented me from delivering this essay, as I had planned, as a paper to the 1994 Commonwealth Fund conference. I am, however, deeply grateful to those who attended the conference, and especially to John Ashworth, Jonathan Earle, Adam Fairclough, Eric Foner, Michael F. Holt, Melvyn Stokes, and Peter Way for their valuable comments on the paper I did deliver, a related study of William Leggett. Their advice and criticisms inform this essay as well. Special thanks go to Mr. Earle, whose forthcoming dissertation on antislavery politics in the 1830s and 1840s promises to give the Jacksonian dissidents their full due.

1. There are several essays that trace the twists and turns of Jacksonian historiography. See, for example, Charles G. Sellers, Jr., "Andrew Jackson versus the Historians," *Mississippi Valley Historical Review* 24 (1958): 615–34; Ronald P. Formisano, "Toward a Reorientation of Jacksonian Politics: A Review of the Literature, 1959–1975," *Journal of American History* 63 (1976): 42–65; Sean Wilentz, "On Class and Politics in Jacksonian America," *Reviews in American History* 10 (1982): 43–63.

2. Roosevelt quoted in Arthur Schlesinger, Jr., *The Age of Jackson* (Boston, 1945), p. x.

3. C. Vann Woodward, "The Populist Heritage and the Intellectual," in Woodward, *The Burden of Southern History* (Baton Rouge, La., 1960), p. 143.

4. Jackson and his supporters have not, to be sure, *entirely* lacked defenders. See above all the numerous works of Robert V. Remini, and especially the third volume of his biography *Andrew Jackson and the Course of American Democracy, 1832–1845* (New York, 1984).

5. Harry L. Watson, *Liberty and Power: The Politics of Jacksonian America* (New York, 1990), pp. 242–43. See also Charles Sellers, *The Market Revolution: Jacksonian America, 1815–1846* (New York, 1992), esp. pp. 293, 295, 401–5, 426–27. Among the recent highly critical appraisals of the Jacksonians, several works stand out, including Richard H. Brown, "The Missouri Crisis, Slavery, and the Politics of Jacksonianism," *South Atlantic Quarterly* 65 (1966): 55–72; Michael Paul Rogin, *Fathers and Children: Andrew Jackson and the Subjugation of the American Indian* (New York, 1975); Leonard L. Richards, "The Jacksonians and Slavery," in Lewis Perry and Michael Fellman, eds., *Antislavery Reconsidered: New Perspectives on the Abolitionists* (Baton Rouge, La., 1979), pp. 99–118; Alexander Saxton, *The Rise and Fall of the White Republic: Class Politics and Mass Culture in Nineteenth-Century America* (London, 1990); David R. Roediger, *The Wages of Whiteness: Race and the Making of the American Working Class* (London, 1991). Related interpretations appear in George M. Fredrickson, *The Black Image in the White Mind: The Debate on Afro-American Character and Destiny* (New York, 1971); Ronald M. Takaki, *Iron Cages: Race and Culture in Nineteenth-Century America* (New York, 1979); and Daniel Walker Howe, *The Political Culture of the American Whigs* (Chicago, 1979). No two of these interpretations are identical, and I shall try to be as specific as possible in assessing their respective claims.

6. Saxton, *Rise and Fall*, pp. 142, 144.

7. The general concept of herrenvolk democracy, introduced by Pierre L. Van den

Berge in *Race and Racism: A Comparative Perspective* (New York, 1967), has been best developed in the United States context by Fredrickson in *Black Image*. The idea is pushed even further, in modified form, by Saxton in *Rise and Fall* and by Roediger in *Wages*.

8. Brown, "Missouri Crisis"; Rogin, *Fathers and Children*. Rogin's introduction to the 1986 reprint of his book contains a revealing account of the political mood that affected his writing.

9. Roediger, *Wages,* esp. pp. 43–95 (quotation on p. 74); Saxton, *Rise and Fall,* pp. 153–54.

10. See, for example, Schlesinger's remarks in *Age of Jackson,* pp. 424–27.

11. John M. McFaul, "Expediency vs. Morality: Jacksonian Politics and Slavery," *Journal of American History,* 62 (1975): 24–39.

12. In part, this image has derived from grandiose readings of the latter chapters of Edmund S. Morgan's important *American Slavery, American Freedom: The Ordeal of Colonial Virginia* (New York, 1975).

13. Frederick Robinson, *Address to the Voters of the Fifth Congressional District* (n.p., [1862]), p. 11. See also Eric Foner, *Free Soil, Free Labor, Free Men: The Ideology of the Republican Party before the Civil War* (New York, 1970), pp. 149–68.

14. Saxton, *Rise and Fall,* p. 154. For related interpretations, see Sellers, *Market Revolution,* pp. 426–27; Eugene H. Berwanger, *The Frontier against Slavery: Western Anti-Negro Prejudice and the Slavery Extension Controversy* (Urbana, Ill., 1967); James A. Rawley, *Race and Politics: "Bleeding Kansas" and the Coming of the Civil War* (Philadelphia, 1969); V. Jacque Voegeli, *Free But Not Equal: The Midwest and the Negro during the Civil War* (Chicago, 1967). A more judicious, if highly critical, assessment of antislavery Democratic racism appears in Eric Foner, "Racial Attitudes of the New York Free Soilers," in his *Politics and Ideology in the Age of the Civil War* (New York, 1980), pp. 77–93. The most thorough study of political antislavery in the 1840s and early 1850s is Richard H. Sewell, *Ballots for Freedom: Antislavery Politics in the United States, 1837–1860* (New York, 1976).

15. *Congressional Globe* (hereafter *CG*), 29th Cong., 2d sess. (1847), appendix, p. 317, quoted in Saxton, *Rise and Fall,* p. 154; Charles B. Going, *David Wilmot, Free-Soiler: A Biography of the Great Advocate of the Wilmot Proviso* (New York, 1924), pp. 174–75 n.; Sewell, *Ballots,* pp. 172–73; Foner, "Racial Attitudes."

16. For a good summary, see Richards, "Jacksonians and Slavery." For a somewhat more heated account, see Lorman Ratner, *Powder Keg: Northern Opposition to the Antislavery Movement* (New York, 1968).

17. Leonard L. Richards, *"Gentlemen of Property and Standing": Anti-Abolition Mobs in Jacksonian America* (New York, 1970), pp. 30–33, 112–29, 131–35; Saxton, *Rise and Fall,* esp. pp. 67–72.

18. Betty Fladeland, *James Gillespie Birney: Slaveholder to Abolitionist* (Ithaca, N.Y., 1955), pp. 175–89; Sean Wilentz, "Jacksonian Abolitionism: The Conversion of William Leggett," in John Patrick Diggins, ed., *The Agony of American Liberalism* (forthcoming); Stanley Harrold, *Gamaliel Bailey and Antislavery Union* (Kent, Ohio, 1986), pp. 12–40; *(Baltimore) Niles' Register,* Dec. 1, 1838 (Morton quotation); Richards, *"Gentlemen,"* pp. 17, 115; Benjamin Franklin Morris, *The Life of Thomas Morris* (Cincinnati, 1856), pp. 107–67; John A. Neuenschwander, "Senator Thomas Morris: Antagonist of the South,

1836–39," *Cincinnati Historical Society Bulletin* 32 (1974): 123–39; Sewell, *Ballots*, pp. 3–42.

19. John Barkley Jentz, "Artisans, Evangelicals, and the City: A Social History of Abolition and Labor Reform in Jacksonian New York" (Ph.D. diss., City University of New York, 1977); Edward Magdol, *The Antislavery Rank and File: A Social Profile of the Abolitionists' Constituency* (Westport, Conn., 1986); Wilentz, "Leggett"; Richards, *"Gentlemen,"* pp. 91–92; *Register of Debates in Congress*, 24th Cong., 1st sess. (1835), pp. 201–8; Sewell, *Ballots*, pp. 18–19.

20. *(New York) Evening Post*, Aug. 22, Sept. 7, 1835; Leggett to [Theodore Sedgwick, Jr.?], Oct. 24, 1838, in Sedgwick, ed., *A Collection of the Political Writings of William Leggett*, 2 vols. (New York, 1840), 2: 335.

21. In addition to Sewell, *Ballots*, pp. 43–106, see Harrold, *Bailey*, pp. 41–54; Fladeland, *Birney*, pp. 207–51. On Chase, Jacksonianism, and the Democrats, see especially Louis Gerteis, *Morality and Utility in American Antislavery Reform* (Chapel Hill, N.C., 1987), pp. 93–96, 108–9, 110–14. John Niven's new biography of Chase, which appeared just as this essay went to press, discusses Chase's political and intellectual transformations in detail.

22. *(Cincinnati) Philanthropist*, June 15, 1842; Sewell, *Ballots*, 80–106 (quotation on p. 102); Alan M. Kraut, "The Forgotten Reformers: A Profile of Third Party Abolitionists in Antebellum New York," in Perry and Fellman, eds., *Antislavery Reconsidered*, pp. 119–48 (quotations on pp. 143–44); Reinhard O. Johnson, "The Liberty Party in Massachusetts, 1840–1848: Antislavery Third Party Politics in the Bay State," *Civil War History* 28 (1982): 237–65.

23. *(New York) Evening Post*, Feb. 20, 1840; Theodore Sedgwick, Jr., *Thoughts on the Proposed Annexation of Texas* (New York, 1844). The latter source contains pieces that Sedgwick wrote for the *Evening Post* in 1843 and 1844.

24. Sewell, *Ballots*, pp. 107–201 (quotation on p. 130); Joseph G. Rayback, *Free Soil: The Election of 1848* (Lexington, Ky., 1970), pp. 22–33, 56–80, 171–85, 201–59. For a sophisticated quantitative analysis of the Free Soil vote and its larger social and political implications, see Thomas B. Alexander, "Harbinger of the Collapse of the Second Two-Party System: The Free Soil Party of 1848," in Lloyd E. Ambrosius, *A Crisis of Republicanism: American Politics in the Civil War Era* (Lincoln, Nebr., 1992), pp. 17–54.

25. Sewell, *Ballots*, p. 174. The quotation refers directly to the New York Barnburners, whom Sewell, Foner, and others single out as among the more explicitly negrophobic elements in the emerging Free Soil coalition of the mid-1840s.

26. *CG*, 25th Cong., 3d sess. (1839), appendix, pp. 168–69, 175. On the abolitionists, see Ronald G. Walters, *The Antislavery Appeal: American Abolitionism after 1830* (Baltimore, 1978); and Lewis Perry, *Radical Abolitionism: Anarchy and the Government of God in Antislavery Thought* (Ithaca, N.Y., 1973), among other fine works. For a review of more recent writings, see James L. Hutson, "The Experiential Basis of the Northern Antislavery Impulse," *Journal of Southern History* 56 (1990): 609–40.

27. *CG*, 25th Cong., 3d sess. (1839), appendix, p. 168. For later variations on the slave power theme in antislavery writings and speeches, see the convenient summaries in Foner, *Free Soil*, pp. 90–98, and Sewell, *Ballots*, pp. 199–201.

28. *(New York) Plaindealer*, Feb. 25, 1837; *Emancipator*, May 27, 1841. For later material, see Sewell, *Ballots*, pp. 189–99. On the abolitionists' economic critique of slavery, see Walters, *Antislavery Appeal*, pp. 111–28.

29. *(New York) Plaindealer*, Feb. 25, 1837; *Liberty Standard*, Dec. 1, 1841, quoted in Sewell, *Ballots*, p. 102.

30. *(New York) Plaindealer*, Feb. 25, July 29, 1837; *CG*, 25th Cong., 3d sess. (1839), appendix, p. 168; *Albany Atlas*, Apr. 28, 1848; *Cleveland Plain Dealer*, Oct. 20, 1847.

31. *(New York) Plaindealer*, Feb. 25, July 29, 1837; *(Washington, D.C.) National Era*, June 28, 1849.

32. Samuel Clesson Allen, quoted in Schlesinger, *Age of Jackson*, p. 153. There are several fine studies of Jacksonian producerist ideas, of which the most thorough is John Ashworth, *"Agrarians" and "Aristocrats": Party Political Ideology in the United States, 1837–1846* (London, 1983).

33. *Brooklyn Eagle*, Sept. 1, 1847. Giving Roediger's argument the benefit of the doubt here should not be construed as implying agreement with his larger thesis.

34. *CG*, 25th Cong., 3d sess. (1839), appendix, pp. 173–74; *Albany Atlas*, Feb. 15, 1847; *Oliver Dyer's Phonographic Report of the Proceedings of the National Free Soil Convention at Buffalo, N.Y., August 9th and 10th, 1848* (Buffalo, [1848]), p. 13.

35. *CG*, 25th Cong., 3d sess. (1839), appendix, p. 174.

36. *(New York) Evening Post*, Sept. 7, 1838.

37. *(New York) Plaindealer*, Sept. 22, 1838. For a fuller account of antislavery constitutionalism in the 1830s, see William M. Wiecek, *The Sources of Antislavery Constitutionalism in America, 1760–1848* (Ithaca, N.Y., 1977), pp. 150–201.

38. Wiecek, *Sources*, pp. 202–27; *Dyer's Phonographic Report*, p. 19. The Jacksonian dissidents' constitutionalism also made them strong critics of Southern disunionism, on grounds (they claimed) that were the same as Jackson's during the nullification controversy. For early presentiments of these views, see Leggett's remarks in the *(New York) Evening Post*, Aug. 15, 1835; *(New York) Plaindealer*, Mar. 11, 1837. For later statements by antislavery Jacksonians, see Foner, *Free Soil*, pp. 178–81.

39. *(Washington, D.C.) National Era*, Feb. 4, 1847; "Proceedings of the Herkimer Mass Convention of Oct. 26, 1847," in *Albany Atlas Extra*, November 1847, p. 11; *Albany Atlas*, Nov. 9, 1847; Seth H. Hunt to Van Buren, July 13, 1848, Van Buren Papers, Library of Congress. Sewell, in *Ballots*, pp. 190–191, observes that some free-soil Democrats took a more limited view of restriction, and were willing to leave southern slavery intact. Still, he notes, most Free Soilers accepted uncritically the idea that, if slavery did not spread, it would die, and that the Wilmot Proviso was "therefore a sure-fire, if gradual, means of abolition."

40. On the Democratic-Republicans, the best discussion remains that in Foner, *Free Soil*, pp. 149–85. The Jacksonian tradition has come in for a great deal of criticism for its benighted political role in Reconstruction, largely because of the class resentments and racism exhibited by President Andrew Johnson. See especially Kenneth M. Stampp's discussion of Johnson as "the last Jacksonian" in his *The Era of Reconstruction, 1865–1877* (New York, 1965). Yet Johnson was hardly a typical antislavery Jacksonian. Unlike most, he came from a border slave state, he opposed the Wilmot Proviso (although he never publicly defended slavery or slavery's extension), and he served as governor of Tennessee

as a War Democrat, not as a Republican. Some of the antislavery Jacksonians (among them Frank Blair and Gideon Welles) did, indeed, take a conservative line on Reconstruction and on black civil and political rights after 1865, and they played leading roles in the feeble Johnson administration. But other ex-Democrats or men closely aligned with Jacksonian principles—including Salmon P. Chase, Edwin Stanton, Hannibal Hamlin, and (the admittedly idiosyncratic) Benjamin F. Butler—wound up backing black suffrage and, in some cases, gravitated to the Radical Republicans. In relation to Reconstruction, just as in relation to slavery, Jacksonianism left more than one legacy.

41. Preston King to Gideon Welles, Sept. 16, 1858, Welles Papers, Library of Congress.

42. In addition to Walters, *Antislavery Appeal,* and Gerteis, *Morality,* see Victor B. Howard, *Conscience and Slavery: The Evangelistic Calvinist Domestic Missions, 1837–1861* (Kent, O., 1990); Robert H. Abzug, *Cosmos Crumbling: American Reform and the Religious Imagination* (New York, 1994), esp. pp. 129–62.

43. Eric Foner, "Labor and the Abolitionists," in Foner, *Politics and Ideology,* pp. 57–76.

44. Abraham Lincoln to Anson G. Henry, Nov. 19, 1858, in Roy P. Basler, ed., *The Collected Works of Abraham Lincoln,* 8 vols. (New Brunswick, N.J., 1953), 3:339. For an astute analysis of Lincoln's free labor ideas and of their place in his larger antislavery thinking, see Gabor S. Boritt, *Lincoln and the Economics of the American Dream* (Memphis, 1978), esp. pp. 155–93. See also Olivier Frayssé, *Lincoln, Land, and Labor, 1809–60* (Urbana, Ill., 1994).

9

From Center to Periphery: The Market Revolution and Major-Party Conflict, 1835–1880

MICHAEL F. HOLT

THIS ESSAY BRIEFLY EXPLORES a fascinating, yet little-investigated, phenomenon in nineteenth-century American politics: the relegation of economic issues from the center to the periphery of partisan conflict between major parties from 1835 to 1880. The questions raised by this shift can be expressed in a number of ways. Each illuminates a different aspect of the overall problem.

Why did divergent programmatic responses to economic developments in the 1830s and 1840s—a transformation now widely labeled the market revolution—form the crux of two-party conflict during the stable phase of the second party system, whereas for approximately thirty years after 1850 economic issues were relatively tangential to major-party combat during the third or Civil War party system? To be sure, Republicans and Democrats divided against each other over certain economic questions during the late 1850s, 1860s, and 1870s. Nonetheless, just as most historians now agree that sharp disagreement over governmental involvement in the expansion of the market economy constituted the central defining difference between Whigs and Democrats from 1837 to approximately 1850, so most agree that the third party system revolved around a quite different set of issues.[1] Between 1856 and 1872, Republicans and Democrats fought over sectional relations between North and South, the conduct of the Civil War and Reconstruction, and policies toward blacks as slaves or freedmen. After 1876, the system was defined primarily by ethnoreligious divisions in the North and racial polarizations in the South.[2]

Concomitantly, by 1876 in both the North and the South the Republican and Democratic parties relied increasingly on elaborate organizational networks rather than contrasting programmatic orientations or achievements to mobilize their respective electorates. As Morton Keller has put it, "During the 1870s, the character of American politics sharply changed. The passionate, ideologically charged political ambiance of the Reconstruction years gave way to a politics that rested on the perpetuation of party organization rather than the fostering of public policy."[3] In neither chronological phase of the third party system, in sum, did divergent governmental economic policies play the central differentiating and voter-arousing role for the major parties that they had during the second. Why was this so?

To phrase the question differently, why did the depressions inaugurated by the panics of 1837 and 1873 have such vastly different effects in shaping the contours of subsequent major-party conflict? The depression of the 1830s dramatically raised the level and intensity of interparty disagreement over economic policies in both Congress and state legislatures. The sharpening of this programmatic conflict, in turn, helped both Whigs and Democrats incorporate hundreds and hundreds of thousands of previous nonvoters, undecided switchers, and adherents to minor parties into their rank and file and instill in them a passionate partisan loyalty.[4] In contrast, the depression of the 1870s was accompanied by, and probably helped cause, a diminution of coherent partisan conflict over economic issues in Congress and state legislatures by a fragmentation rather than a solidification of Republican and Democratic voter coalitions that raised the possibility of a voter realignment that might end the Civil War party system, and, in its early stages, by a reduction rather than an increase in the rate of voter turnout.[5]

In other words, instead of invigorating, reshaping, and enlarging the voter bases of the existing parties as the panic of 1837 had done, that of 1873 neither produced a realignment nor established economic issues as the axis around which the existing party system revolved. Instead, we got what different historians have termed the politics of Tweedle Dum and Tweedle Dee, or a politics based on the conflict of irreconcilable ethnoreligious values rather than alternative economic programs, or, in the South, a politics that drew the line between parties on the issue of race, not economics.[6] We got a politics based on emotional appeals to biases and social cleavages in the electorate, not on conflict over coherent and distinctive partisan economic policies. Why did similar economic stimuli produce such different political results?

To ask the question still another way, why was it that every third party formed in the antebellum period after 1837, other than the highly localized and tiny Anti-Rent movement in New York, focused on noneconomic issues, whereas every third party after the Civil War, other than the Prohibition party, organized around some economic program or other? Since the very emergence of third parties indicates the failure of existing major parties to aggregate and articulate the concerns of portions of the electorate, this dramatic difference in the orientation or organizing principles of third parties in the antebellum and postbellum periods is highly significant. It suggests that, after 1837, for a time Whigs and Democrats monopolized debate and action on questions of political economy and provided an efficacious outlet to those with economic needs or grievances, while after 1865 Republicans and Democrats did not.

More precisely, analyses of roll-call votes in Congress and state legislatures during the late 1830s and 1840s demonstrate that Whigs and Democrats took sharply different stances on governmental economic policy. Other evidence shows that the parties publicized those contrasting voting records to the electorate. Millions of copies of long, detailed, and often exceedingly boring congressional speeches on specific economic policies like tariffs or the Independent Treasury Act were distributed during campaigns, and both parties issued legislative addresses at the close of state legislative sessions that specified how the members of the rival parties had voted during the roll calls of that session. As a result, those with conflicting attitudes toward banking and currency, corporate privileges, tariffs, federal land policy, state and federal subsidization of internal improvements, and even ten-hour laws for labor found the rival Whig and Democratic parties adequate vehicles through which to pursue goals and vent resentments.[7] Yet additional evidence of this fact is the failed attempt of President John Tyler in the early 1840s to stake out middle ground between Whigs and Democrats on national banking policy by pushing his abortive exchequer scheme and subsequently resorting to a totally different kind of issue—Texas annexation—on which to build a third party. Manifestly, after the panic of 1837, conflict over economic policy was channeled through the major parties and was central to the very existence of the second party system.

Conversely, during the 1860s and 1870s those with specific economic agendas, be they railroad regulation, antimonopoly reform, business regulation, currency inflation, or prolabor legislation, palpably did not view the Republican and Democratic parties as adequate vehicles to secure action from government. Instead, they turned to third parties—Reform, Independent, Anti-Monopoly, National Labor Reform, Greenback, and Greenback-Labor parties—or else to ostensibly nonpartisan or bipartisan pressure groups like the Grange or lobbying efforts that sought to influence legislators from both major parties rather than using one of them to secure their agendas.[8] Granted, third parties were more prevalent in the North than in the South during those decades. Nonetheless, reform parties dedicated to retrenchment, tax relief, and clean government also mushroomed in Dixie, as did Readjuster movements dedicated to partial repudiation of state debts in Virginia and a few other states at the end of the 1870s and in the early 1880s.

Why, then, was conflict over governmental economic policies central to the life of the second party system after 1837, but peripheral to that of the third after the close of the Civil War and especially during the depression decade of the 1870s? This issue is all the more puzzling because the general orientations of the rival parties toward the active use of governmental power remained constant from the second party system to the third. Both the Whig party and the postwar Republican party, despite their different constituencies, advocated positive state activism to promote economic development, whereas Democrats from the 1830s to the 1870s and far beyond harped on the dangers of governmental activism and espoused negative state doctrines. Despite this continuity in ideological polarization from the second party system to the third, economic questions were far more vital to the life of the former than to that of the latter. Why?

In raising these questions I make several assumptions about the operation of the political system in the nineteenth century and especially about the relationship between governance or actions of the state and popular voting behavior. I firmly believe that voter allegiance to one or the other of the major parties in any two-party system was dependent on the clarity of differences, especially programmatic differences and conflicts, between them. I also believe that political leaders in the nineteenth century understood the necessity of contrasting their parties with their rivals in order to mobilize voter support. Otherwise they would never have gone to the enormous expense and effort of alerting voters to what the rival parties said and did in Congress and state legislatures. I am also convinced that third parties mushroomed when, and only when, blocs of voters believed that the existing major parties did not offer sufficiently clear or precise programmatic alternatives on specific matters of concern to them. Finally, time series analyses of votes for congressmen during the twentieth century reinforce a common-sense perception that economic issues are and were far more salient to the electorate during depressions or hard times than during periods of prosperity.[9]

If these assumptions are correct, the differential impacts of the depressions of the 1830s and 1870s on the policy agendas and electoral strategies of the two-party systems in existence when they occurred are all the more mystifying. Republican and Democratic leaders on the eve of the panic of 1873 faced exactly the same strategic problem that Whig and Democratic leaders confronted on the eve of the panic of 1837. In both eras, party leaders had to find new issues to replace the original ones that had given birth to the second and third party systems and that had initially allowed the rival parties that constituted each to differentiate themselves for the electorate.

In the case of Whigs and Democrats, the original defining issue was the presidency of Andrew Jackson, on which Whigs and Democrats were far more coherently opposed to each other than they were on economic issues before 1837 and which ended two months before the outbreak of the panic.

While Jackson and congressional Democrats denounced the evils of the Bank of the United States in particular and of privileged monopolies in general, for example, Democratic state legislators in New Hampshire, New York, New Jersey, Pennsylvania, and elsewhere were chartering banks and other corporations and promoting economic development just as avidly as Whigs. As a result, partisan conflict over economic policies in state legislatures was muted prior to 1837. Only after the panic that year did Democrats achieve coherence and congruence between the state and national levels on economic policy, while the conditions of depression gave far more force and urgency to the Whigs' programs of state and congressional activism to promote economic recovery and growth. After 1837, therefore, quantitative indices of legislative conflict soared.[10] Whigs and Democrats, in sum, brilliantly seized on the opportunity provided by the panic of 1837 to define a new dimension of issue difference to replace the original axis of partisan conflict—support for or opposition to Andrew Jackson himself. And it was the shift in the defining issue agenda that explains why the rate of voter participation in presidential elections nationally jumped from 55.4 percent in 1832 and 57.8 percent in 1836 to 80.2 percent in 1840 and 78.9 percent in 1844.

Republican and Democratic leaders responded quite differently to the panic of 1873. They confronted the declining electoral salience of the sectional and race-related policy agenda that had defined the Civil War party system between 1856 and 1872, that had generated such polarized and ideologically fused legislative behavior during the Civil War and the first six years of Reconstruction, and that, as Dale Baum has shown in the case of Massachusetts, produced such dramatic rigidity or stability in the rival parties' voter coalitions until about 1870.[11] Granted, even after the economic crash, roll-call votes in Congress on civil rights and other Reconstruction measures generated higher levels of interparty conflict than other legislation, but those measures virtually disappeared from the agenda of at least the House of Representatives after March 1875 and concrete votes on policies related to questions of war, Reconstruction, and race had disappeared from the agendas of at least northern state legislatures years before that. Instead, economic issues raised by the depression increasingly pressed for the attention of congressmen and state legislators, and on those, in sharp contrast to the case of the 1830s, Republican and Democratic policymakers were far less internally united and polarized against each other along partisan lines than they had been before the outbreak of the panic.[12]

Of greater importance, Republican and Democratic campaigners clearly abandoned programmatic conflict over race and Reconstruction policies as the issue on which they sought votes before the programmatic conflict itself abated. Michael Perman has argued, for example, that while the southern elections of 1867 and 1868 constituted virtual referenda on congressional Reconstruction policies, after 1868 the Whig centrists who dominated both the Republican and the Democratic parties in most southern states declared a cease-fire on the issue of accepting or rejecting Reconstruction itself as the platform on which they sought votes. Until 1873 the dominant Republicans, in fact, took up an economic issue—railroad promotion to restore prosperity—to appeal for votes, while Democrats, apparently, did little to oppose that program in state legislatures prior to the 1873 panic and instead competed at the polls by running prominent former Whigs as candidates.[13]

Similarly, as William Gillette and others have demonstrated, from December 1865 onward northern Republican policymakers in Congress always focused primarily on the North, not on the South. Hence, they were mainly interested in Reconstruction policies for ex-Confederate states as platforms to run on in the North, as guarantees to the northern electorate that they would not sacrifice the fruits of northern victory in the Civil War and allow the Confederacy and the men who ran it to rise again. Therefore, after 1870, when the enforcement of Reconstruction policy became increasingly unpopular with the northern electorate, northern Republican campaigners increasingly distanced themselves from policies for the South and on behalf of blacks as their major platform.[14] Simultaneously, when northern Democrats finally comprehended that attacks on Republican Reconstruction programs simply provided ammunition for Republican "bloody shirt" attacks on them as Confederate sympathizers, they too abandoned Reconstruction policy, or their opposition to it, as their major appeal to voters. This congruence on Reconstruction policy was symbolized in 1872 when Democrats formally adopted the New Departure and congressional Republicans, in part to minimize the anticipated Liberal Republican bolt, supported an amnesty act that removed political disqualifications from all but a handful of former Confederates. Not coincidentally, this blurring of the major line that had separated the parties for sixteen years resulted in the lowest turnout in a presidential election since 1852, the last time voters had perceived no important differences between the parties.[15]

After 1872, of course, Republicans continued to wave the bloody shirt and Democrats continued to race bait whenever possible. Increasingly, however, these appeals, though demonstrably potent, were rhetorical rather than substantive. Democrats no longer promised to overturn Reconstruction legislation and repeal the Thirteenth, Fourteenth, and Fifteenth Amendments, and most Republican campaigners in the North when seeking votes no longer demanded additional legislation or executive action to punish ex-

Confederates or help the freedmen. The South, of course, was an exception to this rule. There Republicans, embarrassed by the collapse of their economic program, tried to mobilize their core black constituency by pointing to state civil rights laws and the civil rights bill of 1874 that Republicans had passed, a tactic that only abetted Democrats in drawing a race line between the parties.[16]

Among other things, the abandonment of programmatic conflict over Reconstruction policies as their principal campaign tactic by northern Republicans and Democrats after 1872 confutes an obvious answer to the questions raised here. One could argue that economic issues moved from the center to the periphery of major-party conflict after 1850 simply because voters and politicians became obsessed with the sectional questions that led to the Civil War and whose salience was reinforced by the war and Reconstruction. That is undeniably true of the period between 1856 and 1872, but not after it. The outbreak of panic in 1873, moreover, thrust economic questions and demands into the political arena and displaced the cluster of issues surrounding Reconstruction and race from the center of congressional and state legislative agendas.[17]

On certain economic questions that emerged in Congress after 1872, the two parties did take distinguishably partisan stands, as Whigs and Democrats had done earlier. In 1874 Republicans, over the opposition of most Democrats, raised tariff duties that they had lowered in 1872 to deter Liberal Republican defections, and they pointed, though not strenuously, to higher tariff rates as a programmatic response to unemployment and economic decline. Similarly, partisan lines on the adoption of the Specie Resumption Act in 1875 and Democratic attempts to repeal it in 1876 were far sharper than on many previous votes concerning the vexed money question. The clarification of party lines on at least these two questions undoubtedly helped Republicans and Democrats reaggregate their previously disintegrating voter coalitions during the presidential campaign of 1876, when the rate of voter turnout leapt from the 71.3 percent of 1872 to 81.8 percent.[18]

Nonetheless, when votes on economic issues as a whole during the 1870s are examined, Republicans and Democrats achieved far less internal cohesion and were dramatically less polarized against each other, not only than Whigs and Democrats had been in the late 1830s and 1840s, but also than Republicans and Democrats themselves had been on roll-call votes concerning economic policy in the 1860s.[19] Despite the emergence of relatively clear partisan lines on the Specie Resumption Act in 1875 and 1876, for example, as soon as the major parties subsequently confronted the issue of monetizing silver, indices of internal cohesion and interparty conflict plummeted.[20] As a result of that collapse and of the labor turbulence associated with the strikes of 1877, the Greenback-Labor vote surged to its apex in the state and congressional elections of 1878, just as splinter parties had mushroomed in subpresidential elections between 1870 and 1874 in response to the major parties' failure to promote coherent and distinctive economic policies prior to 1875.

Of far greater importance, whatever semblance of partisan responsibility for economic policy emerged in Congress after the panic of 1873, no similar clarification developed in northern or most southern state legislatures. In many southern states, even before the outbreak of the panic, Republicans made no attempt to defend their failed railroad program, and instead they competed with Democrats in a shouting match as to which party would cut taxes and expenditures faster and further.[21] In retrospect, indeed, the most important impact of the panic of 1837 on the second party system was to establish a system-wide fault line on questions of political economy so that Whigs and Democrats were sharply divided against each other in the same ways at the state and national levels. No such system-wide fault line emerged on economic issues in the 1870s. So far as unifying each major party and setting them against each other on economic policy, that is, the impact of the panic of 1873 was the reverse of that of the panic of 1837.

The original question then reappears. By 1873, Republican and Democratic leaders, at least in the North, patently needed new issues to replace the ones that had previously differentiated the parties and that both were now abandoning. The depression that broke out in 1873 offered them the same opportunity to formulate contrasting economic programs that it had offered Whigs and Democrats thirty-six years earlier, and to use those programs as the platforms on which they campaigned. Except for the tariff and specie resumption, however, they did not or could not. Why?

Several answers to this question come to mind, but most can be dismissed as unconvincing. As already suggested, preoccupation with sectional relations diverted the attention of politicians and voters between 1856 and 1872, but not between 1850 and 1856 or after 1872. The very mushrooming of economically or reform-oriented third parties after 1870 and the punishment of the incumbent Republicans after depression ensued by angry voters in the 1874 congressional elections show that.[22] Another possibility is that, after their jarring emergence during the Jacksonian period, rapid economic development and the market revolution simply lost political salience with all but the fractious minorities who supported third parties. Economic transformation, in effect, became self-perpetuating. It ceased to require, or possess a dimension relevant to, action by the state. Simultaneously, after the traumatic dislocation caused by the initial spread of the market economy from 1815 to 1850, people adjusted to and were no longer so troubled by the pace of change.

To state these assertions, however, is simultaneously to demonstrate their untenability. After 1850, just as before it, different economic actors—railroad corporations, bankers and other businessmen, farmers, and labor—continued to look to government at different levels of the federal system for positive aid, legal advantages, or redress of grievances. It is equally implausible to suggest that the dislocations generated by economic change somehow became less traumatic after 1850 than they had been before that date. We know, for example, that during the decade of the 1870s in the North the pace of industrialization, the adoption by manufacturers of the factory system that used capital-intensive power-driven machinery, and the resulting reduction of the labor force from the status of self-employed artisans to wage-earning, semi-skilled employees increased at an exponential rate.[23] Qualitatively different but equally disruptive and pervasive economic changes shook the South after the Civil War. A major subtheme of Eric Foner's magisterial history of the Reconstruction, indeed, is that the Civil War, emancipation, and Reconstruction altered class relations in both sections and created a new agenda for government to address.[24]

Clearly, that is, *policy* questions concerning political economy did not disappear from the purview of government between 1850 and 1880. Republican and Democratic officeholders still had to deal with them. The critical difference from the experience of the second party system was not the presence or absence of economic issues on government's platter. Rather, it was how cohesively and distinctively the rival parties before and after 1850 responded to those issues and the degree to which they made use of those responses, rather than something else, when appealing for votes. As numerous scholars have demonstrated, indeed, postwar economic issues, especially the money question, split both parties along geographical and interest group lines rather than uniting them against each other. That was the critical difference from the 1830s and 1840s.

In his book on the prewar Republican party, Eric Foner extends this transformation back into the 1850s when examining the problems of coalition building. He argues that Republican leaders consciously avoided a partisan policy response to the panic of 1857 because ex-Democrats and ex-Whigs in the new party disagreed with each other so sharply on traditional economic questions like banking and the tariff. Instead, they emphasized the free-soil, anti–slave power platform on which all Republicans could agree.[25] But an emphasis on the divergence of Whig and Democratic views on economic, and especially financial, policy and on the need delicately to arrange intraparty compromises does not really explain why party lines on most economic questions collapsed in the 1850s even before the emergence of the Republican party. Nor does it explain why Republicans in both Congress and state legislatures achieved quite high levels of cohesion on certain economic policies during the Civil War, but fragmented on many that arose in the 1870s. That is, if ideological legacies inherited from the Jacksonian period divided former Whigs and former Democrats on economic policies, why would Republicans have been more united in the 1860s than in the 1870s?

Nonetheless, Foner's stress on the tactical needs of party leaders who were determined to hold together a heterogeneous coalition as an explanatory variable is immensely valuable. It suggests that the decisions of political leaders are one place to look for the reasons why economic issues spawned by economic change and depression had such different impacts on the major parties in the Jacksonian and post–Civil War periods.

Foner's prize-winning synthesis on Reconstruction is an even richer source of clues. Contending that altered class relations in both the North and the South created new demands on the state, he also recognizes that by the 1870s those new demands could not be channeled through existing party lines. "Gradually," he writes, "Reconstruction gave way to issues arising from the economic legacy of the war and the impact of capitalism's rapid expansion— questions defined by shifting alliances along East-West, urban-rural, and occupational lines rather than Radical-moderate or even Democrat-Republican divisions." Consequently, "The fact that Republicans remained internally divided on virtually every other question heightened the importance of the Civil War and Reconstruction as touchstones that transcended local differences and served as a continuing definition of the party's identity." Only a few pages later, Foner, echoing other historians, cites the emergence of Liberalism as another deterrent to coherent programmatic partisan responses to economic issues. Liberalism repudiated the activist state associated with the Republican party in both the North and the South in the late 1860s and promoted instead retrenchment, lower taxes, and limited, honest government. Hence it constricted the options available to Republican leaders, since most advocates of Liberalism were themselves Republicans.[26]

These observations strike me as exceptionally fertile. Again Foner suggests that the ideological and political context in which party leaders operated shaped what they did, even if their short-term goal remained holding an electoral coalition together. To this, however, is added the important point that the nature of economic issues themselves was somehow different in the 1870s. Implicitly, and correctly in my judgment, Foner therefore rejects Richard L.

McCormick's insistence on the continuity of distributive economic policies that sustained mass party conflict from the 1830s until the early twentieth century during what McCormick labels "the party period" of American political history. As stimulating as McCormick's argument is, his stress on the similar nature of economic issues throughout the party period cannot account for the different patterns of political conflict they engendered in the 1830s–40s and the 1860s–70s.[27]

Clearly one answer to the questions I have raised, in sum, is that the economic issues generated by the market revolution in the 1830s and 1840s allowed the rival Whig and Democratic parties to cohere internally on opposite sides of them, whereas the economic issues of the 1870s divided members of both parties against each other. As a result, Whigs and Democrats used their programmatic responses to questions of political economy to arouse voters, whereas Republican and Democratic leaders shunned economic issues when possible and looked elsewhere for appeals to mobilize voters.

Though descriptively accurate, this statement hardly qualifies as news to anyone who has studied the nineteenth century. More to the point, it begs the crucial question. *Why* were the economic issues of the late 1830s and 1840s conducive to the formulation of clear and contrasting partisan programmatic responses, whereas those of the 1870s were not? More precisely, why did the internal party divisions produced by economic questions take such different forms in the 1830s–40s and in the 1860s–70s? While Whigs were largely united behind the party's economic policies, at least after the small group of southern states' rights Whigs were driven out of the party with John Tyler, throughout the late 1830s and 1840s Democrats divided along hard money– soft money, antibanking-probanking, antibusiness-prodevelopment lines. Yet those battles were played out primarily within state parties, and once the hard-money forces achieved dominance in the party after 1837 and many conservative Democrats defected to the Whigs, they failed to deter the remarkably high levels of partisan polarization over economic policy in both state legislatures and Congress that historians have noted. In contrast, the clearest manifestations of internal party divisions over economic issues in the 1860s and 1870s took the form of sectional and, among northerners, East-West divisions on votes in Congress and at national party conventions where representatives from different sections confronted each other. They did not generate coherent factional warfare within state parties.[28]

Put differently, factionalism within the Democratic party over economic issues in the 1830s and 1840s was nationwide; advocates of the hard- and soft-money positions could be found in almost every state, although their proportions in each clearly varied. In contrast, Republican and Democratic divisions in the 1860s and 1870s, on at least the banking and currency question, seemed to pit entire regions against each other, not divide the parties in those regions internally.[29] What accounts for this difference?

To explain this and the other changes in partisan conflict over the economic issues detailed above, one must focus on two distinguishable but related transformations between the 1830s–40s and the 1860s–70s. The first occurred in the political and ideological context and in the tactical political imperatives that confronted party leaders in the two periods. The second involved the nature of the economic issues themselves. Together these changes help explain the relegation of programmatic conflict over economic issues from the center to the periphery of major-party politics between 1835 and 1880.

Two interrelated changes in the political context strike me as most important. First, the parties that constituted the Civil War party system were far more mature in terms of mobilizing the potential electorate and instilling in their followers a strong sense of party loyalty when the panic of 1873 occurred than were those of the second party system in 1837. Second, the party that advocated the activist state, first the Whigs and then the Republicans, was out of power in 1837, but in power in 1873.

By 1873, the Republican party was seventeen years old. It had already used the issues of war and Reconstruction to cement and enlarge its voter base, and it had held control of the national government and most northern state governments since 1861 and most southern state governments since 1868. Consequently, the major tactical imperative of Republican leaders when depression ensued was to retain the voter coalition already in place, not build a new one. Like any party in power during a depression, the Republicans could expect a backlash from angry voters who blamed their record for causing or aggravating economic hardship, and they experienced it in 1874 when the Democratic vote soared from its artificially depressed levels of 1872 while former Republican voters simultaneously abstained in droves or, where possible, bolted to splinter parties that often fused with Democrats.[30] The top priority of northern Republican leaders, therefore, especially as one southern state after another was falling into Democratic hands, was to prevent the northern protest vote of 1874 from turning into a permanent realignment.

To the extent that new, first-time voters could be mobilized from an electorate that was already highly politicized, the Democrats seemed far more likely to get them, since Republicans presided over the economic disaster. The Republicans' job was to reconstruct the coalition that had kept them in power from 1860 to 1872. Somehow they had to bring back to the Republican column previous supporters who had abstained or bolted to other parties, be

they the Liberal Republican defectors of 1872 or the angry farmers and workers who had supported protest parties in 1873 and 1874.

Conversely, Whig leaders had every reason to promote a realignment and
mobilize first-time voters in response to the panic of 1837. The party was only
three years old. Its voter base as well as that of its Democratic rival was still
unstable, and the Whigs were a minority party that had lost not only the
presidential election, but also most state and congressional elections in 1836.[31]
To capture control of government, the Whigs had to enlarge their voter base
by luring defectors from the majority Democrats and especially by mobilizing
new recruits from the very large fraction of the potential electorate that still
did not vote.

The Whigs' task of promoting a realignment was made easier and the Republicans' task of preventing one in the 1870s was made far more difficult
because the Whigs were the "outs" and the Republicans the "ins" when the
economy went wrong. This difference in circumstance also helps explain why
the depression of the 1830s engendered partisan programmatic conflict and
that of the 1870s did not. In each instance, the "in" party at the time of the
panic found it necessary to abandon or repudiate its own policies that could
be blamed for causing or aggravating economic hardship. But in the first
instance the party that already distrusted governmental activism did so, while
in the second the party of activism itself had to recant. In effect, because the
Whigs were such a new party and out of power when the panic broke, they
had no baggage in terms of an incriminating legislative record to discard; the
Republicans, who had been in power for twelve years in the North and five
years in the South, did have baggage, and in abundance.

The Democrats held power in Washington in 1837, as they had for the eight
previous years, and they wanted to divert blame for the crash from Jacksonian policies like the Bank War and the Specie Circular to the recklessness
and greed of bankers and speculators. Hence, they abandoned the minimal
amount of national governmental intervention in the private economic sector
that they had previously tolerated—namely, the deposit of federal funds in
pet state banks, a system that had been codified by the Deposit Act of 1836,
which also, significantly, called for the distribution of the federal surplus to
state governments. This repudiation was encapsulated in Martin Van Buren's
Independent Treasury plan, which remained the chief economic issue in national politics from the fall of 1837 until its enactment in July 1840 and
repeal in June 1841, and in Van Buren's message to the special session of
Congress in September 1837 that demanded cessation of surplus payments
to the states and fully articulated the Democratic doctrine of the negative
state.

Simultaneously, heightened fear of the market economy and inflamed antagonism toward paper money and bankers spawned by the nationwide suspension of specie payments allowed hard-money, antibusiness elements in the Democratic party to overwhelm its probusiness wing in most state organizations. Replacing the Democrats who had previously chartered banks and other corporations in state legislatures, antibanking Democrats used their new power to punish the banks that had suspended, stop new charters of incorporation, impose unlimited liability on stockholders, and end state subsidies to internal improvements in order to prove to the electorate that the Democratic party had no sympathy for the villains on whom they blamed the panic. In sum, the panic for the first time forced Democrats to take a coherent and congruent stance on economic policies at both the state and national levels in order to escape the wrath of their own voters.

This sharp, defensive swing of the "in" Democrats in an antibanking, negative state direction allowed the Whigs, who were seeking ways to enlarge their own coalition, to draw a programmatic contrast by pushing for positive legislation to expand credit and the money supply, promote private investment by giving tariff protection to manufacturers and by limiting stockholder liability, and subsidize development of the infrastructure. It must be emphasized, however, that during the remainder of the 1830s, when the Whig party enjoyed its most spectacular growth, the top priority of Whigs with regard to congressional or national policy was not to enact programs of their own. Rather, it was to stop the Democrats from contracting the currency supply still further by enacting the Independent Treasury proposal. This tack was significant, for it allowed the Whigs to achieve one of their tactical imperatives—converting conservative Democrats to Whig ranks.

To arouse previous nonvoters, the Whigs relied primarily on promises that if given political power they would enact positive governmental economic policies that would restore prosperity. To understand the resonance of this appeal, one must underline a little-noted but absolutely crucial feature of the Whig agenda, one that the Republicans forty years later could not possibly duplicate. In heralding the virtues of governmental activism, the Whigs in effect promised voters a free lunch. However ideologically repellent Democrats found Whig proposals, those proposals inflicted no direct economic pain on the citizenry in the form of new taxes to pay for them. Only the indirect costs of higher prices that might result from tariff increases required any kind of payment from Americans for the Whig program. And to a generation who saw themselves primarily as producers or wage earners who suffered from plummeting prices, not as consumers who benefited from them, that threat seemed distant indeed. The Whigs' chief responses to hard times were not fiscal policies that required taxation. Rather, they were monetary, expanding or at least stopping the contraction of the money supply by protecting and enlarging the system of private, note-issuing banks, and legal, using state charters of incorporation to encourage the aggregation of private funds and promoting a national bankruptcy act to succor debtors.

To be sure, the state bond issues that Whigs like New York Governor William Henry Seward advocated to fund internal improvements bore the potential of requiring tax increases to meet interest payments. But Seward and other Whigs almost always accompanied these proposals with a promise that when they captured control of the national government—and this was another reason, they cried, why the Whigs should be given control of it—they would distribute federal land revenues to the states, thus obviating the need to raise local and state real estate taxes. Not only did this promise draw a contrast with Van Buren's demand for a cessation of federal subsidies to the states, but the mirage of tax-free economic development did not seem as implausible then as it would later. As Harry N. Scheiber and others have shown, virtually none of the canal construction completed by 1837 had been done at the immediate expense of taxpayers. Rather, states had borrowed the money by selling bonds, and they had relied on tolls and pyramiding schemes of new bond issues to pay them off.[32]

From the perspective of the 1870s, the astonishingly low direct tax burden on Americans in the 1830s and 1840s assumes critical importance in explaining why two-party conflict could revolve around contrasting economic programs in the earlier period but not the latter. By the 1870s, Americans no longer believed that positive government was or could ever be tax free. First to conduct the Civil War and then to promote economic development and rebuilding after it, Republicans had issued huge amounts of bonded debt at all levels of the federal system and levied unprecedentedly high local, state, and national direct, excise, and income taxes in order to pay the annual interest due on it. During the war, these bond issues and taxes had not provoked much criticism from propertied interests or partisan conflict in Congress, although they initially did in some state legislatures. For the wealthy who bought their own or their sons' way out of military service, criticism would have seemed unseemly indeed. Paying taxes was a way to expiate guilt and demonstrate patriotism.[33] Besides, they were the ones buying and profiting from most of the bonds. As Leonard Curry and Jean H. Baker have shown, moreover, Democrats readily joined Republicans in Congress in supplying and funding northern armies.[34] Concomitantly, the chief purpose of local and state bond issues was initially to pay enlistment bounties for volunteers and, by 1863, to pay commutation fees that exempted local men from the draft. As Iver Bernstein has shown in his study of the New York City draft riots, this latter purpose was especially popular with working-class Democrats, and the resort by local Democratic officials to bond sales established the mechanism that would later fund the graft that oiled urban Democratic machines.[35]

By the early 1870s, however, the debt and tax burdens associated in the public mind to a degree with the Democrats, but especially with the Republicans, became increasingly loathsome to taxpayers. In particular, they resented high taxes because of the widespread exposures of corruption committed by Republican and Democratic officeholders alike. Corruption, of course, was not a new phenomenon in American politics, especially at the local and state levels, but never before had the public funds with which politicos lined their pockets appeared to come so directly from taxpayers' own pockets.[36] Thus, even before the outbreak of the panic of 1873, anger at excessive and corrupt public expenditures and the high taxes that funded them led to the drive for retrenchment, tax relief, and reform that historians have labeled Liberalism. Conversely, a movement like Liberalism, which so constricted the possible programmatic responses of the Republicans to the depression of the 1870s and so gravely complicated their tactical task of retaining intact the coalition that had kept them in power from 1860 to 1873, would have been simply inconceivable in the 1830s and 1840s precisely because the burden of taxation, which fueled its intensity in the 1870s, was so low prior to the war.

The panic of 1873 further complicated the Republicans' task. Few people blamed Republican policies for causing the depression, and, as will be shown later, Republican policies for paying off the debt were largely responsible for confining the damage caused by the depression to only certain sectors of the economy.[37] But hard times increased the bite of the high taxes for which Republicans were primarily responsible and made those taxes a severe political liability. Thus, in self-defense Republicans had to repudiate taxes and spending programs just as Democrats in 1837 repudiated the banking policies they believed had helped produce that panic. Nor, quite unlike their Whig predecessors, could Republicans raise the hope of funding development with revenue from federal land sales, for Republicans had already given away much of that latent resource to homesteaders, railroad corporations, and states for land-grant colleges. In sum, a positive programmatic Republican response to the depression that depended on fiscal stimulus was politically impossible. Instead, Republicans joined Democrats and Liberals in demanding retrenchment, tax relief, and an abandonment of governmental activism, a demand that, among other things, produced a wave of new state constitutions, North and South, that curtailed the ability of state governments to spend or borrow money. As a result, state parties thereafter could not fight over what state government could not do.[38]

Some Republicans, of course, wanted to pursue a monetarist response to depression by inflating the currency supply, although, significantly, their mechanism for doing so differed from that of the Whigs some thirty-five years earlier. Except for the Republicans' brief rally behind, and the Democrats' brief rally against, the Specie Resumption Act in 1875 and 1876, however, these efforts divided the Republican party internally and, more important, failed to differentiate Republicans from Democrats.[39] Perhaps the most glaring difference between the 1830s–40s and the 1860s–70s, indeed, was that partisan disagreements over money and banking were so sharp during the former period and so muddled during the latter.

One *political* reason for that difference stemmed from the changed stance of Democrats on the money issue. Some Democrats may have supported Greenbackism and later silver monetization in the 1870s for the same reason that Democrats supported hard money in the 1830s and 1840s, namely, to strip private bankers of their control over the currency supply by relying exclusively on government-issued money. This purpose did indeed differ from that of soft-money Republicans who wanted to lower interest rates, expand the credit and capital available for investment in business enterprises, and bolster the protective impact of tariff duties by increasing the premium on gold. Nonetheless, from the perspective of the electorate little seemed to separate parties that both wanted to expand or at least prevent contraction of the currency supply. In sharp contrast, Democratic hard-money schemes and the Independent Treasury plan in the 1830s and 1840s manifestly would have contracted the amount of paper currency in circulation, whereas the Whigs wanted to expand it. That was a partisan distinction voters could readily grasp.

A second and more important political reason why the money and banking question generated less clear-cut partisan responses in the 1870s than in the 1830s–40s derived from the tactical imperative that confronted Republicans after 1872. They had to reassemble their previous coalition by stopping defections and wooing back bolters. As is well known, however, the attitude of the Liberal Republican bolters of 1872 on the money question differed sharply from that of Republican farmers and workers whose enthusiasm for Greenbackism soared after 1873 and who sat on their hands in disgust or defected to third parties in protest after Grant vetoed the Inflation Act of 1874 in order to woo back Liberals.

The modest tariff increase of 1874 and the ingenious intraparty compromise represented by the Specie Resumption Act may have reconciled the interests of manufacturers with those of bankers and merchants, but there is little reason to believe that they appeased the grievances of either farmers or industrial workers who had once voted Republican. Those groups represented a far larger voting bloc than businessmen of any kind, but to prevent their realignment behind the Democrats the Republicans dared not directly meet their demands for concrete legislative redress of grievances. For one thing, some of those demands were anathema to business elements the Republicans were also trying to retain. For another, as many historians have noted, they affronted the ideological belief of many Republicans, but especially the Liberals, that the purpose of government was to provide equal rights before the law, not special-interest legislation that went beyond equality.[40]

Forced in any event to abandon activist government by the prevailing ethos against high taxes, corruption, and governmental intervention, neither the Republicans nor the Democrats could rely on programmatic policy output to rally voters for the impending presidential election of 1876. Instead, both turned to symbolism, appeals to social cleavages in the electorate, and organizational politics. Both nominated squeaky-clean "reformers" for president in 1876 to get on the right side of the corruption issue. To remobilize previous supporters, and especially army veterans, Republicans waved the bloody shirt and Democrats reciprocated in kind by race baiting, especially in the South. ·

But the Republicans' biggest innovation in 1875 and 1876 was consciously and dramatically to exploit the hatred between Protestants and Catholics that had helped power the realignment of the 1850s only to be submerged by later events. That supposed "baby politician" Ulysses Grant himself initiated this offensive by proclaiming at a reunion of the Army of the Tennessee, in September 1875, that the Catholic threat to the public school system now posed the biggest menace to the republic. Republican candidates in the fall of 1875, like Ohio gubernatorial candidate Rutherford B. Hayes, took up the anti-Catholic cry, and James G. Blaine continued the assault in the succeeding congressional session by introducing a constitutional amendment to forbid public tax support of parochial schools, an amendment that was featured prominently in the Republican national platform of 1876.[41]

The self-conscious reinstigation of religious animosities by the Republicans is the major reason why they were able to reaggregate their northern electoral coalition in the 1876 campaign. Granted, it did not stop a surge of angry working-class voters to the Greenback-Labor party in the off-year elections of 1877–78, but, as Republican and Democratic leaders soon discovered, the religious animosities first instigated by Republicans had such powerful salience with both Republican and Democratic voters that the major parties did not need coherent and distinctive programmatic positions on economic questions to mobilize their respective electorates. They had the luxury of tolerating intraparty differences on economic issues at the policymaking level because they usually could retain their electorate despite those divisions. They had discovered a device to differentiate the parties from each other and get voters to the polls that was just as effective as, if not more effective than, the programmatic conflict over divergent economic policies employed by the Whigs and the Democrats. Thus they would use ethnoreligious, not economic, issues to replace the Civil War and Reconstruction as the central axis of interparty conflict.

Yet if political changes from the 1830s–40s to the 1860s–70s help explain the movement of economic issues from the center to the periphery, changes in the nature of economic issues themselves over that period were even more important. Or, to put the matter more precisely, the market revolution demanded, or allowed, a different kind of policy response from government before 1850 than it did after that date. I have already mentioned the differential impact of direct taxes on policy options before and after the Civil War and its role in facilitating or constricting programmatic conflict between the parties. Here let me focus on another matter that was intrinsic to the most important feature of American politics and governance in the nineteenth century: federalism.

The single most important cause of the transformation I have outlined is that the economic issues of the 1830s and 1840s engendered a system-wide fault line between major parties, while those of the 1860s and 1870s did not. In the earlier period, that is, the Whigs and the Democrats contended over the same cluster of issues on which they took the same sides at both the state and the national levels of the federal system. Not only were issues inextricably intertwined in terms of their potential impact on the two levels—for example, the potential impact of the Independent Treasury on state banking and the supply of currency or of the distribution of federal land revenues on the ability of states to pay off bonds—but the simultaneous struggle over them at two levels reinforced their salience and the distinctions between the two parties in the minds of the electorate. That was why programmatic conflict was so central to the life of the second party system after 1837.

Conversely, by the 1860s and 1870s conflict over economic issues no longer coincided at the two levels of the federal system. The economic agendas of state and national politics differed. Thus, state and national conflict over economic policy lost the cumulative impact that it had possessed earlier. In addition, both state and national economic issues split the two major parties along lines of region versus region, locality versus locality, or interest group versus interest group. Instead of reinforcing the image of partisan coherence and distinctiveness, the economic issues of the 1860s and 1870s reinforced the impression of partisan incoherence and similarity. Instead of allowing the construction of geographically broad and inclusive voter coalitions, they threatened to blow such coalitions apart if either party as a whole took a stand on one side or the other of those issues. That is why the Republican and Democratic parties could not use programmatic responses to them in order to rally voters, and that is why economically oriented third parties mushroomed instead.

Both governmental decisions and economic changes produced this difference. The most obvious example of the former concerns the related questions of banking and currency. These questions formed the crux of partisan conflict after 1837 because state-chartered private banks issued most of the circulating currency and because the decisions of both Congress and state legislatures impinged on their ability to do so. And because state legislatures, not just Washington, could influence how much paper money circulated, or at least could be issued by banks, within the borders of individual states, the factionalism between hard-money and soft-money Democrats was fought out primarily within state organizations, not between regional blocs in Congress.

Once Congress nationalized the money and banking questions during the Civil War, however, they ceased to be fodder for partisan conflict at the state level. State legislatures could not determine the amount of greenbacks in circulation or the regional allocation of national banknotes or the remonetization of silver. And, while the tax on state banknotes contained in the 1865 revisions of the National Banking Act did not drive state-chartered banks completely out of existence, those that remained in business were primarily in the East and relied on checks drawn on deposits, not note issue, anyway. The areas that were starved for banking facilities and currency because of the gross maldistribution of banknotes had to look to Washington, not state legislatures, for charters, and banks with such charters were impervious to attacks from state legislatures. At the same time, it was the maldistribution of national banknotes that fueled the Greenback movement and fostered the sectional divisions, as distinct from intrastate factional divisions, over the contraction issue as well as over the later question of remonetizing silver.

Since control of the currency supply had become virtually the exclusive preserve of national authorities—at least so far as governmental policy could affect it, that is—it ceased to be a source of partisan conflict within states. Or, to phrase the matter differently, with regard to banking and currency, the movement of political authority from the periphery to the center of the federal governmental system resulted in its movement from the center to the periphery as a source of partisan conflict.

Since Congress had always had exclusive authority to levy tariff duties, one might argue that the relative marginalization of the tariff issue as an object of partisan conflict in the 1860s and 1870s undermines the case I am making for the crucial importance of federalism with regard to the ability of parties to engage in programmatic partisan conflict.[42] But that argument assumes that the tariff issue had identical economic and ideological connotations before and after the Civil War, and that assumption is erroneous. In the 1830s and 1840s the tariff was viewed as absolutely integral to the entire range of issues Whigs and Democrats fought over at the state and national levels, whereas in the 1860s and 1870s it was seen as largely irrelevant to state issues.

At the simplest level, tariff rates were connected to land prices prior to the Civil War because they formed the sole sources of federal revenue, and land revenues were integral to the ferocious partisan struggle over Whig proposals to give them to state governments to fund bonds for internal improvements. That is what connected the distribution provision of the Land Act of 1841 to the fights over tariff increases in 1841 and 1842. After the Civil War, however, as already noted, distribution of land revenues to the states was a dead issue, and the government no longer relied so exclusively on tariff duties for revenue. In 1874 and thereafter, some Republicans would use the promise of protection to protect wages and jobs, but as a practical matter tariff schedules were shaped by conflicting interest groups who found advocates in both parties.[43]

Interest groups also fought over tariff schedules in the 1840s, of course, but tariff battles evoked sharper partisan conflict then than later because of the tariff's perceived implications for the simultaneous battle over banking and currency that was fought out primarily at the state level. To understand this requires another look at the nature of the conflict between Whigs and Democrats over economic policy and at how it was rendered obsolete after 1850 by developments both inside and outside the political arena.

It has become a historiographical commonplace to say that the Whigs wanted to use state power to foment the spread of the market economy and the Democrats wanted to stop its spread. In its broad implications that formulation is accurate, but the core of the partisan struggle was narrower and more focused. The Whigs did indeed want to promote economic development, and, since they believed that the nation's economy remained underdeveloped because of the dearth and atomized distribution of private capital, they advocated governmental policies that would supply capital directly or facilitate its aggregation in private hands.

To Whigs, banks and tariffs were integrally linked as keys to growth and prosperity, for they believed that the oil that lubricated the engine of economic growth was credit. For Whigs, the ability of individuals to borrow beyond their existing resources and to use those loans to transport products, start businesses, meet weekly payrolls, buy land to farm, and earn the profits from which loans could be repaid generated expansion and opened opportunity for upward mobility. Banks and businesses provided the necessary credit, and, since the specie resources of the United States were limited, it had to be advanced primarily in the form of paper banknotes, bills of exchange secured by goods in transit, or promissory notes.

Yet the credibility of those various forms of paper credit ultimately depended on the assurance that they could, if necessary, be redeemed in specie. Thus, the supply of credit and the rates of interest at which it could be obtained ultimately depended on the nation's specie reserves. That is why the Whigs regarded the tariff as so crucial. To them the biggest threat to the nation's specie reserves and thus to the availability of credit was an unfavorable balance of foreign trade. If the value of what Americans imported exceeded the value of what they exported, the Whigs feared, specie would be drained abroad, and credit, the lubricant of the economy, would dry up. Hence protective tariffs were necessary not simply to shield American manufacturers, miners, and laborers from foreign competition, but to limit imports, slow the exodus of specie, and preserve the credit supply that could free men to pursue their economic ambitions beyond the limits of their restricted individual financial capabilities.[44]

Most Democrats castigated this program as baneful and unnecessary. They viewed credit from its dark flip side, as debt, as a trap rather than a release. They denounced its public form, bonds, as a burden on taxpayers and its private forms as threats to individual autonomy, as insidious inducements to self-enslavement. Credit, in sum, was precisely the feature of the market economy they most feared, and thus they launched a comprehensive assault on all the measures Whigs felt necessary to expand it. They attacked banks and other corporations as privileged monsters that violated equal rights before the law. They vilified paper money as a cheat and a fraud. They dismissed protective tariffs as pandering to manufacturers who would inevitably raise prices to unjustified and unjustifiable levels. And to Whig cries that positive state activism was necessary to expand and protect the credit supply in order to fuel growth, they answered, nonsense. "There is, perhaps, no more dangerous heresy taught in our land than that the prosperity of the country is to be created by its legislation," intoned Pennsylvania's new Democratic governor, William L. Bigler, in January 1852. "The people should rely on their own individual efforts, rather than the mere measures of government for success."[45]

While Whigs and Democrats battled over a wide range of specific policy alternatives and the broad question of governmental involvement in the economy, therefore, what provided ideological intensity to those conflicts was not so much divergent attitudes toward the market or growth itself. Rather conflict centered on the mechanisms by which the market might spread and the government's role in creating them. And of these none was more crucial than credit, which the Whigs regarded as essential and the Democrats condemned as insidious.

Elsewhere I have tried to outline the political and economic developments between 1849 and 1854 that undermined programmatic economic conflict between Whigs and Democrats even before the emergence of the Republican party.[46] Now I would emphasize far more than I once did that the new gold supplies pouring from California after 1849 and the huge increase in British investment in the American economy ended conflict over credit, or at least over the necessity of the concrete programs the Whigs had advocated to provide and protect it. Specifically, the tariff lost relevance as a guardian of the credit supply. Thus it lost its connection to the banking and money issues. Of vast importance, moreover, this development was true not just of the boom during the early 1850s, but also of the latter part of that decade and the 1860s and 1870s.

During the 1880s, of course, partisan disagreements over the tariff between Republicans and Democrats would assume vast symbolic importance, but even then the tariff lacked the connection to other kinds of economic issues that it had formerly had and that had once facilitated programmatic partisan conflict. More to the point, after 1850 the tariff never regained its economic, and therefore ideologically charged, role as guarantor of the credit supply. Indeed, credit itself never regained the place at the ideological core of partisan conflict that it had once occupied.

At least two reasons can be offered for this development, although others are conceivable. First, the state itself either directly supplied or obviated the need for credit. This statement will seem counterintuitive or flatly wrongheaded to those who know the work of economic historians that shows that the years between 1861 and 1866 witnessed a net decline in the supply of capital in the private economic sector as government bond issues sucked huge supplies of money out of it.[47] But a wartime economy was not a peacetime economy. Not only did the government create a new supply of money with its greenback issues, but it spent money at unprecedented levels to pay for supplies and soldiers' wages.[48] These measures, of course, did not fully compensate for the amount of money taken out of the private sector through bond sales, but the economy was so awash in money that inflation, not a credit crunch, seemed the chief danger.

In part for this reason, wartime tariff increases were justified as compensation for the new excise taxes on American manufacturers, not as a means to protect the credit supply. The tariff had in effect become an interest group or microeconomic measure, not a macroeconomic instrument. Equally important, as noted earlier, during the war the instruments of governmental debt, the bonds, did not become a partisan issue because Democrats saw merit in them.

More important, as Jeffrey Williamson has shown in his truly seminal article, when the war ended wartime taxes stayed in place but expenditures stopped.[49] By 1866, the federal government was running a surplus ranging from 1 to 2 percent of the GNP a year, and it spent that surplus on buying back bonds, thus pumping back into the private economy the money it had taken out of it during the war with interest, since bonds that had been purchased in greenbacks were repaid in gold. Thus ample supplies of capital and credit for potential investment were available in the 1870s that were not attributable to the tariff. How the tariff had its impact, Williamson shows, was by inducing investment in machinery for manufacturing rather than in something else. That investment, in turn, not only explains why manufacturing output increased during the depression decade, but it also probably helps explain why manufacturing elements in the Republican coalition were so quickly reconciled to the slow currency expansion implicit in the Specie Resumption Act. In effect, the inundation of long-term capital investment obviated their dependence on banks and short-term credit for working capital.[50]

By the late 1860s, of course, portions of the Democratic party were bitterly protesting the privileges of bondholders and demanding that debts be scaled or repaid in greenbacks rather than gold. Yet no historian, so far as I am aware, suggests that this government policy of using its surplus to buy back bonds drew explicit criticism. To understand why, one need look no further than the analysis and mind-boggling diagrams presented in Richard Bensel's *Yankee Leviathan,* which illustrate how the government's intervention in the bond and gold markets worked. Few politicians, let alone voters, could have possibly understood this mechanism. The policy was simply too complex to be grasped or politicized. It could not be fodder for partisan conflict even if allowance is made for the fact that elements of the Democratic party also benefited from it.[51]

Complexity that rendered economic issues virtually immune to coherent partisan manipulation also characterized other policy choices that emerged

in the 1870s, particularly those at the state level. This was true largely because
of the second economic transformation after 1850, which accompanied resolution of the credit problem. Although the spread of the market economy
between 1815 and 1880 never ceased to have dislocating consequences, the
proportions of Americans involved in it surely grew over time. And the fewer
Americans who remained outside the market over time, the more the nature
of the economic issues changed and the greater the difficulty of the major
parties in providing coherent yet distinctive policy responses to them
became.

The central ecological or demographic fact that underlay partisan conflict
between Whigs and Democrats in the 1830s and 1840s was that a significant
fraction of the population still had not experienced the market revolution.
Without joining the continuing debate about how intransigent the ideological opposition of those outside the market economy was to commercial activity per se, we can agree that preserving their personal economic autonomy
was a top priority of those whom we call, for purposes of convenience, subsistence farmers and that they perceived certain mechanisms of the market
economy, especially the credit-debt nexus, as a threat to it. Thus, broadly put,
the Democratic party was a coalition of those inside the market sector who
had been victimized by it and those outside it who feared its encroachment,
whereas the Whigs attracted those who wanted to expand the market sector
because they had already enjoyed its benefits or hoped to do so in the future.
The relative equality in size of these two blocs and the easily comprehensible
relevance to them of the programs advanced by the Whigs and the Democrats
helps vastly to explain why the parties stressed that programmatic conflict
when they sought to mobilize votes.

In contrast, at the end of the Civil War and in increasing proportions until
1880, the great majority of the American population was absorbed, voluntarily
or involuntarily, into the market economy.[52] Thus the questions of whether
the market should spread and, if so, what role government should play in
fostering that spread were moot. The expansion of the market revolution was
a fait accompli. Now at issue was its variegated impacts and how to adjust to
or compensate for them. And those questions, quite unlike the easily politicized earlier issue, did not divide Americans in terms of where they stood on
the market or the preservation of economic autonomy or the advantages and
disadvantages of credit. Instead they pitted interest group against interest
group or locality against locality. Because both the Republican and the Democratic coalitions that emerged from the Civil War and Reconstruction included members from each rival interest group and each rival locality, neither

dared take a position as a party on those issues lest it alienate crucial members of its coalition.

After the Civil War the money question fell into this category of issues, as did the tariff, and one could cite other issues, like the southern disputes over fence laws, that defied the formulation of coherent statewide party lines. Let me close, however, by briefly discussing three issues that emerged at the state level after 1850 and proved indigestible to the major parties: railroad construction and regulation; regulation of fire and life insurance companies; and labor's demands for eight-hour laws.

If banks and the credit they provided spearheaded the penetration and expansion of the market economy before 1848, railroads clearly played that role after that date. Yet from the beginning the scramble for charters and attempts to dictate routes in state legislatures pitted region against region or locality against locality, not party against party. Thus it was impossible for parties as statewide organizations to take positions on those debates without risking the loss of more support than they gained.[53] Similarly, the demand for the regulation of railroad rates and competitive practices that resulted in the misnamed Granger laws in midwestern states in the 1860s and 1870s did not align party against party or even farmers against railroads. Rather they set legislators who represented merchants and other shippers from areas that already had railroads and wanted regulation against legislators representing localities that still lacked railroad connections, wanted them, and feared that state regulation would deter further railroad construction. No statewide party dared touch that hornet's nest.[54]

Similarly, attempts by the New York legislature in the 1870s to regulate the insurance industry pitted "haves" against "have nots." Larger firms there wanted the state government legally to establish standards regarding minimal capitalization and policy redemption practice in order to drive out reckless competitors in the business who offered cheaper premiums, but consequently lacked the resources to pay off claims. Because both the Republican and Democratic parties drew support from the owners of both kinds of firms, to say nothing of their policyholders, this was hardly the kind of question they could take to the electorate in campaigns for statewide office or even members of the legislature. Again the complexity of the new issues precluded the coherent programmatic response possible to the issues of the 1830s and 1840s. But they were also less conducive to partisan manipulation than even something like the creation by New York Republicans over Democratic opposition of a Metropolitan Fire Department and a Metropolitan Board of Health for New York City in the mid-1860s. For, as James C. Mohr has brilliantly shown, those policies had an overt partisan purpose—the weakening of the Democratic machine in New York City and the creation of an identity for the radical wing of the state Republican party.[55]

Finally, as David Montgomery has shown, workers' demands for eight-hour laws after the Civil War did not spawn partisan polarization over the issue. Rather, where laws were enacted at all, they were generally toothless, unenforceable measures that had bipartisan backing. In part, that backing reflected the healthy respect that both parties had for the growing political militance of labor and a fear of offending it. For the same reason, both parties nominated laboring men for local offices to show that they were on the side of the angels. Yet that backing also reflected the fact that pressure for such laws often came from local manufacturers who had been forced by their own workers to reduce the length of the workday and who found themselves at a competitive disadvantage against manufacturers elsewhere who had not done so. In sum, for state legislative parties, the eight-hour law campaign of labor assumed the same dimension of have versus have not, locality versus locality, as railroad and insurance regulation. That alignment could destroy statewide electoral coalitions if any party was so foolhardy as to take a statewide stance on it.[56]

In sum, just like the money issue at the national level, the economic questions that percolated into the political arena at the state level in the late 1860s and early 1870s, and as early as 1850 with regard to railroads, were not as conducive to coherent programmatic partisan conflict as the economic issues of the late 1830s and 1840s.[57] And it was the combination of changes in both the economic and the political context that explains why they were not. Together those changes moved economic issues from the center to the periphery of major-party conflict between 1835 and 1880.

NOTES

1. For partisan conflict over the market revolution during the stable phase of the second party system, see Harry L. Watson, *Jacksonian Politics and Community Conflict: The Emergence of the Second American Party System in Cumberland County, North Carolina* (Baton Rouge, La., 1981); Harry L. Watson, *Liberty and Power: The Politics of Jacksonian America* (New York, 1990); Charles Sellers, *The Market Revolution: Jacksonian America, 1815–1846* (New York, 1991); William R. Brock, *Parties and Political Conscience: American*

Dilemmas, 1840–1850 (Millbrook, N.Y., 1979); and John Ashworth, *"Agrarians" and "Aristocrats": Party Political Ideology in the United States, 1837–1846* (London, 1983).

2. On the Civil War party system as a whole, see Paul Kleppner, *The Third Electoral System, 1853–1892: Parties, Voters, and Political Cultures* (Chapel Hill, N.C., 1979) and Dale Baum, *The Civil War Party System, The Case of Massachusetts, 1848–1876* (Chapel Hill, N.C., 1984). For developments in the South, however, see Michael Perman, *The Road to Redemption: Southern Politics, 1869–1879* (Chapel Hill, N.C. 1984).

3. Morton Keller, *Affairs of State: Public Life in Late Nineteenth Century America* (Cambridge, Mass., 1977), pp. 238–83 (quotation on p. 238); Keith I. Polakoff, *The Politics of Inertia: The Election of 1876 and the End of Reconstruction* (Baton Rouge, La., 1973); and Perman, *Road to Redemption,* pp. 123–77.

4. Thomas B. Alexander, *Sectional Stress and Party Strength: A Computer Analysis of Roll-Call Voting Patterns in the United States House of Representatives, 1836–1860* (Nashville, 1967); Herbert Ershkowitz and William G. Shade, "Consensus or Conflict? Political Behavior in State Legislatures during the Jacksonian Period," *Journal of American History* 58 (1971): 591–622; Peter Levine, "State Legislative Parties in the Jacksonian Era: New Jersey, 1829–1844," *Journal of American History* 62 (1975): 591–608; M. Philip Lucas, "The Development of the Second Party System in Mississippi, 1817–1846" (Ph.D. diss., Cornell University, 1984); William G. Shade, "Political Pluralism and Party Development: The Creation of a Modern Party System, 1815–1852," in Paul Kleppner et al., eds., *The Evolution of American Electoral Systems* (Westport, Conn., 1981), pp. 77–111; Ronald P. Formisano, *The Transformation of Political Culture: Massachusetts Parties, 1790s–1840s* (New York, 1983), pp. 173–320; Michael F. Holt, *The Political Crisis of the 1850s* (reprint, New York, 1983), pp. 26–27; and Michael F. Holt, "The Election of 1840, Voter Mobilization, and the Emergence of the Second American Party System: A Reappraisal of Jacksonian Voting Behavior" in Michael F. Holt, *Political Parties and American Political Development from the Age of Jackson to the Age of Lincoln* (Baton Rouge, La., 1992), pp. 151–91.

5. I shall attempt to document these assertions about decline in the levels of partisan conflict on roll-call votes in Congress and state legislatures as I proceed with this essay, but a disruption or turbulence in the electoral coalitions of both Republicans and Democrats between 1870 and 1876, as well as a decline in turnout in the early 1870s, is well documented. See Kleppner, *The Third Electoral System,* pp. 16–142, esp. pp. 16–47 and Tables 4.4, 4.5, and 4.7, and pp. 127, 129, and 141; Baum, *Civil War Party System,* pp. 145–210; and Walter Dean Burnham, *Critical Elections and the Mainsprings of American Politics* (New York, 1970), pp. 16–17. No historian has attempted quantitative analyses of southern voting patterns during the 1870s comparable to those performed for the north. Nonetheless, from the beginning of 1870 until the end of 1874 and even later in a few states, talk of impending realignment that would replace the Republican and Democratic parties was rampant, attempts to form new biracial parties of the center were constant, white scalawags moved from the Republican camp to the Democratic camp, and previously apathetic whites were mobilized by Democrats. See Perman, *Road to Redemption,* pp. 108–77.

6. Kleppner, *The Third Electoral System,* pp. 143–356; Perman, *Road to Redemption,* pp. 149–77.

7. The studies of roll-call voting in state legislatures cited in note 4 above indicate less partisan disagreement on votes concerning labor legislation than on other issues in this

list. Nonetheless, squabbling over the implementation of ten-hour laws could provoke sharp partisan conflict. See, for example, my *Forging a Majority: The Formation of the Republican Party in Pittsburgh, 1848–1860* (New Haven, Conn., 1969), pp. 66–69.

8. On lobbying of state legislatures by interest groups, see, for example, James C. Mohr, *The Radical Republicans and Reform in New York during Reconstruction* (Ithaca, N.Y., 1973), pp. 21–114 and passim; and Seymour Mandelbaum, *Boss Tweed's New York* (New York, 1965), pp. 141–46.

9. I cite some of this extensive literature in my essay on Jacksonian voter behavior, cited above.

10. Holt, *The Political Crisis of the 1850s,* pp. 26–27.

11. Baum, *Civil War Party System,* pp. 20–21, 60–72, 114–15, 141–43.

12. Baum, *Civil War Party System,* pp. 145–210; Terry L. Seip, *The South Returns to Congress: Men, Economic Measures, and Intersectional Relationships, 1868–1879* (Baton Rouge, La., 1983), pp. 112–268; Carl V. Harris, "Right Fork or Left Fork? The Section-Party Alignments of Southern Democrats in Congress, 1873–1897," *Journal of Southern History* 42 (1976): 471–506; Richard J. Piper, "Party Realignment and Congressional Change: Issue Dimensions and Priorities in the U.S. House of Representatives, 1871–1893," *American Politics Quarterly* 11 (1983): 459–90; Jean H. Baker, "A Loyal Opposition: Northern Democrats in the Thirty-seventh Congress," *Civil War History* 25 (1979): 139–55; and, for the disappearance of race and Reconstruction issues from the agendas of at least two northern state legislatures, Lex Renda, "The Polity and the Party System: Connecticut and New Hampshire, 1840–1876," (Ph.D. diss., University of Virginia, 1991).

13. Perman, *Road to Redemption,* pp. 3–107; Mark W. Summers, *Railroads, Reconstruction, and the Gospel of Prosperity: Aid under the Radical Republicans, 1865–1877* (Princeton, N.J., 1984). For an interpretation of southern politics between 1868 and 1873 that rejects Perman's notion of a "politics of the center," see Eric Foner, *Reconstruction: America's Unfinished Revolution, 1863–1877* (New York, 1988), pp. 412–59.

14. William Gillette, *Retreat from Reconstruction, 1869–1879* (Baton Rouge, La., 1979). The obsession of northern Republicans with their own electoral fortunes in the North and their lack of serious interest in fostering a Republican party in the South is also a theme of Richard H. Abbott, *The Republican Party and the South, 1855–1877: The First Southern Strategy* (Chapel Hill, N.C., 1986) and Seip, *The South Returns to Congress.*

15. The national rate of voter turnout sank from 78.1 percent in 1868 to 71.3 percent in 1872; in 1852 it had been 69.6 percent. U.S. Bureau of the Census, *The Statistical History of the United States from Colonial Times to the Present* (New York, 1976), p. 1072.

16. The difference between the Republican party's national platform of 1872 and that of 1876 well reflects the Republicans' retreat from specificity regarding the implementation of Reconstruction. The two platforms can be found in the appendices to the essays on the elections of 1872 and 1876 in Arthur M. Schlesinger, Jr., and Fred Israel, eds., *History of American Presidential Elections, 1789–1968,* 4 vols. (New York, 1971), Vol. 2.

17. Harris, "Right Fork or Left Fork?"; Piper, "Party Realignment and Congressional Change."

18. Irwin Unger, *The Greenback Era: A Social and Political History of American Finance, 1865–1879* (Princeton, N.J., 1964), pp. 259, 409–13, and passim. While Republicans mentioned both their pledge to resume specie payments and the tariff in their 1876 national

platform, their tariff plank was tepid. Nowhere did they use the code words *protection* or *discrimination,* which had been so central to protariff propaganda in the antebellum period. Instead they simply called for duties "which, so far as possible, should be so adjusted as to promote the interests of American labor and advance the prosperity of the whole country." This soft-pedaling undoubtedly reflected nervousness about holding those Liberal Republicans who had returned to the party after 1872.

19. Piper, "Party Realignment and Congressional Change," pp. 472–75; Harris, "Right Fork or Left Fork"; and Ballard C. Campbell, "Party, Policy, and Political Leadership in Congress during the Nineteenth Century" (unpublished paper, Project 87, Conference on Congress, 1981).

20. Compare, for example, the partisan dimension of the votes on Senate and House passage of the Specie Resumption Act in Unger, *The Greenback Era,* pp. 259, 409–13, with that of the House vote to remonetize silver in July 1876, the House vote to pass the Bland Silver Purchase Bill in November 1877, the Senate vote to add the Allison amendment to Bland's bill in February 1878, Senate adoption of the Bland-Allison Act, and House concurrence in the Bland-Allison Act listed in Harris, "Right Fork or Left Fork?"

21. Perman, *Road to Redemption,* esp. pp. 143–48; Summers, *Railroads, Reconstruction, and the Gospel of Prosperity;* and J. Mills Thornton III, "Fiscal Policy and the Failure of Radical Reconstruction in the Lower South," in Morgan Kousser and James McPherson, eds., *Region, Race and Reconstruction: Essays in Honor of C. Vann Woodward* (New York, 1982).

22. While Paul Kleppner insists that hostility to prohibition hurt Republicans more than hard times in the elections of 1873–74 and William Gillette argues that a racist backlash against the civil rights bill of 1874 hurt northern as well as southern Republicans that year, Eric Foner's contention that "only the depression can explain the electoral tidal wave that swept over the North in 1874" is surely on the mark. See Foner, *Reconstruction,* p. 523.

23. David Montgomery, *Beyond Equality: Labor and the Radical Republicans, 1862–1872* (New York, 1967), pp. 3–14; Jeffrey Williamson, "Watersheds and Turning Points: Conjectures on the Long–Term Impact of Civil War Financing," *Journal of Economic History* 34 (1974): 636–61.

24. Foner, *Reconstruction,* esp. pp. xxiii–xxvi, 1–34. Foner treats the North on pp. 460–524.

25. Eric Foner, *Free Soil, Free Labor, Free Men: The Ideology of the Republican Party before the Civil War* (New York, 1970), pp. 168–85.

26. Foner, *Reconstruction: America's Unfinished Revolution,* pp. 487, 488–89. David Montgomery also stresses the importance of Liberalism in *Beyond Equality,* pp. 379–86. In effect, both provide an ideological explanation for the retreat from activist, program-oriented politics that Morton Keller seems almost to attribute to innate inertial forces in *Affairs of State,* pp. 161, 238–83, and passim.

27. Richard L. McCormick, "The Party Period and Public Policy: An Exploratory Hypothesis," *Journal of American History* 66 (1979): 279–98. See also McCormick's book of collected essays with the same name, *The Party Period and Public Policy: American Politics from the Age of Jackson to the Progressive Era* (New York, 1986). One might note here that Joel Silbey's similar stress on a single-party period from 1838 to 1893, which emphasizes

the continuity of pre- and postwar politics, also fails to explain the movement of pro-grammatic conflict over matters of political economy from the center to the periphery of that system. See Joel H. Silbey, *The American Political Nation, 1838–1893* (Stanford, Calif., 1991).

28. Terry Seip, in his *The South Returns to Congress,* has made a valuable contribution by demonstrating that the well-known East-West split in the Republican party was not its only sectional division. On many economic questions northern and southern Republicans also voted against each other.

29. To the extent that these assertions are accurate, they may simply reflect the fact that we know far more about Congress than about state legislatures in the 1860s and 1870s. As I shall try to show, state-oriented economic issues did indeed divide both parties, al-though far more along lines of locality versus locality and interest group versus interest group than of coherent factionalism.

30. Kleppner, *The Third Electoral System,* pp. 121–42.

31. The instability of both Whig and Democratic electoral coalitions prior to 1837 is demonstrated by the correlation analysis in Shade, "Political Pluralism and Party Development."

32. Harry N. Scheiber, *The Ohio Canal Era: A Case Study of Government and the Economy, 1820–1861* (Athens, Ohio, 1969). My allusion to Seward's promise of a bonanza of federal money to pay off the new bonds he wanted to issue to fund expansion of the Erie Canal network is taken from draft chapters of a forthcoming book by my colleague Professor Charles W. McCurdy on the legal ramifications of the Anti-Rent movement in New York.

33. The chief rationale of Republican policymakers who adopted the income tax during the war was to deflect criticism from the wealthy who profited from the conflict while refusing to fight it by showing they shared in the sacrifice required by the war. See Robert Stanley, *The Dimensions of Law in the Service of Order: Origins of the Federal Income Tax, 1861–1913* (New York, 1993), pp. 27–43, 234. Stanley's unusually passionate book also shows that the income tax, like other economic issues, did not polarize Republicans and Democrats along party lines; he also provides a highly sophisticated analysis of debates and roll-call votes over the tariff after 1865.

34. Leonard P. Curry, "Congressional Democrats, 1861–1863," *Civil War History* 12 (1966): 213–29; Jean H. Baker, "A Loyal Opposition: Northern Democrats in the Thirty-seventh Congress," *Civil War History* 25 (1979): 139–55.

35. Iver Bernstein, *The New York City Draft Riots: Their Significance for American Society and Politics in the Age of the Civil War* (New York, 1990), pp. 64–65, 69–70, 195–236; Mandelbaum, *Boss Tweed's New York.*

36. The best study of corruption in the antebellum period is Mark W. Summers, *The Plundering Generation: Corruption and the Crisis of the Union, 1849–1861* (New York, 1988).

37. Foner notes the uneven impact of the depression on overall economic performance in *Reconstruction,* pp. 512–24. See also Williamson, "Watersheds and Turning Points."

38. Keller, *Affairs of State,* pp. 319–21; Perman, *Road to Redemption,* pp. 178–220.

39. Unger, *The Greenback Era,* pp. 410–11; Seip, *The South Returns to Congress,* p. 195.

40. Montgomery, *Beyond Equality;* Foner, *Reconstruction,* pp. 488–524.

41. Kleppner, *The Third Electoral System*, pp. 227–37. The order of the extraordinarily broad range of appeals in the Republican national platform is fascinating. The first three planks referred to the Republicans' success in winning the war and their determination not to sacrifice its fruits. The fourth pledged specie resumption, the fifth condemned the spoils system, the sixth vowed that Republicans would prosecute corrupt officials, the seventh endorsed the Blaine anti-Catholic amendment, and the eighth was the tepid endorsement of tariff increases. The fourteenth said that pledges to soldiers and sailors, presumably for pensions, "must be fulfilled," and the fifteenth and sixteenth heavy-handedly reminded voters of the Democratic party's affiliation with the South and the Confederacy.

42. Here I use *federalism* as an abbreviation of the rather cumbersome formula I spelled out above. Party lines on economic questions were congruent between the state and national levels and therefore reinforcing in the 1830s and 1840s, but incongruent and therefore disaggregating in the 1860s and 1870s.

43. The fact that the tariff had become an interest group issue rather than a strictly partisan one is reflected in the relatively low indices of disagreement tariff votes prompted in the House and the Senate throughout the 1870s. See Stanley, *The Dimensions of Law in the Service of Order*, pp. 45–99, and Harris, "Right Fork or Left Fork?"

44. This summary of the Whig position is based on years of research in Whig sources, but the Whigs' obsession with protecting credit became particularly clear in 1846 when they faced the one-two punch of the Democrats' Independent Treasury Act and Walker Tariff. In congressional speeches, party newspapers, and the pages of the Whig *American Review*, they hammered away at the Democratic assault on credit. For that particular episode, see my "Winding Roads to Recovery: The Whig Party, 1844–1848," in my *Political Parties and American Political Development*, pp. 224–27.

45. *(Philadelphia) Public Ledger*, Jan. 21, 1852.

46. Holt, *The Political Crisis of the 1850s*, pp. 106–13.

47. See, for example, Susan Previant Lee and Peter Passell, *A New Economic View of American History* (New York, 1979), pp. 234–35.

48. I have not included the $300 million worth of national banknotes authorized during the war in this list, because those notes were themselves based on bonds. And, since they represented only 90 percent of the face value of bonds, they contributed marginally to the net withdrawal of money from the private sector.

49. Williamson, "Watersheds and Turning Points."

50. As Robert F. Dalzell, Jr., has brilliantly shown, Massachusetts' largest textile manufacturers had freed themselves of dependence on bank loans for working capital to meet weekly payrolls long before the Civil War by establishing their own insurance company to supply it. This ingenious solution to the constant need for credit, in turn, may explain why large textile manufacturers like Abbott and Amos Lawrence or Nathan Appleton were distinctively less insistent about the need for protective tariffs than they had been earlier. See Joseph Grinnell to John J. Crittenden, Jan. 31, 1849, John J. Crittenden MSS, Library of Congress; Robert C. Winthrop to John P. Kennedy, Dec. 24, 1851, copy, Robert C. Winthrop MSS, Massachusetts Historical Society; and Robert F. Dalzell, Jr., *Enterprising Elite: The Boston Associates and the World They Made* (Cambridge, Mass., 1987).

51. Richard Bensel, *Yankee Leviathan: The Origins of Central State Authority in America, 1859–1877* (Cambridge, Eng., 1990), pp. 254–302. The relevant diagrams are on pp. 256, 260, and 262.

52. This development is quite properly a central subtheme of Foner's book on Reconstruction.

53. For a trenchant analysis of how localistic conflict over railroad construction and related policies concerning state real estate taxes disrupted New Jersey's Whig party in the 1850s, see Lex Renda, "Railroads, Revenue, and Reform: Decline of the New Jersey Whigs" (M.A. thesis, University of Virginia, 1984).

54. George H. Miller, *Railroads and the Granger Laws* (Madison, Wis., 1971). The same dynamic inhibited partisan responses in states whose railroad networks developed after the 1870s. See Margaret S. Holden, "The Rise and Fall of Oregon Populism: Legal Theory, Political Culture and Public Policy, 1868–1895" (Ph.D. diss., University of Virginia, 1993), pp. 148–52.

55. Mandelbaum, *Boss Tweed's New York*, pp. 141–46; Mohr, *The Radical Republicans and Reform in New York during Reconstruction.*

56. Montgomery, *Beyond Equality*, pp. 230–95. On the unenforceability of eight-hour legislation, except by workers themselves through the resort to strikes, see also Bernstein, *The New York City Draft Riots*, pp. 243–57.

57. As greatly as I admire the work of my former student Richard L. McCormick, I believe the analysis presented here undermines his case that the infinitely divisible resources available to governments in the form of charters, other privileges, and subsidies allowed them continually to meet the needs of competing interest groups and thus allowed "distributive" economic policies to sustain mass two-party conflict throughout the "party period." For one thing, not all nineteenth-century economic policies were distributive as McCormick implies. Demands for regulation appeared long before the twentieth century. For another thing, it was precisely the emergence of interest group conflict after the economy had matured that inhibited rather than fostered coherent policy responses from the major parties. Though mass two-party conflict did indeed continue in the late nineteenth century, it was despite of, not because of, this interest group conflict.

PART IV

Religion and the Market Revolution

10

The Market Revolution and the Shaping of
Identity in Whig-Jacksonian America

DANIEL WALKER HOWE

IKE A NUMBER OF PROMINENT HISTORIANS before him, Charles Sellers waited until he had retired before publishing his magnum opus, a
summation of the results of his lifetime of research and teaching. Such
a work is *The Market Revolution: Jacksonian America, 1815–1846*.[1] When I read
this book, two things struck me: first, the interpretive framework was much
the same as I had heard it thirty years before as a graduate student listening
to Professor Sellers's lectures at the University of California; second, for some
reason I *liked* the old lectures better. Of course one couldn't help wondering
why: what was different? Fortunately, there was a published version of the
lectures, so one did not have to rely simply on memory and old notes to make
the comparison.[2]

Thirty years ago, Charles Sellers was arguing that the antebellum era had
been characterized by the formation of a national market economy based
primarily on commercial agriculture and that this national market economy
constituted a transition between the colonial staple-exporting economy and
the industrial economy of modern America. In the colonial economy, he
pointed out, only those people who lived within easy access to water transportation had been able to market their crops, and the rest of the population
had had to be economically self-sufficient, if not within their families, then
within their local communities. The national market economy that came into
being during the antebellum period was made possible by improved transportation and was characterized (as Sellers put it) by "a vast extension of the
division of labor or, in other words, specialization of economic activities.
Areas and individuals that formerly had been self-sufficing," or nearly so,
"began to concentrate on the one product or service they could produce most
efficiently."[3] The expansion of cotton cultivation was particularly momentous. It contributed to such varied and important developments as the rise of
textile manufacturing and the American merchant marine, conflict between
the "five civilized tribes" and white settlers, and political disputes over economic issues: whether to have a protective tariff, how to provide credit to

commercial farmers, and how to fund internal improvements necessary to transport crops to market. Ultimately, this extension of commercial agriculture produced sectional competition over whether it would be slave or free farming that would be expanded. The explanatory model that Sellers described in those lectures, the causal dynamic of commercial agriculture, carried conviction.[4]

Building on the strengths of these lectures, *The Market Revolution* adds an interpretation of the cultural consequences wrought by economic change and relates these, too, to politics. To examine "the expansion of the market, the intensification of market discipline, and the penetration of that discipline into spheres of life previously untouched by it" is a necessary and demanding undertaking that has been addressed by a number of recent historians.[5] Recognizing the importance of religion to antebellum American life, Sellers casts his discussion of the cultural impact of the market largely in terms of religion. Much of the time, his analysis of the interactions among economic, religious, and political history dovetails nicely with the more specialized findings of Richard Carwardine and others.[6]

In *The Market Revolution,* Sellers is at his best in his evocative, sympathetic descriptions of the culture of the subsistence farmers who lived outside the market.[7] Although somewhat romanticized, his presentation also takes account of the dark side of that culture: the oppression of women and children within the household, the bitter hatred of African Americans and Native Americans, the vulnerability to certain kinds of demagogy. (Joseph Smith, the founding prophet of Mormonism, is portrayed as one of the worst of demagogues.)[8] But, despite its virtues, the presentation of cultural history in *The Market Revolution* is so tendentious, so heavily freighted with the determination to show that the market was undemocratic and inhumane, that it fails to convey a comparable understanding of the culture of the new middle class created by the market and embraced by many people. Because we are not made aware of this culture's attractions, we are left even at the end of this massive book wondering why the market revolution succeeded and the opposition to it failed. A more balanced assessment of the costs and benefits entailed by the market revolution would help explain this outcome. Besides critically analyzing the presentation of cultural history in Sellers's book, the present essay will go on to suggest how we can understand the appeal of the market revolution to Americans living between 1815 and 1846.

Invoking the language of theology, Sellers describes a commercial world-view that he calls "arminianism" and a noncommercial, agrarian world-view that he calls "antinomianism." Here is how he explains their opposition: "While arminian moralism sanctioned competitive individualism and the market's rewards of wealth and status, antinomian new birth recharged rural America's communal egalitarianism in resistance. A heresy of capitalist accommodation confronted a heresy of precapitalist cultural revitalization in a *Kulturkampf* that would decide American destiny on the private battlegrounds of every human relationship."[9]

Historically, Arminianism was not defined in opposition to antinomianism; it was defined in opposition to Calvinism. In Christian theology, Arminianism is the doctrine that, even after the Fall, human beings retain sufficient free will to choose whether to accept God's saving grace. The doctrine was advanced among Reformed Protestants in the seventeenth century as an alternative to the High Calvinist position that humanity was utterly depraved and divine grace was irresistible.

Among Dutch, Swiss, and New England Protestants, Arminianism flourished most within prosperous mercantile communities, which indeed raises the question whether their merchant capitalism fostered a sense of human capacity and moral responsibility. Sellers puts it this way: "As God seemed kindlier, the environment more manageable, and their fate more dependent on their own abilities, [Arminians] could no longer see themselves as sinners helplessly dependent on the arbitrary salvation of an all-powerful God."[10] This is a plausible sociological explanation for the rise of what was manifestly a religion affirming a greater measure of human dignity. Another possible explanation is that a higher standard of living diminished the appeal of the austere Calvinist lifestyle. Of course, the two hypotheses are not mutually exclusive. Whatever the causal mechanism, the Calvinist doctrines of total depravity, unconditional election, and irresistible grace were losing their appeal during the course of the nineteenth century, and not only in the United States. It seems likely that, even if early Calvinism fostered what Max Weber termed "the spirit of capitalism," in later generations a market economy fostered higher notions of human dignity and liberty than were compatible with orthodox Calvinism.[11] This much may be conceded by way of overall plausibility to Sellers's association of Arminianism with the market. Whether the connection between theology and economic development was as straightforward and politically manifest as he makes out is something else.

By the nineteenth century, Arminian-like doctrines were growing in popularity among several denominations of American Protestants, having been embraced not only by rationalists like the Unitarians and Universalists and liturgicals like the Episcopalians, but also by such important evangelical groups as the Methodists, "new school" Presbyterians, and Freewill Baptists. However, these assorted kinds of Arminians did not constitute a united front in support of common economic, political, or even religious issues. One convenient test of support for the market revolution was support for the Whig party, but only certain versions of Arminianism were associated with Whig voting. Arminian Unitarians certainly were predominantly Whigs, but Arminian Universalists and Baptists were probably more often Democrats. The politics of the Arminian Methodists are only now being sorted out by Richard Carwardine.[12] Episcopalians—despite their Arminianism and high socioeconomic status—were often Democrats, especially in New England, where they, along with Baptists and Quakers, shared the status of religious dissenters from the Congregational establishments and consequently embraced Jeffersonian principles on the relationship of church and state.[13]

Although many Whigs may have been Arminians, there is no doubt that many other Whigs were Calvinists. The typical Whig reformers, such as the famous Tappan brothers, were evangelical Calvinists. The New England Calvinism of Andover Theological Seminary, founded for the express purpose of resisting Arminianism, was quintessentially Whig. The most uncompromisingly anti-Arminian of all American Calvinists, the Old School Presbyterian faculty of Princeton Theological Seminary, were "Cotton Whig" in their politics. In short, evidence that antebellum theological Arminianism was a stalking-horse for Whig politics or promarket economic policies is difficult to find.

The socioeconomic origins of Arminianism are probably multiple, and the Arminianism of the New England commercial elite, which eventuated in Unitarianism and best illustrates Sellers's thesis, is only one aspect of the story. The growth of Arminianism among the common people has been studied less, although Steven Marini and Nathan Hatch have made an exciting start.[14] It needs to be added that Arminianism, like other theological and philosophical positions, has an intellectual appeal on rational grounds that is independent of socioeconomic predilections, and a balanced historical account will recognize this. The debates carried on in this period over the nature of free will among theological exponents of various schools of thought, Calvinist and Arminian, were remarkable for their intellectual sophistication. Sellers shamelessly reduces these arguments to fronts for economic interest, often distorting them in the process.[15]

Antinomianism, the other of Sellers's categories, also dates from the time of the Reformation. Antinomianism is the doctrine that the moral law does not bind God's elect, since they enjoy the indwelling presence of the Holy Spirit. It has not been a popular teaching, because it seems to license anarchic behavior by fanatics claiming the direct guidance of the Spirit. Sellers does not so much as mention this definition, however; instead he describes antinomianism as the "heresy that God visits ordinary people with the 'New Light' of transfiguring grace and revelation."[16] This is confused: first, because antinomianism is not the same thing as New Light Calvinism; second, because the doctrine Sellers has stated is not heretical. What would make it heretical would be if the revelations of God's will that the believer received were considered to apply to anyone else or to substitute for Scripture or the doctrine taught by the Church.

The only Christian body in antebellum America that subscribed more or less to the heretical form of antinomian doctrine was the Quakers. Yet the Quakers were conspicuously *not* a backwoods denomination or one whose members practiced subsistence agriculture; what is more, they were generally part of the Whig voting bloc. The founders of certain other sects, notably Ann Lee of the Shakers and Joseph Smith of the Mormons, claimed to have received revelations that supplemented the Judeo-Christian Scriptures. Instead of accepting traditional agricultural society, however, they both founded utopian communities, highly regimented, with novel economic and sexual practices. One group of antebellum American Christians did indeed approximate the kind of antinomian peasant *mentalité* Sellers describes, scrupulously rejecting the market and all modernity. These were the Mennonites, including the Amish. But Sellers never mentions them in his book. All in all, antinomianism seems to work even less well as a cultural category in Sellers's book than Arminianism does.

In a footnote, Sellers explains that he does not intend the terms *arminian* and *antinomian* to be taken in their accustomed theological senses, but rather as designating "clashing cosmologies," of which the "narrower theological distinctions" are symbols.[17] By not capitalizing *arminian* and *antinomian,* it is possible that the author may intend to remind us that the terms are not being used in their usual senses. But what is the relationship between "arminianism" and Arminianism, and why use terms in special, esoteric senses? The footnote goes on to say, "The evangelical movement galvanized by the antinomian New Light also contained doctrines susceptible to arminian drift under market pressures, especially the moralism of the Methodist *Discipline,* and the free grace for all believers of Methodists, Free-Will Baptists, and Universalists." This seems to mean that whatever sincere conviction motivated the evangelicals is to be attributed to their antinomianism, while their arminianism (or Arminianism) was an unfortunate lapse "under market pressures." But why should belief in human dignity rather than depravity be presumed hypocritical? And how could one test such a claim?

Sellers evidently adopted his bipolar interpretation of American Christianity from Alan Heimert's book on the Great Awakening of the eighteenth century. Like Heimert, he opposes the Arminianism of the merchant capitalists to the "New Light" evangelical faith of the rural democracy.[18] In his retrospective look at the Great Awakening, Sellers follows Heimert's interpretation. He and Heimert are alike devoted to Perry Miller's most unreliable work, his 1949 intellectual biography of Jonathan Edwards, long since superseded. Sellers goes out of his way to endorse its argument in a summary of Edwards's career.[19] However, Heimert tried to be more sensitive to theological distinctions, denying emphatically that the New Light Calvinists were antinomians. What is more, Heimert argued that the evangelical Calvinists were not hostile to the market, but were simply concerned with democratizing it.[20]

Like Heimert, Sellers identifies New Light theology with communitarian values and Jeffersonian politics. But he exaggerates the extent to which there was an American political ideology celebrating and seeking to protect the noncommercial agrarian way of life. He attributes such an ideology to Thomas Jefferson, distinguishing between the purity of Jefferson's own devotion to noncommercial agriculture and the compromises with commercialism made by his follower Madison. "Jefferson was anxious about the corrupting effect of the market on American farm families," he writes.[21]

It is true that Jefferson and his followers thought that the ownership of property gave a citizen-householder a measure of independence that was politically valuable. The wage earner, like the apprentice, the slave, the minor, or the woman, was by their definition not fully independent and therefore not qualified for political participation. Thus a society consisting of family farms enjoyed, in their eyes, a strong economic basis for free political institutions. However, what was important to this model was that the farm be held in fee simple and be clear of mortgage indebtedness, not that it practice subsistence agriculture. Provided that Americans lived on family farms, they would derive the social and political advantages of Jeffersonian theory regardless of whether those farms produced for local consumption or for export. The Jeffersonian model of property-owning households was readily applicable to commercial farmers and urban artisans producing articles for sale. Indeed, the laissez-faire of Jeffersonian political thought seems to have been intended more as a means to commercial expansion than as a means to the preservation of premarket conditions.[22]

To enlist Thomas Jefferson on behalf of the kind of folk culture Sellers attributes to the noncommercial antebellum farmers is to misunderstand him. Jefferson, who was committed to the right to the pursuit of happiness and defined it as the fulfilling development of one's faculties, would hardly have wished the meager, subsistence way of life on his countrymen. What Sellers describes as the antinomian cosmology—a blend of superstitious su-

pernaturalism, patriarchal repressiveness, and limited intellectual horizons—
had zero appeal for Jefferson. Instead he wished to encourage education, literacy, and religious toleration—in short, a broadening of horizons. Jefferson
was a spokesman of the Enlightenment, not of a provincial peasant *mentalité*.
His vision of human beings as self-directed, autonomous free agents had
much more in common with what Sellers calls arminianism than with what
he calls antinomianism.

The merits of Sellers's Kulturkampf interpretation cannot definitively be settled by an analysis of the true content of Arminianism, antinomianism, and
Thomas Jefferson's political philosophy. Ultimately, the issue is the way Sellers
opposes democracy to commercial life, "the people" to what he reifies as "the
market." In his account, American democrats—those who work with their
hands, whether in the countryside or in cities—courageously resist the temptations of internal improvements, bank credit, and competition. As Sellers
sees it, the conflict between the people and the market came to a climax in
Andrew Jackson's war on the Bank of the United States: "While collective
repression pushed bourgeois hegemony across the North, antinomian democracy—and racist slavery—empowered the patriarchal Hero of New Orleans to bring *Kulturkampf* to a showdown in national politics."[23]

In the remainder of this essay, I should like to accept Sellers's challenge to
locate political conflict within a broader cultural context. In place of adopting
the notion of an apocalyptic Kulturkampf, however, I wish to show how the
new capitalist market was welcomed by a wide variety of people, how it
broadened their horizons and offered them more control over their own lives
than they had ever enjoyed before. The market greatly facilitated what Jefferson had called "the pursuit of happiness," something which, as he so appro-
priately recognized, most Americans valued next to life and liberty.

It is an oversimplification to suppose that "subsistence" and "the market"
posed themselves as stark alternatives to most Americans of the antebellum
period. In rural areas, farm families supplemented their incomes with various
market activities that might include, depending on the time and place, taking
raw cotton from a storekeeper to spin into yarn, distilling grain into whiskey,
churning milk into butter, or sending a daughter off to work in a mill town.
As Christopher Clark has shown so well for western Massachusetts, market
activity presented itself as an additional resource within a complicated family
survival strategy.[24] In small towns, goods and services were for sale, yet the
prosperity of the community depended on that of the neighboring farms. The
ways of the market were not perceived in sharp opposition to customary rural
ways. There were means of combining and synthesizing them: for example,

keeping account-book records of credits and debts was an intermediate step between a cash economy and a barter economy. The struggle of which rural families were aware was the struggle for a livelihood, not necessarily a struggle between two alternative kinds of livelihood.

Sellers's presentation of a political conflict between market and nonmarket regions probably works best in explaining conditions in the South.[25] In the North, commercial versus noncommercial conflict was often overshadowed by ethnic or class conflict. In the cities, the transition between two alternative kinds of commercial livelihood—artisan labor and wage labor—could be more dramatic and traumatic for those who underwent it than the transition between subsistence and commercial farming.[26] Industrialization and the technological changes that went with it, rather than the expansion of the market per se, were responsible for the replacement of the old form of artisan manufacturing with factory production and the proletarianization of the work force. Class conflict emerged in nineteenth-century industrial cities that was unlike anything in eighteenth-century cities, where merchants and artisans, masters and apprentices, had often shared common political interests. Yet the most violent conflicts in Jacksonian America involved racial and religious hostilities: white against black, abolitionist against antiabolitionist, Protestant against Catholic, Mormon against Gentile. Often they pitted workers against workers. In such cases, cultural conflict cut across economic class lines rather than coinciding with them.[27]

Just as the market provided new economic resources for people, it also provided new cultural resources as well. Along with new ways for farmers to supplement their incomes, the market also multiplied schools and colleges and provided cheaper newspapers, magazines, and books, a better postal system, and, beginning with the invention of the telegraph, communication at the speed of light. The market revolution provided the opportunity for people to make choices on a scale previously unparalleled: choices of goods to consume, choices of occupations to follow, educational choices, choices of lifestyles and identities. The ultimate test of autonomy is to be the kind of person one chooses—that is, to be self-constituted. The market brought people new power to shape their own identities.[28]

Sellers conceives of the cultural history he is relating as the subordination of the people to the market: "Where nobilities and priesthoods left folk cultures little disturbed, capital feeding on human effort claimed hegemony over all classes."[29] But the way in which Sellers is here using the neo-Marxist concept of hegemony implies that a false consciousness is being imposed. What if people really were benefiting in certain ways from the expansion of the market and its culture? What if they espoused middle-class tastes or evangelical religion or (even) Whig politics for rational and defensible reasons? What if the market was not an actor (as Sellers makes it), but a resource, an instrumentality, something created by human beings as a means to their ends?

Sellers is right to see that conflicts over culture were of crucial importance to the antebellum period. Whether all of them can be reduced to one titanic Kulturkampf is less clear, although modernization and its discontents were arguably central to the whole Victorian epoch.[30] But Sellers makes no conscientious effort to take account of the advantages as well as the costs of the market revolution and its cultural consequences. The economic costs, the dislocations, the deskilling and proletarianization of workers, the concentration of wealth: all these were real enough. So were the cultural hypocrisies and contradictions of middle-class ideology. But the market revolution also brought real advantages to large numbers of people.

Some of these advantages were material, such as a more varied diet, cheaper clothing, better housing, and new ways of earning a living. Of course, most of the comforts, conveniences, and improvements in medicine that technological progress would bring still lay in the future. In the period Sellers treats, up to 1846, it was not at all clear to contemporaries that the material benefits of the industrial revolution outweighed the costs. But the market revolution was broader than the industrial revolution, and probably affected rural and small-town people more. The material benefits of the expansion of the market were more readily apparent than those of industrialization, because they could give farmers extra income without drastic social dislocations.

Moreover, in assessing the advantages entailed by the market revolution before 1846, the nonmaterial ones seem particularly significant. The market revolution increased individual autonomy, the opportunity to exercise choice. Nineteenth-century Atlantic civilization celebrated the ideal of "careers open to talents," but this ideal required an appropriate variety of careers from which to choose. The market revolution and urbanization multiplied occupations, especially those making use of formal education, far beyond what subsistence husbandry could provide. The market also broadened people's horizons, and therefore enhanced their quality of life. Besides more schools and colleges, better communication, and more printed matter to read, the market revolution provided more (and more beautiful) places of worship, more humane child-rearing practices, more opportunities to encounter the arts.

Precisely because American frontier life was so anarchic and violent, the indigenous social controls to which it gave birth were equally harsh and tough. An uncompromising fundamentalism struggled to contain frontier hedonism like a stern patriarch disciplining unruly sons and daughters—or like a lynch mob confronting cattle rustlers. Andrew Jackson typified the authority figure of the West: violent, passionate, and vindictive, unconstrained by the rules of law (or spelling). Sellers accurately characterizes the culture of the American frontier as patriarchal. The market revolution brought a new middle-class culture that, for all its psychological tensions, held out the promise of deliverance from this narrow world of patriarchy and violence. The historian Louise Stevenson, calling this new culture by its political name, Whiggery, describes it well: "Whiggery stood for the triumph of the cosmopolitan and national over the provincial and local, of rational order over irrational spontaneity, of school-based learning over traditional folkways and customs, and of self-control over self-expression. Whigs believed that every person had the potential to become moral or good if family, school, and community nurtured the seed of goodness in his moral nature."[31] Those who opted for the market and its culture of modernization were not necessarily victims of a false consciousness.

As Sellers well recognizes, party loyalty was strong in the period he treats, and political parties were vehicles for voter self-consciousness. To be a Democrat or Whig could be an important facet of a man's identity. To Abraham Lincoln, for example, being a Whig was part of his self-image and chosen way of life, which was based on education, temperance, self-control, and self-improvement.[32] Lawrence Frederic Kohl has proposed that we look at the Whigs as "inner-directed" personality types and the Democrats as "tradition-directed" ones. This terminology, borrowed from social psychology, is not without its problems (Kohl ignores the way in which these terms were originally defined by David Riesman), but it seems to make the point Sellers wants to make in a way that is less misleading than his own theological terminology of "arminian" and "antinomian."[33]

What the terminologies of both Kohl and Sellers ignore is the importance of the Enlightenment to the Jeffersonian-Jacksonian political orientation. The Enlightenment, with its celebration of natural rights, its insistence on the separation of church and state, and its enthusiasm for laissez-faire and low taxes, must surely be recognized as the ideological fountainhead of the program of the Democratic party. It is not easy to reconcile—or figure out how contemporaries reconciled—these Enlightenment principles with the Democratic party's penchant for racism, patriarchy, and violence, but the problem is not solved by ignoring the Enlightenment.[34] A somewhat different strand of Enlightenment thought emphasizing accommodation with classical learning, Christianity, and polite culture was important to the Whigs.[35]

One important kind of opportunity for voluntary activity in antebellum America was represented by religion. In colonial and antebellum America, the growth of organized religion went hand in hand with the extension of the market. The founding of new churches kept pace with the founding of new towns, and the percentage of the population joining churches increased in parallel with the growth of towns and cities.[36] Sellers recognizes the connection between the market and the expansion of religious revivalism, but not the element of individual autonomy involved. Evangelical Protestantism celebrated the moment of "new birth," or conscious commitment to Christ, as a time when the believer was liberated from sinful dependence by God's grace. Among evangelical Arminians, it was seen as the moment when a person took charge of his or her own life by making a transforming decision. Because society was pluralistic and religion voluntary, even the religious bodies that were not Arminian in principle provided in practice a form of voluntary self-definition.

The wide range of religious options available, both indigenous and imported, had never been equalled in any previous human society. Religion could be a way of preserving an ancestral identity for immigrant ethnic minorities; it could also be a vehicle for upward social mobility. To make a decision for Christ for many young people meant to embrace a new self-definition as sober and responsible members of adult society. On the other hand, a religious commitment might represent the deliberate choice of a counterculture. People could create new religions or synthesize them through syncretistic processes. Religions proliferated for much the same reasons that unconventional schools of thought sprang up in science, medicine, and philosophy: there were Grahamites and Fourierites, phrenologists, mesmerists, and spiritualists. Many people, we sometimes forget, deliberately chose no religion at all—an option that was unprecedented in premodern society, yet one antebellum Americans were free to exercise without fear of reprisal.

The voluntary basis of American religion—economic, legal, and, in the dominant evangelical heritage, theological—was unique in the world. It probably explains why the modernization of American society was not accompanied by a corresponding secularization.[37] Instead, Americans volunteered for service in the army of Christ, just as they volunteered for service in fire brigades, the militia, the Freemasons, the Antimasons, labor unions, sewing circles, political parties, or Washingtonians. This example of a religious yet individualistic and modernized population has persisted in the United States from antebellum times to the present. It is a distinctively American phenomenon, one that has survived the discrediting of so many other alleged cases of "American exceptionalism."[38] In antebellum America, religion was on its way to becoming what it would become more obviously in our own day, a consumer good that members of the public are free to purchase or not in any of a wide variety of brands. Revivalism in such a society can be interpreted as an effective form of the mass marketing of religion to the public.[39]

But the identity that went with a religious commitment was not merely a label to be pinned on. With the identity there went a lifestyle. The parallel between religion and the consumer society of the present day should not mislead one into dismissing religion in antebellum America as merely a form of recreation. Most of the kinds of religion embraced by antebellum Americans required some form of self-discipline. Sellers calls such religious self-discipline "collective repression," and he sees it as an example of the bourgeoisie imposing its values in the interests of "class needs for work discipline, social order, and cultural hegemony."[40]

Paradoxically, however, an increase in social organization provided an arena within which enhancement of personal autonomy could take place. A market society and economic development presuppose a sense of corporate trust and social responsibility in the population just as much as a respect for individual rights.[41] In antebellum America, it was evangelical Protestantism that provided most of the impulse toward social organization. The benevolent empire of voluntary associations provided a model of national, local, and international organization in a society where little else was organized, in which there was no nationwide business corporation but the Bank of the United States and no nationwide government bureaucracy but the post office. The Second Great Awakening promoted both social organization and optimism about progress, sometimes expressed theologically in postmillennialism.[42]

While one should recognize the economic function of a disciplined workforce within a market society, the history of religious self-discipline must take account of much more. Since the Reformation, the members of Protestant sects had recognized the right of their communities to impose church discipline. The "watch and ward" that lay members exerted over each other represented, within their voluntarily constituted communities, a substitute for the hierarchical subordination that maintained order in traditional society. It was a part of the Protestant program of empowering the laity. Even in Jacksonian America, evangelical discipline, both individual and communal, had its liberating and empowering side, as well as its restrictive one. The reforms undertaken by the evangelicals of the time were typically concerned with redeeming persons who were not functioning as free moral agents: slaves, criminals, the insane, drunkards, children, and even—in the case of the most logically rigorous of the reformers—women. Redemption and discipline went hand in hand as aspects of personal autonomy.[43]

Nineteenth-century self-discipline came to a focus in the temperance movement. Temperance represented the confluence of religious discipline with the needs of the marketplace. The economic incentive to temperance involved more than the interests of industrial employers; commercial farmers were just as prominent as manufacturers among the businessmen who joined with New England clergy in originating the movement. Besides religious discipline and workplace efficiency, there was also a third argument for temperance, which was based on secular science. Americans in 1815 drank a great deal more alcohol than was good for them, and the medical profession gave temperance important backing. The temperance movement undoubtedly improved national health standards, just as its proponents claimed it did.[44] Nor was recognition of the evils of intemperance confined to the middle class. Even Sellers notes that the working class had its own temperance movement, exemplified by "indigenous working-class Methodism" and the Washingtonians—an admission that would seem to embarrass, at least a little, his interpretation of temperance as bourgeois "cultural imperialism."[45] Temperance may be taken as an example of how the quest for personal improvement became a prominent feature of American life during this period. Eventually, the movement for personal temperance became a movement for the improvement of society as a whole, employing the coercive power of the state.

Originally, the temperance movement was part of a much larger trend toward the reformation of manners that was by no means simply religious. There was also a new secular code of conduct promoted by the marketplace and practiced by people in their everyday lives. This was middle-class politeness. Given his commendable commitment to merging the public and private sides of history, Sellers curiously neglects the history of politeness. As Paul Langford has shown in his work on England, polite culture was one of the great consequences of the commercial revolution of the eighteenth century and the concomitant rise of the middle class.[46] The rise of politeness was a giant undertaking of voluntary self-reconstruction made possible by the market revolution. As obedience to the discipline of a church defined its membership, good manners defined a person as a member of the middle class— "polite society," as it was termed. Besides self-discipline, the new ideology of politeness also encouraged the cultivation of good taste. Concern with taste was a response to the wider consumer choices and rising material standard of living made possible by the market revolution.[47] Why should we not regard the increasing ability to make such consumer choices as a form of personal empowerment? The principle of voluntarism, which the American separation of church and state had secured for religion, was extended by the market revolution to patterns of consumption.

Unlike the hierarchical code of traditional European society, the new polite culture was inclusive rather than exclusive, open to all who would adopt it. It was part of a program of self-improvement whose patron saint was Benjamin Franklin, a program that included education and economic efficiency. Etiquette books promoting politeness were part of a massive and remarkably successful didactic effort to remake the face of America. They taught a prudential basis for social ethics in which the reason for treating others politely was to demonstrate that one deserved to be treated with reciprocal politeness.[48] The new code of politeness provided a framework for interaction with strangers at a time when the market revolution was bringing people increasingly into contact with strangers. Accordingly, politeness became the cosmopolitan (or metropolitan) code of behavior, as opposed to the folk practices of the provinces.

Middle-class polite culture brought new dignity for women. It did not simply teach men to pay courtesies to women ("ladies first"); it enjoined the subordination of sexuality, along with other forms of emotional indulgence, to principled self-discipline. Sellers is at his most intemperate in his denunciations of nineteenth-century middle-class prudery. (He does not seem to realize that condemnation of masturbation and homosexuality did not originate with nineteenth-century evangelicals.)[49] But what we think of as Victorian prudery can also be seen as a clumsy effort to make men regard women as something other than sexual objects. Although polite culture put women on a pedestal to avoid challenging the prerogatives of men, it represented in important respects an advance over the subjugation of women common in premodern society. In contrast to the patriarchy of folk tradition, middle-class polite society gave women a new role. It made them guardians of polite sensibility, religion, morality, and the home—roles that women themselves gradually amplified and politicized. Most of the early undertakings to provide education for women were conceived in terms of fitting them for this domestic role.[50]

Out of the sphere accorded them by Victorian middle-class culture and the wider scope of economic opportunities outside the home brought by the market revolution, women forged a new autonomy for themselves. Historians have universally acknowledged that women's liberation began in the urban middle class, within Protestant denominations that had encouraged a measure of gender equality (especially Unitarians and Quakers), and among women who had had experience in such other religiously motivated reform movements as those for temperance and antislavery.[51] Economically, the market revolution offered women alternatives to their traditional subjugation within the household. Politically, the early feminist movement occupied, together with abolitionism, what might be called the extreme left wing of the Whig-Republican political orientation.[52] If we are to view antebellum history in terms of a Kulturkampf between the market and the subsistence economy, there can be no doubt which side offered the more attractive option to women. The contribution of the market revolution to increasing autonomy for women is one of the ways in which it was a force for modernity and liberation, in antebellum America as in other times and places.[53]

Polite culture and evangelical religion had much in common: discipline, perfectionism, the impulse to improve the individual and the world. Like the evangelical reform movements of the time, polite culture undertook to make the world a better place by reshaping individuals into better people. Like evangelical religion, politeness taught people to control their appetites and passions and practice consideration for others. In the largest sense, the rise of politeness was linked with the rise of humanitarianism, both of which involve the restraint of antisocial impulses.[54] Together, politeness and evangelical moral reform helped reshape the world into a place where violent behavior was discouraged and commercial relations between strangers would be facilitated. Not surprisingly, both movements often appealed to the same people: the middle class or those who aspired to middle-class identity.

Accordingly, many evangelical Christians embraced politeness and allied with it. The synthesis of evangelical religion with politeness produced the respectable evangelicalism that accepted market society, but tried to reform and sensitize it—the type of evangelicalism Sellers calls "the Moderate Light." *Moderate Light* is the term he invented to distinguish bourgeois evangelicals from New Light folk evangelicals. So far, so good: there were different kinds of evangelicals in antebellum times. Some were ecumenical, polite, reformist, and Whig. Others were particularistic and stern, seeking not so much to reform the larger society (which had been written off as corrupt) as to preserve the distinctiveness of a saving remnant. What Sellers calls Moderate Light revivalism produced the Second Great Awakening that I have argued was an important component of the political culture of the Whig party.[55]

Sellers's bifurcation of evangelicals into New Lights and Moderate Lights makes for confusion, however. The Quakers disapproved of middle-class politeness, yet they strongly supported perfectionist social reforms. Does this make them New Light or Moderate Light? Sellers himself finds many evangelicals sharing characteristics of both; in such cases he attributes their good qualities to the New Light and their bad ones to the Moderate Light in ways that make for little real illumination.[56] And what is the precise relationship between his brand of antinomianism and the New Light? Upon analysis, New Light and Moderate Light seem to be sociopolitical rather than religious categories. Sellers wants the New Light to serve as a Jacksonian counterpart to the Moderate Light of the Whigs, but the category does not really work. It does not take account of the enormous variety of religious positions taken by the Jacksonian Democrats, many of whom were not any kind of evangelical. They could be Catholics, Lutherans, Episcopalians, Old School Presbyterians, freethinkers, or Freemasons. The best way to characterize the Democrats in religious terms is as outsiders. Sean Wilentz, writing of the workingmen of New York City, concludes: "It would be foolish to try to impose unity upon such diverse currents of artisan piety, irreligion, and apathy."[57] Democrats who demonstrated great religious diversity could unite in defense of the separation of church and state, in common opposition to the cultural onslaught of polite, perfectionist, Moderate Light Whiggery—but not in any common "antinomian" New Light theology.

One of the important movements of the period Sellers treats was Antimasonry. As a popular cause with both religious and political dimensions, Antimasonry provides an appropriate test case for the interpretation of politics in terms of religious categories. It has been the subject of considerable recent historical interest.[58] One might expect Antimasonry, therefore, to figure prominently in Sellers's account. But Sellers's treatment of Antimasonry is brief and conventional. He identifies it, in passing, with antinomianism at one point and with the middle-class Moderate Light at another.[59]

One of the principal features distinguishing the Moderate Light revival—accepting for the moment Sellers's terminology—was its broad sense of social responsibility.[60] Moderate Lights were committed to an ecumenical, national, and even international perspective. This commitment reflected a variety of influences, including long-standing Puritan philanthropy and the new, market-fostered, humanitarian concern for suffering outside one's personal encounter that Thomas Haskell has identified.[61] One of the ways in which the market revolution broadened people's horizons was in relation to their racial attitudes. Racism was, of course, pervasive in antebellum America, but there are degrees of racism, and they were reflected in the variety of political positions taken on the slavery question. The position taken by the bourgeois Whig party on slavery varied from one geographical region to another, but in each area the Whig party generally took a less strongly proslavery position than the Democratic party took. (Henry Clay, the party's architect and leader, supported gradual compensated emancipation and colonization as late as the Kentucky state constitutional convention of 1849.) Blacks had no difficulty perceiving which major party was the lesser evil; wherever they could vote, they voted as a bloc against the Democrats.[62] Indian policy was an important political issue when the second party system was taking shape in the 1830s, and policy toward Mexico was important through- out its duration. On both these issues, too, the Whigs espoused a distinctly less racist (and less violent) position than the Democrats.

Sellers's treatment of abolitionism is idiosyncratic. In general, he regards the reforms of the period as examples of sinister bourgeois social control; unlike most of the social-control school of historians, however, he makes an exception for abolitionism. In the case of abolitionism, he sees the reformers as genuinely enlightened and their cause as liberating. To distinguish aboli- tion from other reform movements, he does all he can to link it with "anti- nomian" and New Light influences.[63] Actually, abolitionism is better under- stood as an extreme version of the perfectionist, improving impulse that was so prominent a feature of Whig-market-postmillennial culture. Support for abolitionism has been convincingly correlated with both the practice of com- mercial farming for the market and the adoption of marketplace values. As John Quist has put it, "the moral crusade to abolish slavery was dominated by people who were also preoccupied with self-improvement and bettering the circumstances of their families."[64] That abolition had connections to New Light divinity (e.g., through Samuel Hopkins) is really an indication that the New Light and Moderate Light versions of evangelicalism were not so differ- ent from each other as Sellers makes out.

What Sellers calls New Light revivalism would appear to be more or less what Nathan Hatch has described in his recent book *The Democratization of American Christianity*—that is, the Christianity of American popular culture. There is a major difference between their descriptions of popular revivalism, however. Hatch does not see his New Lights as defenders of tradition against modernity; he sees them as innovators, particularly in their assault on tradi- tional social deference. As Hatch puts it, "Rather than looking backward and clinging to a moral economy, insurgent religious leaders espoused convic- tions that were essentially modern and individualistic. . . . Religious move- ments eager to preserve the supernatural in everyday life had the ironic effect of accelerating the breakup of traditional society and the advent of a social order of competition, self-expression, and free enterprise."[65]

The American exponents of the Moderate Light developed a creative syn- thesis of evangelical Christianity with polite culture, the intellectual basis of which was their adaptation of Scottish moral philosophy to the needs of American denominational colleges.[66] Perhaps Sellers's term *New Light* fits those who rejected politeness as a form of worldly corruption and imposed their own discipline on members as a godly alternative code of behavior. The austere lifestyle of such evangelical outsiders did make them less vulnerable to the seductive consumption patterns of the market, though it seldom deterred production for the market. Generally, the discipline of the groups Sellers calls antinomian was sterner than bourgeois polite discipline. Sellers's insistence on blaming all repression of impulse and passion on the bourgeois elite does not take account of this.[67] For example, temperance began as a polite and elite movement that was concerned with promoting moderation in the consumption of alcohol and endorsing wine as an alternative to whiskey. As it became less elite-dominated, the movement became more extreme in its demands, which culminated in total abstinence and legal prohibition. On the other hand, the "primitive" Baptists were not only antimission in an evangelistic sense, but also antitemperance, and so they seem to illustrate a version of the antireform, antipolite kind of religion more in keeping with what Sellers calls antinomianism.[68]

The competition among different forms of evangelical, polite, and traditional cultures provides some of the most interesting historical examples of Kulturkampf, not only in the United States, but throughout the western world.[69] Sometimes denominations started out resisting the market revolution and its culture only to reach an accommodation with it—the most dramatic reversal being that of the Mormons, who switched at the turn of the last century from defending an autonomous enclave of polygamy and socialism to embracing monogamy, capitalism, and the Republican party. The struggles over culture, however, are not simply more complicated, but also more morally ambiguous than is conveyed in Sellers's book.

In conclusion, we need to articulate why some Americans were suspicious of the market revolution, and even hostile to aspects of it like banks and bank currency. This Sellers does for us, eloquently. It is also important, however, to know why such suspicions and hostilities were overcome. In the United States during the Whig-Jacksonian period, white people were achieving greater autonomy and opportunity for self-definition than ever before. Sellers is right to characterize belief in human autonomy—what he calls arminianism—as basic to the culture of the market. What he does not do is make it clear how the market enhanced autonomy and why so many contemporaries found this attractive. Ultimately, most Americans welcomed the economic benefits of the market and rose to the opportunities presented by it, often on a piecemeal basis. But it would take a civil war and tumultuous reconstruction for African Americans to be incorporated into market participation. As and when it happened, it formed part of the national recognition of their full humanity. For them, even more than for other Americans, market participation was indeed a revolution and a means of liberation.

There is a tendency today among some intellectuals in the western world to romanticize traditional society and undervalue modernity. Professor Sellers's book is an example of this tendency. Sellers's conception of antinomianism seems to contain both the anthropological concept of a traditional society awaiting modernization and a vision of fraternal, participatory democracy that can serve as a model for our own time.[70] But American frontier society and religion do not really serve his didactic purposes well. Like most premarket societies, the American hinterland was even more ethnocentric and patriarchal than bourgeois society, and Sellers is too good a historian not to notice this. Nor did the antinomian religion that Sellers celebrates constitute such a marked traditional contrast to that of the modernizing Moderate Lights. The New Light denominations, like those of the Moderate Lights, were descended from the Reformation. A sect like the Baptists, when compared with, say, Finneyite revivalism, simply represented an earlier historical version of the growth of individual autonomy associated with modernization.

Charles Sellers's political sympathies lie with the Jacksonian Democratic party, and the history he writes properly reflects this. But, even given this commitment, the intellectual—and, yes, the moral—utility of Sellers's concept of antinomianism is open to question. The most constructive, admirable aspect of the Jefferson-Jackson political impulse in the antebellum United States was not its defense of traditional society in the face of an evil market revolution; it was its support for individual freedom and equality, which it expressed in Enlightenment terms of natural rights. All in all, then, Charles Sellers's analysis of the impact of the market revolution on the United States was sounder before he added to it the anachronistic, ambiguous, and misleading categories "antinomian" and "arminian."

NOTES

1. Charles Sellers, *The Market Revolution: Jacksonian America, 1815–1846* (New York, 1991).

2. The lectures are available in the form of a superb brief textbook that Sellers wrote with a colleague: Charles Sellers and Henry F. May, *A Synopsis of American History* (Chicago, 1963). Sellers wrote the antebellum and May the postbellum chapters.

3. Sellers and May, *Synopsis,* p. 110.

4. One may question, however, whether the "market revolution" contributed as much to economic growth, as distinguished from social, political, and economic change, as Sellers implied. See Thomas Weiss, "The American Economic Miracle of the Nineteenth Century," paper presented to the American Historical Association (January 1994), and Paul David, "The Growth of Real Product in the United States Before 1840," *Journal of Economic History* 27 (1967): 151–97.

5. Quotation from Thomas Haskell, "Capitalism and the Origins of the Humanitarian Sensibility," *American Historical Review* 90 (1985): 339–61 and 547–66. See also the illuminating "Forum" discussion among Haskell, David B. Davis, and John Ashworth, *American Historical Review* 92 (1987): 797–878.

6. Richard J. Carwardine, *Evangelicals and Politics in Antebellum America* (New Haven, Conn., 1993).

7. E.g., Sellers, *Market Revolution,* pp. 8–19.

8. Sellers, *Market Revolution,* pp. 217–25.

9. Sellers, *Market Revolution,* p. 31.

10. Sellers, *Market Revolution,* p. 30.

11. See Daniel Walker Howe, "The Decline of Calvinism: An Approach to Its Study," *Comparative Studies in Society and History* 14 (1972): 306–27. If I were to rewrite this article, I should complicate its line of argument, taking account, among other things, of a resurgence of Calvinism in the eighteenth century.

12. Carwardine, *Evangelicals and Politics,* especially pp. 113–126, 222–29.

13. After the disestablishment of religion by the New England states (a process not completed until 1833), Episcopalians still found the Democratic party a congenial refuge from evangelical moral reform crusades. See Robert Bruce Mullin, *Episcopal Vision/ American Reality: High Church Theology and Social Thought in Evangelical America* (New Haven, Conn., 1986), p. 200.

14. Steven Marini, *Radical Sects of Revolutionary New England* (Cambridge, Mass., 1982); Nathan Hatch, *The Democratization of American Christianity* (New Haven, Conn., 1989).

15. For example, Sellers, *Market Revolution,* p. 210.

16. Sellers, *Market Revolution,* p. 30.

17. Sellers, *Market Revolution,* pp. 452–53, n. 44.

18. Alan Heimert, *Religion and the American Mind: From the Great Awakening to the Revolution* (Cambridge, Mass., 1966).

19. Sellers, *Market Revolution,* pp. 203–4, is a précis of Perry Miller, *Jonathan Edwards* (New York, 1949). For a more reliable understanding of Edwards's ideas, see Norman Fiering, *Jonathan Edwards' Moral Thought and Its British Context* (Chapel Hill, N.C., 1981).

20. Heimert, *Religion and the American Mind,* pp. 55 and 56.

21. Heimert, *Religion and the American Mind,* p. 39.

22. See Joyce Appleby, *Capitalism and a New Social Order: The Republican Vision of the 1790s* (New York, 1984); John R. Nelson, *Liberty and Property: Political Economy and Policymaking in the New Nation, 1789–1812* (Baltimore, 1987); and Richard Vernier, "Political Economy and Political Ideology: The Public Debt in Eighteenth-Century Britain and America" (D. Phil. diss., Oxford University, 1993).

23. Sellers, *Market Revolution*, p. 268.

24. Christopher Clark, *The Roots of Rural Capitalism: Western Massachusetts, 1780–1860* (Ithaca, N.Y., 1990). See also James Henretta, "Families and Farms: *Mentalité* in Pre-Industrial America," *William and Mary Quarterly* 35 (1978): 3–32; John Mack Faragher, *Sugar Creek: Life on the Illinois Prairie* (New Haven, Conn., 1986); and Lacy K. Ford, *Origins of Southern Radicalism: The South Carolina Upcountry, 1800–1860* (New York, 1988).

25. See Charles Sellers, "Who Were the Southern Whigs?" *American Historical Review* 59 (1954): 335–46; J. Mills Thornton III, *Politics and Power in a Slave Society* (Baton Rouge, La., 1978); Harry Watson, *Community Conflict and Jacksonian Politics* (Baton Rouge, La., 1981).

26. The best account is Sean Wilentz, *Chants Democratic: New York City and Rise of the American Working Class, 1788–1850* (New York, 1984).

27. See, for example, Michael Feldberg, *The Turbulent Era: Riot and Disorder in Jacksonian America* (Oxford, 1980). Sellers tries to blame this violence on bourgeois instigation; it would be more accurate to say that employers took advantage of ethnic hostilities among workers than that they created them. See *Market Revolution*, pp. 386–89.

28. See Richard D. Brown, *Knowledge Is Power: The Diffusion of Information in Early America, 1700–1865* (New York, 1989), chap. 9. On the importance of creating the power of choice in the modern world, see David Apter, *The Politics of Modernization* (Chicago, 1965), pp. 9–11.

29. Sellers, *Market Revolution*, p. 237.

30. As I have argued in *Victorian America* (Philadelphia, 1976).

31. Louise Stevenson, *Scholarly Means to Evangelical Ends: The New Haven Scholars and the Transformation of Higher Learning in America, 1830–1890* (Baltimore, 1986), pp. 5–6.

32. Sellers is good on this. See his *Market Revolution*, p. 395.

33. Lawrence Frederick Kohl, *The Politics of Individualism: Parties and the American Character in the Jacksonian Era* (New York, 1989).

34. On why people might legitimately welcome both market economics and the political program of the Enlightenment as enhancing their autonomy, see Joyce Appleby, *Liberalism and Republicanism in the Historical Imagination* (Cambridge, Mass., 1992).

35. On the contrasting ideological positions of the Democratic and Whig parties, see John Ashworth, *"Agrarians" and "Aristocrats": Party Political Ideology in the United States, 1837–1846* (London, 1983); Major L. Wilson, *Space, Time, and Freedom: The Quest for Nationality and the Irresistible Conflict* (Westport, Conn., 1974); and Daniel Walker Howe, *The Political Culture of the American Whigs* (Chicago, 1979).

36. On urbanization and Christianity, see Steve Bruce, ed., *Religion and Modernization: Sociologists and Historians Debate the Secularization Thesis* (Oxford, 1992); Patricia Bonomi, *Under the Cope of Heaven: Religion, Society, and Politics in Colonial America* (New York, 1986); and Timothy Smith, *Revivalism and Social Reform in Mid-Nineteenth Century America* (New York, 1957).

37. See Roger Finke, "An Unsecular America," in Bruce, ed., *Religion and Modernization*, pp. 145–69.

38. See Byron Shafer, ed., *Is America Different: A New Look at American Exceptionalism* (Oxford, 1991); Ian Tyrell, "American Exceptionalism in an Age of International History,"

American Historical Review 96 (1991): 1031–55; and Michael Kammen, "The Problem of American Exceptionalism," *American Quarterly* 45 (1993): 1–43.

39. See Terry D. Bilhartz, *Urban Religion and the Second Great Awakening: Church and Society in Early National Baltimore* (Rutherford, N.J., 1986), and R. Laurence Moore, *Selling God: American Religion in the Marketplace of American Culture* (New York, 1994).

40. Sellers, *Market Revolution,* pp. 259 and 266–68.

41. See Nathan Rosenberg and L. E. Birdzell, Jr., *How the West Grew Rich: The Economic Transformation of the Industrial World* (New York, 1981), pp. 123–26.

42. See Daniel Walker Howe, "The Evangelical Movement and Political Culture in the North During the Second Party System," *Journal of American History* 77 (1991): 1216–39.

43. See Howe, "Evangelical Movement."

44. See Ian R. Tyrell, *Sobering Up: From Temperance to Prohibition in Antebellum America, 1800–1860* (Westport, Conn., 1979); and W. J. Rorabaugh, *The Alcoholic Republic: An American Tradition* (Oxford, 1979).

45. Sellers, *Market Revolution,* p. 267.

46. Paul Langford, *A Polite and Commercial People: England, 1727–1783* (Oxford, 1992), chap. 3.

47. See Richard Bushman, *The Refinement of America: Persons, Houses, Cities* (New York, 1992).

48. See John F. Kasson, *Rudeness and Civility: Manners in Nineteenth-Century Urban America* (New York, 1990).

49. Sellers, *Market Revolution,* pp. 246–52.

50. On the education of women for their role as "republican mothers," see Linda Kerber, *Women of the Republic: Intellect and Ideology in Revolutionary America* (New York, 1980).

51. See Ross Paulson, *Women's Suffrage and Prohibition* (Glencoe, Ill., 1973); Nancy Cott, *The Bonds of Womanhood: "Woman's Sphere" in New England, 1780–1835* (New Haven, Conn., 1977), pp. 126–59; Mary Patricia Ryan, *Cradle of the Middle Class: The Family in Oneida County, New York, 1790–1865* (Cambridge, Eng., 1981); Anne C. Rose, *Transcendentalism as a Social Movement, 1830–1850* (New Haven, Conn., 1981); Barbara Epstein, *The Politics of Domesticity: Women, Evangelicalism, and Temperance in Nineteenth-Century America* (Middletown, Conn., 1981); Nancy A. Hewitt, *Women's Activism and Social Change: Rochester, New York, 1822–1872* (Ithaca, N.Y., 1984).

52. Cf. Ellen DuBois, *Feminism and Suffrage: The Emergence of an Independent Women's Movement in America* (Ithaca, N.Y., 1978), p. 75.

53. An excellent new treatment of the connections among women's rights, party politics, and the new culture of respectability is Norma Basch, "Marriage, Morals, and Politics in the Election of 1828," *Journal of American History* 80 (1993): 890–918.

54. See the wonderfully wide-ranging work of Norbert Elias, *The Civilizing Process,* trans. Edmund Jephcott (Oxford, 1982; first published in German, 1939).

55. Howe, *Political Culture of the Whigs,* esp. 150–80, and "Evangelical Movement."

56. Sellers, *Market Revolution,* pp. 210–12, 225–36.

57. Wilentz, *Chants Democratic,* p. 83.

58. Recent analyses of Antimasonry include Paul Goodman, *Towards a Christian Republic: Antimasonry and the Great Transition in New England, 1826–1836* (New York,

1988); Robert O. Rupp, "Parties and the Public Good: Political Antimasonry in New York Reconsidered," *Journal of the Early Republic* 8 (1988): 253–79; Kathleen Smith Kutolowski, "Antimasonry Reexamined: Social Bases of the Grass-Roots Party," *Journal of American History* 71 (1984): 269–93; William Preston Vaughn, *The Antimasonic Party in the United States* (Lexington, Ky., 1983); and Donald Ratcliffe, "Antimasonry and Partisanship in Greater New England, 1826–1836" *Journal of the Early Republic* 15 (1995):197–237.

59. Sellers, *Market Revolution*, pp. 282 and 405.

60. See George M. Thomas, *Revivalism and Cultural Change: Christianity, Nation-Building, and the Market in the Nineteenth-Century United States* (Chicago, 1990); George M. Marsden, *Religion and American Culture* (San Diego, Calif., 1990); and Randolph A. Roth, *The Democratic Dilemma: Religion, Reform, and the Social Order in the Connecticut River Valley of Vermont, 1791–1850* (Cambridge, Eng., 1987).

61. Haskell, "Capitalism."

62. Howe, *Political Culture of the Whigs*, pp. 17–18 and 133–37.

63. E.g., Sellers, *Market Revolution*, pp. 233 and 402.

64. John Quist, "The Michigan Abolitionist Constituency of the 1840s," paper presented to the Organization of American Historians, Apr. 1993; see also Eric Foner, *Politics and Ideology in the Age of the Civil War* (New York, 1980), pp. 57–76.

65. Hatch, *Democratization*, p. 16.

66. See Mark A. Noll, *Princeton and the Republic, 1768–1822* (Princeton, N.J., 1989); Donald Harvey Meyer, *The Instructed Conscience: The Shaping of the American National Ethic* (Philadelphia, 1972); Robert M. Calhoon, *Evangelicals and Conservatives in the Early South* (Columbia, S.C., 1988); Brooks Holifield, *The Gentlemen Theologians: American Theology in Southern Culture, 1795–1860* (Durham, N.C., 1978).

67. Sellers, *Market Revolution*, pp. 245–59.

68. Rorabaugh, *Alcoholic Republic*, p. 209.

69. See, for example, Dickson D. Bruce, *Violence and Culture in the Antebellum South* (Austin, Tex., 1979), and Leigh Eric Schmidt, *Holy Fairs: Scottish Communions and American Revivals in the Early Modern Period* (Princeton, N.J., 1989).

70. Implicit throughout, this becomes explicit in the last sentence of the book. See Sellers, *Market Revolution*, p. 427.

11

"Antinomians" *and* "Arminians": Methodists and the Market Revolution

RICHARD CARWARDINE

N O ONE CAN DOUBT the profound significance of the flowering of
evangelical religion in the United States during the early national period. Intellectual and church historians have long regarded the waves
of revival that comprised the Second Great Awakening as expressing and accelerating a major ideological and theological reorientation, as well as demonstrating the American churches' extraordinary practical energy and enterprise in the years following disestablishment.[1] More recently, exponents of
the "new social history" have contributed a variety of painstaking and impressive local studies that have done much to anatomize the religious life of
particular communities in the early republic.[2] Even those who favor a primarily ideological explanation of the Awakening see the value of pursuing
the linkages between evangelical-revivalist culture and an expanding market
economy whose salient features included better communications, urban
growth, incipient industrialization, increasing class tensions, changing gender roles, and a mobile population.[3] In both the United States and Great Britain, the early decades of the nineteenth century saw social and economic
changes that transformed an older rural, preindustrial order, touching the
lives of hundreds of thousands of men, women, and children; both societies
simultaneously witnessed so massive a burgeoning of evangelical Protestantism that the relative strength of their churches was greater than at any time
before or since.[4]

In his grand interpretation of the era, Charles Sellers builds on these specialized studies to offer the most ambitious attempt yet at integrating what we
know of Jacksonian Americans' religious experiences and the realities of their
economic and political lives. Sellers contends that American society in the
early republic was fundamentally divided by the experience of capitalist market revolution. On one side in this Kulturkampf stood the traditional rural,
democratic order of subsistence farmers, marked by communal cooperation,
family obligation, patriarchal authority, honor, and independence. Rapidly
making inroads into this culture by 1815 was the world of market production,

characterized by specialization, division of labor, competitive individualism, enterprise, and boom and bust.[5]

Sellers makes religion functionally pivotal in this analysis: only religious fervor, he argues, could "nerve" Americans for their "stressful passage from resistance [to the capitalist revolution] through evasion to accommodation." He explains the ecstatic "New Light" revivals over the period of a century—from the mid–eighteenth-century Great Awakening through the turn-of-the-century Great Revival to the culminating Second Great Awakening of the 1820s and 1830s—as an "antinomian" reaction against the advance of capitalist enterprise by a subsistence world valuing egalitarianism, democracy, plainness, and communal love; the market, on the other hand, with its competitive ethic and its rewards of wealth and status, was nourished by an "arminian" heresy that related salvation to human capability and effort. Some disaffected evangelicals (the Shakers, for example), driven by "millennial fantasy," chose to "come out" of a corrupted world altogether; but far more chose to mobilize against the new economic order through the primary agency of the New Light churches, especially those of the Baptists and Methodists, plebeian movements of subsistence farmers and working people. New Lights found political expression in Jacksonism, discovering in the hero of New Orleans a "moral preeminence" that could be asserted against cosmopolitan elites.[6]

The merchants and fashionable congregations who made up those elites were often Unitarians, believing in a God who had given them power to fashion their earthly success. But, Sellers continues, far more influential among Yankee merchants, millers, and other entrepreneurs was "a Moderate Light tenuously blending the self-discipline of arminian effort with antinomian love." Here the agent of transformation was the inspirational Charles Grandison Finney. The upstate New York attorney-turned-revivalist took the theological inheritance of Jonathan Edwards, Joseph Bellamy, and Samuel Hopkins—that is, their New Divinity of moderate antinomianism and "disinterested benevolence"—and among the transplanted Yankee communities of the "burned-over district" "met head-on the climactic antinomian challenge to the culture of capitalist accommodation." Finney jettisoned conventional Calvinism, "refocus[ing] the Moderate Light by appropriating the . . . universalism" of the antinomian sects, especially the Methodists. In due course, in a celebrated progress, he was to reach New York's Broadway Tabernacle and achieve unimagined fame, preaching capitalist discipline to the working class and asceticism to their employers. Ultimately he would retreat, disillusioned by the social conservatism of capitalist culture, but not before he had "nerved Americans for the personal transformation required by a competitive market."[7]

Sellers's integrative approach is deeply imaginative, provoking us to look anew at familiar materials. But his interpretation of popular religion raises as many questions as it tries to solve. A minor issue is one of terminology, since he deploys familiar labels in unfamiliar ways. A more serious difficulty arises over the way he implicitly attaches significance to religion only insofar as it operates as a function of economic change and as a validation of economic self-interest: to this issue, and its restrictive implications for analyzing electoral behavior, we shall return. Most problematic, however, is that the evidence on which Sellers builds his bipolar cultural conflict between "antinomianism" and "arminianism" is less emphatic than he seems to suppose. At the heart of his antimarket coalition sit the Methodists, institutionally nonexistent in America at the time of Jackson's birth, but the fastest-growing and largest denomination in the country by the time he reached the presidency. Sellers describes the Methodists as "the main bearers of antinomian universalism" outside New England in the aftermath of the panic of 1819; they appear as core members of the democratic insurgency that took Jackson to the White House in 1829; only later (Sellers offers no date) did the Methodists' "ethical athleticism" open their denomination up to capitalist imperatives and "obliterate from the[ir] memory . . . their origins in a massive cultural mobilization against the market and its ways."[8]

But how far, in practice, were the Methodists the defenders of a "parochial and fatalist" subsistence culture against the developing momentum of the capitalist market? Were the Methodists' values really at odds with the competitive individualism of "arminian" entrepreneurs? How substantial was the philosophical distance between Methodist revivalists and the refocused Moderate Light religion of Finney? These questions bear investigation. Methodist "antinomianism" is essential to the purity of Sellers's model of cultural bipolarity: without it, his interpretation of Jacksonian religion would lose much of its force.

The origins of Methodism as a church of the poor and common people are so well established they need little rehearsal here.[9] Early Methodist preachers held meetings anywhere they could secure a hearing: in barns, yards, private houses, schoolrooms, and public streets. To plebeian audiences of rural laborers, subsistence farmers, mechanics, journeymen, and artisans they proffered a gospel of salvation and the means of finding "liberty." Usually farmers and artisans themselves, and lacking formal theological training, these preachers spoke the language of the common folk they addressed, openly and implicitly criticizing worldly ostentation and the love of money and display. John Sale, a Virginia-born presiding elder in early Ohio, rejoiced at having moved to a part of the country "where there is so much of an Equallity & a Man is not thought to be great . . . because he possesses a little more of this Worlds rubbish than his Neighbour."[10] Self-denial in matters of dress was the primitive Wesleyan rule for both preacher and people. One early southern preacher, Nicholas Snethen, spoke contemptuously of slave-holding urbanites as "soft, effeminate and sensualised, the willing captives of every delusion which is covered with a thin veil of external decency."[11]

Convinced that secular trading corrupted devotional exercise, presiding elders worked strenuously to prevent the selling of goods at camp meeting grounds. As the commercial revolution advanced, reflective and prayerful Methodists grieved over Sabbath trading. Freeborn Garrettson, from the vantage point of Rhinebeck, New York, lamented "the many boats on the Lords-day scraping the shores of the great Canal, and the north river gathering up the sabbath-breakers, either for business or pleasure."[12] Alarmed at the profane influences at work on those laboring in the multiplying workshops, northeastern Methodist ministers scheduled factory preaching into their itineraries.[13] When cotton looms were stopped for revivals, as in Otsego and in Troy in 1828, or when protracted meetings were held thrice daily over a period of several weeks, the tension between the demands of enthusiastic Methodist religion and the needs of productive industry was plain enough.[14] According to historians Teresa Murphy, William Sutton, and Jama Lazerow, Methodism provided evangelical artisans and other workers with secure congregational communities; an ethic that condemned excessive profits, the abuse of wealth, and the exploitation of the powerless; and the inspiration to oppose the injustices associated with the social relations of emerging capitalism.[15]

Looking back on the early days of the movement through which some of them had lived, many mid–nineteenth-century Methodists reflected warmly on the church's original simplicity of spirit, manners, and forms of worship. Critics of change like Beverly Waugh extolled the communalism and "brotherly love" that the early Methodists had fostered in the intimacy of class meetings. Even the unsentimental George Peck, writing in 1866, agreed that "there was more equality of social position, and, of course, more familiarity, in former times than at present." As Methodism won converts among the wealthy, the educated, and the socially influential, and as its own members rose in society and began to wear "gold and costly apparel," so it seemed that its primitive character had evaporated. By the 1850s, the earlier indifference to formal education had yielded to institution building on an elaborate scale: in their Address of 1856 the Bishops of the Methodist Episcopal Church proudly listed nineteen colleges and universities, sixty-eight academies offering "literary advantages" to both sexes, and two theological seminaries.[16]

The status that Benjamin Tefft was pleased to claim for his denomination in his triumphalist *Methodism Successful* was reflected in the building of more ornate churches whose steeples and bells proclaimed Methodist splendor; at the same time, the members of existing churches were spending thousands of dollars "remodeling and beautifying" their meeting-places. The introduction of organs and other musical instruments alarmed those fearful that the expense of sustaining music would mean that "rich men become necessary to us." Symbolizing the denomination's increasing status was the advance of the pew-rent system, which was introduced in the 1840s in Baltimore, Richmond, and other major urban centers of Methodist strength and which by the late 1850s was evident in towns of all sizes from the East Coast to the Mississippi Valley. Conscious that even the free Methodist churches in New York and other cities might seem too luxurious for the very poor, Abel Stevens and other church leaders grew alarmed that the general population might have ceased to see Methodism as "the common religion of the common people." Midcentury Methodists could speak without embarrassment about riches, adopting a tone apparently alien to Wesleyan or Asburian primitivism. Phoebe Palmer explained that she had "no sympathy with that querulous spirit which is ever denouncing the rich, merely because they are so; or perhaps oftener than otherwise, because the denouncer is not possessed of the same means, and who, were he possessed of them, would be less faithful than those whom he denounces. . . . There are gradations in society which always have been, and doubtless always will be, till the end of time."[17]

The stark contrast between turn-of-the-century Methodism and its midcentury gentility seems to suggest that the movement had experienced a huge cultural shift and that Sellers is correct in pointing to a betrayal of its anti-market origins as it succumbed to "capitalist imperatives." But this interpretation raises the question, Why did the process of embourgeoisement provoke so little resistance in the church? The great Methodist schisms of the first half of the century concerned episcopal authority, the rights of laymen, the relationship of whites and free blacks, and the place of slavery within the denomination. Only one minor schismatic group, the Stillwellites, can be said to have originated primarily in resistance to the growing respectability of Methodism. In New York City, the issue of lay independence was compounded in the 1820s by a conflict over the rebuilding of the mother church on John Street. Its lavish refurbishing, which included the addition of a carpeted altar, appeared to one of the trustees, Samuel Stillwell, and his nephew William to represent a betrayal of the primitive simplicity of Methodism. The resultant new sect grew rapidly for a while, and William Stillwell, along with a number of other radical Methodists, developed a "producerist" philosophy and a scriptural critique of industrial capitalism that he propagated through the pages of his weekly family magazine, *The Friendly Visitor.* At first the new connection grew and spread into neighboring states, claiming two thousand members by 1825. But it was never more than a minority strand of Methodism and would eventually die out.[18]

Significantly, Methodism experienced no schism of similar dimensions to the conflict within American Baptist churches through the early nineteenth century, which culminated in the split at the Black Rock Convention in 1832, as "Primitive" Baptists sought to uphold the true historic faith against Arminian softening by corrupted modernizers; rooted in the rural South and West, the Primitives represented an atavistic reaction against "modernism" in their churches. Nor was there an American version of the English Primitive Methodist schism by which the victims of industrial and agrarian upheaval sought to sustain the revivalist enthusiasm of early Wesleyanism against "Buntingite" Toryism and early Victorian respectability. When British missionaries attempted to introduce Primitive Methodism into the United States, the effort failed, not the least because, as one Primitive Methodist minister ruefully and tellingly reported, "all sorts of labor (*except Primitive Methodist preaching*) is paid higher than in England."[19]

The truth is that American Methodism experienced no searing conflicts over its churches' embourgeoisement because, although the early Methodists were poor, they were far from hostile to enterprise and the capitalist ethic. The movement was indeed a radical, egalitarian counterculture, but it was reacting against genteel patriarchalism and aristocratic pretension, creating its own community against a world of deference and honor, and not against industrious effort and self-improvement.[20] It was a community whose *Discipline* encouraged its members to buy and sell to each other, and to give employment to Methodists whenever possible.

From its early days, and emphatically from the turn of the century, the denomination comfortably embraced a number of socially prominent and economically successful members. In Maryland these included, for example, a number of leading Delmarva Peninsula planter families as well as merchants, professionals, and successful craftsmen.[21] The Methodists embraced Thomas Worthington, United States senator from Ohio, a member of the Chillicothe Methodist Church and a promoter of cotton, wool, and flax manufacturing in the town.[22] They numbered Philip Gatch, a pioneer Methodist evangelist who, after he had "located" from the itinerant ministry, settled as a slave-owning planter in Maryland and Virginia and then moved to Ohio. He served in Ohio's first state constitutional convention and encouraged the immigration of enterprising southern Methodists who, like him, were disenchanted with slavery and alert to the opportunities for commercial agriculture in southern Ohio ("We shall not want for trade in this Countrey," he declared in 1802). One of those he tried to tempt was Edward Dromgoole, who never wholly succumbed to "Ohio fever," but who speculated in Ohio lands and managed them from Virginia through the Pelham family. Peter Pelham and his eight children had moved to Greene County in 1807; they saw no tension between their Methodist convictions (Pelham more than once acted as host to Asbury) and enthusiastically embracing the opportunities presented by commercial agriculture. They bought and improved lands, hired laborers, sold wheat and corn, established (with other leading Methodists) an interest in woolen and cotton manufacturing, opened a grocery store, and appear to have edited and published Xenia's first newspaper in 1810.[23]

Such socially and economically successful early Methodists, and those who observed them, saw no contradiction in declaring their skepticism about human riches while simultaneously striving for improvement of themselves and their families. In one breath Philip Gatch declared, "I generally look at a mans Spirit more than his wealth. [t]his may fail, but charity never failith, this includes the first and second command, which will abide forever." But at the same time Gatch reflected thoughtfully on commercial opportunities and made no attempt to conceal his pleasure when his daughters married "industrous" men. Though the itinerant minister John Sale might declare himself an enemy of worldly accumulation, he also lauded the fertile soil and good communications for trading in agricultural and other goods in early Ohio. Another Methodist itinerant, Bennett Maxey, urging Edward Dromgoole to leave Virginia for good, reflected with evident satisfaction on his four years in the "good land" of Ohio. You could, he reported, "do well by keeping a retail store in this country[;] three years ago our merchants began the wourld with little or nothing. This spring they opened . . . [their] stores with a large assortment. You may git farmers to cultivate your land." Dromgoole's profits might not be as gratifyingly large as they were under slavery, but, Maxey insisted, "I believe the . . . [far] greater parte that have come from Virginia have ad[d]ed fore fold to their property with industry and frugality. They live as well as heart could wish for."[24]

These examples suggest that Sellers's portrayal of Methodists' thought world is both partial and misleading. Sellers emphasizes the movement's democratic egalitarianism and communalism, the values most congruent with his definition of subsistence culture. It is true that, in rejecting the doctrines of election and of Christ's limited atonement, Methodists did indeed proffer a radical, democratic, and inclusive alternative to the perceived restrictions and inequalities of Calvinist orthodoxy: Christ, they insisted, had died for all men and women; no one had been excluded from the offer of his love and the Spirit's grace. Here was a philosophy wholly in harmony with the antielitist, democratic ethos of the early republic. But these were not the only emphases in Methodist ideology. Asbury's itinerants bore a further message, one that underscored individual responsibility and ability. God's grace was freely given as well as universally offered. What prevented its reception were human obstinacy and prevarication. These barriers were reinforced by the stultifying Calvinist doctrine that sinners had to wait passively for the operations of the Holy Spirit. But, Methodist preachers insisted, the initiative lay with sinners themselves. Although no one could experience the new birth without the intervention of the Holy Spirit, it was open to every sinner to take the steps that would put him or her in the way of salvation. At the core of Methodism, in other words, lay the empowerment of the individual.[25]

Determined to force Methodists into the mold of "antinomian" critics of Arminian heresy, Sellers is thus driven to ignore their primary defining characteristic: the trumpeting of Arminius's view of conversion as a process involving human enterprise. In a purely theological sense, at the very least, Methodists were thoroughgoing Arminians. They deemed the salvation of their own souls, the energetic pursuit of the conversion of others, and the prosecution of revivals as their paramount business, and to this end they had fashioned their highly centralized and effective connectional organization of circuits and stations, districts, and annual and general conferences. Faith in human ability and responsibility led them to seek out potential converts under the most daunting conditions and in all corners of the union, however remote, and to get there before their competitors; it underpinned the proliferation of camp meetings and their introduction of new, decision-inducing techniques of evangelism. Revival-focused Methodists put their faith in itinerancy before pastoral care; in the repetition through pointed, colloquial preaching of the need for repentance; and in multiplying and protracting services until hearers achieved "liberty." Sinners were repeatedly told, "If you are damned, it is your own fault" and "All things are *now* ready." The preachers' quintessential revivalist tool, resolutely constructed on the foundations of human ability, was the "call to the altar" or to the "mourners' bench." By this means the "anxious" unconverted hearers separated themselves physically from the body of the congregation (who, even so, continued to look on), to open themselves to the instruction and prayers of those who would guide them to a liberating salvation. First adopted in a variety of frontier and urban settings at the end of the eighteenth century, the call to the altar was to become a standard element in Methodist spiritual engineering by the second decade of the new century.[26]

Methodism was both a perfect metaphor for the emergent capitalist market of the early republic and indeed the principal beneficiary of the free spiritual market that superseded the colonial system of energetic government support for religion. When state assistance to a single favored denomination was replaced not, as first seemed possible, by multiple establishment, but by an entirely voluntary system of church support, the initiative passed to those whose denominational institutions proved most flexible and muscular. In 1780 the Methodists had perhaps 50 congregations, as compared with the Congregationalists' 750, the Presbyterians' nearly 500, and the Baptists' and Episcopalians' 400 each. Taking advantage of the end of legal constraints, though continuing to suffer considerable persecution in New England, the Methodists proved the most successful of the liberated groups, growing even more quickly than their principal competitors, the Baptists, the other denomination notably freed by voluntarism to proffer its spiritual wares on the open market. By 1820 the enterprising Methodists had so successfully "sold" their religious doctrines—and, in the significant language of their critics, "manufactured" revivals and converts—that they boasted 2,700 congregations, the same number as the Baptists, having easily overtaken the Presbyterians and Congregationalists, who counted 1,700 and 1,000 respectively. The Methodists prized every new convert and every indication of growth. The membership returns to the annual conferences became the balance sheets of the organization, and they were scrutinized for evidence of weakness or, more usually, stunning growth. In the "market revolution" in religion, the Methodists were the chief beneficiaries.[27]

The entrepreneurial instincts of Methodist ministers were not restricted to matters spiritual. As the market revolution advanced, many espoused the capitalist ethic. It was not unusual for poor itinerants, dependent on the hospitality of the laity, to lodge with rich laymen—often commercial farmers or manufacturers—or their wealthy widows. Traveling preachers carried in their saddlebags books for sale, books that were the production of an influential, competitive, and (ultimately) prosperous Methodist Book Concern that had been established in 1789 as the first denominational publishing house in the United States.[28] Church leaders launched denominational newspapers and took such good advantage of their connectional system that the New York *Christian Advocate and Journal*, first published in 1826, quickly established itself as the most successful weekly newspaper in the world. Methodist ministers also entered the educational marketplace to win custom for their colleges; some institutions went to the wall, but many others flourished through the enterprise and determination of their administrators.

Despite Asbury's admonitions, the attractions of making a living from the market proved too powerful for many poorly paid Methodist itinerants. Reminiscing in 1818 after over forty years in the ministry, Freeborn Garrettson regarded the practice of preachers "locating" as the bane of early Methodism, a constant weakening of the itinerancy. Some left for marriage, others for relief from ill health, and others still, wearying of the arduous, penurious traveling life, for the attractions of business and material prosperity. For some, like John Hogan, all three influences combined. Hogan was an Irishborn orphan who had been raised under Methodist influence in Baltimore. Had he died young, in the late 1820s, he would have been remembered as a typical frontier preacher who spent several years itinerating on horseback around huge circuits in Indiana, Illinois, and Missouri. Eventually he was assigned the St. Louis Circuit, a vast, wild, dangerous, and largely unsettled territory extending along the south bank of the Missouri river from St. Louis itself to Boonville. Traveling fifteen miles a day on horseback from one log cabin settlement to another, reading as he rode (when not disturbed by Indians or wild beasts), holding two services daily for small congregations, sleeping in primitive accommodations, and rarely having a room to himself, Hogan faced great hardships and privations, and eventually he suffered a serious breakdown in his health. In 1830, he located. The following month he married, and soon afterward he began a general merchandising business in Illinois with his brother-in-law. It quickly prospered. Moving to Alton, the largest town in southern Illinois, he established a successful wholesale grocery house and became president of the Alton branch of the State Bank of Illinois. Hogan lost his fortune in the panic of 1837–38, but in the 1840s he established a wholesale grocery partnership with his uncle in St. Louis, importing sugar and coffee. Extending his interests into insurance, banking, railroads, and manufacturing, "Honest John Hogan" was to become one of the wealthiest and best-known men in Missouri. He remained a Methodist local preacher to the end of his enterprising life.[29]

Ordinary members of Methodist congregations showed no less eagerness than locating preachers in pursuing the rewards of the market. Early nineteenth-century itinerants commonly complained of members' laxness over Wesley's and Asbury's prescriptions regarding dress and material temptations. Yet Methodists' seizing of market opportunities was a corollary of the very doctrines and values that ministers propounded and that helped make the church so attractive to Americans of the era: individualism, self-discipline, and self-improvement. Love feasts and revival services may have provided social networks, mutual support, and communalism, but Methodist doctrine also encouraged the atomistic and competitive elements integral to the early republic's liberal individualism. George Peck was skeptical about the supposedly selfless equality and brotherly love of early Methodism. This latter attribute, he asserted, "arose from the smallness of the social circle, and a sense of mutual dependence, as much as from real brotherly love," he wrote half a century later. "Methodists then were few, and were much persecuted, and they were naturally forced together. They were poor and mutually dependent, and they had motives for being kind to each other of a selfish nature which they have not at present." Methodists were not communitarians. The essential method for doing good, explained a writer in the *Christian Advocate* only a few months after Jackson entered the White House, was to "make every individual take care of himself." He posed the rhetorical question, "Can the good of the nation be secure in any other way than by first securing the good of those individuals which compose the nation?" Each person had an obligation to make his or her individual spiritual pilgrimage. Each, according to the formal articles of Methodism, had the right to the enjoyment of his or her private property. Not even the earliest and poorest Methodists favored the doctrine of community of goods.[30]

Methodism, like other evangelical movements of the era, also extolled and inculcated habits of self-discipline, industry, and temperance. With its concern for decency in personal behavior and encouragement of spiritual development, it both generated and helped slake a widespread "thirst for improvement" (as Freeborn Garrettson put it) among the young in particular. That improvement connoted both moral and material achievement. Sellers points to the correction that Methodism offered to "the patriarchal vices of drinking, swearing, gambling, and fighting" and its challenge—by giving women and slaves a more equal role—to narrow subsistence patriarchy. But he shies away from the conclusion that such corrections represented more a push toward the market's competitive individualism and material improvement than an endorsement of the fundamentals of premarket society. In his *Autobiography,* a work that is in many ways a jeremiad for the passing of a lost era, the elderly circuit rider Peter Cartwright recalled the case of a miserly Illinois farmer who was saving all his money to buy land, and with three hundred dollars already hoarded still kept his Methodist family in the most primitive of conditions. The preacher told the husband to refurbish his cabin with decent chairs, beds, eating implements, and so on, and to provide his wife and daughters with smart clothing. "You ought to know," Cartwright told him, "that the Discipline of our Church makes it the duty of a circuit rider to recommend cleanliness and decency everywhere; . . . and you ought to attend to [these things] for your own comfort, and the great comfort of your family." Though the farmer called Cartwright a proud preacher and told him "he knew I was proud the moment he saw me with my broadcloth coat on," he did later refurbish his cabin and provide the women with new calico dresses. The instincts of each of the parties involved in this story were beckoning them into one sector of the market or another, yet Sellers chooses to see the primary meaning of the story in the enforcement on the husband of communal (that is, subsistence) standards of behavior. But surely its main lesson is that the Methodists' concern for decency and self-improvement accelerated rather than resisted the advance of the capitalist market.[31]

In his recent study of rural religion in the early settlement and development of upstate New York, Curtis Johnson looks for evidence that might link Methodism and areas of subsistence agriculture. In Cortland County, which witnessed a rapid shift to commercial farming between 1810 and 1830 and which shared in the era's canal fever, he examines the church's strength in areas high in the production of homemade cloth (an indicator of subsistence economy). Far from flourishing in these communities, Methodism was much weaker than it was in areas of market penetration. In fact, "Methodism grew in strength as the market penetrated the county's farthest reaches," and by 1860 it was the largest denomination: "Arminian theology with its emphasis on individual free choice had conquered the Calvinist doctrine of election."[32]

By the 1820s, the decade of Jackson's insurgency and a period when the Methodist Episcopal Church almost doubled its membership from a quarter-million to nearly half a million, it is clear that the movement had come to embrace many from the ranks of the socially well regarded. The more Methodists took pains to prevent "rant, extravagance, or 'strange fire' " in their revivals, the more they boasted converts who included "men of talents, science, and of the highest and most respectable standing."[33] At some camp meetings they had to protect themselves against "the baser sort of the community." Many joined the church "without laying off any of the garniture which characterizes the fashionable of the first grade." More refined revivalists like John Newland Maffitt found their natural constituency among "respectable" citizens who would protect them against "the baser sort."[34]

There are, then, strong grounds for believing that Methodism in the era of the Jacksonian revolution was already infused with a capitalist and market ethic. Even if, as Sellers contends, first-generation Methodism demonstrated a number of "antinomian" features—in its communalism, egalitarianism, and location in premarket areas—it was also "arminian" in its understanding of human ability, its stress on individual responsibility, and its stimulus to self-improvement and enterprise. It was certainly not *anti*market. By the 1820s the movement had entered its second generation. Though there were those who resisted its self-conscious pursuit of respectability, many others took heart from their own social betterment, from the movement's evident capacity to attract new members of wealth and status, and also from its contribution to the discipline of the market and of the new industrial arena. Methodist reports of the religious revival in 1827 at Bozrahville, Connecticut, of which it was claimed that fewer than ten of the employees of the cotton factory were immune to religious reformation, happily extolled prayerful Methodism's capacity to fashion an attentive, industrious workforce.[35] The denomination embraced many who conspicuously welcomed the new economic order. Its spokesmen saw the country's commercial growth (as well as its climate, natural resources, and republican institutions) as an earnest of the Almighty's grand design for the nation.[36]

In their capacity for embracing modernity and economic improvement, the Methodists showed themselves members of a church with a national, not local or merely congregational, vision. Methodist connectionalism—involving the countrywide transfer of information through denominational publications and networks like the Sunday School Union, as well as the itinerating ministry—worked to inform and broaden the horizons of ordinary members. "Until after the period in which I became a subscriber to your useful and valuable paper," explained a reader of the *Christian Advocate and Journal,* "my views were entirely local." Sellers treats Methodism as part of the "magical spirituality of a parochial and fatalist countryside against the cosmopolitan and activist market." Yet few agencies in the early republic could boast Methodism's capacity for national integration and the breakdown of localism.[37]

It is only in recent years that writing on religion in the early republic has ceased to serve a "Calvinist synthesis"—that is, the perception that Calvinism is the shaping force in American religious culture, and that other expressions of Christianity, and non-Christian religions, are either marginal or warrant exploration principally in relation to Calvinist experience. Sellers's evident sympathy for the egalitarianism and communalism of "antinomian" culture, and his placing early Methodism at its heart, suggests his own break with that Calvinist-centered tradition; so, too, does his recognition of "antinomian" Methodist influence on the revolutionary Finney. Yet he does not wholly escape that tradition, for it is to Calvinists of the Moderate Light that he attributes the reconciliation of "the anxious antinomian majority to a capitalist world."[38] He devotes considerable space to the conflict within Calvinism, in

New England and its diaspora, over the response to the market, but only a sentence or so to the ultimate embourgeoisement of Methodism. He develops a model of middle-class clerics and entrepreneurs combining to impose capitalist values and "collective repression" on reluctant antinomians who sought to remain loyal to rural ways; he misses the possibility that the Methodist lives of ordinary folk may have provided them with their own channel of self-improvement. He regards the conflict in Finney's burned-over district as one between Presbyterians and antinomian rebels; but the differences between the fast-growing Methodists and the "Presbygationalists" had more to do with missionary zeal in the spiritual marketplace, with conflict over style and comportment in the competition for souls, and with the residual theological conflict between Arminianism and Calvinism.

The triumph of Arminianism (in the conventional doctrinal sense, not Sellers's Jacksonian variant) over Calvinism was the crucial ideological reorientation brought about by the Second Great Awakening.[39] As the principal purveyors of Arminian doctrine, the Methodists engaged in bitter conflict with their evangelical competitors. No reader of the diaries and reminiscences of the popular preachers of this period can avoid their interdenominational polemics. Methodists saw themselves engaged in a battle not just against sin, but against false doctrine, principally Calvinism, and their principal targets among their Calvinist adversaries were the Baptists. Far from being commonly engaged in an "antinomian" battle against the market, Arminian Methodists and Calvinist Baptists were antagonistically locked into one of the fiercest popular conflicts of the first half of the century as each strove to become the preeminent denomination of the common people. Peter Cartwright's struggle with various stripes of Baptists provides a leitmotif for his recollections of early Methodism in Kentucky, Tennessee, and Illinois. In a similar vein, Allen Wiley's memoirs are a celebration of the Methodists' achievement in becoming the principal denomination in the Whitewater Valley and other regions of Indiana where the Baptists had earlier predominated (a story made all the more pointed by Wiley's having been raised a Baptist). Similar conflicts marked upstate New York.[40]

Nowhere was sectarian antagonism more bitter, however, than in southern Appalachia. In Tennessee, Methodist growth and proficiency in revivals provided a target for Calvinists from the early 1800s to the late antebellum years: both Baptists and Presbyterians regularly abused Methodist organization, theology, and morality, especially in the pages of Frederick Augustus Ross's *Calvinistic Magazine* and James R. Graves' *Tennessee Baptist.* Interminable theological wrangles over complete immersion, the baptism of infants, and Calvinistic predestination jostled side by side with salacious charges and countercharges of debauchery, drunkenness, and sexual seduction. Methodist allegations that Baptists were ignoramuses opposed to formal learning confronted Baptist claims that Wesley's troops were unscrupulous recruiters who would make any promise—even rebaptize their adult members by immersion—to secure their church's supremacy. Venomous polemics reached their climax in the 1850s when Graves published a compilation of his newspaper articles, which had denounced Methodism as an autocratic, overcentralized, and cryptopapist organization, under the title of *The Great Iron Wheel, or, Republicanism Backwards and Christianity Reversed.* This elicited a reply in kind from "Parson" William Gannaway Brownlow. In *The Great Iron Wheel Examined,* the combative Methodist preacher and editor mixed invective, personal insult, and innuendo in a bellicose riposte that confirmed his status as southern Appalachia's most redoubtable polemicist. Reflecting on these sectarian contentions, Brownlow—an Arminian pot bubbling alongside Graves's Calvinist kettle—concluded that "there is, perhaps, more of the spirit that prevailed in Geneva [when Servetus was burned] . . . in East Tennessee, than in any other place in this Union."[41]

These conflicts between the two principal popular denominations undoubtedly expressed more than competing certainties over baptismal practices. In part they represented a conflict between the Methodists' energetic connectionalism and the Baptists' localism, in part a conflict between Arminian self-advancement and Calvinist determinism. In part, too, they may have been related to differing attitudes toward the market and economic development. Brownlow and his fellow eastern Tennessee Methodists were much more strongly identified than Baptists with Whiggish enterprise in moral and economic affairs. Brownlow, Samuel Patton, and (in western North Carolina) David R. McAnally typified Methodist leaders who regarded their part of the southern highlands as "the garden spot of the Union, and the El Dorado of America," which needed only investment and internal improvements to link it to a wider market and realize its economic potential. As Whig-Methodist boosters they connected religious, social, and economic improvement. "The interests of Education, Agriculture, and Commerce," one of them explained, "are more nearly allied to the prosperity of Christ's Kingdom than most men, perhaps, are willing to admit." Conversely, Baptists in the same region, particularly but not exclusively those "hard shell and iron sided" believers who made up the Primitive Baptists, seem more often than not to have been Jacksonians. High Calvinists, the Primitives (or "Antimission" Baptists) were strenuously opposed to Arminian "effort" and denounced theological education, temperance and missionary societies, "new measure" revivalism, "steam religion," and a "money-hunting" Protestant priesthood; they had no enthusiasm, as one elder explained, for plans "for the improvement of the moral, intellectual, and physical condition of mankind." James R. Graves and the "Missionary" Baptists shared many of the Primitives' perspectives on the Methodists, lamenting the heterodoxy of their preaching ("you can get religion and lose it at pleasure") and the threat to local autonomy and congregational independence from their centralizing ecclesiastical machinery. There was a history of Tennessee Baptists' rebuking Methodist preachers for their finery and warning the people to beware those who "wore black broadcloth coats, silk jackets[,] . . . fair-topped boots, and a watch in their pockets; [and] that rode fine fat horses." *The Great Iron Wheel* can be seen as a Baptist-Democratic manifesto for republicanism, decentralization, and provincialism in the face of a movement that Baptists saw as despotic, open to cosmopolitan corruption, and too energetically nationalist. These ideological and cultural antipathies ran deep. They produced in Anderson County in eastern Tennessee what the Methodist circuit rider Frank Richardson judged "the bitterest denominational prejudice I have ever known anywhere." At the county seat, Clinton, the two communities "had no dealings with each other whatever": each had its own churches, schools, taverns, stores, blacksmith shops, and even ferries across the river. "Most of the Methodists were Whigs," Richardson noted, "and most of the Baptists were Democrats."[42]

If, then, the Methodists cannot be easily classified as "antinomian" opponents of the capitalist market, and indeed in some incarnations have rather to be seen as its allies, how is one to explain their loyalty to Jackson and his party? Accepting that Methodists in 1828 were mainly Jacksonians in politics, we do not have to suppose that those who voted for Old Hickory as Methodists did so because they saw him as their best defense against the market's advance. As I have argued at greater length elsewhere, evangelicals' motivation in voting was highly complex and varied, and their party preferences depended considerably on context.[43] But there is no doubt that many saw in Jackson's party, as they had earlier seen in Jefferson's, their best defense against illegitimate religious power—that is, against the influence of "formalist" denominations, including those that had previously benefited from the statutory alliance of church and state and that sought to impose legal controls on moral and religious behavior. The ranks of the Methodists—and the Baptists—were made up very largely of those who emphasized the primacy of personal piety, believed churches' main responsibility was to save souls, saw social change as coming through the Holy Spirit working in the hearts of individuals, and tended to distrust governmental schemes for social reform. Politically they sought the best means of sustaining the laissez-faire principles by which churches fought for members on equal terms and sustained themselves by their own voluntary efforts.

Methodists' experience at the hands of Calvinist orthodoxy had a profound effect on their partisan allegiance. In New England, in the early years of the young republic, they were forced to pay taxes to sustain the Congregationalist Standing Order; poor ministers faced heavy fines for conducting marriage ceremonies; hostile mobs intimidated worshippers, broke up services, destroyed meeting places, and attacked as "incarnate demons" itinerant "intruders into the land of steady habits." In areas of Yankee settlement outside New England, though they suffered no legal disabilities, Methodists faced social discrimination from higher-status Calvinists: in the Western Reserve, for example, an informal establishment of "Presbygationalists" strove to hobble them by closing off preaching places. In consequence, it was hardly surprising that most Methodists became enthusiastic Jeffersonians, not because they cherished Jefferson's personal religious beliefs, of course, but because his party provided a principled defense of religious pluralism against Federalist church establishments.

The motives that made Methodists Democratic-Republicans under the first party system—in particular their determination to defend Arminian truth against Calvinist arrogance and bigotry—similarly drew many into Jacksonian Democracy, especially in the party's early years.[44] Political managers were no strangers to the truth expressed by a writer in the *Farmer's Herald*: "To subserve the interests of party, different sects must be made to hate, and villify each other."[45] The Democrats offered a home to those who, encouraged by Jacksonian publicists in the 1828 election, believed that John Quincy Adams's National Republicans and subsequently the early Whig party represented the Calvinist establishment in new clothing. Methodists' anxieties over political favoritism to formalist churches revealed themselves especially in reactions during the 1820s and 1830s to campaigns for Sabbatarian and temperance legislation. Presbyterian and Congregationalist demands for a state-supported Sabbath and for the prohibition of the liquor trade seemed to many Methodists, as to Baptists and others who also had suffered at the hands of a religious establishment, to be part of a momentum that would bring the young republic's delicate structure of civil and religious liberty crashing to the ground. Methodists' strong Democratic loyalties persisted in many areas into the late antebellum period, sustained in part by these earlier antagonisms.[46] William X. Ninde recalled that even into the 1850s Democratic politicians continued to exploit the residual tensions between Congregationalists and Methodists in Connecticut and "went in heart and soul to help the Methodists. It was a sort of 'you tickle me, and I'll tickle

you' system, a kind of see-saw arrangement. When the Whigs and the Congregationalists went down the Democrats and the Methodists went up and
vice versa."[47]

Yet by no means all Methodists were Jacksonians, even in the early days of
the second party system, and as the years passed the Democrats' hold on the
denomination grew increasingly less assured. "Lord deliver us from Whiggery!" prayed a Tennessee Methodist preacher at a camp meeting; "God forbid!" came the response. It is impossible, given the well-established problems
of identifying the church affiliations of aggregated anonymous voters, to be
precise about the number or proportion of anti-Democratic Methodists. But
there were plenty who shared the perspective, if not the exhibitionism, of the
"violent Anti-Jackson preacher" of the Baltimore Conference who visited the
White House with colleagues in 1831, and took the opportunity to pray that
the general might be converted, "which he did so loud that he could be heard
at the President's gate." Some, like William Winans, followed Henry Clay
from Antifederalism through National Republicanism to Whiggery. Others
took a route that led through Antimasonry. Paul Goodman's analysis of that
movement in New England suggests substantial Methodist support for Antimasonry, morally and electorally, especially in Maine and Vermont, where
Methodists contributed a number of prominent leaders. Subsequently a majority of Antimasonry's supporters, including Methodists, amalgamated with
the new Whig party. An examination of Methodists' published and manuscript diaries and journals makes it clear that, by the 1840s, many denominational leaders regarded Clay's party as a truer heir of Jeffersonian Democracy than the Locofocos. So, too, do some of the sparse survivals of individual
voting records: one analysis indicates that 74 percent of Methodists in Green
County, Illinois, voted Whig; another points to a similar orientation in parts
of Rhode Island.[48] The Indiana Conference was said to be mainly of that
outlook by 1840. James Dixon, a British Wesleyan representative at the General Conference of the Methodist Episcopal Church in 1848, was clear that the
vast majority of Methodists that he met on his travels were Whigs.[49]

There can be little doubt, as Brownlow's example has already suggested,
that Whiggery's attraction lay to some degree in its posture as the party of
economic and social improvement. But it is also clear that a major element
of its appeal was its standing as a party of Christian—or, more specifically,
Protestant—integrity. Inheriting the Jeffersonian mantle of defenders of religious pluralism and freedom of conscience, Jacksonian Democrats found
themselves charged with moral myopia in a society increasingly threatened—
as it seemed—by paganism, rationalism, and degraded theology. Whigs
played mercilessly on Jacksonians' readiness to shelter freethinkers and het-

erodox Christians. Thus William Crane, a Methodist minister and devoted free trader and internationalist, chloroformed his economic conscience and voted Whig through the 1830s, despite "their cardinal doctrine" of a protective tariff, because the Whigs offered evangelical Protestant Americans a more secure morality than their free trade opponents. The Jacksonians, he believed, were irredeemably flawed since "they despised no man for his sins." Crane and other Methodists froze at the names of Fanny Wright, Abner Kneeland, Robert Dale Owen, and other Locofoco heirs of Tom Paine. Significantly, Crane had been sympathetic to Antimasonry, a movement that had successfully played on fears of a spreading conspiracy against orthodoxy and that acted for some as a route into Whiggery.[50]

Most threatening of all the groups embraced by the Democrats, it seemed, were the burgeoning communities of Irish and German Catholics. The smoldering embers of the Methodists' historic antipathy toward Romanists burst into open flame through the 1830s and 1840s, fanned by the energetic propaganda of skilled publicists. Few were more vitriolic than Parson Brownlow, who charged Catholic immigrants and the papal hierarchy with near-unanimous support of the corrupt Locofocos and denounced Van Buren as a Romish sycophant. More temperate in language, but equally clear about the political logic of Catholic leaders' attempts to secure state funding for their schools in New York City and elsewhere, was the *Christian Advocate and Journal:* "The school question is now made a political one . . . with the Romanists claiming the aid of the Democrats, and the Whigs asking the help of Protestants. . . . The Protestants have not done this. . . . the Romanists are the aggressors." The Methodists were also aggrieved by the Jacksonians' complicity in the Irish Catholic efforts to secure the repeal of the Anglo-Irish Union of 1800.[51]

To counter this convergence of Methodism and evangelically oriented Whiggery, the Democrats stressed their opponents' "Federalist" roots and their threat to the separation of church and state, but with decreasing effect. In the early years of the century, the fear of Federalism and state-supported Calvinism had been sufficient to bind within the Republican party both Methodism and, as Alfred Brunson recalled, "the infidel portion of the community, though these classes were antipodes in all things pertaining to religion."[52] By the 1830s, however, some Methodists were ready to support a party that also embraced the very Calvinists they had once had cause to fear. A number of Methodists were beginning to question their faith in moral suasion alone as a means of preserving a Protestant social order and came to see the legitimacy of and need for legal measures, whether to prohibit liquor selling or protect camp meetings from outside disturbance. Those Methodists who were afraid that such measures represented a threat to the separation of church and state, and a betrayal of their historic credo, were reassured by church spokesmen who sought to distinguish between an improper sectarian establishment and an entirely proper subjection of legislation to Christian influence. As Benjamin Tefft explained, "No enlightened Christian wishes to see Church and State united in government; but if men [are] to do all things to the glory of God, they must be constantly governed by the moral law of God; and hence religious principle must be made the basis of political action."[53]

That important body of Methodists who traveled into Whiggery from Jeffersonian Republicanism and Jacksonian Democracy were moving from being cultural outsiders to insiders; their journey was associated with the increasing social status of Methodists and the Arminianization of Calvinism, which made political coalition with non-Methodists all the more possible. There is, however, little evidence to suggest that it had to do with Methodists' latter-day conversion to the merits of the market, for they had long been in tune with the individualist, entrepreneurial values of capitalism. Sellers is critical of liberal historians who argue for an early nineteenth-century capitalist consensus, and he may well be right in relating political division in Jacksonian America principally to the responses to the market.[54] But Methodists provide a more feeble support than his argument supposes. They do not fit comfortably into his "antinomian"–"arminian" dichotomy. Their experience suggests that capitalist values were shared across the partisan divide. But this does not make those political divisions artificial or insubstantial. Methodists' partisan allegiances were neither accidental nor incidental. They were to a considerable degree shaped by meaningful ideological conflict between competing religious groups. The concerns underlying Methodists' political allegiance in the early national period were shaped as much by the religious as by the economic marketplace.

NOTES

1. In two influential works William G. McLoughlin discusses the ideological shift effected by the Second Great Awakening and relates it to deep cultural change. He sees each of America's awakenings "as a period of fundamental social and intellectual reorientation of the American belief-value system, behavior patterns, and institutional structure." In

the early nineteenth century American Calvinism had to be "revitalized" as society moved toward a new cultural era emphasizing independence and self-reliance. William G. Mc-Loughlin, Jr., *Modern Revivalism: Charles Grandison Finney to Billy Graham* (New York, 1959), pp. 3–121, and *Revivals, Awakenings, and Reform: An Essay on Religion and Social Change in America, 1607–1977* (Chicago, 1978), pp. 10 (quotation), 98–140.

2. Representative of the genre are Paul E. Johnson, *A Shopkeeper's Millennium: Society and Revivals in Rochester, New York, 1790–1865* (New York, 1978); Mary P. Ryan, *Cradle of the Middle Class: The Family in Oneida County, New York, 1790–1865* (Cambridge, Mass., 1981); Randolph A. Roth, *The Democratic Dilemma: Religion, Reform, and the Social Order in the Connecticut River Valley of Vermont, 1791–1850* (Cambridge, Eng., 1987); David G. Hackett, *The Rude Hand of Innovation: Religion and Social Order in Albany, New York 1652–1836* (New York, 1991). All draw inspiration from a classic work: Whitney R. Cross, *The Burned-Over District: The Social and Intellectual History of Enthusiastic Religion in Western New York* (Ithaca, N.Y., 1950). Other valuable local and regional studies include John B. Boles, *The Great Revival, 1787–1805: The Origins of the Southern Evangelical Mind* (Lexington, Ky., 1972); Terry D. Bilhartz, *Urban Religion and the Second Great Awakening: Church and Society in Early National Baltimore* (Rutherford, N.J., 1986).

3. Curtis D. Johnson, in *Islands of Holiness: Rural Religion in Upstate New York, 1790–1860* (Ithaca, N.Y., 1989), relates the growth of evangelical churches in Cortland County to the experience of rapid economic change, but attaches primary importance to ideology in fostering revivalistic religion. Hackett, in *The Rude Hand of Innovation*, p. 164, also emphasizes how ideological conflict "directly influenced the course of social change."

4. Richard Carwardine, "The Second Great Awakening in Comparative Perspective: Revivals and Culture in the United States and Britain," in Edith L. Blumhofer and Randall Balmer, *Modern Christian Revivals* (Urbana, Ill., 1993), pp. 84–100.

5. Charles Sellers, *The Market Revolution: Jacksonian America, 1815–1846* (New York, 1991), pp. 5–6, 9–33.

6. Sellers, *Market Revolution*, pp. 137–38, 157–61, 164–65, 178, 299–300.

7. Sellers, *Market Revolution*, pp. 202–36.

8. Sellers, *Market Revolution*, pp. 158, 161.

9. Particularly valuable in understanding the status and world-view of early Methodists are Nathan O. Hatch, *The Democratization of American Christianity* (New Haven, Conn., 1989); Donald G. Mathews, *Religion in the Old South* (Chicago, 1977), esp. pp. 28–37; Russell E. Richey, *Early American Methodism* (Bloomington, 1991); and William Henry Williams, *The Garden of American Methodism: The Delmarva Peninsula, 1769–1820* (Wilmington, Del., 1984). See also George Claude Baker, Jr., *An Introduction to the History of Early New England Methodism 1789–1839* (Durham, N.C., 1941); Emory S. Bucke, ed., *The History of American Methodism*, 3 vols. (New York, 1964).

10. John Sale to Edward Dromgoole, Feb. 20, 1807, in William Warren Sweet, *Religion on the American Frontier 1783–1840*, Vol. 14, *The Methodists* (1946; reprint, New York, 1964), p. 160.

11. Nicholas Snethen to George Roberts, Dec. 31, 1801, Methodist Manuscript Collection, Methodist Center, Drew University (hereafter MCDU).

12. Freeborn Garrettson to Bishop George, Aug. 1, 1825, MCDU. See also *(New York) Christian Advocate and Journal* (hereafter *CAJ*), Dec. 7, 1827.

13. J. Tackaberry, "Day Book" and "Journal," 1:8–9, MCDU.

14. *CAJ*, Jan. 25, 1828. See also, for example, issues for Mar. 14, 1828, Jan. 13, Feb. 25, and Apr. 15, 1831; [?] Smith to G. Coles, May 12, 1842, MCDU.

15. Teresa Anne Murphy, *Ten Hours' Labor: Religion, Reform, and Gender in Early New England* (Ithaca, N.Y., 1992); Jama Lazerow, "Spokesmen for the Working Class: Protestant Clergy and the Labor Movement in Antebellum New England," *Journal of the Early Republic* 13 (1993): 323–54; William R. Sutton, "Tied to the Whipping Post: New Labor History and Evangelical Artisans in the Early Republic" (*Labor History*, forthcoming). See also Ronald Schultz, "The Small-Producer Tradition and the Moral Origins of Artisan Radicalism in Philadelphia, 1720–1810," *Past and Present* 127 (1990): 84–108. Murphy is especially sensitive to the complexities and ambiguities of the evangelical response to industrialization, and explores both the disruptive and disciplining elements of Methodist revivals: "Religion was . . . a strongly contested terrain in which working people and employers had very different interpretations and goals." See Murphy, *Ten Hours' Labor*, p. 82. By contrast, the socially controlling, self-disciplining, and restrictive effects on mechanics and factory workers of evangelicalism in general and Methodism in particular is the principal, though not the sole, burden of Paul Johnson, *A Shopkeepers' Millennium*; Bruce Laurie, *Artisans into Workers: Labor in Nineteenth-Century America* (New York, 1989), and *Working People of Philadelphia, 1800–1850* (Philadelphia, 1980); and Anthony F. C. Wallace, *Rockdale: The Growth of an American Village in the Early Industrial Revolution* (New York, 1978). Sean Wilentz, like Murphy, also sees the "gamut of impulses" deriving from Methodism "all tied to the tensions between submissiveness and egalitarianism that lay at Methodism's core." Ultimately, though, he sees Methodism becoming "more closely identified with efforts to enforce an industrious morality of self-discipline." See Sean Wilentz, *Chants Democratic: New York City and the Rise of the American Working Class, 1788–1850* (New York, 1984), pp. 80–81. Cf. Barbara M. Tucker, *Samuel Slater and the Origins of the American Textile Industry, 1790–1860* (Ithaca, N.Y., 1984), pp. 163–85.

For a parallel debate on the influence of Methodism on English social relations during the industrial revolution, see Edward P. Thompson, *The Making of the English Working Class* (London, 1963), and, in response, Thomas W. Laqueur, *Religion and Respectability: Sunday Schools and Working-Class Culture, 1780–1850* (New Haven, Conn., 1976) and David Hempton, *Methodism and Politics in British Society, 1750–1850* (London, 1984). Sellers writes, "Urban stress converted the antinomian ecstasy of Methodist conversion into the arminian effort of capitalist discipline, and a 'changed heart' was most clearly evidenced by the capitalist virtues. Spiritual intensity functioned to motivate and sustain the personal transformations required for survival under intensifying market relations." See his *Market Revolution*, p. 285.

16. Beverly Waugh to George Coles, Aug. 25, 1856, MCDU; George Peck, *The Past and the Present: A Semi-Centennial Sermon: Preached before the Oneida and Wyoming Conferences at Ithaca, N. Y., April 19, 1866* (New York, 1866), pp. 10, 24–27, 32; *CAJ*, May 12, 1827, June 12 and July 31, 1829, Apr. 8, 1831, Jan. 5, 1848, May 15, June 12, and Aug. 7, 1856, Jan. 1, 1857.

17. Benjamin F. Tefft, *Methodism Successful, and the Internal Causes of Its Success* (New York, 1860); *CAJ*, July 27, Sept. 15, 1841, June 14 and July 5, 1843, Oct. 25, 1848, Feb. 21 and

Mar. 13, 1856, June 11, 1857; Richard Wheatley, *The Life and Letters of Mrs. Phoebe Palmer* (New York, 1876), p. 600.

18. Sutton, "Tied to the Whipping Post," 27; Bucke, *History of American Methodism* 1: 629. Methodism suffered divisions over the Church's proper response to Freemasonry in the late 1820s and the early 1830s. Insofar as the Antimasonic movement can be seen (as Paul Goodman argues) as a passionate reaction against the transition to a new industrial society and consumerism, its Methodist supporters might seem to be antimodernists and Methodist Masons part of an emergent bourgeoisie. But that conclusion has to be tempered by the fact that many New England Methodists were drawn to Freemasonry primarily because of its devotion to religious tolerance and that, as a predominantly Calvinist movement, Antimasonry was not a natural refuge for Arminian Methodists.

19. Bucke, *History of American Methodism* 1:633.

20. For Methodists and patriarchy, see Richey, *Early American Methodism*, pp. 25–26, 56–57. Donald Mathews argues that early southern Methodism "was a means through which a rising 'new' class sought authentication outside the archaic social hierarchy." Methodists tried to replace class distinctions based on worldly honor, but they could not escape the social system in which they were moving to better farms and improving their status. See Mathews, *Religion in the Old South*, pp. 37–38.

21. Williams, *The Garden of American Methodism*, pp. 99–105.

22. Peter Pelham to Edward Dromgoole, Jr., June 21, 1811, in Sweet, *Religion on the American Frontier*, 4:196–97. See Rutsen Suckley to J. B. Wakeley, May 7, 1866, MCDU, for the friendship of Asbury, Coke, and Garrettson with Suckley's Methodist father, the American agent and managing partner of the Sheffield-based manufacturers, Newbould and Holy.

23. Peter Pelham to Edward Dromgoole, June 20 and July 27, 1807, Apr. 16, 1810, June 21, 1811, in Sweet, *Religion on the American Frontier* 4:163–67, 172–74, 187–88, 196– 97. The family of Frederick Bonner, friend of Gatch and Asbury, presents a similar Greene County mix of staunch Methodism, land acquisition, manufacturing, and openness to the market. Frederick Bonner to Edward Dromgoole ["Drumgole"], July 19, 1807, in Sweet, *Religion on the American Frontier*, 4:170–71.

24. Philip Gatch to Edward Dromgoole, June 1, 1805, John Sale to Edward Dromgoole, Feb. 20, 1807, and Bennett Maxey to Edward Dromgoole, July 27, 1807, in Sweet, *Religion on the American Frontier*, 4:157, 159–60, 174–75.

25. For Methodist doctrine and its implications for human ability, see, for example, Hatch, *The Democratization of American Christianity*, pp. 171–72. George M. Thomas discusses the tension between Calvinists' predestinarianism and their daily experience of the market; Methodists, by contrast, enjoyed a doctrine of human ability and control that was wholly compatible with their daily economic and political lives. See George M. Thomas, *Revivalism and Cultural Change: Christianity, Nation Building, and the Market in the Nineteenth-Century United States* (Chicago, 1989), pp. 7–8. Hackett, in *The Rude Hand of Innovation*, pp. 90–95, 98–99, also relates the conflict between Calvinist and Methodist to the changing socioeconomic order of the early Republic and sees Methodist ideology appealing to Albany's rising poor through its "new insistence on individual autonomy."

26. *CAJ*, Nov. 18, 1831; Richard Carwardine, "The Second Great Awakening in the Ur-

ban Centers: An Examination of Methodism and the New Measures," *Journal of American History* 59 (1972): 327–40.

27. Jon Butler, *Awash in a Sea of Faith: Christianizing the American People* (Cambridge, Mass., 1990), pp. 268–82.

28. When the New York Book Concern burned down in 1836, the loss of building and stock was so great that the New York insurance companies almost collapsed. Bucke, *History of American Methodism* 1:579.

29. Freeborn Garrettson to [?], Dec. 22, 1818, June 15, 1824, MCDU; Sophia Hogan Boogher, *Recollections of John Hogan by His Daughter* (St. Louis, 1927), pp. 8–29, 51.

30. Peck, *The Past and the Present*, p. 32; *CAJ*, July 24, 1829; A. A. Jimeson, *Notes on the Twenty-five Articles of Religion, as Received and Taught by Methodists in the United States* (Cincinnati, 1855), pp. 362–66. Cf. Phoebe Palmer, *Faith and Its Effects, or, Fragments from My Portfolio* (London, 1856), pp. 192–97.

31. Freeborn Garrettson to [?], Dec. 22, 1818, MCDU; Sellers, *Market Revolution*, pp. 155, 160; Peter Cartwright, *Autobiography of Peter Cartwright: The Backwoods Preacher*, ed. W. P. Strickland (New York, n.d.), pp. 251–54.

32. Curtis D. Johnson, *Islands of Holiness: Rural Religion in Upstate New York, 1790–1860* (Ithaca, N.Y., 1989), pp. 82–85.

33. *CAJ*, Feb. 3, 1827 (on the Ithaca revival of 1826–27), Oct. 10, 1828 (on the Hempstead, Long Island, revival). See also, for example, *CAJ*, Apr. 8, 1831, which states that the Troy revival brought in "men in their prime . . . high in talent, office, influence and wealth."

34. *CAJ*, Oct. 7, 1826, July 31, 1829; J. N. Maffitt to G. Coles, n.d., MCDU.

35. *CAJ*, Apr. 7, 1827.

36. Methodists' enthusiasm for the new economic order did not make them blind to the greed and exploitation of the capitalist market, but in general its Methodist critics sought to Christianize or sanitize the new order, not resist it. The efforts of Methodists in both the United States and Britain to devise Christian rules for commercial practice deserve analysis in their own right, and are necessarily beyond the scope of this essay. Attention to stewardship, voluntary giving, and schemes of private, systematic benevolence was an ever-present element of midcentury Methodists' discourse. For quintessential examples, see Jimeson, *Notes on the Twenty-five Articles of Religion*, pp. 204–12 ("Good Works"), 362–70 ("Of Christian Men's Goods"); Andrew Carroll, "Proper Use of the Mammon of Unrighteousness," in Maxwell P. Gaddis, ed., *The Ohio Conference Offering, or, Sermons and Sketches of Sermons, on Familiar and Practical Subjects, from the Living and the Dead* (Cincinnati, 1854), pp. 95–109; Calvin Kingsley, "Practical Benevolence," in William Hunter, ed., *Original Sermons by Ministers of the Pittsburgh, Erie, and Western Virginia Conferences of the Methodist Episcopal Church* (Pittsburgh, 1850); *Memorial of E. P. Williams, Late Member of the Oneida Conference of the M.E. Church: Being a Choice Collection of the Sermons and Sketches of Sermons, with a Brief Biographical Sketch* (Syracuse, N.Y., 1959), pp. 54–78 ("Christian Benevolence"). *The Successful Merchant* (London, 1852), William Arthur's well-regarded prescription for the blending of commercial and Christian values, enjoyed an extensive transatlantic circulation among Methodists during the 1850s. See, for example, *CAJ*, Mar. 13, 1856.

37. *CAJ*, Sept. 23, 1826, Feb. 17, 1827, Aug. 31, 1827; Sellers, *Market Revolution*, pp. 30–31.

38. Sellers, *Market Revolution*, p. 204.

39. McLoughlin, *Revivals, Awakenings, and Reform*, pp. 113–40. For a recent discussion, see Johnson, *Islands of Holiness*, pp. 33–52, which shows that the decades of Cortland County's rapid economic development were also years when Arminians won "an astonishing victory over their Calvinist opponents" and when Calvinism itself was Arminianized. But "the popularity of Arminian ideas . . . was more a secondary consequence than a primary cause of new attitudes [of individualism, self-determination, and free will] among the general population" (p. 51).

40. Cartwright, *Autobiography*, pp. 64–72, 107–10, 118–22, 133–38, 147–51, 215–19, 226–28; Elizabeth K. Nottingham, *Methodism and the Frontier: Indiana Proving Ground* (New York, 1941), pp. 41–55; Johnson, *Islands of Holiness*, pp. 43–52.

41. Richard Carwardine, "Religious Revival and Political Renewal in Antebellum America," in Jane Garnett and Colin Mathew, eds., *Revival and Religion Since 1700: Essays for John Walsh* (London, 1993), pp. 145–46.

42. Carwardine, "Religious Revival and Political Renewal in Antebellum America," pp. 138–51; Frank Richardson, *From Sunrise to Sunset: Reminiscence* (Bristol, Tenn., 1910), pp. 107–8. Yet it is hard to press all Baptist-Methodist conflict into the mold described here, given that so many Baptists in various parts of the Union were pursuing and enjoying the benefits of the market, too.

43. Richard J. Carwardine, *Evangelicals and Politics in Antebellum America* (New Haven, Conn., 1993), pp. 97–132. For a judicious and persuasive analysis of voters' characteristics in Jacksonian America based on lists of identifiable voters in New England, see Paul Goodman, "Politics in Jacksonian America," *Journal of the Early Republic* 6 (1986): 23–58. Goodman stresses the importance of context in voting behavior and sees the important connections between class and religion without reducing denominational conflict to economics alone.

44. For Methodists' strongly Democratic preferences in early Jacksonian New Hampshire, Maine, Vermont, and Massachusetts, see Paul Goodman, *Towards a Christian Republic: Antimasonry and the Great Tradition in New England, 1826–1836* (New York, 1988), pp. 109–19, 130, 153–54.

45. Quoted in Goodman, *Towards a Christian Republic*, p. 130.

46. William E. Gienapp, in *The Origins of the Republican Party* (New York, 1987), pp. 432–34, concludes that, though Methodist ministers in the free states may have been vocally Republican by 1856, lay Methodists "seem not to have backed the Republican cause to any decisive degree." Some rallied to Fillmore, but many remained loyal to the Democrats, especially in western states. Even in 1860, large numbers of Methodists continued to adhere to the Democratic party, and of all the evangelical bodies in the North Methodists were the least strong for Lincoln. William E. Gienapp, "Who Voted for Lincoln?" in John L. Thomas, ed., *Abraham Lincoln and the American Political Tradition* (Amherst, Mass., 1986), p. 75.

47. Mary L. Ninde, *William Xavier Ninde: A Memorial* (New York, 1902), pp. 50–51.

48. Carwardine, *Evangelicals and Politics*, pp. 125–26; Goodman, *Towards a Christian Republic*, pp. 116, 130; Ronald P. Formisano, *The Transformation of Political Culture:*

Massachusetts Parties, 1790s–1840s (New York, 1983), p. 219. Ronald P. Formisano cites John M. Rozett's study of Green County in his comments on Robert Kelley, "Ideology and Political Culture from Jefferson to Nixon," *American Historical Review* 82 (1977): 573. Goodman, in "Politics in Jacksonian America," p. 55, offers data from East Greenwich and Providence, R.I., that suggest Whig support among Methodist church members of 47 percent and 75 percent, respectively.

49. James Dixon, *Personal Narrative of a Tour through a Part of the United States and Canada, with Notices of the History of Methodism in America* (New York, 1849), pp. 62–63.

50. William W. Crane, *Autobiography and Miscellaneous Writings* (Syracuse, N.Y., 1891), pp. 85–86; Carwardine, *Evangelicals and Politics*, pp. 108–9.

51. William G. Brownlow, *A Political Register Setting Forth the Principles of the Whig and Locofoco Parties in the United States* (Jonesboro, Tenn., 1844), pp. 77, 109–11, 113–16; *CAJ*, Apr. 27 and Nov. 18, 1842; *(Cincinnati) Western Christian Advocate*, Nov. 12, 1841, and July 8, 1842.

52. Alfred Brunson, *A Western Pioneer, or, Incidents in the Life and Times of Rev. Alfred Brunson*, 2 vols. (Cincinnati, 1880) 1:43, 285–86.

53. Benjamin F. Tefft, *The Republican Influences of Christianity: A Discourse* (Bangor, Maine, 1841), pp. 10–11.

54. Sellers, *Market Revolution*, p. 268.

PART V

The Market Revolution in Perspective

12

Capitalism and Democracy
in American Historical Mythology

CHARLES SELLERS

THE PARADIGM OF DEMOCRATIC RESISTANCE to a stressful market revolution in the Jacksonian United States derives from a strikingly British-American group of historians working independently along parallel lines. The 1994 Commonwealth Fund Conference at University College London brought many of us together and allowed us to vet our work with a distinguished assemblage of scholars from both sides of the Atlantic. The concept of market revolution seemed to pass muster, at least to the extent of linking economic transformation with equally profound transformations of society, culture, and politics. In particular, the rich scholarship in rural social history, capped by the work of Christopher Clark, has apparently prevailed over the long-standing (and ideological) assumption that the United States never had a precapitalist populace to be transformed.

Clark's essay in this volume extends his perceptive analysis of the market revolution's social impact into the later nineteenth century, and his argument here introduces other provocative papers on the concept's post-Jacksonian reach. In addressing politics, the slavery–free-soil controversy, the South, and gender, some of these are structured by and derive insight from the concept, while others attest to its fit with analysis not greatly dependent on it. The concept organizes the remaining essays on the Jackson period, four on politics, one on religion, and one on culture. Unfortunately, the urgent task of addressing the daunting confusions that bedevil Jacksonian historiography permits more than passing reference only to those essays most critical to the market revolution paradigm.

Only Clark addresses the paradigm itself. He is surely right to warn against losing historical complexities in its overarching uniformities. Credible paradigms must be grounded in and constantly corrected by the kind of close, theoretically informed analysis he so signally demonstrates. But neither should paradigmatic meaning be lost in the manifold discontinuities of the historical reality from which it is abstracted. My conception of the market revolution would incorporate many of Clark's discontinuities as arising from inherent and ongoing contradictions between capitalist market relations and human needs.

Clark's reluctance to see the Jacksonian market revolution as capitalist, as a process rather than a series of events, makes me uneasy that too much paradigmatic meaning may be lost. The evidence remains convincing to me that a process of capitalist market revolution impacted most relations of production, including family farming, when it "took off" in Jacksonian days as self-accelerating and hegemonic.[1] Discontinuities should not blind us to the relentlessly commodifying process of ongoing capitalist transformation, which seems unstoppable as long as its energizing Jacksonian constellation of avid capital, expanding free market, and captive polity holds.[2]

While Clark's keen eye for the critical theoretical issues helps scholars define their own view of the market revolution, the major point of substantive contention is the resistance this revolution met. How much was there, and how did it figure in Jacksonian politics and evangelical religion? Because this question goes to the merits of capitalism, it cannot be realistically addressed without also addressing interpretive bias. With British scrupulosity tempering Yankee zeal at the London conference, what the transnational perspective highlighted for me was Jacksonian history's special and too-little-acknowledged proneness to bias. But bias, I hope to show, has both uses and abuses.

For a century and a half American identity and destiny have been contested between capitalism and democracy, making their simultaneous Jacksonian takeoff a historical storm center. Between these two poles Jacksonian interpretation has oscillated ever since, following major swings in the political climate and caught up in the broader contention over national self-definition. Jacksonian democracy was denigrated by patrician historians as a threat to capitalist progress through the Gilded Age, then rehabilitated by "progressive" historians as a middle-class defense against capitalist abuse in the climate of Progressivism and the New Deal, and finally domesticated by "consensus" historians as a politics of democratic capitalist enterprise during the Cold War.[3] Now the spirited engagement, diverse paradigms, and fresh ideas of this book herald a new round of debate over this perennially contested era.

Interpretive bias seems inescapable for the Jacksonian historian who lives in an American political world still structured by the contradictions between capitalism and democracy. As both citizen and historian, I took alarm when consensus historians armed the United States for Cold War by purging class from consciousness. Muffling exploitative capital in appealing democratic garb, their mythology of consensual democratic capitalism purged egalitarian meaning from democracy. I winced when Ronald Reagan evoked "democracy" against the Evil Empire though clearly meaning capitalism. I grieved when public discourse translated democracy into "freedom" ("liberty" in the academic mode)—typically meaning freedom to aggrandize yourself without any concern for people who lack the gumption, social advantages, or luck to do the same. The political reactions of other citizen-historians, though different, are no less heartfelt. Hence the Yankee zeal that bemuses British colleagues.

On this politically charged Jacksonian ground, the warring assumptions are particularly illuminated by Daniel Walker Howe in Chapter 10 of the present volume. The capitalist market was too manifestly beneficial to be rationally resisted, he argues. Although he acknowledges substantial costs, he thinks them outweighed by liberation from Andrew Jackson's "narrow world of patriarchy and violence" to an open world of autonomy and choice. Cultural commitments structure Howe's catalog of changes that conferred this premier market boon: more occupational choices ("especially those making use of formal education"), more consumer choices ("a form of personal empowerment"), more schools and colleges, more printed matter, more ("and more beautiful") churches, more humane child rearing, "more opportunities to encounter the arts," and "the cultivation of good taste." Howe sees self-discipline as the other great boon of market culture, and the ancillary benefits he describes include the "culture of politeness" and the array of evangelical churches and voluntary organizations that reinforced "the subordination of sexuality, along with other forms of emotional indulgence, to principled self-discipline."

The implicit argument is that rational people could not have resisted such self-evident benefits. But Howe's hierarchy of values is self-evident only within the bourgeois middle-class culture it defines. It was not self-evident to the Jacksonian majority, and it is not self-evident to this historian. The underlying conflict of values over the merits of bourgeois middle-class culture reaches to the merits of capitalism. Where Howe's assumptions suggest that I undervalue capitalism's benefits and attractions, my assumptions suggest that he underestimates its costs and coercions. Yet by standing so manifestly on the personal (and class?) values that structure his argument, this learned, fair-minded, and honest historian sets an example that could make the next round of Jacksonian debate unusually productive.

My corresponding values, I ought therefore to avow, derive in the first instance from my experience of bourgeois middle-class autonomy as driven, self-repressive, and intensely competitive. Capitalism commodifies and exploits all life, I conclude from my life and all I can learn. Relations of capitalist production wrench a commodified humanity to relentless competitive effort and poison the more affective and altruistic relations of social reproduction that outweigh material accumulation for most human beings. A life of competitive relationships dehumanizes all.

Howe's consensus narrative—"Market delivers eager self-improvers from stifling Jacksonian barbarism"—is blind to the coerciveness of both capitalist transformation and its culture. More plausible to me is "Go-getter minority compels everybody else to play its competitive game of speedup and stretchout or be run over." In my narrative, both conscripts and converts (including, perhaps, a few historians) need bourgeois–middle-class–evangelical culture and its mythologies both to cope with the naked egotism of capitalist life and to reinforce a new level of self-disciplined effort.

The present historic moment of bourgeois triumphalism is not auspicious for questioning capitalism, and my implicit critique is not accepted by some (for example, Richard E. Ellis) who otherwise credit my argument in *The Market Revolution*.[4] Yet understanding capitalism's human costs, along with democracy's majoritarian limits, has never been more urgent. As corporate capital rides a spreading free market to world dominion, competitive stress intensifies, the fruits of free-enterprise autonomy sour with job flight and social breakdown, environmental disaster looms, politics gridlocks, and huckster-driven media increasingly dominate public consciousness. Democracy's last chance to challenge or chasten the capitalist market could be slipping away. The essays of John Ashworth, Christopher Clark, and Amy Dru Stanley give hope that capitalism's cost-benefit bottom line may be more realistically calculated once Cold War rigidities ease and the Stalinist bogeyman recedes as the only conceivable alternative. Meanwhile every historian may calculate it for herself or himself.

But historical understanding of the market revolution turns less on the abstract merits of capitalism than on the Jacksonian facts. Historians' primary commitment is to the "ascertainable facts," to use Lee Benson's phrase, and logical inference from them. Of course, facts would be meaningless without interpretation, and interpretation is inevitably biased by values and assumptions from personal experience, especially, in Jacksonian historiography, those of class. Historical integrity requires both self-scrutiny of one's bias and readiness to adjust interpretation and bias to the ascertainable facts.

Yet, while bias distorts, especially if unconscious or unacknowledged, it also generates the paradigms that guide us to such historical truth as we can know. Because dominant paradigms are usually biased to reinforce existing relations of power and privilege, truer history requires multiple paradigms arising from a broader range of human experience and perception. No paradigm has a wide enough lens to absorb the whole meaning of any past, while every paradigm that is focused by honest experience and faithful to the ascertainable facts opens some new perspective on *wie es eigentlich gewesen ist.*

Preeminent among the Jacksonian facts is the transformation of politics and culture by massive upwellings of populism and evangelicalism. The critical test of any paradigm is how well it fits and explains these momentous developments in politics and religion where the broadest spectrum of Americans becomes historically visible.

On the main interpretive battleground, politics, some chapters of the present volume and most current scholarship reveal that consensus history's death, like Mark Twain's, has been greatly exaggerated. In answer to Donald J. Ratcliffe's complaint in Chapter 7 of this book that I write "as if Lee Benson had never issued his call to make political history more scientific," I hope to show that so did Benson himself.[5] Only by transcending his own injunction did he redeem short-run error with enduring insights. The consensus history that reached its definitive formulation in his *Concept of Jacksonian Democracy,* however misleading in substance, opened most of the new historical vistas we now explore, including that of market revolution.[6] The problems that surface in some essays in this book must be addressed at their source in the still regnant consensus paradigm, especially as perfected by Benson.

The consensus perspective was provoked by the red flag of class when Arthur M. Schlesinger, Jr., in *The Age of Jackson,* set off a critical feeding frenzy unparalleled in American historiography.[7] Schlesinger was the first historian to dig so deeply into the (mainly northeastern) Jacksonian political correspondence and newspapers. There he discovered both the hard-money ideology at the core of Jacksonism and the roots of insurgent democracy in disruptive economic change. With the New Deal climate attenuating progressive historiography's ambivalence about class, he boldly announced that Jacksonian politics pitted antibank farmers and workers against credit-hungry businessmen. In his liberal paradigm, business excesses periodically mobilized the rest of society for political reform, usually through the Democratic party.

Amid relentless critical assault on *The Age of Jackson,* the consensus paradigm was enunciated in a 1948 essay by Richard Hofstadter. It was received with uncritical acclaim, although not much buttressed by research until Bray Hammond's magisterial history of the politics of banking appeared nine years later. Jacksonians were proclaimed "expectant capitalists" epitomizing an era of exploding entrepreneurial avidity. This proposition was supported less by new ascertainable facts than by an interpretive tour de force: Jackson's Democrats, Hofstadter announced, destroyed the restrictive Bank of the United

States in order to multiply free-lending state banks and entrepreneurial opportunity.[8] A number of Hofstadter's colleagues at Columbia University
mounted a flank attack on Schlesinger's claim that labor supported Jackson.[9]

The zeal to discredit Schlesinger and the uncritical enthusiasm for the consensus paradigm registered a national ideological shift intersecting a sociological shift in the production of historical scholarship. As New Deal liberalism succumbed to Cold War hysteria, an able and energetic cohort of World
War II veterans flooded the historical profession, impatient to jump-start
postponed careers, and often experiencing upward mobility in a flourishing
academy, thanks in part to the educational generosity of the GI Bill of Rights.
Consensus history validated for much of my academic generation the ideal of
"careers open to talents." While meritocratic competition sharpened and research grants blossomed under federal largesse, McCarthyism muted dissent.
Many scholars enlisted in the CIA's cultural Cold War to sell capitalist democracy to intelligentsias around the world by covert means.[10] Consensus
history was born in a Cold War academic atmosphere of intellectual mobilization and keen ideological demand for a mythology of consensual democratic capitalism. Schlesinger himself left Jacksonian class politics to its critics
as he moved into anticommunist Cold War liberalism and New Deal–Came-
lot hagiography.[11]

My encounter with this contested terrain as an apprentice historian best
explains my understanding of how lived experience interacts with paradigm
and ascertainable facts. Fresh from the brutalities of race and class in the
depression South as a Harvard undergraduate, I was puzzled by an academic
history oblivious to racism and class conflict, and only gradually developed
the intellectual self-confidence to trust my own experience of social reality.
Although I encountered Schlesinger only glancingly at Harvard, I was drawn
to history by the class realism of *The Age of Jackson* and captivated at first by
his rationale for a humane liberal politics.[12] Thinking him then, as I do now,
more nearly right than his critics, but weak on the South and the West, I
undertook to test and broaden his analysis in a dissertation on James K. Polk.
My Schlesinger paradigm spoke to the ascertainable facts in focusing research
and selecting facts.

But then the facts started speaking to the paradigm. They confirmed Schlesinger's class politics, though with a larger antibank, hard-money role for
southern and western farmers than Schlesinger allowed and far more slippage
between the pronouncements and actions of Democratic politicians. The ascertainable facts, moreover, supported many consensus themes, some not yet
put forward: a rampant and bipartisan commitment to enterprise, a politically alienated working class, ethnocultural politics, and constraints imposed

by the constitutional-party system. The sources also attested to the major economic transformation posited by both paradigms; and, in my need for a paradigm consistent with all the facts, new insights from economic history prompted speculation about a "market revolution."[13]

Meanwhile, overtaking facts were threatening Hofstadter's thesis with the reality of class. The Jacksonian centrality and broad appeal of hard money proved undeniable, not only in Bray Hammond's study of banking politics, but also in the study of Jacksonian rhetoric and ideology by Hofstadter's perceptive doctoral student Marvin Meyers. Meyers tried to explain it away. Ingeniously, he made conflict safe for consensual capitalism by banishing it from class to an ambivalent Jacksonian psyche. Destruction of the national bank resolved inner conflict, he argued, by simultaneously appeasing precapitalist conscience and unleashing state banks to satisfy capitalist appetite. Although this insight illuminates Jacksonian cross pressures, they were seldom resolved in individual breasts. Instead the genie of conflict, as the facts compelled Meyers to recognize, escaped the psychic bottle to polarize a class politics of hard money. When Meyers conceded that Whigs spoke more to capitalist hopes and Democrats to precapitalist anxieties, consensus history faltered.[14]

Hammond, too, abandoned Hofstadter's claim that Jacksonians in general were "expectant capitalists." But, in conceding Jackson and the Democratic rank and file to the unaccountable atavism of hard money, he turned the spotlight on Democratic politicians. Like Meyers, he was propelled by a paradigm under pressure into new insight. Hammond saved the consensus idea from class politics by blaming the destruction of Philadelphia's national bank, and therefore financial stability, on Democratic politicians linked with inflationary state banks and their would-be borrowers. At the center of this alleged conspiracy were Wall Street jealousy, Martin Van Buren's Tammany-Bucktail Democrats, and their state banks.

Hammond appropriated this narrative and much else from the partisan polemic broadcast by New York Whiggery's brilliant editor-strategist Thurlow Weed. It is contrary to fact. Andrew Jackson and his grassroots army were not, as Hammond implied, duped into destroying the Bank by scheming politicians. It was the other way around. Only voter pressure forced many Democrats to support Jackson's inexplicably popular Bank veto after a Democratic Congress rechartered the national bank. Many, and often most, Democratic congressmen braved voter retribution in standing shoulder to shoulder with united Whiggery to defend both national and state banks against their chieftain and infatuated constituents. Hammond's astute focus on Democratic politicians points, in fact, to a structural feature of capitalist, two-party

democracy that is critical to Jacksonian politics: majority rule's slippage between insurgent majorities and the business-oriented politicians (typically
lawyers) who profess or attempt to represent them.[15]

When Lee Benson selected New York as the test case for his imaginative
and wholesale reconstruction of the tottering consensus paradigm, he had
obviously drunk even more deeply than Hammond from Thurlow Weed's
fount of ideology and rhetoric. The problem was the need to stave off class.
If Democrats could not be made the bearers of democratic capitalism, Weed
presented Whigs as promising candidates—New York Whigs, that is, who
were uniquely dependent on democratic Antimasonry for most of their votes.
The Empire State also promised an alternative to class as the basis for party
division. It was almost unrivaled in ethnic diversity and conflict, and Benson
improved this advantage by deriving his analysis of voting patterns from the
1844 election, when savage nativist–Irish Catholic conflict climaxed. He did
not, of course, weigh his strategic choices in this consciously ideological way.
Both his errors and their longevity demonstrate instead the unconscious
force of paradigm imperatives, class, and ideological climate, even for highly
creative historians on full alert against the pitfalls of what Benson called "impressionistic" history. Most of us accept what we want to believe with far less
scrutiny than we lavish on challenges to our assumptions.

Benson was refreshingly candid about his a priori commitment to consensual democratic capitalism. "The spirit of enterprise flourished," he asserted
on impressionistic faith, "before enterprise itself felt the invigorating effects" of economic takeoff. Egalitarianism spread with canals and railroads
(the critical Weed narrative) as enterprising Americans demanded an equal
chance at glittering new opportunities. Therefore, because Americans agreed
on "the economic virtues of capitalist culture" (the critical Hofstadter narrative), they divided politically over a host of secondary differences. "Since
the United States is highly heterogeneous, and has high social mobility," Benson's argument wound up, "I assume that men tend to retain and be more
influenced by their ethnic and religious group membership than by their
membership in economic classes or groups."[16]

Whiggery was the true people's party in the Weed-Benson narrative, and
the true bearers of democracy were the egalitarian Antimasons who joined
the Whigs to champion equal entrepreneurial opportunity. Antimasons were
mainly upstate farmers of New England heritage whose patriarchal, egalitarian lifestyle was disrupted when the Erie Canal brought market revolution
and its train of bankers, bosses, lawyers, land speculators, and their ilk. Upstate fury at the secret Masonic fraternity of these agents of enterprise transformed New York politics. Antimasonry—aptly characterized by Benson as

"an impassioned, leveling attack by members of the 'lower classes' against the village and urban 'aristocracy' "—expressed for Yankee farmers averse to a Masonic and slaveholding president the democratic impulse that elsewhere rallied around Jackson.[17]

Equal opportunity was Weed's talisman for translating the patriarchal equality cherished by antibank Antimasons into the entrepreneurial opportunity demanded by bank-hungry canal-town enterprisers. While rhetorically appropriating the Antimasons' egalitarianism, he turned their susceptible suspicions of "monster" institutions (Masonry and the national bank) against the "aristocrats" of Martin Van Buren's Albany Regency and their fictitious "monopoly" of "monster" state banks. Although Masons had been prominent in all political parties, Van Buren's Bucktail-Tammany Democrats were especially vulnerable because they had been so long entrenched, as a reward for bringing white male democracy to New York, that their power reached into every village establishment. Their ties with Albany's important Mechanics and Farmers Bank lent some credibility to Weed's diatribes, despite the Whiggery of most banking interests. The Weed-Benson narrative purloined democracy from the vulnerable Bucktails and ascribed it instead to a rising tide of small enterprisers evoked by the spreading market and driven to egalitarian Antimasonic insurgency by resentment of monopolies and special privileges (banks allegedly Bucktail) that blocked their upward path.

Thus Weed's brilliant opportunism divided and almost neutralized an otherwise irresistible Bucktail-antibank-democratic majority while reaping for threatened enterprise the boon of equal (that is, free-banking, soft-money) opportunity. In the process he fathered (with major input from his editorial soul mate Horace Greeley) both consensus history and the mythology of consensual democratic capitalism. Unlike Benson, the Whig ideologists knew perfectly well that they were contending against the reality of class politics. "All of the advocates of a higher destiny for labor, . . . all the social discontent of the country, has been regularly repelled from the Whig party, and attracted to its opposite," Greeley warned Weed privately, and the Whigs were doomed unless they could counter their reputation as "the bulwarks of an outgrown aristocracy." When the adroit polemic tailored to this purpose became the master text for Weed's academic heirs, the "wizard of the lobby" must have chuckled in whatever Valhalla his matchless political skills ensconced him.[18]

Benson followed the partisan Weed-Greeley line into gross distortions of New York political history,[19] and his strategy for a more scientific "multivariate analysis" was undercut by the paucity and ambiguity of available data.[20] In this creative historian, a genius for paradigmatic imagination competed with a passion for scientific exactitude. He started out with a contagious enthusiasm for radically shrinking the zone of interpretive doubt and disagreement by means of the rigorously empirical methods of social science research he had learned at Columbia University.[21] His conscious purpose, paradoxically, was more to make history scientific than to rescue the consensus paradigm whose congenial assumptions were self-evident and universally conceded in the ideological climate he inhabited.

Benson demonstrated ethnicity's importance in Jacksonian politics (especially in the Northeast) so convincingly that it could no longer be ignored. But his jerry-built, multivariate evidential base could not sustain his weighty proposition that ethnicity and religion, not class, determined most votes.[22] In the two counties he selected to demonstrate this by full examination (a banner county for each party), the empirical poverty and paradigm bias of multivariate analysis are apparent. Even from his data, each seems more explicable by my understanding of class.[23]

Ethnicity and class cannot be divorced, in fact, and their cross pressures, along with those of religion and culture, were complexly mixed at the Jacksonian ballot box. Antimasonic Yankee farmers were an ethnic group in Benson's terms that were acting as a class in my terms—that is to say, as a group sharing a common situation in the relations of production. And whatever the reason for their dramatic Antimasonic insurgency, it was unquestionably prompted—this much Weed and Benton concede to class, though not in my terminology—by a market revolution dramatically impacting relations of production. The Antimasons who did fit the Weed-Benson formula were sons of the rural majority like Weed who were rising as clerks, mechanics, and lawyers in booming canal towns and resented the establishment banks that denied them the credit they required for success. Invoking rural egalitarianism to support their demand for equal opportunity, they gradually drew rural kin into both commodity markets and market culture, preparing the next generation to carry Daniel Howe's bourgeois middle-class "Whig" culture to hegemony on the Great Lakes prairies.

In all these ways, Antimasonry was mainly about class (relations of production), leaving for ethnocultural factors (more cultural than ethnic in this case) to explain why Yankees were such apt adapters to the market. But culture, too, and its permutations, are rooted in class relations of production. These are among the ascertainable facts indicating (in the light of my paradigm, to be sure), that for most of Jacksonian America, including New York, politics was structured mainly by class.

Benson's flawed paradigm has proved more fruitful, I have to conclude, than his elaborate exercise in multivariate analysis. His refurbished consensus history, although muddying the Jacksonian foreground until ascertainable facts can overtake it, has pointed historians in productive new directions, for which his multivariate facts provide some specification. Paradigm led him to ethnicity, and ethnicity led him to culture. Understanding that ethnicity involved more than ancestral genes, he devised the term *ethnocultural* to wrap it in a penumbra of culture ranging from religion, family structure, and shared experience to foodways and ghost stories. Where Benson thought of culture as mainly cohering around ethnicity and usually around religion as well, followers of his insight learned to see it more broadly, as an inherent component of human society that coheres around many social formations, including class (the early mechanic culture and later plebeian street culture of Jacksonian cities, for example), and even political parties (Daniel Howe's Whig culture versus the more raffish, libertarian, class-conscious, and racist political culture of Jean Baker's Democrats).[24]

The Concept of Jacksonian Democracy cast a long historical shadow. From it flowed not only a new cultural history and an ethnocultural perspective that permeated and revitalized post-Jacksonian history, but a new political history that has dramatically elevated the sophistication and realism of historical political analysis. Political historians have been busy ever since exploring his pioneering insights into the dynamics of two-party politics, particularly the stability of party attachments and therefore party balance, and the critical importance of the brief realignment phases that unpredictably interrupt the two-party drift toward electoral parity at every level.[25] Benson and Schlesinger are the historians from whom I have learned most.

Blindness to class disarmed consensus history in the face of the critical Jacksonian question, What caused the upwelling of grassroots democracy that transformed American politics? As consensus scholarship fell back for reinforcements to Revolutionary-Jeffersonian terrain, the elements of a better answer were emerging.[26] A new interest in "history from the bottom up" flowered amid the ferment of the 1960s, producing rich "new" histories of labor, rural society, and women and gender. This profusion of new ascertainable facts and insights, when juxtaposed to both the explosion of entrepreneurial energy discovered by consensus history and the hard-money thrust of Jacksonian politics discovered by Schlesinger, at last promised an explanation of the upheaval that culminated in Jacksonian politics.

The only paradigm I can conceive that answers the critical Jacksonian question and is compatible with all the ascertainable facts begins with a stressful capitalist transformation astride a market galvanized overnight into accelerating expansion. When market stresses climaxed in the panic of 1819, a confused and substantially precapitalist populace, especially subsistence farmers and urban workers, rose in political rebellion against banks, conventional politicians, and "aristocrats." Drawn to the presidential polls in 1824 on an unprecedented scale by a spectacular maverick who invoked democracy and seemed by experience and temperament more amenable to their concerns, they delivered a popular mandate for Andrew Jackson. Robbed of their victory by "bargain and corruption," they doubled 1824's turnout four years later to install their hero in the White House by the largest popular majority in the nineteenth century.[27]

No president in American history (for reasons more personal than political) had a keener ear for the popular pulse, and none was more ready to follow popular opinion so far in defiance of all respectable opinion. This rosy morning of democratic millennium radiated the popular hope that ordinary people could rule, and in this singular historic moment they actually tried to do so. Targeting banks as epitomizing the governmental favoritism through which market forces threatened the cheap-land yeoman republic of patriarchal independence and equality, they actually tried to choke off capitalism's lifeblood, credit. They were prevented from doing so mainly by an unresponsive two-party system, which Bensonian political history enables us to understand, and by the endemic sensitivity of politicians to highly motivated, articulate, and well-heeled elites, which requires a dash of realism about class to understand. Deflated millennial expectations, as Michael Holt's long-range analysis of nineteenth-century politics in this book suggests, meant that Americans would never invest such hope in democratic politics again.

Jackson's hard-money assault on the lifeblood of enterprise becomes, in this view, the critical test of whether a majority (even of white males) can actually rule. This view calls up for reconsideration the most defining and pervasive assumptions about American history and identity. Democracy arose in resistance to capitalism, not as its natural political expression. But the majority does not seem to rule, at least on the most important matters.

The Jacksonian upwelling of evangelical Protestantism could become as important as the Jacksonian upwelling of democracy for understanding American experience—if we could only explain it. A brief final comment seems called for, therefore, about my awkward "antinomian-arminian" appropriation from theology, as discussed in earlier chapters by Richard Cardwine and Daniel Walker Howe. Having wrestled with this problem ever since a senior thesis on "The Great Awakening in North Carolina," I am convinced that evangelicalism was a two-phase phenomenon, "New Light–Moderate Light" in my terminology. It began as an "antinomian" mobilization and revitalization of traditional precapitalist culture against threatening change. Under market pressures it evolved into an "arminian" mode of adaptation to capitalist imperatives. All agree that the arminian phase encouraged striving, self-discipline, self-improvement, and the other capitalist virtues in shaping Howe's bourgeois middle-class culture.

What was centrally at stake in the original evangelical upwelling, I suggest, was spirituality—or, more broadly magic, the vividly experienced everyday presence and agency of the supernatural. As early Americans defined the problem in the available terms of Protestant theology, the antinomian conviction that God spoke directly to individuals in dispensing magical grace arose against the God-diminishing arminian doctrine of human ability. In these terms the transition to capitalism was fought out for most Americans. New Light evangelicalism tended to be rural, communal, and democratic, and Nathan O. Hatch has richly delineated its democratic thrust, but its energy derived from its antinomian spiritual core.[28] I understand, with Carwardine and Howe, that my terminology, unless taken in the metaphorical sense in which I proffer it, seems to bowdlerize the long and complicated history of antinomianism and Arminianism as technical theology. I struggled for, and will happily embrace, any more accessible terminology that captures as well the spiritual or magical core of cultural resistance to capitalist transformation.

I readily grant to Carwardine, from whom I learned most of what I know about Methodism, the Arminian theological core that ultimately shaped it. But I suggest, as does his rich documentation for an earlier, somewhat different Methodism, that Wesley's theology was drowned out at first by antinomian camp-meeting ecstacy. A further wealth of ascertainable facts leads John H. Wigger to argue, "For earlier American Methodists who found themselves struggling to come to terms with unprecedented social and cultural changes and with frequently hostile resistance from the broader society, popular enthusiasm in many ways represented a more important theological construct than did Arminianism."[29] This granted, I will look to Carwardine for understanding of how and when Methodism changed. For Methodists, like other evangelicals, this great transmutation was more than an institutional shift from "cult" to "denomination" and "more beautiful" churches. It mobilized American psyches for an anxiously competitive capitalist life.

As custodians and guarantors of collective memory, American historians owe careful consideration to the neglected issues of power and justice raised by Jacksonian history. But as successful competitors in the academic marketplace, are they too often mesmerized by a national mythology that begs for critical analysis? Why was Schlesinger's class interpretation so instantly and

massively assailed, while hosannas greeted the consensus denial of class and
its errors went so long uncorrected? A history embedded in national mythology cries out for more critical perspectives.

Understanding of American society has been most distorted by the political correctness that has long banned class from history and consciousness.
But the "PC" defenses of American mythology are beginning to be breached
as a wider range of ethnic, class, and gender experience addresses illuminating paradigms to the American past. "Objective reality we know we can never
altogether reach," as I concluded my first take on Schlesinger and his critics,
but multiplying paradigms promise "ever closer vantage points for discern-
ing its salient features."[30]

NOTES

1. By midcentury, for example, falling birthrates and nucleating families indicated that
many farmers were well along the slow road from family-powered subsistence through
commodity production using supplemental hired hands to modern agriculture's highly
capitalized mechanization and sweated stoop labor. Clark's least compelling argument in
his chapter of this book is that new forms of collectivity counteracted market atomization.
It seems more likely to me that the mass anonymity of the new spectator sports and
popular culture bespeaks isolation, while churches flourished by enforcing a new level of
conformity. Nor do I see the relevance, let alone the accuracy, of blaming class-based
judicial instrumentalism on the ideological kit bag of Jacksonian judges, especially in view
of the havoc they wrought on their venerated common law.

2. The impressionable are too easily terrified by the incomprehensible anathema "reifi-
cation," which is loosed regularly against scholars who see a "Marxist" constellation of
forces as driving a long series of developments.

3. Charles Grier Sellers, Jr., "Andrew Jackson versus the Historians," *Mississippi Valley
Historical Review* 44 (1958): 615–34.

4. Charles Sellers, *The Market Revolution: Jacksonian America, 1815–1846* (New York,
1991).

5. Ratcliffe's Ohio studies are among the best in teasing out the social, economic, and
cultural dimensions of partisan voting patterns. See especially Donald J. Ratcliffe, "Politics
in Jacksonian Ohio: Reflections on the Ethnocultural Interpretation," *Ohio History* 88
(1979): 5–36. Although he works within the market revolution paradigm, he postpones its
political impact to the mid-1830s boom-and-bust crisis. Political change certainly peaked
during the crisis years to crystallize a durable party realignment, but it was rooted in the
rising tide of democratic disaffection that was precipitated by the panic of 1819, was sharp-

ened by state struggles over banking and debtor relief during the 1820s, and gradually overcame Radcliffe's undeniably sectional organization of politics to coalesce politically around Jackson (and in "Yankee" regions of the rural northeast around Antimasonry). Other debatable aspects of current scholarship that inform his analysis are mainly attributable to Benson.

6. Lee Benson, *The Concept of Jacksonian Democracy: New York As a Test Case* (Princeton, N.J., 1961).

7. Arthur M. Schlesinger, Jr., *The Age of Jackson* (Boston, 1945).

8. Richard Hofstadter, *The American Political Tradition and the Men Who Made It* (New York, 1948), chap. 3; Bray Hammond, *Banks and Politics in America: From the Revolution to the Civil War* (Princeton, N.J., 1957).

9. They found ambiguous election returns and even greater confusion about who constituted "labor." We now understand, from the new labor history stimulated by their questions, that the old mechanic class was fracturing between rising mechanic bosses and a growing wage proletariat. Boss mechanics and rising skilled journeymen were often Whig, it seems; labor militants were skeptical about both major parties until inspired by Jackson's Bank War; and the urban unskilled probably voted preponderantly Democratic, especially after the Bank War.

10. Sociologists of historical knowledge may yet explain why consensus history emanated almost exclusively from Dwight D. Eisenhower's Columbia University, with Bray Hammond just downtown at the Federal Reserve Bank. Benson worked out his analysis under the influence of Paul Lazarsfeld at Columbia's Bureau of Applied Social Research. Columbia's consensus warriors (some graduate students at the time) included, besides Benson and Hofstadter, Joseph Dorfman, Walter Hugins, Marvin Meyers, Richard B. Morris, Edward Pessen, and William A. Sullivan.

11. At the dawn of the Cold War, Schlesinger helped organize Americans for Democratic Action (for which I worked briefly between college and graduate school) to purge liberalism of Communist taint. Although ADA helped put civil rights on the national agenda (with Schlesinger at the forefront, both in Washington and in his influential call for a history of slavery and abolitionism premised on human equality), it functioned mainly, as I finally understood, to blunt Henry Wallace's third-party effort against Truman, preclude any criticism of bipartisan Cold War policy beyond a discredited radical fringe, and consolidate a climate of Cold War ideological mobilization that fostered McCarthyism. My disappointment with Schlesinger for giving liberal cachet to Cold War excess in the Kennedy administration was greater because his work played a role in defining for me a liberal faith that was shattered in the civil rights and antiwar struggles of the 1960s. This experience was critical, of course, in recontouring my paradigm to revised assumptions about American society. Truth is served, I suggest, when life experience of whatever kind jostles an occasional academic historian a little beyond the bourgeois middle-class assumptions that so powerfully and unconsciously constrain our historical vision.

12. Schlesinger defined class in the conventional categories of progressive historiography: farmers, workers, and businessmen. Although these broad categories have some uses with reference to cross-class coalitions, it seems far more useful for historical purposes to define a class as those similarly situated as to mode and relations of production, regardless

of whether they exhibit class consciousness or conflict. This definition distinguishes, for example, subsistence farmers from commercial farmers, rising entrepreneurs from those with established wealth, unskilled wage workers from mechanic bosses.

13. See, for example, George Rogers Taylor, *The Transportation Revolution, 1815–1860* (New York, 1951); Douglass C. North, *The Economic Growth of the United States, 1790–1861* (New York, 1961).

14. "The Whig party spoke to the explicit hopes of Americans as Jacksonians addressed their diffuse fears and resentments. . . . The Whigs distinctively affirmed the material promise of American life as it was going; and they promised to make it go faster." See Marvin Meyers, *The Jacksonian Persuasion: Politics and Belief* (Stanford, Calif., 1957), esp. pp. 1–10 (quotation on p. 9). Similarly, the facts caused Edward Pessen to reverse consensus history's initial skepticism about the authenticity and radicalism of Jacksonian labor organizations and leaders. See Edward Pessen, *Most Uncommon Jacksonians: The Radical Leaders of the Early Labor Movement* (Albany, N.Y., 1967).

15. Hammond, *Banks and Politics.* For Hammond's errors, see Frank O. Gatell, "Sober Second Thought on Van Buren, the Albany Regency, and the Wall Street Conspiracy," *Journal of American History* 53 (1966): 19–40. As an official of the New York Federal Reserve Bank and defender of central banking against the entrepreneurial abuse of credit that perennially cripples American capitalism, Hammond was projecting into the Jacksonian period the struggle he had discovered in the early republic between the responsibly restrictive national bank and the irresponsibly inflationary state banks controlled by avid would-be borrowers. Thus he was insensitive to a critical turning point. As the Bank maneuvered for recharter early in the Jackson administration, its president, Nicholas Biddle, effected a rapprochement with the state bank interests (that is, most local business communities) by easing its restraints on credit expansion. As a result most state banks, including the Wall Street suspects, supported recharter, and a unified business perspective pervaded not only the National Republican–Whig opposition, but many if not most Democrats elected on Jackson's coattails. In addition to rechartering the Bank, Democratic Congresses resisted Jackson's removal of the federal deposits (until the Bank's irresponsibility forced even Whigs to abandon it) and sabotaged his hard-money restraints on state banks (until he roused "the people" to "take it up"). Grassroots pressure from "Democrats in principle" eventually forced "Democrats by trade" to mouth the hard-money line or bolt. The real division over banking aligned Jackson and his grassroots adherents against politicians—all Whigs and probably a majority of those who called themselves Democrats. Hammond also failed to understand that Biddle, by inflating the currency to consolidate business elites behind the Bank, set in train (along with a flood of British credit) the runaway inflation and crash of the mid-1830s. Again, following Whig polemic, Hammond (and most historians) blamed economic disaster on the inflationary irresponsibility of Democratic politicians.

16. Benson, *Concept of Jacksonian Democracy,* pp. 12–13, 165, 273. Cited in support of these critical assumptions are quotations from H. St. John de Crèvecouer and Hezekiah Niles, along with the interpretations of Hofstadter and consensus history's godfather, Louis Hartz. Hartz's *The Liberal Tradition in America* (New York, 1955) argued that Americans differed from Europeans in being "born free," which frustrated all effort to push

political theory or debate beyond the liberal consensus. I first contested the consensus perspective in a dazzling undergraduate seminar conducted by Hartz.

17. Quotation from Benson in his *Concept of Jacksonian Democracy*, p. 14.

18. Michael J. Lebowitz, "The Significance of Claptrap in American History," *Studies on the Left* (1963): 85. The more conventionally business-minded New York Whigs paid a heavy price for indispensable Antimasonic votes. Antimasonic Whigs and orthodox Whigs were constantly at loggerheads, notably over the Bank of the United States and its leading advocate, Henry Clay, a Mason who lost his best chance for the presidency in 1840 as a consequence. New York's Antimasons will continue to puzzle historians until they are given the insightful scrutiny and "great transition" perspective that Paul Goodman has applied so fruitfully to their copartisans in New England. See Paul Goodman, *Towards a Christian Republic: Antimasonry and the Great Transition in New England, 1826–1836* (New York, 1988).

19. The Weed-Benson line errs most in (1) making Van Buren an opponent of democracy rather than its critical champion in the historic constitutional convention of 1821, (2) confusing the worker radicalism of the original Workingmen's party with the faction of boss mechanics and invading politicians who co-opted its name for Whig coalition, (3) equating Workingman-Antimasonic opposition to banks with a ruling passion for equal entrepreneurial opportunity, (4) grossly exaggerating Bucktail complicity with state banks when most banking interests were Whig, (5) explaining the Bucktails' campaign against the national bank as a defensive response to Weed's polemic against their alleged state banking monopoly, and (6) blurring the critical distinction between the Democratic Locofocos' hard-money free banking and the Whigs' soft-money version. For further discussion of these and other errors, see Lebowitz, "Significance of Claptrap," pp. 79–94.

20. Benson's solid data for percentages of Democratic-Whig voters by county (albeit in an election skewed by ethnic strife and a decade beyond the Jacksonian realignment) had to be compared with nonpolitical variables for which data were fugitive and crude: for religion, the number of churches or seating capacity by denomination; for wealth and class, the average value of town dwellings in 1855 and 1865; and, for both these and ethnicity, whatever his ingenious assiduity could cobble together from gazetteers, antiquarian county histories, and other impressionistic sources. Conclusions from multivariate data, moreover, are almost as subject to distortion by paradigm as more impressionistic data. Vast gaps in the scant data must be bridged by assumptions, estimates, and projections whose subjective imprecision is disguised by the deceptively concrete percentages in which outcomes are reported.

21. My rewarding and cordial engagement with Lee Benson began in 1960 at the Center for Advanced Study in the Behavioral Sciences. He inscribed my presentation copy of *The Concept of Jacksonian Democracy* to "a damned fine historian, even if he is a Jacksonian." Under his influence, I have put a lot of effort into testing the efficacy of social science perspectives for my patch of the past. I trust it is apparent that I engage his work with enormous respect.

22. Benson was able to deny class politics in upstate New York because the large class of antibank farmers were split by Antimasonry between the parties. This does not deny class politics; it hides the class politics that occurred within the parties, as well as between

them. Farmer Antimasonic Whiggery sabotaged commercial Whiggery's darling Henry Clay and blocked its dearest hope, revival of the Bank of the United States. Downstate, Benson had to concede that the correlation of wealth with Whiggery in New York City wards suggested class division. But "further analysis" exorcised the demon by ascribing the votes of most ethnically identifiable groups exclusively to their ethnicity. Although the most Democratic groups "also happened to be lower class," this is pronounced on unconvincing grounds to be "casual rather than causal." See Benson, *Concept of Jacksonian Democracy*, pp. 142–64.

23. Benson, *Concept of Jacksonian Democracy*, pp. 86–109. Democratic Rockland County seems to me a classic case of an old farming community whose Antifederalist-Republican-Democratic politics had long defended the independence and equality of its patriarchal families against taxes and outside authority. Whig Chautauqua, by contrast, was recently settled by Yankee farmers whose abnormal Whiggery expressed unusually fervent Antimasonry.

24. Daniel Walker Howe, *The Political Culture of the American Whigs* (Chicago, 1979); Jean H. Baker, *Affairs of Party: The Political Culture of Northern Democrats in the Mid-Nineteenth Century* (Ithaca, N.Y., 1983).

25. This no-longer-so-new political history refined and nationalized Benson's cycles of party balance, identifying in the process a succession of distinctive party systems that emerged from widely spaced realignment phases. It has taught us much else: how the constitutional environment structures the party system to mandate two-party politics, the inescapable heterogeneity of both party coalitions, the importance of close party competition in politicizing voters and raising turnout, and the momentum of the parties' institutional cultures and will to survive. Yet this fertile scholarship betrays its consensus origins by tendencies to muffle issues of power and justice; ascribe too much to institutional dynamics and too little to interests, electoral pressures, and class; and reinforce the illusion that politicians represent the majority. Often it smacks of inside dopester awe at such a marvelously self-regulating system for resolving conflict among interests, muting discontent, and confining politics to a safe and narrow spectrum. Here, perhaps, consensualism found its most sophisticated and insidious form.

26. Joyce Appleby, *Capitalism and a New Social Order: The Republican Vision of the 1790s* (New York, 1983); Gordon S. Wood, *The Radicalism of the American Revolution* (New York, 1992). Richard E. Ellis's chapter in the present volume incorporates Appleby's extremely valuable insights while doing justice to the Jeffersonian majority she slights. Like Benson, the intellectually protean Wood raises more issues than can be briefly characterized. The greatest diversion of early American historical scholarship from historical reality has been the interminable flogging of ideological republicanism. Although the political language most available to the Revolutionary/Jeffersonian generation has been usefully illuminated, it is so notoriously adaptable to so many uses that its causal effect has been greatly exaggerated. Like too much intellectual history, this mystifying preoccupation smacks of resort to ideology as a refuge from class, largely ignoring the class forces that generated and sustained the ideology.

27. Richard E. Ellis is particularly insightful about the 1820s in Chapter 6 of this book.

28. Nathan O. Hatch, *The Democratization of American Christianity* (New Haven, Conn., 1989).

29. John H. Wigger, "Taking Heaven by Storm: Enthusiasm and Early American Methodism, 1770–1820," *Journal of the Early Republic* 14 (1994): 169–94 (quotation on p. 191). Nathan Hatch, cited above, leads the acknowledgements of assistance to Wigger, who is a doctoral student in Hatch's department at Notre Dame.

30. Sellers, "Andrew Jackson versus the Historians," p. 634.

Conclusion

MELVYN STOKES

ROM THE VERY BEGINNING of the national history of the United States—if not long before—Americans revealed a fascination with facts and figures. One of the first acts of the new federal Congress in 1789 was to establish, in accordance with article 1, section 3, of the new Constitution, a census bureau to carry out the decennial surveys need for apportioning direct taxes and representation in the House of Representatives. Other organizations were created in subsequent years to gather figures on a range of matters other than population. The statistics amassed by such bodies, however inadequate by today's standards of information gathering, do give an approximate guide to the changes that occurred as the Union grew from sixteen to thirty-eight states between 1800 and 1880.

In 1800, the new nation covered an area of 864,746 square miles; by 1880, it had grown (by 243 percent) to 2,969,640 square miles. Population growth was even more startling: the 5,297,000 estimated inhabitants of 1800 had risen almost tenfold to 50,262,000 in 1880. Centers of population grew sharply in number and size. In 1800, there were only 33 towns or cities with a population of more than 2,500, and just one of more than 50,000. By 1880, there were 939 communities with more than 2,500 inhabitants; 35 of these were over 50,000 and one was over a million. Statistics covering economic factors also showed remarkable expansion during these decades: the net tonnage of ships entering U.S. ports went from 804,000 in 1800 to 18,011,000 in 1880 (a 2,140-percent growth), exports from $71 million to $853 million (an increase of 1,101 percent), and imports from $91 million to $761 million (up by 736 percent).[1]

Statistics of this kind help delineate the social and economic changes that took place as the United States evolved from an agrarian nation bounded by the Atlantic seaboard, the Great Lakes, and the Mississippi River into a continental republic with an increasingly broad manufacturing base. The United States, in 1880, was producing 3.835 million tons of pig iron and 1.397 million tons of steel (an industry in which it was poised to overtake the United Kingdom during the next decade as the world's largest producer).[2] In 1880, the American economy as a whole was linked by some 93,267 miles of railroad track.[3] This network not only made possible the introduction of mail order in 1872, it helped tie the country together through telegraph lines (which were commonly built alongside the railroad tracks). It was the railroads, indeed, perhaps more than any other single factor, that were responsible for transforming the United States into a national market. It was highly appropriate, therefore, that it should have been the railroads that both recognized that national market and began to regularize it through the introduction of the standard time zones (1883) and a common track gauge (1886).

The major transformation in American life brought about by the market revolution attracted both supporters and critics. One of the earliest—and most optimistic—of the former was George Washington. "I cannot avoid reflecting with pleasure," he wrote some fifteen years ahead of the period covered by this book, "on the probable influence that commerce may hereafter have on human manners and society in general." Just two years after the ending of the War of Independence, Washington looked forward to the time when the human race would be "connected like one great family in fraternal ties" and believed "that the period is not very remote, when the benefits of a liberal and free commerce will, pretty generally, succeed to the devestations and horrors of war."[4] Some, like Washington, believed that social and international solidarity would be the fruits of commercialization. Others, however, surveying its effects, criticized it for fostering inequality, helping to divide society, and posing a threat to democracy. "We hold it best," declared George Bancroft in a speech marking the fiftieth anniversary of American independence, "that the laws should favor the diffusion of property and its acquisition, not the concentration of it in the hands of the few."[5]

The disagreements between contemporaries and near-contemporaries over the requisite costs and benefits of the market revolution are reflected in this book. The convictions of Charles Sellers and Daniel Walker Howe place them at opposite ends of the spectrum on this issue. Sellers sees the economic changes of the early nineteenth century as having powerful negative effects: they undermined the security, dignity, and personal autonomy of subsistence life, substituting the pressures of the competitive marketplace for the characteristic independence and neighborliness of the subsistence economy. Howe, by contrast, emphasizes the darker side of the subsistence world, seeing the market revolution as a liberating process that broadened horizons and expanded individual autonomy by creating a far wider range of choice.

It is, of course, true that the market revolution had both a good and a bad side, and historians are just beginning to come to terms with the latter. While propagandists for commercial progress drew attention to opportunities for personal fulfillment and the rewards of material success (the 1840s saw the coining of the term *millionaire* to describe one small but favored group), the reality of the market revolution for many had more to do with debtors' prisons and bankruptcy proceedings.[6] Dreams of success were balanced by the new fear of failure. Tocqueville thought that failure carried no particular stigma: men who had undergone the experience usually set out again on the sometimes fruitless search for material success. But more research is needed to prove or disprove his belief. We also need to know more about the way in which the credit system worked in different areas of the United States and the impact of the monetary system (no uniform currency existed until the 1860s, and some estimates had it that the amount of counterfeit money in circulation at times reached 40 percent of the total).[7]

Another possible area for future research arises from the fact that the market revolution was not merely a national, but also an international, phenomenon. Many countries were going through their own versions of these economic changes at the same time. This suggests the possibility of useful comparative studies of parallel social, economic, and political developments. There already exist a number of works comparing the history of the British and American economies for a slightly later period.[8] An interesting new tendency, apparent in work by Shearer Davis Bowman and Colleen A. Dunlavy, has been to compare aspects of the economy and society of antebellum America with their counterparts in *Vormärz* Prussia.[9] But, as the financial panics and subsequent depressions of 1819, 1837, and 1873 showed, the United States was increasingly part of an international economy that was linked together through investment, finance, and trade. Another conceivable approach would be to analyze elements of the American market revolution in their international context—in the way that scholars, for example, have investigated the existence of an international bourgeoisie in the nineteenth century or the creation of a world market in rice.[10]

A range of domestic issues raised by the market revolution also require more research. What was the role played by taxation, which demanded payments in monetary form, in pushing subsistence farmers into endorsing a more market-oriented way of life? At what point, indeed, did a subsistence farmer raising a surplus for sale become converted into a commercial farmer? If southern farmers were split into a dual economy, were northern farmers more united in response to the market revolution?[11] And to what extent did the changes wrought by the market revolution affect landscape and ecology?[12]

A decade ago, much of the interest in the debate over the economic transformations of the early nineteenth century revolved around their consequences for daily life. Since then, attention has increasingly moved to their impact on party formation and politics. One problem, however, is that there is no agreement—even among the contributors to this book—on the time when the market revolution had its principal impact on national politics, or on why that impact eventually diminished. Unlike both Ellis and Sellers, for example, Ratcliffe rejects the view that the rise of Jacksonian Democracy in the 1820s was essentially an expression of voters' dissatisfaction with the market revolution. In view of the fact that the revolution happened at differing speeds, in different places, and at different times, he does not see it as exerting a major influence on the national political scene until the mid- or late 1830s. Holt addresses the different issue of why the importance of market-related issues declined in politics in the period between the 1830s depression and that of the 1870s. His answer, while thorough and thought-provoking, does not cover one possibility implicitly suggested in the essays of Foner and Ashworth: that the market revolution encouraged a focus on slavery as antithetical to free labor, and this in turn crowded out interest in other economic issues.

Those who dominated the nineteenth-century political process, of course, were both white and male. One of the most promising directions for future research, however, may be to combine the market revolution thesis with new perspectives gained from the study of race and gender. We hope this book will help encourage such efforts. Harry Watson, for example, reviews recent literature on the ways African-American slaves were influenced by—and themselves influenced—the market revolution. Amy Stanley shows the inadequacy, as an interpretative tool, of distinctly separate, gendered spheres for this period. Sellers's own work deals with the relationship between Native Americans and the market revolution, yet there is clearly far more research to be done on that issue. Historians still do not know enough about differences within groups (gendered, racial, ethnic, and religious) in attitudes toward expanding markets, or about the ways in which some groups (such as the Mormons) came to embrace the market after having initially resisted it.

In broader terms, the market revolution offers—as Charles Sellers indicates in the previous chapter—a new perspective on the relationship of capitalism and democracy. Consensus historians, influenced by the Cold War, saw capitalism in the United States as democratic and consensual by nature, its position sustained by a liberal ideology in which almost all Americans believed. What seemed to these scholars an exceptionalist American ideology has become, with the ending of the Cold War and the disintegration of capitalism's most threatening adversary, the dominant ideology across much of the world. Some historians have hailed this development as a triumph: Francis Fukuyama, in particular, has seen the growing global influence of democratic liberalism allied to capitalist economies as "good news."[13] In sharp contrast, Charles Sellers advocates a better understanding of the costs—as well as the benefits—of capitalism's rise. The record of the market revolution in the United States demonstrates that the benefits of capitalist transformation were far from obvious to everyone involved. That there was democratic resistance to that transformation is a fact now accepted by most historians of the nineteenth century, although probably only a minority of these would share Sellers's faith in the ability of present-day democracy to challenge or at least to modify the capitalist marketplace.

NOTES

1. These figures are calculated from tables in *The Statistical History of the United States: From Colonial Times to the Present,* with an introduction by Ben J. Wattenberg (New York, 1976), pp. 8, 11, 760, 885–86.

2. Ibid., pp. 600, 694; Charles Wilson, "Economic Conditions," in F. H. Hinsley, ed., *The New Cambridge Modern History,* vol. 11, *Material Progress and World-Wide Problems 1870–1898* (Cambridge, Eng., 1962), p. 50.

3. John Stover, *American Railroads* (Chicago, 1961), p. 224. Europe, by comparison, had 105,017 miles (169,000 kilometers) of railway track which reached from the Atlantic to the Ural mountains. Wilson, "Economic Conditions," p. 51, n.1.

4. Washington to Lafayette, Aug. 1785, quoted in Jack P. Greene, *Imperatives, Behaviors, and Identities: Essays in Early American Cultural History* (Charlottesville, 1992), pp. 313–14.

5. Bancroft, quoted by William Miller, "The Realm of Wealth," in John Higham, ed., *The Reconstruction of American History* (London, 1962), p. 151.

6. Ibid., p. 137.

7. Michael O'Malley, "Specie and Species: Race and the Money Question in Nineteenth-Century America," *American Historical Review* 99 (1994): 374.

8. See Philip S. Bagwell and G. E. Mingay, *Britain and America 1850–1939: A Study of Economic Change* (London, 1970); Graeme M. Holmes, *Britain and America: A Comparative Economic History, 1850–1939* (Newton Abbott, Eng., 1976). For a study of a more specialized aspect of the American and British economies from a comparative perspective, see H. J. Habakkuk, *American and British Technology in the Nineteenth Century* (Cambridge, Eng., 1967). For cultural comparisons, see Daniel Walker Howe, ed., *Victorian America* (Philadelphia, 1976).

9. Shearer Davis Bowman, "Antebellum Planters and *Vormärz* Junkers in Comparative Perspective," *American Historical Review* 85 (1980): 779–808; Colleen A. Dunlavy, *Politics and Industrialization: Early Railroads in the United States and Prussia* (Princeton, N.J., 1994).

10. Charles A. Jones, *International Business in the Nineteenth Century: The Rise and Fall*

of a Cosmopolitan Bourgeoisie (Brighton, Eng., 1987); Peter A. Coclanis, "Distant Thunder: The Creation of a World Market in Rice and the Transformations It Wrought," *American Historical Review* 98 (1993): 1050–78.

11. Did the tenant farmers of upstate New York, for example, react in the same way to commercial pressures as Clark's Massachusetts farmers?

12. For pioneering studies of these issues, see Carolyn Merchant, *Ecological Revolutions: Nature, Gender, and Science in New England* (Chapel Hill, N.C., 1989); William Cronon, *Nature's Metropolis: Chicago and the Great West* (New York, 1991), esp. chaps. 3–5; Theodore Steinberg, *Nature Incorporated: Industrialization and the Waters of New England* (Cambridge, Eng., 1991).

13. Francis Fukuyama, *The End of History and the Last Man* (New York, 1992).

Contributors

John Ashworth is the author of *"Agrarians" and "Aristocrats": Party Political Ideology in the United States, 1837–1846* (1983) and *Slavery, Capitalism, and Politics in the Antebellum Republic,* vol. 1, *Commerce and Compromise, 1820–1850* (1996). He is Senior Lecturer in American History at the University of East Anglia.

Richard Carwardine writes on nineteenth-century religious history. He has published *Transatlantic Revivalism: Popular Evangelicalism in Britain and America, 1790–1865* (1978) and *Evangelicals and Politics in Antebellum America* (1993). He teaches at the University of Sheffield.

Christopher Clark helped launch the concept of the market revolution in a seminal article in 1979. His *Roots of Rural Capitalism: Western Massachusetts, 1780–1860,* was published in 1990 and *The Communitarian Moment: The Radical Challenge of the Northampton Association* in 1995. He is Senior Lecturer in History at the University of York.

Stephen Conway has published a number of articles in the *William and Mary Quarterly.* He has edited three volumes of Jeremy Bentham's *Correspondence.* His *War of American Independence, 1775–1783* was published in 1995. He teaches history at University College London, where he helped organize the Commonwealth Fund Conference on American history for 1994.

Richard E. Ellis has published *The Jeffersonian Crisis: Courts and Politics in the Young Republic* (1971) and *The Union at Risk: Jacksonian Democracy, States' Rights, and the Nullification Crisis* (1987). He is Professor of History at the State University of New York at Buffalo.

Eric Foner's books include *Free Soil, Free Labor, Free Men: The Ideology of the Republican Party before the Civil War* (1969; reissued with a new introduction in 1995), *Tom Paine and Revolutionary America* (1977), *Politics and Ideology in the Age of the Civil War* (1980) and *Reconstruction: America's Unfinished Revolution* (1988). He was Harmsworth Visiting Professor at Oxford University in 1993–94. A former president of the Organization of American Historians, he is currently DeWitt Clinton Professor of History at Columbia University.

Michael Holt is the author of *Forging a Majority: The Formation of the Republican Party in Pittsburgh, 1848–1860* (1969) and *The Political Crisis of the 1850s*

(1978). His collection of essays *Political Parties and American Political Development: From the Age of Jackson to the Age of Lincoln* was published in 1992. He was Pitt Visiting Professor at Cambridge University in 1993–94. He teaches at the University of Virginia.

Daniel Walker Howe is the author of many scholarly works, including *The Political Culture of the American Whigs* (1979) and *Virtue, Passion, and Politics: The Construction of the Self in American Thought* (1996). He is Rhodes Professor of American History and Institutions at the University of Oxford.

Donald J. Ratcliffe has published numerous articles on the politics of the Jacksonian period, and is currently completing a book on early Ohio politics. His most recent publication is "Antimasonry and Partisanship in Greater New England, 1826–1836," *Journal of the Early Republic* 15 (1995): 199–239. He is Senior Lecturer in History at the University of Durham, England.

Charles Sellers is the author of *James K. Polk, Jacksonian, 1795–1843* (1957), *James K. Polk, Continentalist, 1843–1846* (1966), and, most recently, *The Market Revolution: Jacksonian America, 1815–1846* (1991).

Amy Dru Stanley teaches at the University of Chicago. She has published articles in the *Journal of American History* and is completing a book entitled *Bonds of Contract: Wage Labor and Marriage in the Age of Slave Emancipation,* to be published by Cambridge University Press.

Melvyn Stokes is coeditor of *Race and Class in the American South since 1890* (1994). He has published articles on reform movements, progressive thought, historiography, and film history. He is currently completing a book on progressive discourse before the First World War. He teaches American history at University College London, where he has organized the Commonwealth Fund Colloquium/Conference since 1988.

Harry Watson is the author of *Jacksonian Politics and Community Conflict: The Emergence of the Second Party System in Cumberland County, North Carolina* (1981) and *Liberty and Power: The Politics of Jacksonian America* (1990). He teaches at the University of North Carolina.

Sean Wilentz has published *Chants Democratic: New York City and the Rise of the American Working Class, 1788–1850* (1984), *The Kingdom of Matthias* (1994), coauthored with Paul E. Johnson, and many scholarly articles. He is Professor of History at Princeton University.

Index